The Economics of Project Analysis

A Practitioner's Guide

William A. Ward
and
Barry J. Deren
with
Emmanuel H. D'Silva

The World Bank
Washington, D.C.

The Economic Development Institute (EDI) was established by the World Bank in 1955 to train officials concerned with development planning, policymaking, investment analysis, and project implementation in member developing countries. At present the substance of the EDI's work emphasizes macroeconomic and sectoral economic policy analysis. Through a variety of courses, seminars, and workshops, most of which are given overseas in cooperation with local institutions, the EDI seeks to sharpen analytical skills used in policy analysis and to broaden understanding of the experience of individual countries with economic development. Although the EDI's publications are designed to support its training activities, many are of interest to a much broader audience. EDI materials, including any findings, interpretations, and conclusions, are entirely those of the authors and should not be attributed in any manner to the World Bank, to its affiliated organizations, or to members of its Board of Executive Directors or the countries they represent.

Because of the informality of the series and to make the publication available with the least possible delay, the manuscript has not been edited fully as would be the case with a more formal document, and the World Bank accepts no responsibility for errors.

The backlist of publications by the World Bank is shown in the annual *Index of Publications*, which is available free of charge from the Distribution Unit, Office of the Publisher, The World Bank, 1818 H Street, N.W., Washington, D.C. 20433, U.S.A., or from Publications, Banque mondiale, 66, avenue d'Iéna, 75116 Paris, France.

William A. Ward is director of international programs, Division of Agriculture and Natural Resources, Clemson University, Clemson, South Carolina, U.S.A.
Barry J. Deren is an economist with the consulting firm of HJP International, Ltd., Ledbury, Herefordshire, U.K.
Emmanuel H. D'Silva is a research analyst in the Agriculture and Rural Development Division of the World Bank's Economic Development Institute.

Library of Congress Cataloging-in-Publication Data

Ward, William A. (William Augustus), 1942–
        The economics of project analysis : a practitioner's guide /
    William A. Ward and Barry J. Deren, with Emmanuel H. D'Silva.
            p.   cm. — (EDI technical materials)
        Includes bibliographical references and index.
        ISBN 0-8213-1751-2
        1. Economic development projects—Developing countries—
    Evaluation.   I. Deren, Barry J., 1959–   .   II. D'Silva, Emmanuel
    H., 1950–   .   III. Title.   IV. Series.
    HC59.72.E44W37   1991
    338.9′0068′4—dc20
                                                                    90-25058
                                                                        CIP

Contents

Preface

The Economics of Project Analysis: A Practitioner's Guide is written for project practitioners, for instructors in agricultural project economic analysis, and for students of that subject. The *Practitioner's Guide* extends and complements the discussion of project and policy economics contained in the second edition of *Economic Analysis of Agricultural Projects,* by J. Price Gittinger—referred to throughout this volume as Gittinger (1982).

Gittinger (1982) was written primarily with the noneconomist in mind. Its objective was to assist agricultural project practitioners in carrying out the financial and economic appraisal of projects in their sector. Chapter 7 of that text provides the guidance needed for project appraisers—whether they be economists or noneconomists—to carry out the economic analysis of the most common types of agricultural projects in developing countries. However, Gittinger does not attempt to teach noneconomists how to derive the shadow prices that have come to be called "national economic parameters." Nor does Gittinger deal with the more complicated issues sometimes associated with estimating project-related shadow prices (e.g., those for fuelwood or for fresh milk—dealt with in Part V of this volume), or conduct the broader analysis of policy issues regarding the sector (except in "Trade Policy Signals from Project Analysis," pages 271-278).

Since Gittinger (1982) was published, several changes have taken place in the economic situation facing trainers and agricultural project practitioners around the world. Among the more important of these changes have been the following:

a. Changes in the world trade and monetary situation have led to the development of increasingly distorted trade, fiscal, and financial policies in many developing countries, increasing both the importance and the difficulty of deriving and using shadow prices in project economic analysis.

b. In recent years, greater emphasis has been placed on policy-based financial assistance by donors and on assessing projects in terms of the policy environment of the sector.

The combination of more distorted sets of prices and of more attention being paid to policy issues has made the old style of economic analysis—i.e., "second best" shadow pricing of projects, often conducted in isolation from the broader issues affecting the sector and the economy—increasingly inappropriate. This has meant that it is more difficult to conduct project economic analysis with the limited understanding of project economics that was judged sufficient in 1981/82.

At the same time that the world in which project appraisal takes place was becoming more complicated, a second change was also occurring. After more than a decade of providing training in agricultural project appraisal to government officials, the Economic Development Institute (EDI) of the World Bank began to focus more on conducting policy seminars and on training national trainers to take over the agricultural project appraisal courses that EDI no longer gives in Washington. This second phenomenon has meant that most project appraisal training is now conducted at the national level rather than within the international context that EDI was able to provide and that the training is provided by national trainers rather than by World Bank staff.

This change has had both good and bad effects. On the one hand, it has meant that project appraisal training can be increasingly tailored to local problems and to local needs. On the other hand, it has also meant that some of the richness of the international experience and perspective has been partly lost. EDI has sought to deal with the problems posed by these changes in several ways. One of the measures taken by EDI is represented by the *Practitioner's Guide*. In addition to this book, other materials—e.g., on agricultural sector analysis and on agricultural policy analysis—are being prepared for use by trainers and practitioners in the field. These materials are designed to assist trainers and practitioners in dealing with policy changes in economic management.

Because of the increased importance placed on the policy environment of project appraisal, the *Practitioner's Guide* takes the reader a bit further into economic theory to provide the background for project economic analysis. This journey is necessary because it is the basic theory of economic efficiency that provides the link with the other policy measures needed for dealing with the economic and social issues facing the agricultural sector. The *Practitioner's Guide* will not by itself provide the guidance necessary to conduct sector or policy analysis, but it will help the project planner to better understand the relationship between project and policy analysis and between project interventions and policy interventions.

While one objective in bringing out this book is to provide more information on the economics of shadow pricing, it is also the objective to maintain consistency with the pragmatic approach taken in Gittinger (1982). The *Practitioner's Guide* does so by providing in Part V several examples of shadow pricing to help demonstrate how economic theory is used in the project planning context.

It is intended that both noneconomists and economists find the *Practitioner's Guide* understandable and useful. Like Gittinger (1982), this book was written primarily with the practitioner in mind. It is the practitioner—whether an economist, agriculturalist, or other technician—who must implement the approaches that are discussed in this book, if they are to be implemented. It is the practicing economist who must train other practitioners in the application of project economic analysis. The ultimate aim of the *Practitioner's Guide* has to be to augment the understanding of project economic analysis by those in the field who must not only deal with the day-to-day problems that arise with agricultural projects but must also keep asking the question, "What are the broader economic objectives of these projects?" This book must assist in this function—for the process of reconciling on-the-ground realities with a rational, overall, economic game plan is a function that must be performed by someone. In order to do this, the project planner needs not only an understanding of the nuts and bolts of agricultural project appraisal that were dealt with in Gittinger (1982): he or she also needs to understand the basic economic theory that underlies the economic interventions that the projects and the policies in the sector represent.

The *Practitioner's Guide* is designed to provide the practitioner with part of that understanding by:

a. Linking the estimation and use of shadow prices in project economic analysis with the policy context of the project and its sector;

b. Defining and demonstrating the derivation of shadow prices in the more prominent methods of project economic analysis that are practiced by the major international development organizations;

c. Providing a historical context within which practitioners may be better able to understand the various recommendations that are made on project economic analysis methods; and

d. Providing examples of shadow pricing problems that have been faced by World Bank staff in the process of carrying out the Bank's project lending activities in recent years.

This book is divided into five parts. Part I provides a brief outline of the neo-classical theory of the public sector to put into context the reason for deriving shadow prices and to help the reader understand what it is that a government should be trying to do when it "intervenes" in the economy by planning a project. It is the contention of the authors that all project analysis and all policy analyses should begin with a return to the theory of the public sector. The analyst should always ask the related questions, "What market failure is this intervention intended to address?" and "How is the intervention going to correct for that particular market failure?" Pursuing this line of questions will, almost automatically, orient the project planning process more toward policy analysis.

The *Practitioner's Guide* uses neoclassical economics to conduct project and policy analysis. It takes the neoclassical perspective because that approach has been prominently applied by international organizations, such as the World Bank, in analytical work related to economic assistance to developing countries during the 1980s. The concern with improving economic efficiency in both industrial and developing economies has taken on increased importance in the current world economic environment and has led to a resurgence of the notions of economic efficiency that are embodied in neoclassical economic theory. The resurgence of neoclassical economic doctrine has made it important that economic planners in central and sectoral agencies fully understand the basics of this approach to project and policy analysis. However, some economists may find the neoclassical approach too limiting and may wish to pursue other approaches to economic management. We encourage them to explore other approaches as well.

Part II describes experiences of the World Bank and other organizations in applying project economic analysis in developing countries. Developments in the use and interpretation of "willingness to pay" analysis and "foreign exchange numeraires" are discussed in some detail. In Part III, cost-benefit analysis is discussed in terms of the strategic planning model.

Part IV extends Gittinger's discussion of the impact of time on the analysis of projects. The problems caused by inflation—both domestic and foreign— are discussed in some detail, and suggestions are made for dealing with its impacts. Additional recommendations on setting up project accounts are presented. Exchange rate forecasting is addressed in terms of the "purchasing power parity" model of trade theory—the most widely used model for forecasting exchange rates in project appraisals. The issue of the discount rate for project economic analysis is also taken up.

Part V presents many concrete examples of economic valuation problems faced by World Bank analysts in recent years. The examples cover a wide range of countries and valuation issues. These are intended for use by both practitioners and trainers—as examples to guide the former in the search for answers to difficult practical problems of their own, and as classroom examples, exercises, and cases for use by trainers and educators.

This book is not intended to be encyclopedic nor to break new theoretical ground. An attempt has been made to keep the main part of the text as straightforward and practical as possible. Theoretical discussions, where unavoidable, have been relegated to the Technical Notes at the end of the volume. Still, university faculty members will find much in the book to recommend it as supplementary reading for their students, many of whom may eventually become the practitioners and trainers for whom the *Practitioner's Guide* was written.

Theoretically inclined readers will find the Technical Notes useful, though the book breaks no new theoretical ground. Others will find that the area of project risk analysis—only thinly covered in Gittinger (1982)—has barely been discussed in this volume. Project social analysis has been accorded much the same fate. The authors can only take refuge in the knowledge that agricultural project appraisal is a big subject covering many separate skills. The *Practitioner's Guide* has focused on a few of the skills which have been accorded insufficient coverage in other texts.

William A. Ward
Barry J. Deren
Emmanuel H. D'Silva

Acknowledgments

Erdmann Zimmer-Vorhaus first suggested the book and provided early support and guidance. J.A. Nicholas Wallis continued this support and was the driving force behind the completion of the book. Tufan Kolan, Voltaire Andres, and Yahaya Doka provided additional financial assistance for materials development through the training programs for World Bank staff. Michael O'Farrell did the same through support for work on International Finance Corportation (IFC) staff training activities. Bill Peterson assisted the effort in the process of carrying out training programs for the staff of the Asian Development Bank (ADB).

An intellectual debt is owed to hundreds of officals and their trainers from developing countries who participated in EDI seminars out of which the materials in this book grew. In addition, staff of the World Bank, the IFC, the ADB and numerous other institutions who participated in project appraisal workshops in these organizations have contributed greatly to the evolution of the ideas and presentational techniques contained in this volume.

A number of former EDI colleagues assisted in the development of the material and ideas over a long period of time. The list includes J. Price Gittinger, Maxwell Brown, Nicholas Burnett, Janet S. de Merode, Orlando Espadas, Vincent Hogg, John Huang, Frank Lamson-Scribner, Gopi Puri, Walter Shaefer-Kehnert, Arnold von Ruemker, Irving Sirken, V. Srinivasan, Jack Upper, Lilina Williams, and Bob Youker. Michalann Greenway checked bibliographic citations. Patrick Lavey helped with the presentational aspects of the book.

The authors are responsible for any errors that remain.

PART I

Neoclassical Economics
and the
Theory of the Public Sector

*Foundations of Project
and Policy Economics*

1. Defining Economic Efficiency

Summary. *To an economist, the objective of economic activity is to maximize the value of society's consumption over time. "Economic efficiency" is attained when the economy is functioning in a way that maximizes that value. In the neoclassical economic model, "value" is measured by society's "willingness to pay" for the goods and services that are consumed as outputs or used as inputs, or both.*

Project economic analysis and policy dialogues between the World Bank and its member governments have tended to focus on the promotion of economic efficiency. The "shadow prices" (also called "accounting prices") used in project economic analysis are designed to move the economy closer to meeting the conditions necessary to achieve improved efficiency. Economic efficiency has three elements: static, dynamic, and distributional. Project social analysis focuses on all three elements of efficiency, while project economic analysis tends to focus largely on static and dynamic efficiency

---

Economists normally work from the presumption that the objective of economic activity is consumption. In economics, the concept of efficiency relates to conditions under which the value of a society's consumption will be maximized over time. Current-day texts on neoclassical economics tend to define three kinds of economic efficiency. These texts are discussed below and follow Musgrave and Musgrave (1980), Killick (1981), and Meier (1983).

Static Efficiency.
Defined by the existence of three simultaneous conditions:

1. Full employment;

2. Use of "right" combination of inputs;

3. Production of the "right" combination of outputs.

"Right" is defined in terms of relative values, where "relative values" are measured by society's willingness to pay for each unit of the good or service.

Static efficiency relates to the conditions of full employment, in which the economy is not only using all of its resources, but is also using them "correctly" by producing the "right" combinations of output, and using the "right" combinations of inputs (see Technical Note 1 at the end of this volume). The "right" combinations in all cases is defined in terms of what the market is willing to pay for a marginal unit of each output and each input—i.e., the marginal demand prices. This will be true for inputs (i.e., producer goods) as well as for outputs (i.e., consumer goods).

The demand for inputs is derived from the demand for the products the inputs can be used to produce (see Technical Note 2). Thus, input prices and the optimal combinations of inputs are also determined by consumers' willingness to pay. There is, obviously, a strong "consumer sovereignty" bias in this neoclassical approach to defining efficiency.

In the traditional economic efficiency analysis of projects, all inputs and all outputs would be valued in terms of these willingness to pay prices, rather than the prices that are actually paid. (You should note that in an undistorted market, we normally expect the prevailing market price and the willingness to pay price to be the same. "Distorted" and "undistorted" markets will be defined in later sections of Part I.)

In Gittinger (1982), for example, it is suggested that nontraded project outputs be shadow priced in terms of marginal willingness to pay. [If you are using border prices in the willingness to pay numeraire, these willingness to pay prices must then be converted to border prices using appropriate conversion factors—Gittinger (1982), pages 253-265; if you are using the domestic price version of the willingness to pay numeraire, then the willingness to pay prices do not need to be converted to border price equivalents. These points are discussed further in Chapter 7 of Gittinger and in Part II of this volume.]

The neoclassical economic model demonstrates that the value of present consumption to society will be maximized when the following three conditions relating to static efficiency are met:

   a. making full use of the nation's resources;

   b. producing the "right" combinations of outputs; and

   c. using the "right" combinations of inputs
      (see Technical Notes 3 and 4).

Dynamic efficiency relates to whether the economy (specifically, consumption) is growing at the "right" rate. Again, the "right" rate is defined by the willingness of society to save and invest rather than to consume—or said in another way, it relates to society's choice of present consumption over future consumption, since future consumption is the objective of present saving and investing (see Technical Note 5). In a society characterized by perfectly functioning financial markets, both the choice between present and future consumption and the opportunity cost of capital (at the margin, of course, in both cases) would be indicated by the market rate of interest.

The economics literature discusses various distortions that may dictate the use of interest rates other than the prevailing market rate [see Gittinger (1982), pages 313-315; Sandmo and Dreze (1971); and Atkinson and Stiglitz (1980), pages 474-80]. In any case, some discount rate is needed in project planning to compare future consumption with present consumption. This is necessary, because we must be able to tell whether the "with project" option

Willingness to Pay. *The price that society would be willing to pay for each succesive unit of a good or service, indicated by marginal demand prices.*

Dynamic Efficiency. *A condition in which the economy is growing at the "right" rate, where "right" is defined in terms of society's choice between present and future consumption.*

or the "without project" option is more efficient in terms of a society's willingness to pay for the different consumption streams that result from the alternative uses of the resources that will be tied up by the project.

In the simplest applications of economic efficiency analysis, the economic opportunity cost of capital is traditionally used as the discount rate in choosing from among the project alternatives. Gittinger (1982) briefly discusses different approaches to choosing the discount rate (pages 313-315), but does not suggest that any of the alternatives be selected in isolation. In general, the agricultural project planner should use the rate that is suggested by the Planning Office. This suggestion has a rational basis, since both static and dynamic efficiency require that all agencies use the same discount rate in appraising their projects. Some of the issues surrounding the discount rate and some of the approaches that have been used to estimate it are discussed in Chapter 21.

Static and dynamic efficiency are generally treated together by economists. The reasons become obvious once we give a little thought to the three aspects of static efficiency mentioned earlier. First, the issue of the "right" combination of outputs immediately raises questions about producing consumer goods versus investment goods. The question about what the right combination of these outputs is cannot be answered until we have a mechanism for valuing future consumption (the object of the investment goods) against present consumption (the object of the consumer goods). Second, the issue of the right combination immediately raises the question of the economic cost of producer durable inputs like machinery versus the economic cost of nondurable inputs like labor.

Much of the "policy dialogue" between international development agencies and governments of developing countries takes place over the issue of static and dynamic efficiency. For example, fertilizer subsidies are sometimes challenged because they tend to distort the relative prices of inputs and to lead to the "wrong" combinations of inputs being used. Similarly, administered prices for foodgrains tend to distort the relative prices of outputs and to lead to the "wrong" combinations of outputs being produced. For instance, a subsidized price for wheat may lead to overproduction of wheat and underproduction of rice, relative to consumers' willingness to pay for the two commodities; at the same time, the wheat subsidy may lead to production of wheat on land that is far better suited to production of rice or other food crops (see Technical Note 6).

By the same token, subsidized interest rates often have a detrimental effect on both static efficiency and on dynamic efficiency. In static

Traditionally, the economic opportunity cost of capital is used as the discount rate in choosing from among the project alternatives. However, the agricultural project planner should use the rate that is suggested by the Planning Office.

efficiency terms, subsidized interest rates may lead to the use of the wrong combination of inputs—specifically, the use of too much capital (e.g., machinery) and too little labor. In dynamic efficiency terms, subsidized interest rates may disturb financial markets to the point of actually reducing incentives to save and distorting the choices between present and future consumption (see Technical Note 7).

Distributional efficiency relates to whether a society feels that its total output (consumption) is optimally distributed. There are no willingness to pay prices to serve as references in determining whether this aspect of efficiency is being met. Thus, distributional efficiency is vulnerable to criticism on grounds of being subjective (see Technical Note 8).

The social analysis introduced by OECD (1969) and by UNIDO (1972) sought to incorporate considerations of distributional efficiency into the cost-benefit analysis of projects. These two works did not totally invent the concern with equity, of course: government officials, as well as many economists, had been concerned with these questions long before the OECD Manual was published. We should note, however, that distributional efficiency did not have a prominent place in the texts used in teaching "principles of economics" before the 1970s. [See Lal (1974) for a comparison of the OECD and UNIDO methodologies.]

The neoclassical approach to economic policy has tended to focus on static and dynamic efficiency and to leave distributional efficiency issues to politics and philosophy. In fact, a group of economists who view themselves as "positive scientists"—generally labeled the "positivists," and led by Nobel laureate Milton Friedman (1966)—argue that economists can tell politicians about the distributional implications of economic policies; but, the positivists argue, positive science should not tell politicians what the proper income distribution should be, nor should they say what the value of a rupee of income be to one individual compared to another. The addition of income distribution objectives to cost-benefit analysis, then, appears to the positivists to be a journey into normative judgments—a venture which many positive scientists would not be willing to undertake (see Technical Note 9).

Cost-benefit analysis has only one objective—economic efficiency—and uses a form of economic efficiency numeraire to focus on static efficiency and dynamic efficiency. It ignores distributional efficiency. In other words, economic efficiency analysis assumes that each rupee of income is equally important to each individual in society. In this analysis, each rupee of income receives an income weight of 1—regardless of who receives it.

Distributional Efficiency.
A condition in which general agreement exists that the output of society is equitably distributed.

Distributional efficiency is not taken into account until we get to the third step in the Squire-van der Tak method—the social analysis. [Squire and van der Tak (1975) divide the project appraisal process into three sequential steps: financial analysis, economic efficiency analysis, and social analysis.] Gittinger (1982) does not discuss the details of this third step, and so we shall not pursue it further in this volume.   (For an idea of how economic prices might be used to reflect the distributional concerns in project analysis, see Case 14 in Part V, which discusses the economic values of white and yellow maize in The Philippines.)

2. Market Failure and the Government Role

Summary. *Under certain conditions, free markets will automatically achieve economic efficiency. However, there are many cases in which markets depart from these conditions. Neoclassical economics defines those departures as "market failures."*

In the face of market failure, neoclassical theory prescribes "optimal interventions" to restore the requisite conditions (or to substitute for those conditions) so that efficiency will be restored. In the neoclassical model, the government's role is to undertake these optimal interventions. In real life, however, government intervention is often nonoptimal—that is, it does not optimally correct for market failures. In addition, governments often intervene in cases in which the market has not failed on its own; and the intervention itself disrupts efficiency.

In this chapter, nonoptimal interventions and unwarranted interventions are grouped together under "government failure." If all interventions were warranted and optimal, the resulting financial prices would approximate economic values, and shadow pricing would not be required in projects involving marketable goods and services (such as most agricultural and industrial projects). When government failure exists, some form of shadow pricing may be required in planning and appraising projects.

In neoclassical economic theory, freely functioning markets will automatically lead to static and dynamic efficiency, so long as certain conditions are met [Killick (1981)]. These conditions are generally referred to as the conditions of "perfect competition."

Perfect competition basically means that:

   a. Each market is characterized by a large number of buyers and a large number of sellers of undifferentiated products. (Current-day market analysts would term these products "commodities.")

   b. Each product has the attributes of a private good:

   • The owner can exclude others from using it.
   • Title to the good or service can be bought and sold in a market.
   • Producing and using the good affects nobody other than the buyer and the seller.

   c. All market transactions are entered into freely (i.e., without coercion or interference by outside parties) by both buyer and seller.

Perfect Competition. *A condition in which large numbers of buyers and sellers engage in voluntary transactions for a private good.*

7

Neoclassical economics recognizes that "market failures" may prevent static and dynamic efficiency from being achieved. Market failures relate to situations in which markets for particular goods and services fail to meet the conditions of perfect competition mentioned earlier.

In the case of market failure, the government should intervene in the economy in a manner that will correct for those failures and which will lead to static and dynamic efficiency being achieved. In other words, the government's role in the economy (via projects, programs, and policies) should be to produce "optimal interventions" to correct for market failures. (A distinction will be made later between market failure and government failure. See also Technical Note 10).

When markets fail, the prices that are paid in those markets may lead to consumption and production decisions which do not contribute to national economic efficiency (i.e., static and dynamic efficiency). Shadow prices are used in project economic analysis to partially correct for the misallocations that occur in the economy because of distorted prices resulting from market failures.

Government interventions may be viewed as "optimal" when they help restore the conditions needed to achieve economic efficiency. Interventions which disrupt economic efficiency, or which do not fully restore the conditions for economic efficiency, may be viewed as "nonoptimal interventions." Unfortunately, in many countries, government actions—rather than correcting for the distortions caused by market failures—often worsen the distortions. Frequently, governments add new distortions by initiating policies, such as protective tariffs, import bans, and export subsidies; and by taking various measures to change prices in markets which—in many cases—would otherwise meet the requisite conditions to be considered competitive markets. In particular, they include restrictions on international trade in products in which border prices represent an effective, inexpensive, and equitable mechanism for regulating producers and consumers in the public interest.

Market failure.
Failure to attain the conditions of perfect competition, such that some form of societal intervention is required to ensure that social welfare is maximized— a condition that neoclassical theory demonstrates would occur naturally in the absence of market failure.

Examples of market failure fall under four broad headings:

a. monopolistic elements (which include natural monopolies such as public utilities and imperfect competition);

b. external economies;

c. public and quasi-public goods; and

d. the paradox of thrift and fallacies of composition.

These items are discussed in the later sections.

Government failure can be divided into two categories:

a. interventions designed to correct for market

a. failures but which, in practice, turn out to be inappropriate, insufficient, or excessive; or

b. interventions which disrupt otherwise efficiently functioning markets.

The accounting prices that are used in project economic analysis are designed to partially correct for the distortions caused by market and government failure. In other words, these prices allow us to recommend projects that improve the degree of static and dynamic efficiency.

In agricultural projects, the shadow pricing often tends to focus on correcting distortions caused by government policies. One important reason for this is that the agricultural sector in most countries comes closest to meeting the economists' model of perfect competition—i.e., large numbers of buyers and sellers, producing undifferentiated products, and so forth. In many developing countries we find that, in practice, corrections for policy-induced distortions tend to be one of the more important corrections involved in the shadow pricing exercise.

Shadow pricing may be viewed as a correction for government failure of either the first or the second type defined earlier. The need to use accounting prices may be looked upon as a criticism of the government for failing to optimally intervene in the economy. In some sense this is true, since accounting prices would not be needed if governments could find a way to restore in every market the requisite conditions for economic efficiency.

However, we must also recognize that economic efficiency is not the only objective of society; and it is not the only objective of the government. Thus, we should not seek to make it the only factor to consider in project and policy analysis; and the economic efficiency accounting prices that we shall discuss shortly cannot be the only "values" that count. However, we should also keep in mind that the economic conditions faced by most countries in the latter half of the 1980s make it more important than in the past two decades that economic efficiency issues be given prominence in the economic planning and management processes of all countries.

To plan with economic efficiency in mind requires that we understand the circumstances under which economic efficiency is achieved, the circumstances which disrupt economic efficiency, and how to judge interventions in the agricultural sector in terms of whether or not they help us restore the requisite conditions for national economic efficiency.

The Theory of Market Failure

In project economic analysis, we talk about economic values based

Government Failure.
1. Interventions which are designed to correct for market failure, but which are either inappropriate, insufficient, or excessive; or 2. Interventions which disrupt an otherwise efficiently functioning market.

Shadow Pricing.
In project planning and appraisal, the use of prices other than existing "market" or administered prices to correct for distortions that exist because of market and government failure.

on society's willingness to pay for the inputs and for the outputs that are involved in a project. We have already said that taxes, for example, do not normally represent real resource flows in the financial accounts. So, one of the first things to do in conducting economic analysis is to delete the taxes from the accounts, since they do not represent real resource flows. Similarly, subsidies (e.g., export subsidies) also do not represent real resource flows; therefore, they should also be ignored. Such taxes and subsidies constitute "transfer payments," not real flows of resources (see Technical Note 11).

But what about the other "money flows"? Do they constitute real resource flows? After all, they (unlike the taxes and subsidies) are payments made on a per unit basis for real inputs and for real outputs. Don't they measure for us the willingness to pay, since they obviously represent payments that people make for actual goods and services?

The answer is that financial payments other than the taxes and the subsidies may or may not accurately represent the real willingness to pay for the project's inputs and outputs. The practical question is whether the prices that are actually paid accurately measure the willingness to pay. Let us discuss this issue further. First we will talk in theoretical terms. Then we will get down to specifics.

Economic values reflect the values that society would be *willing* to pay for a good or a service. Financial values, in contrast, are the prices that people *actually* pay. In project economic analysis, the task, of course, is to convert the financial prices into economic values, or to "adjust" the financial prices so that they more accurately represent economic values. So an understanding of the difference between what is actually paid and the willingness to pay values is very important.

Economic Efficiency.
In economics, the concept of efficiency relates to conditions under which the value of a society's consumption will be maximized over time.

Economic values may differ from financial values for a variety of reasons:

    a. market failure;

    b. government failure; and

    c. merit goods and demerit goods.

Economic Prices.
These are the values that society would be willing to pay for a good or a service.

In the presence of these factors, the prices actually paid may differ from what people would be willing to pay for those same items. For example, because of subsidies, consumers may pay less than they would be willing to pay. If we took the financial price as the indication of the real value of that item, we would end up undervaluing that item.

Financial Prices.
These are the prices that people actually pay.

Market failure occurs because of the specific characteristics of a particular good or service, or because of the production technology for that good or service. Public utilities which are "natural monopolies," represent examples of market failure. Another example is industries that pollute air or water and, thus, impose uncompensated costs on other people.

In principle, the government needs to intervene to restore "socially optimal" production, consumption, and pricing (where pricing is possible) of the good or service affected by market failure [Musgrave and Musgrave (1988)]. For example, natural monopolies —such as telecommunications, electricity, and water distribution— normally are regulated or owned by the government. The objective is to ensure that these companies behave in socially beneficial ways [Saunders, Warford, and Wellenius (1983)].

Government failure, in contrast, results from "nonoptimal" intervention by the government. It constitutes interventions that do not correct for market failure, or interventions that actually make society worse off.

Merit goods represent goods or services considered necessary for a "decent" standard of living. (Demerit goods—e.g., tobacco and alcohol—are viewed as having a negative social merit.) Merit goods represent an apparent departure from the willingness to pay measure of value. The willingness to pay is usually based on an amalgamation of individual values that are expressed in consumer demand. The concept of a merit good is based on the idea that there are values that are held in common by society—values that are different from those expressed in individual demands [Musgrave and Musgrave (1988)].

Examples of merit goods include public housing, support for the arts, and minimal subsistence. They may also include access to educational opportunities and adequate health care. In many cases, these values come to be accepted as basic human rights. Governments generally assume responsibility for providing these goods and services. Attempts to subsidize the availability of foodgrains, for example, are often justified as attempts to provide a merit good. We will see later that merit goods are particularly difficult to deal with in the project economic analysis.

Monopoly Elements

Natural monopolies occur when major economies of scale exist for a nontradable good or service. *Economies of scale* means that the average cost of supply decreases over a wide range of production scales. Economies of scale tend to be important in the provision of services that have large and costly distribution systems, such as power grids, natural gas pipelines, water distribution systems, and the like. It is "natural" to monopolize the provision of these services, since it does not make sense to duplicate their very great costs in several firms as a way of having competition.

Merit Good.
A good or service for which "society" chooses to interfere with private individual choices in decisions regarding the provision or consumption of the good. A merit good may be either a "public good" or a "private good" in terms of its other characteristics.

Demerit Good.
A merit good in which the "merit" is negative— for example, alcohol consumption.

The cost considerations are important since natural monopolies tend to have a large element of fixed costs (e.g., the transmission and distribution networks for electricity, irrigation, and urban water supply). Many of the public utilities have high fixed costs—primarly because of the cost of distribution systems like pipelines and transmission lines. As a result of these fixed costs, the average cost of supply in these sectors tends to decrease as output increases. This is what is meant by "economies of scale." Because of this tendency for average cost to decrease as scale increases, there will tend to be only one firm in the sector—hence, the sector will be "monopolistic" by nature.

A free market would fail to provide an economically efficient outcome in the case of natural monopolies, because there would be no competition—neither local nor international—to regulate the behavior of the monopoly in the interest of society. For a free market to work efficiently and in the interest of society, the market for that good must have certain characteristics. One of these is that there must be a large number of buyers and a large number of sellers of the product so that competition will protect society from predatory practices (see Technical Note 12).

In neoclassical economics, economic activity is seen as an interplay between motivating forces and regulating forces. Neoclassicists believe that individuals' desire to improve their own and their family's welfare is the primary motivating force in any economy. This motivating force is assumed to be based on an inherent drive for personal gain. Because the "natural" drive to improve their own welfare may lead individuals to behave in ways that are costly to others, society will need some regulating force to prevent individuals from taking advantage of other people.

The neoclassical theory presents convincing evidence that competition, where it can be achieved, is a very effective and low-cost regulator; and where competition exists on both sides of the market for a pure private good—i.e., "perfect competition"—the interplay between the motivating force of individual drive and the regulating force of competition will help maximize society's welfare.

Of course, this natural interplay between motivation and regulation occurs only in cases of perfect competition. In other cases, some other form of regulation may be needed. In the case of natural monopolies, for example, the regulatory force of competition will not be present. Often, the government will step in to play the role of a regulator. In those cases, government regulation, in principle, should attempt to do the same things that real competition would do—were it possible to have positive competition.

These regulatory objectives are meant to lead the supplier to:
  a. build the most efficient scale of plant;

Natural Monopolies.
These occur when major economies of scale exist for a nontradable good or service. It is "natural" to monopolize the provision of power grids, natural gas pipelines, and other costly distribution systems, since it does not make sense to duplicate their very great costs in several firms as a way of having competition.

Economies of scale.
Means that the average cost of supply decreases as output increases. The cost considerations are important since natural monopolies tend to have a large element of fixed costs.

b. operate the plant at its lowest cost level of output;

c. price the service to meet the objectives of:

- economic efficiency;
- financial mobilization; and
- equity; and

d. be responsive to the needs of its customers.

In the best interests of society, the government should intervene to regulate the natural monopoly "optimally." The economics literature contains hundreds of volumes dedicated to helping public utility managers operate these firms in a socially optimal fashion [e.g., Munasinghe and Warford (1982); and Saunders, Warford, and Wellenius (1983)]. For a variety of reasons, it is a difficult task to accomplish.

However, if the public monopoly is regulated optimally, then the financial price of, say, electric power would represent the economic value of that electricity. No accounting price would be needed in appraising projects which use electric power as inputs (see Technical Note 13). Government intervention would have corrected for the market failure and the monopolistic power company would have been behaving in the same way that it would under perfect competition.

Unfortunately, we will find that natural monopolies are not regulated optimally. Generally, electric power is provided to consumers at a price below its replacement cost and below the price that the user would be willing to pay for that amount of electricity. In Egypt, for example, consumers pay a price that is approximately one-third of the cost of supplying electricity. In a project which used this electric power as an input, we would have to shadow price the electric power—i.e., use an economic value which was different from the financial value (see Case 1 in Part V).

Imperfect Competition. Monopoly elements may exist in other ways than through natural monopolies (or public utilities). Various forms of imperfect competition may exist for a wide range of products. Imperfect competition tends to be more common in manufacturing and in marketing services than, for example, in agricultural activities. Nonetheless, we may still find imperfect competition existing at the local level in the supply of inputs or services to farmers, or in the collection and marketing of agricultural outputs. For example, a developing country may have only six domestic foundries that produce pumps for irrigation. If those six firms collude either explicitly or tacitly to fix the price of pumps, social welfare may be affected. So we may have to shadow price the cost of pumps in making an economic analysis of the agricultural project. And if we need to shadow price the outputs of a sector, then we may also wish to recommend that a sector or

Imperfect competition may force financial prices to diverge from economic values and make it necessary for us to estimate accounting prices. If estimating the accounting prices is very complicated, we might have to go beyond project analysis and start looking into policy reforms as well.

policy analysis be conducted for that sector (see Chapter 8).

The need to shadow price the pumps may lead us (or the project planner in the country concerned) to recommend policies for dealing with monopolistic elements in the foundry sector. We should not overlook these "policy implication" aspects of the project analysis. No one will be in a better position than the project analyst to identify the positive and negative effects that government policies have on the subsector, because no one else in the government is likely to have the detailed micro-level understanding of that subsector. In all cases involving the use of shadow pricing, a more desirable alternative would be to design an optimal intervention to correct for the underlying market failure that leads us to use an accounting price.

Any form of imperfect competition may force financial prices to diverge from economic values and may make it necessary for us to estimate accounting prices in conducting project economic analysis. And when competition is so imperfect as to complicate the estimation of the economic values, we should begin to think beyond project analysis and start looking into the need for policy reforms as well. Economics includes more than the theory of shadow pricing: there are specialized areas which deal with the theory of regulation in each of the areas of market failure discussed in this chapter. Shadow pricing and project planning should not be carried out in isolation from work being done in the country based on knowledge from these other areas of economic analysis.

External Economies

A second group of market failures involves "external economies." [A very useful reference for this section is Cornes and Sandler (1986).] An *external economy* occurs when an economic activity affects a "third party"—someone other than the producer and the buyer. The result of an external economy is that some production or consumption impacts will not be "internalized" in the financial price

---

A Review of Natural Monopolies

Let us quickly review our discussion of natural monopolies.

• We have said that economic values will sometimes differ from financial values. This might occur because of the second type of government failure: the failure to intervene optimally to correct for the natural monopoly type of market failure.

• In the case of a natural monopoly, the government should design optimal interventions—including optimal prices.

• Sometimes the government will not regulate prices to optimal levels in these natural monopolies; therefore, "accounting prices" will have to be used in the economic analysis. In this case, the economic values would be different from the values that were used in the financial analysis.

that is paid for the good. By "internalized" we mean that some costs or benefits are not included in the financial statements of the supplier or of the buyer. Rather, they occur "external" to these statements and affect a third party.

Technological Externality. A "third party" impact, or an external economy, might occur in a feedlot operation, for example. The third party might be downstream users of the water from a small stream that was polluted by wastes run off from the animal stalls. In this example, the financial cost of producing meat would not reflect the true cost to society—unless, of course, the government were to intervene to impose a "socially optimal pollution tax" on the meat producer. (To be "optimal," the tax should be equivalent to the net real costs borne downstream and not otherwise reflected in the price of the meat.) Economists call the type of external economy dealt with in this example a "technological externality."

In most countries, "socially optimal pollution taxes" do not exist, though environmental economists have argued for such policies for many years. Thus, in principle, the shadow pricing for the project economic analysis should try to reflect the downstream externalities as well as the "internalized" costs borne by the producer. The economic cost of the meat produced in the feedlot would include not only the cost of the animal feed (which would already be internalized in the financial value), but also the costs borne by the downstream users of the water (which would not be "internalized" in the financial value). Thus, the economic cost of the meat would be higher than its reported financial costs. The "internal economies" (i.e., those values that accrue to the buyer or seller) will be reflected in the financial values, so they will be relatively easy to determine. However, it will usually be difficult to estimate the full cost, or full value, of external economies.

Linkage Economies. Some economists include "intersectoral dependencies," or "linkage economies," under the heading of external economies and suggest that these linkage economies represent justification for government activity. Examples of linkage economies are often found in the natural resource development sector—particularly in mining and large-scale timber operations. Linkage economies also form an important reason for the attempts at integrated planning, such as the regional planning system implemented in the Philippines over the past decade.

As an example of linkage economies, let us discuss a proposal to develop a large-scale ore mine in an undeveloped area of a developing country. The export of the ore might require investment in three separate sectors:

   a. in the ore mine itself;

   b. in a rail link to tie the mine to the nation's rail network; and

Externality.
This occurs when an economic activity affects a "third party"—someone other than the producer or the consumer. The result is that some costs or benefits are not included in the financial price paid for the good.

c. in a port expansion to handle the additional load on the port.

Expansions in these three linked sectors—mining, railways, and the port—should, ideally, be planned together. Many economists argue that such integrated planning is best undertaken by the government. But, in addition to the problem of integrating the planning, each link in the ore exporting system might represent a monopolist vis-à-vis the other links. And the system might have difficulty functioning if there were three or even two separate private firms involved.

Some governments have therefore decided that such interlinked operations should be owned or controlled by the state. A moment's thought will show why this conclusion has been reached. A private mine facing a private railroad would involve a monopolist facing a monopsonist. The outcome would likely be determined by the one with the most financial, political, or—perhaps—private military power. Ultimately, the more powerful firm would likely end up buying the assets of the weak at less than their original cost. And the battle in between might be costly to society.

Thus, where such intersectoral dependencies exist, governments often step in to undertake the development of the linked sectors, or at least to participate in the planning and in controlling their development. The government might choose to own part of the interlinked system—e.g., the rail link and the port. Similarly, in irrigation supply, governments often choose to be the monopolistic provider of water in that closely interlinked production system.

Information Economies. Sometimes, information economies is included under the heading of external economies. Information often readily becomes part of the public domain. Not only is it difficult to control information for private use (e.g., research findings), it may also be undesirable to do so. This is particularly true in the case of information which might affect the health or welfare of a large part of society.

The government often engages in activities designed to generate and to distribute information. Agricultural research and extension are examples of such activities. Similarly, the government often assists in providing market information to agriculturalists and others by sponsoring radio programs which provide timely information to producers.

It is difficult to put a willingness to pay value on any of the forms of external economy that we have discussed—in particular linkage economies and information economies. In this respect, they are similar to the public and quasi-public goods that we shall discuss shortly. Yet, like these goods, we will sometimes have to deal with them in agricultural and, in particular, rural development activities. In a later section, we will discuss various means for dealing with items, such as these, that are difficult to value in willingness to pay terms.

Pecuniary Externalities. Production and purchase decisions often have third-party effects which occur through the prices paid or received by others. For example, the decision by a wealthy eccentric to buy and hoard canned goods may cause the price of canned goods to rise in the short run. The increase in price may have negative impacts on other consumers. Likewise, a government's decision to build a hydroelectric dam may cause the price of cement to rise. This effect on the price of these goods may be viewed as a "third party impact," just as are the technological externalities discussed previously. These impacts on the price are termed "pecuniary externalities."

Pecuniary externalities obviously can have an impact on the distribution of purchasing power in society; they are normally ignored in economic efficiency analysis, because the increase in price that harms one party usually benefits another. If both the payer and the payee of the higher price are citizens of the country, then the pecuniary impacts may be viewed as netting out to zero. However, if the pecuniary externalities relate to a good that the country imports or exports, then it should be taken into account as an aspect of market failure for which government intervention would be appropriate.

If the country is a major exporter of an item (e.g., Bangladesh jute, Brazil coffee, Malaysia tin and rubber, Egypt long-staple cotton, Ghana cocoa, and Thailand rice), then the optimal policy for that sector may be to impose an export tax to force exporters to internalize the pecuniary impact their incremental exports will have on other producers (see the case of Egyptian cotton in Part V).

Increasing and Decreasing Returns to Scale. Scale economies are sometimes discussed under the heading of external economies. The presence of increasing returns to scale and competitive input markets is likely to lead to monopoly. This problem has been discussed in the preceding section on natural monopoly. In principle, it is possible to treat all aspects of market failure as forms of external economies.

Public and Quasi-Public Goods. A third category of market failure involves "public goods" and "quasi-public goods" [see Cornes and Sandler (1986)]. Public and quasi-public goods will not be provided in optimal quantities by private markets because of two characteristics that make them different from "private goods." [See Schmid (1978 and 1987), pages 40-42, for an iconoclastic discussion of conceptual problems surrounding the definitions of "private" and "public" goods.]

Pecuniary Externalities. *"Third party" effects that arise from the production or purchase decisions of individuals or the government through the prices paid or received by others. These externalities can have an impact on the distribution of purchasing power in society.*

A *pure public good* has two distinctive characteristics. First, people who do not buy the good or service cannot be excluded from consuming the good or service. For example, a clean environment is available to everybody, once it is provided. So is national defense. This is called the "nonexclusion" characteristic of a public good. Second, one person's consumption of a public good does not come at the expense of another person's consumption. Up to the point of congestion, my enjoying a beautiful view does not deprive you of being able to enjoy it. This aspect is called the "noncompetitiveness in consumption" characteristic of a public good.

A *quasi-public good* has some attributes of a public good, but does not have all of the required characteristics to be considered a pure public good. Examples of quasi-public goods include education, public health, police protection, and fire protection.

A *private good*, by comparison, is different from a public good in that, first, a private good can be made available to one person at a time—i.e., it can be "titled." The title can be transferred and nonpurchasers can be excluded from the benefits of consuming it. An automobile is an example of a private good. So is a bottle of soft drink. This is called the "exclusion principle" and must be met for a good or a service to be provided in private markets. Second, one person's use of a private good deprives some other person from using it. By consuming a soft drink, the user deprives someone else of the opportunity to do so. This is called "competitiveness in consumption." It means that each person who wants to consume the good must pay for the right to do so—there is none of the "free rider problem" associated with public and quasi-public goods.

Public and quasi-public goods usually are provided by the government and are paid for through government expenditure. This is as much for practical reasons as it is for reasons of principle. Because of the free rider problem and the nature of the demand for public goods, these goods must be provided by the public sector, and they cannot be sold like private goods. Thus, usually, there will not be a financial price paid for these goods.

The Free Rider Problem. Once public goods are provided to some individuals, others cannot be excluded from access to those goods. For example, once the air is made clean, everyone can enjoy the clean air—whether or not they paid for the cleanup. Economists refer to this as the problem of "nonexcludability;" and it gives rise to a second problem—the free rider problem. Joint public action will be required in dealing with public goods: the free rider problem will cause everybody to sit back and wait for others to pay for the provision of public goods, resulting in their underprovision.

The Nature of the Demand for Public Goods. Public goods cannot be broken into individually consumable units. For example,

Pure public good.
Has two characteristics:
1. People who do not buy the good cannot be excluded from consuming it;
2. One person's consumption of this good does not come at the expense of another's.

many of the most effective means of controlling water-borne diseases cannot be divided and sold in packages to individual consumers. This "indivisibility" problem affects our ability to derive a total demand function from the individual demand functions for public goods. For private goods, the total demand is derived by adding the number of units demanded by each consumer at each price—i.e., by "horizontally adding" individual demands.

Public goods, in contrast, do not exist in units. Thus, to derive the total demand for public goods, the willingness to pay by each individual for the total availability of the good is added—by "vertically adding" the individual demands. In concept, this determination of the total demand is important, because one of the functions of economic analysis is to assist in deciding on the optimal amounts of each public good to provide.

If a project produces a quasi-public good, or uses it as an input, there will be no "reference point" for estimating the willingness to pay value, because there will be no financial price for the good. Thus, goods of this sort tend to create the greatest difficulty in conducting project economic analysis.

Paradoxes and Fallacies

The Paradox of Thrift. The neoclassical list of market failures was augmented by John Maynard Keynes' "discovery" of the paradox of thrift. Many economists consider this to be one of Keynes' greatest contributions to economic thought [Amacher and Ulbrich (1986), p. 204]. The paradox of thrift is related to the fallacy of composition discussed below.

The problem, according to Keynes (1936), is that planned savings, if undertaken on a large scale by a number of individuals, may cause a reduction in aggregate demand and lead to a reduction in incomes from which actual savings will occur. The result may be that both income and actual savings will be lower than anticipated.

In the Keynesian approach to economic management, the government's function is to undertake macroeconomic interventions in the form of fiscal and monetary policies to correct for the impacts that such a paradox might have on the employment, income, and price levels in the economy.

The Fallacy of Composition. It is "a fallacy in which what is true of a part is, on that account alone, alleged to be also necessarily true of the whole" [Samuelson and Nordhaus (1989), p. 14]. This fallacy is most apparent in the agricultural sector in the behavior of commodity prices. If one farmer succeeds in increasing his output through, say, increasing his crop yields, then his revenue would be expected to increase. However, given the

Paradox of thrift.
Planned savings, if undertaken on a large scale, may reduce aggregate demand and reduce incomes.

inelastic demand for many agricultural commodities, increased yields by all farmers might result in lower revenues for each farmer.

Many issues of trade policy revolve around understanding the implications of the fallacy of composition. For example, imposing a protective tariff may help producers of the protected product and may even improve the balance of payments (at least in the short run). However, large-scale use of tariff protection may raise the cost of exports, hurt other producers of tradable goods, and actually worsen the balance of payments situation [see Harberger (1989)].

Similarly, when a country is a major producer of an exportable commodity (e.g., Egyptian long-staple cotton—see Case 11 in Part V—or Thai rice or Bangladesh jute), individual farmers may increase their incomes by increasing production for the export market. However, large-scale increases in the production of price-inelastic commodities may make all exporters worse off.

This "augmented" neoclassical theory of market failure, then, sees two sets of roles for the government:

    a. sector and market-level interventions designed to correct for market failures which occur market by market; and

    b. macroeconomic interventions designed to maintain full employment, stability of price levels, and external balance [see Dornbusch and Helmers (1988)].

A Review of Market Failure

Let us summarize again. There are three categories of market failure where shadow pricing may be required:

- monopolistic elements;
- external economies; and
- public and quasi-public goods.

Natural monopolies may not require shadow pricing, if government intervention is "optimal." However, experience has shown that there are few examples of such optimal intervention. Output prices may not reflect the actual willingness to pay by consumers of the natural monopoly's output; then economic values will be different from the financial values. It might sometimes be difficult to estimate the appropriate economic values for the outputs of public utilities, but it is basically a research problem and is not impossible by any means. It is time consuming, though.

Imperfect competition may require that financial prices be adjusted in determining real economic values. This too is basically a research undertaking, which usually can and should be done where the "imperfect competitor" is important as a supplier of project inputs, or as a purchaser of project outputs. ("Important" is usually defined, for practical purposes, to mean more than 10 percent of project costs or benefits.)

External economies will almost always involve costs or values which are not reflected in the financial values. It will also be difficult, in most cases, to accurately estimate the actual extent and values of these external economies. At least in the case of technological externalities, this too is a research problem; but it is usually a more difficult one than that for natural monopoly or imperfect competition valuation. For linkage economies and information economies, the valuation problems can be particularly difficult.

Public and quasi-public goods are, by their nature, generally not subject to market provision and market pricing. Thus, it will usually be very difficult to estimate the willingness to pay value of these types of goods. As a result, they will often be treated as "intangibles" in the cost-benefit analysis. And, if economic analysis is done, the form of economic analysis used for projects producing primarily public or quasi-public goods outputs will be either "least cost" analysis or "cost effectiveness" analysis.

Paradoxes and fallacies in relating individual behavior to aggregate economic performance lead many economists to argue that government intervention is required in managing the macroeconomy. The existence of unemployment resulting from macroeconomic imbalances may lead to the need for shadow pricing labor in the analysis of project and policy interventions. Disruptions in the foreign exchange market may suggest shadow prices to correct for temporary shocks that distort the exchange rate through temporary capital account flows.

3. Government Failure and the Need for Shadow Pricing

Summary. *Government failure occurs when the government intervenes in the economy in an unwarranted, inappropriate, or nonoptimal manner. Government failure creates "distortions" in the financial prices faced by producers and consumers, which lead them to make production and consumption decisions that are not economically efficient. These distortions are broken down into two elements: "border distortions" and "domestic distortions." A distinction between these two terms would be useful in deriving and using the accounting prices for correcting price distortions; these topics are discussed in the chapters that follow.*

The introduction of the concept of "merit goods" clouds the definition of government failure and, along with the inclusion of distributional issues in project planning introduced in Chapters 1 and 2, provides a background for the emergence of the social analysis (or the multi-objective approach) to be discussed in Part III. When merit goods and political and other considerations lead to large-scale intervention by the government, the economy may become "thoroughly distorted," which makes rational planning and appraisal of projects increasingly difficult. Optimal intervention should include both project and policy interventions, and development planning should focus on both of these approaches. When government failure has created a thoroughly distorted economy, policy reform will generally be more productive than will additional project investments in the distorted environment.

Government failure, as defined in Chapter 2, occurs when government intervention is "nonoptimal"—i.e., when government intervention is either inappropriate or should not have been undertaken. Government failure may occur, for example, when the government uses a "nonoptimal" import tariff to protect a favored producer at the expense of domestic consumers, or when it uses a tariff to collect revenues for running the government.

In both cases, the tariffs may be important to other objectives, but they nonetheless impose economic costs on society. Government failure may also occur when the government bans the export of a consumer item—as Pakistan did with eggs in the late 1970s— resulting in a net reduction in the welfare of society. Though some consumers might benefit in the short run, it would be at the expense of producers; and it would also be at the expense of consumers in the long run and detrimental to the country's need for foreign exchange. So, the overall result is a net loss in society's welfare. [For a survey of policy-imposed distortions in product and factor markets and the effects of such distortions on the efficiency of resource allocation and growth in developed, developing, and socialist countries, see Balassa (1984).]

Varieties of Government Failures

The presence of government failures will require that we estimate economic values; these values will usually be different from financial values. Economic distortions caused by government failure will generally fall under two headings:

    a. border distortions; and

    b. domestic distortions.

Border distortions include distortions such as export subsidies and import bans, which tend to sustain an overvalued exchange rate (i.e., keep high the official rate at which local currency exchanges for foreign currency). Border distortions affect the relationship between "border prices" [i.e., cost, insurance, and freight (CIF) and free-on-board (FOB) prices] and "domestic prices." Border distortions in developing countries tend to increase domestic prices relative to border prices. This raising of domestic prices, incidentally, is the mechanism through which the government is able to maintain an overvalued exchange rate.

The economic valuation process will have to somehow adjust for this distortion between border prices and domestic prices, because the distortion will affect the relative values of traded goods versus nontraded goods. Using the "shadow exchange rate" (instead of the "official exchange rate") in the economic analysis is one way of adjusting for the distortion between traded and nontraded goods. Using a shadow exchange rate in developing countries usually places higher values on foreign exchange and, thus, on traded goods relative to nontraded goods.

By comparison, the official exchange rate, would place a lower value on foreign exchange and, thus, a lower value on traded goods relative to nontraded goods. It is the distortion in the official exchange rate that is adjusted for in the economic analysis. Using conversion factors is an alternative way to deal with border distortions in the project economic analysis. We will discuss both of these methods in a later section.

Domestic distortions affect relationships among domestic prices. For example, a minimum-wage law will tend to raise the price of labor covered by the law relative to the cost of machinery, other inputs,

Border Distortions.
Include export subsidies and import bans, which sustain an overvalued exchange rate. These distortions affect the relationship between border prices and domestic prices.

Domestic Distortions.
These affect relationships among domestic prices. Minimum wage laws and subsidized interest rates are examples of domestic distortions.

and labor not covered by the law. Minimum-wage laws tend not to be applied to agricultural labor in developing countries. Thus, they tend to raise industrial wages, reduce employment in industry, and as a result lower agricultural wages. By the same token, a subsidized interest rate will tend to lower the cost of machinery relative to the cost of unskilled labor. This may be an important concern in many developing countries, where labor tends to be the abundant factor while capital tends to be a relatively scarce factor of production.

Merit Goods, Demerit Goods, and Market Failure

Merit goods can be viewed as a form of "intentional" government failure—in the sense that the government rejects the functioning of the market for that good in favor of controlling provision of the good through the public sector. The market has thereby been defined to have failed, even though none of the attributes of market failure are present. We could say that merit goods represent an attempt to define as a public good some good which has the characteristics generally associated with a private good. Public housing is an example of such a good. Various foodgrains represent other common examples.

By treating a good or service as a merit good, the government rewrites the rules of market failure on a basis that at times can be quite arbitrary. In Bangladesh, for instance, government projects dominate the marketing of hand pumps—not only those used for village drinking water, but also those used for minor irrigation (see Chapter 8).

A major problem with merit goods is that we have no clear-cut rules for defining which goods should be merit goods and which ones should not be. This is a different situation from the one we face in dealing with market failure, where we have developed over time a set of guidelines for determining when the market is failing to function efficiently.

By treating a good as a merit good, the government rewrites the rules of market failure on a basis that may seem arbitrary. A major problem is that there are no clear-cut rules for defining which goods should be merit goods and which ones should not be.

Merit goods pose two particularly difficult problems. First, the very concept of a merit good rejects the willingness to pay values that individuals place on those same goods through their individual buying actions. But we have no other source of information on the willingness to pay by society for these goods. Thus, they are difficult to value in the economic analysis apart from using the willingness to pay values that the government seems to have rejected already.

Second, we have no ready means for determining when a good

should be defined as a merit good; and we have no ready measure of the worth of merit goods in comparison with their costs. Thus, by accepting the idea of merit goods, we create an opportunity for those in positions of political or bureaucratic power to impose their own wishes in the name of society. This provides a potential for the practice of elitism, paid for with the use of society's resources. Publicly provided housing for public officials and publicly supported municipal orchestras in the capital city can sometimes be examples of such abuse.

In the agricultural sector, merit goods arguments can be used to justify policies which create government failure rather than provide socially optimal supplies of agricultural goods. For example, some agricultural pricing policies may nominally be aimed at providing low-cost food to society. But these policies may end up actually reducing the amount of food that is produced; or the policies may cause food to be produced at higher cost than would be possible using alternative sources or alternative technologies.

Basic Needs. However, the idea of merit goods is not totally without value. Products often defined as merit goods are also often described as "basic needs." The market demand for these basic needs generally reflects the existing income distribution, while the government may wish to meet the basic needs of each member of society, regardless of that person's ability to pay. For example, many countries subsidize the production of foodgrains. A disadvantage of this policy is that the subsidies sometimes cause foodgrains to be produced in areas which have very low productivity for foodgrains, but which have high productivity for other uses. The saline estuaries of Bangladesh and other countries, for example, are much better suited to producing prawns for export than they are for producing salt-tolerant varieties of rice. Much more rice can be imported by using the foreign exchange earned from prawn exports than can be produced in some of these coastal areas.

Merit Goods and Distributional Efficiency. The provision of many merit goods can be linked to concerns about the distribution or consumption in society (e.g., public housing and food subsidies). In cases where such a linkage exists, the provision of merit goods may represent an attempt by planners to bring considerations of distributional efficiency into the planning process.

As we noted earlier, distributional efficiency gives economists particular difficulty in applying positivistic methods of analysis. Recall that the idea of willingness to pay, which economists widely use to measure "value," basically ignores the distribution of income

Basic Needs.
These are essentially merit goods the market demand for which reflects existing income distribution. In trying to meet the basic needs of each member of society, the government rejects the "willingness to pay" measure of value in favor of the member's "ability to pay."

that underlies the demand schedules from which willingness to pay for private goods is derived. Still, whatever case may be made for merit goods, governments must be careful not to convert merit goods into more serious cases of government failure. But such care is needed in any case of government intervention.

Now let us return to our previous discussion of what we may call "truly meritorious" merit goods and look at the problems that they create for us—problems which occur even without "nonoptimal" intervention. Those merit goods which are really nothing more than basic needs may involve rejecting the willingness to pay measure of value because, for these goods, the "ability to pay" issue is considered more important. While we may find reasonable examples of true merit goods—and basic needs may be a good case in point—we must nevertheless keep in mind that each merit good creates two difficulties for economic planners in developing countries.

First, merit goods in low-income countries create difficult planning choices for governments. When per capita incomes are low and government budgets are small, there will likely be a gap between human needs (in terms of which merit goods often will be defined) and the resources available to the government to meet those needs. In these cases, choices must be made among merit goods as well as between consumption and investment. Government expenditures on one class of merit goods may carry high opportunity costs in terms of other classes of merit goods and in terms of increases in future consumption for all members of society.

Second, merit goods create difficult valuation problems for the project analyst. Once we have defined something as a merit good, we have—to a greater or lesser extent—taken it out of the category of "tangible" project impacts and put it into the category of "intangibles." As we shall see later, these intangibles are much less amenable to quantitative analysis than are the tangible inputs and outputs with which we are more accustomed.

When Do Financial Values Represent Economic Values?

We have discussed market failures which lead to financial values differing from economic values. You may wonder whether there are cases in which the market for a product does not fail. In other words, if there are cases in which financial and economic values are the same (cases in which financial values represent social values).

Financial values equal economic values when there is a perfectly functioning market which has none of the aspects of market failure.

Let us pose the same question in a different way: When can we say that what consumers actually pay is exactly equal to what they would be willing to pay? And when is that value exactly equal to the "social value" of a good? The answer is: when there is a perfectly functioning market which has none of the aspects of market failure.

Such a perfectly functioning market would need to have the following characteristics:

a. A large number of independent buyers and a large number of independent sellers must exist, and they must not collude to take advantage of others (No monopoly elements).

b. The good or service must be capable of being "titled" and transferred—i.e., it must be possible to market it (The exclusion principle must hold).

c. People who pay for the good must be able to prevent nonpayers from benefiting from the good (No "free rider" problem—related to the exclusion principle).

d. Use of the good by one person must prevent another person from using the good (Competitiveness in consumption).

e. Production and consumption of the good or service must not cause uncompensated benefits or costs to be borne by people who are not engaged in the production or consumption of the good (No externalities).

f. Government intervention must not be economically "nonoptimal" so that financial values do not differ from economic values (No government failure).

e. The good must not have the attributes of major merit or demerit goods.

Obviously, few markets meet all of these criteria. [Perhaps no markets meet all of these requirements all of the time; see Schmid (1978)]. This is true in developed countries, as well as in developing countries.

Elements of market failure are widespread. Monopoly elements are found in every country—particularly in developing countries where the size of the market for many products is small and thus very easily monopolized. The need for government intervention—through projects, programs, and policies—to correct for these market failures is readily apparent. However, that intervention should be planned and analyzed very carefully.

But, government intervention is not always carefully planned and

Elements of market failure are widespread. Monopoly elements are found in every country. The need for government intervention to correct for these market failures is therefore important.

analyzed. Often, it is undertaken to meet narrow interests rather than to meet the broader social interest. Again, this is true in both developed and developing countries. Government failure can create distortions in the economy which are more serious than those caused by market failure. In economies which have serious distortions of this type, it is very difficult to plan and implement projects (see Technical Note 14).

We can make three generalizations regarding countries which have serious government-induced price distortions:

a. It will be difficult to plan and implement viable projects in such an environment.

b. It will be difficult to estimate the economic values to use in project analysis in such an environment.

c. Changing the policy environment which is responsible for the price distortions will often be more productive than implementing another project in the existing, highly distorted environment.

Project planning and analysis comprise just one part of development planning. Equally important—perhaps, more so—is the policy environment that the government creates and is expected to maintain. [Consider, for example, the case of Colombia where, depending upon the trade policies the government pursues, a tradable commodity may be valued as if it were intrinsically a nontraded good. See Case 8 in Part V; see also Marsden and Belot (1987)]. The extent to which we must carry out shadow pricing—i.e., substitution of economic values for financial values—when we conduct project economic analysis tells us to what extent the policies being pursued by the government are the correct ones from the standpoint of society's economic welfare.

We would not have to conduct an economic analysis separate from the financial analysis of the project (i.e., financial values and economic values would be the same) under the following circumstances:

a. Market failures were corrected by economically optimal government intervention.

b. There were no government failures, because the government did not intervene in markets which did not have some element of market failure.

c. The government was able to raise the revenues necessary to carry out its optimal interventions without having the taxes themselves create (major) distortions.

Government failure can create distortions in the economy which are more serious than those caused by market failure. In economies which have serious distortions of this type, it is very difficult to plan and implement projects.

Obviously, it would be very unusual to find that all the values in the project financial accounts could be accepted as representing real economic values. Thus, we will usually have to shadow price at least some of the values in the project financial accounts in conducting the project economic analysis. We will also have to use the knowledge that we achieve in that process to assess policy options that would increase the efficiency with which that sector functions. [See Singh, Squire, and Kirchner (1985) and their references to some techniques under development at the World Bank to assess the impacts of alternative agricultural pricing policies in individual countries.]

Optimal Taxation and Shadow Pricing

Up to now, we have treated the shadow pricing problem as though it would go away if governments would simply manage economies correctly. This has been the traditional approach to project economic analysis (partly by choice, and partly out of necessity). In this approach, the need for shadow prices presumably derives from the forms of government failure. This approach to economic analysis has generally been viewed as a necessary expedient— necessary, because of the lack of an implementable theory of shadow pricing based on a fully developed theory of trade and of public intervention. The need for shadow pricing generally has been accepted by practitioners, because of the widely held view that correcting for inappropriate government interventions was, in practice, the most important job to be done in project economic analysis.

At the same time that this approach to shadow pricing was being practiced, work continued on broader issues related to the theories of trade and the public sector. Much of the latter work was published under the heading of the "theory of taxation." (The Newberry and Stern volume, cited in the Bibliography at the end of this volume, provides a good summary of the status of that work at this writing. Also, Technical Note 25 discusses the development of project appraisal techniques within this body of work.)

In simple terms, work on the public sector starts from the premise that it is practically impossible for a government to act to remove all distortions in the economy. Indeed, the very act of removing one distortion will create another. Thus, in practice, the problem is essentially one of determining the "best" set of distortions, since we know that there will be distortions; this is referred to as the broader economic problem of second best. In this, much more complicated environment, "second best shadow prices" represent the prices which take into account several inherent conflicts and trade-offs facing managers of the public sector.

The need for shadow prices derives from government failure. Practitioners of development regard correcting for inappropriate government interventions to be the most important job in project economic analysis.

However, later work on the public sector has assumed that since there will be distortions, the problem is one of determining the "best" set of distortions, referred to as the "broader economic problem of second best." The "second best shadow prices" take into account conflicts and trade-offs that public sector managers face.

A fundamental conflict exists in the various functions of government that are postulated in most contemporary texts on public finance, a subfield in economics that is increasingly being referred to as "economics of the public sector" [see Musgrave and Musgrave (1988)]. These functions include:

    a. the allocation function (i.e., static and dynamic economic efficiency, the subject of this text);

    b. the stabilization function (i.e., macroeconomic management); and

    c. the distribution function (i.e., equity, including attention to income distribution issues).

The first fundamental conflict occurs because government is given the role of providing public goods to meet the allocation function. A basic problem is that to provide public goods, government requires access to finance. It is difficult to find sources of revenue which are "nondistorting."

The classic lump-sum tax (such as the "head" tax) approach to raising revenues in a nondistorting manner in efficiency terms may well constitute a regressive tax, and thus be in conflict with the distribution function of government. It is unlikely that "corrective taxes"—discussed in the preceding section and included under the allocation function—will raise sufficient revenues to compensate for the distortions as well as to finance the provision of public and quasi-public goods. Additional revenues will have to be raised, and these will (in principle) be applied according to the one or both of the two classic principles of taxation:

    a. the benefit principle, which states that citizens should pay taxes according to the benefits they receive from public sector activity; and

    b. the "ability to pay" principle, which states that citizens should be taxed according to their ability to pay.

These principles of taxation imply that taxes are unlikely to be "neutral"—i.e., nondistorting in the pure efficiency sense. Indeed, some taxes may be imposed for "corrective" reasons to meet income distribution objectives. Similarly, conflicts will exist between economic efficiency and the government's objectives of stabilization and growth.

A fundamental conflict can occur between the allocative and distributive functions of a government. This conflict will occur when the government tries to provide public goods, but cannot raise revenues in a "nondistorting" manner to pay for those goods.

Because of these fundamental conflicts, we do not consider it feasible to follow the "first best" approach of correcting for distortions in terms of allocative efficiency only—the attitude taken in the simplified approaches to public intervention and to project economic analysis addressed in most manuals, guidelines, and training activities directed at practitioners. In this simplified approach, the term "first best" is often used to refer to cases in which the shadow prices would have been estimated in terms of equilibria which would exist after optimal correction of all distortions; while the term "second best" is often used to refer to prices which do not assume that these corrections have occurred, or will occur.

In this volume, we use the term "second-best shadow prices" in the simplistic sense implied in the preceding paragraph, while bearing in mind the general problem of second best implied by the still-developing theory of optimal taxation. In the Technical Notes at the back of this volume, we discuss and review this latter work in more detail for the theoretically oriented readers. We have assumed that the main text will be of interest to practitioners and to economists just beginning the study of these complex matters. To a large extent, the body of the main text relates to actual current practice, while the Technical Notes discuss attempts to develop the next generation of practice.

4. The Willingness to Pay Numeraire

Summary. *If projects are to be judged on the basis of their contribution to national economic efficiency, then the contributions must be measured by some common denominator, or a "numeraire." Two kinds of numeraires are widely used: the willingness to pay (WTP) or aggregate consumption numeraire, and the foreign exchange numeraire.*

The WTP numeraire values nontraded goods and services on the basis of what society is willing to pay; and it values traded goods and services in foreign exchange at border prices, which must then be converted into local currency to make them additive with the values of nontraded goods. In the WTP numeraire, much attention must then be paid to the definition and calculation of the exchange rate used for the conversion. Usually, some form of shadow exchange rate (SER) is used; and that SER often is approximated by some measure of the "willingness to pay" value for some basket of goods and services that incremental foreign exchange would be able to provide.

There are many ways to conduct a project appraisal using an economic efficiency approach. The two most prominent of these can be viewed as alternative ways of defining the economic efficiency numeraire. We will call the first of these methods the "willingness to pay analysis" because it values all inputs and all outputs in terms of what society (really, the market) would be willing to pay for them. We will call the second method the "generic foreign exchange" numeraire, because it seeks to convert all inputs and outputs into foreign exchange.

We use the term "generic" because no distinction is made regarding who has control of the incremental foreign exchange in the economic analysis formulation. (Note that we do not have to be specific about beneficiaries of the foreign exchange impacts, because we are dealing only with the economic efficiency objective. Were we to add income distribution or increasing government income as objectives, we would have to differentiate between the beneficiaries of the foreign exchange impacts. Thus, the foreign exchange would not be generic.)

There are advantages and disadvantages to using both the willingness to pay numeraire and the generic foreign exchange numeraire; these are discussed in the sections that follow. While the willingness to pay approach appeared to be the most prominent

Numeraire.
In cost-benefit analysis, the numeraire is the common denominator for measuring benefits and costs. The two prominent forms of numeraire in economic efficiency analysis are the "willingness to pay" numeraire and the "foreign exchange" numeraire.

method at the time the Gittinger (1982) was written, in recent years increasing use is being made of the foreign exchange numeraire in the economic efficiency analysis. In this chapter, we look at the willingness to pay version of the economic efficiency numeraire. In Chapter 5, we shall look at the foreign exchange version of the economic efficiency numeraire.

Valuing Nontraded Goods

When we work in a willingness to pay numeraire (also called the consumption numeraire), we attempt to value all inputs and all outputs on the basis of what society (consumers really) would be willing to pay for each unit of each good or service being valued. Note that what society would be willing to pay and what is actually paid will often be different—in which case some degree of shadow pricing may be necessary. In this approach, units of output are valued at prices reflecting the marginal willingness to pay, and units of input are valued at the marginal willingness to pay for the forgone outputs that the inputs would have produced without the project.

The prices of nontraded goods that are produced and sold in undistorted markets will already be expressed in the willingness to pay numeraire. However, nontraded goods whose prices are distorted by market or government failures will not be expressed directly in the willingness to pay numeraire. In addition, the border prices of traded goods (where there are trade distortions) will have to be adjusted, or shadow priced, to express them in the willingness to pay formulation of the economic efficiency numeraire. [Gittinger goes into some degree of detail in explaining how each category of traded and nontraded goods would be valued in this version of the economic efficiency numeraire; and he discusses the steps involved in expressing the economic efficiency values either in domestic prices or in border prices. See Gittinger (1982), pages 250-271.]

Valuing Traded Goods

In shadow pricing traded goods, the first thing that we do is delete the taxes and subsidies from the financial values. We talk about the willingness to pay as being the important concept in this approach to shadow pricing, but then we take the tariffs and subsidies off of the traded goods, and reduce them to border values rather than leave them at their market values. Of course, we are not finished with shadow pricing the traded goods after this step, but noneconomists find this intermediate step in getting to the willingness to pay values very confusing. If you are an instructor of project economic analysis, you may find this a sticky point in classroom presentations and might have to once or twice remind

Willingness to Pay, or Consumption Numeraire.
A numeraire in which all benefits and all costs are valued in terms of impacts on society's consumption over time. The accounting price for each unit of output would be based on the marginal willingness of the market to pay for the good. Future consumption is discounted to present values by using a discount rate which reflects the rate of fall of the value of consumption over time.

Foreign Exchange Numeraire.
A numeraire in which all benefits and all costs are measured in units of foreign exchange. A "generic" foreign exchange numeraire does not take account of who in the society gains or loses from the use of incremental units of foreign exchange.

your participants of the logic involved. The logic is contained in the following paragraphs (see also Technical Note 11).

First of all, remember that taxes and subsidies normally do not represent real resource flows; thus, they usually are deleted from the financial values in determining economic values. After they are deleted, we are left with the border values. (Plus or minus, of course, any related local transport and marketing costs which must themselves be shadow priced. Let us ignore these local elements of cost for the moment.)

Having reduced traded goods to border prices (i.e., to foreign exchange impacts), we must convert these values into willingness to pay terms. This may be looked upon as a process of converting "foreign exchange impacts" into "consumption impacts." (Note that, if we had been using the generic foreign exchange numeraire, we would leave the traded goods in border prices and would instead convert the willingness to pay values of the nontraded goods into foreign exchange equivalents. We discuss this approach in Chapter 5.)

In the willingness to pay analysis, traded goods affect consumption (willingness to pay) indirectly. Imported project inputs use foreign exchange that, in their alternative use, could have been used to import consumer goods that would have increased domestic consumption. What would be the value of the alternative domestic consumption that was forgone? The answer, of course, is what society would have been willing to pay for those goods. Or the foreign exchange might have been used to import intermediate goods—such as raw materials—which could have been used to produce consumer goods. How much added consumption would that have generated? To determine this, we take the marginal value product (MVP) of the intermediate goods that would have been imported with the alternative use of the foreign exchange. That will tell us how much those alternative imports would have contributed to final consumption (i.e., the willingness to pay value of the final consumption that those intermediate goods would have produced).

In shadow pricing traded goods, the first step is to delete the taxes and subsidies from the financial values. The traded goods are now reduced to border values. The next step is to convert these values into willingness to pay terms.

Similarly, exported outputs, or import substitutes, increase the foreign exchange available to the country; and, thus, they make additional imported goods available for consumption. How much are those additional goods worth in economic terms? They are worth what society would be willing to pay for them. Remember that in a true willingness to pay analysis, everything is worth what society would be willing to pay—i.e., the demand price. (For a producer good, of course, the demand price will be derived from the producer good's MVP. See Technical Note 15.)

Foreign Exchange and Traded Goods

When we are dealing with traded goods in the willingness to pay approach, we are really dealing with increases or decreases in the amount of foreign exchange that is available. We can value that foreign exchange—and, thus, the traded goods—by making reference to the amount of added consumption (measured in willingness to pay terms) that the foreign exchange will make available.

In the process, we will calculate a shadow exchange rate (or a standard conversion factor) which expresses the relationship between the willingness to pay value of nontraded goods and the border price (i.e., foreign exchange) of a traded good. It will tell us the price relationship, or "exchange rate," between traded and nontraded goods. This average exchange rate between traded and nontraded goods may be expressed either as the shadow exchange rate (SER), or as the standard conversion factor (SCF):

$$\text{SER1} = \frac{\text{Willingness to pay prices in rupees}}{\text{Border prices in dollars}} \tag{4.1}$$

$$\text{SCF} = \frac{\text{Border prices in rupees at OER}}{\text{Willingness to pay prices in rupees}} \tag{4.2}$$

Note that the SER we use in project economic analysis (let us call it SER1) is a specialized one. There are other variants. For instance, macroeconomists and international trade experts often talk about another version of the shadow exchange rate in attempting to estimate the exchange rate that would balance trade (let us call this second one SER2); they will also speak of a third shadow exchange rate in terms of the exchange rate necessary to balance payments on current account (let us call the third one SER3). SER2 and SER3 may be vastly different quantitatively from the SER1 that we use in project work; the uses of SER2 and SER3 are quite different from our use of SER1. The different definitions of the SER are given in the box on page 36.

No matter which formula we use in the willingness to pay numeraire, we will end up with a conversion of foreign exchange into willingness to pay values. If we use the SER formula, we will be doing so at one price level—the domestic price level. If we use the SCF, we will convert foreign exchange into willingness to pay values at a different price level—the border price level. The first of these is the approach that Gittinger (1982) calls "the shadow exchange rate method;" the second is "the conversion factor method."

When we are dealing with traded goods in the willingness to pay approach, we are really dealing with increases or decreases in the amount of foreign exchange that is available.

In describing both of these approaches in Gittinger, the numeraire that is applied is the willingness to pay numeraire.

A willingness to pay numeraire can be applied in two ways:

    a. a domestic price level calculation using the SER; and

    b. a border price level calculation using the SCF.

It is important for us to understand that the border price level calculation in Gittinger (1982) is just as much an application of the willingness to pay numeraire as is the domestic price level calculation. It is important, because we may have to explain the difference to other economists who may jump to an erroneous conclusion based on their knowledge of the UNIDO Guidelines and the OECD Manual.

Different Definitions of Shadow Exchange Rates

SER1   Measures the degree of distortion between traded and nontraded goods (called "border distortions" in later sections). A "de facto" exchange rate, in that it measures the actual rate at which traded and nontraded goods exchange for each other, on average.

SER2   Estimate of the official exchange rate (OER) needed to balance *trade*. An estimated "equilibrium" rate. If there is a trade deficit in existence, then SER2 would be expected to be higher than SER1.

SER3   Estimate of the OER needed to balance *payments* on the current account. In the presence of capital flight, SER3 is expected to be higher than SER2 and to be unstable and difficult to predict. SER4, the "black market exchange rate" is sometimes advocated as the measure of the SER. However, this is seldom an appropriate measure of the SER for project appraisal, though it may be used on occasion in "fine tuning" the estimate of the SER. Generally, the "black market" (or "informal market" as it is also called) is too thin and specialized and does not accurately reflect the goods and services that represent inputs and outputs of public sector projects. This might be the appropriate SER in some "thoroughly distorted" economies, where the OER is ridiculously overvalued and where practically no trade takes place at the OER (see Technical Note 16). Uganda may be regarded as an example of a country of this type.

The UNIDO Guidelines uses the domestic price level version of the willingness to pay analysis. In contrast, the OECD Manual uses a version of the foreign exchange numeraire; all values in the OECD method end up in border prices. Because of this difference in these two widely known methods of analysis, economists generally expect a domestic price level calculation to be an application of the willingness to pay analysis; and they normally expect a border price level calculation to be an application of the foreign exchange numeraire.

5. The Foreign Exchange Numeraire

Summary. *In agricultural projects, the issue of the exchange rate can be avoided by working in a foreign exchange numeraire rather than the willingness to pay (WTP) numeraire discussed in Chapter 4. The foreign exchange numeraire requires that nontraded goods be valued in terms of their indirect impact on foreign exchange, while traded goods be valued in terms of their direct effects on foreign exchange. Thus, in this numeraire all goods and services are treated as either directly or indirectly traded.*

Calculating the foreign exchange impacts of nontraded goods requires either tracing down the direct and indirect foreign exchange used in producing those goods, or finding traded goods for which the nontraded goods are substitutes. This tracing will usually be possible in agricultural and industrial projects, though not necessarily in water and sewerage or urban services projects.

In the (perhaps, perverse) value system of economics, the end objective of all economic activity is consumption. We said in preceding chapters that foreign exchange can be used for consumption purposes in the sense that it can buy additional consumer goods for the society (or producer goods which will contribute to future consumption). We can convert this foreign exchange into consumption values by using some variant of a shadow exchange rate, or a standard conversion factor (see Chapter 4).

Obviously, if we can convert foreign exchange into willingness to pay values (or domestic consumption values), then we can use the reverse process to convert domestic consumption values into foreign exchange. In other words, we can turn the numeraire around and express it in foreign exchange—rather than in willingness to pay terms—and we will still be measuring economic efficiency.

The foreign exchange numeraire requires that the nontraded goods be valued in terms of their indirect impact on foreign exchange, while traded goods be valued in terms of their direct effects on foreign exchange.

One advantage of the generic foreign exchange formulation of the economic efficiency numeraire is that it is easier to understand what it is that is being counted. Units of foreign exchange tend to be more easily understood than are units of consumption valued at what the market is willing to pay for them. By the same token, the foreign exchange numeraire is also easier to explain to politicians and administrators.

Converting Nontraded Goods to the Foreign Exchange Numeraire

In the foreign exchange numeraire, the CIF and FOB prices of traded goods—or their parity price equivalents—will already be expressed in foreign exchange. [Parity prices are discussed in Gittinger (1982), pages 78-83.] The problem then will be to convert the nontraded goods into foreign exchange equivalents. In each of the two numeraires discussed herein, the problem lies in accurately reflecting the other category of goods in the selected numeraire—and to do so consistently. In other words, in the willingness to pay formulation, the problem is to convert traded goods values into a valuation system comparable to that of the nontraded goods (i.e., convert foreign exchange into willingness to pay).

From the preceding paragraphs we know that this is done by determining the foreign exchange impacts of the traded goods and then calculating a consumption value equivalent for the foreign exchange. In the generic foreign exchange formulation, in contrast, the problem is the opposite: it is to convert the nontraded goods into equivalent foreign exchange impacts. To do this, two different approaches are used, depending upon whether the nontraded item being valued is a project input, or a project output.

Nontraded Project Inputs. In applying the foreign exchange numeraire, project inputs normally will be converted to foreign exchange by tracing the foreign exchange used directly and indirectly in producing the project inputs—i.e., by breaking the project's inputs down into their inputs, round after round, *ad infinitum*. (This procedure is discussed more fully in later chapters.)

When the process is completed, we will be left with direct and indirect foreign exchange impacts, nontraded labor, and land (i.e., natural resources). The foreign exchange valuation process will then be completed by converting the nontraded labor and land into foreign exchange and adding these foreign exchange costs to the direct and indirect foreign exchange costs of the other direct and indirect inputs. The procedure for converting labor and land to foreign exchange equivalents is discussed in a separate section.

What is important is to remember that, for nontraded project inputs, the approach involved is to convert them to foreign exchange by tracing the inputs of the inputs backward in the transaction process, round after round, until there are no nontraded items of any significance left to be broken down (see Technical Note 17).

Nontraded Project Inputs.
In applying the foreign exchange numeraire, project inputs will be converted to foreign exchange by using the foreign exchange utilized directly and indirectly in producing the project inputs.

Nontraded Project Outputs. Nontraded project outputs are converted to foreign exchange in a different way. They cannot be traced backward, round after round, as are the nontraded inputs: To do so would make no sense. Rather, they are converted to foreign exchange impacts by determining the traded goods for which they substitute in domestic consumption.

For example, it may be determined that nontraded vegetables produced by a project actually substitute in consumption for imported wheat. That is, had the project not increased the output of vegetables, the farmers would have consumed bread instead. Since the country was a net importer of wheat, the bread consumption would have led to increased imports of wheat. Or by providing vegetables for on-farm consumption, farm families may eat more vegetables and less rice, and the project may release domestic rice production for export. Each of these alternatives would involve foreign exchange impacts brought about by the project's production of nontraded vegetables.

The point to remember is that, in the foreign exchange numeraire, nontraded agricultural outputs ultimately substitute for some traded good. We must find those substitutes so that we may use their border prices in deriving the foreign exchange impacts of the nontraded goods output produced by the project (see Cases 5, 6, 12, and 13 in Part V).

❖

Nontraded Project Outputs.
In applying the foreign exchange numeraire, project outputs will be converted to foreign exchange impacts by determining the traded goods for which they substitute in domestic consumption.

6. The Exchange Rate in the Two Numeraires

Summary. *The willingness to pay (WTP) numeraire involves the use of a shadow exchange rate (SER), while (for agricultural and industrial projects) any exchange rate can be used in the foreign exchange numeraire. In practice, the SER calculation usually is based on some form of a weighted average tariff rate (WATR) estimate. In either numeraire, the correction for border distortions may be made by either raising border prices up to domestic price levels, or by decreasing domestic WTP values to border price levels. Thus, comparisons of all values may be made in either domestic prices, or in border prices. The common practice is to denominate a foreign exchange numeraire in border prices. In mathematical terms, it does not matter which denomination is used. In practice, the domestic price level denomination makes it easier to separate out and explain the domestic and border distortions, while the border price level denomination makes international price comparisons easier.*

The Exchange Rate in Willingness to Pay Analysis

The shadow exchange rate (SER) is a critical variable in the willingness to pay analysis. This is true because the foreign exchange impacts of traded goods must be converted into consumption values—i.e., into willingness to pay values. The rate at which that conversion is made is critical to the resulting value of the objective function. As we shall see later, the exchange rate issue is not nearly as critical a parameter when we use the generic foreign exchange numeraire (except in projects which produce nontraded outputs for which no substitutes exist, such as urban water supply, urban sanitation, and so forth). Because the SER is so critical to the willingness to pay numeraire, let us discuss this point further.

Let us keep in mind what is actually being done when a SER is used in a willingness to pay approach. The SER represents the capability of a unit of foreign exchange to create domestic consumption value. The domestic consumption value is based on the willingness to pay for the good that could be provided by having an extra unit of foreign exchange available.

Since an extra unit of foreign exchange may be used to provide a wide range of traded goods, the average of the willingness to pay values of all of these goods may be included in calculating the SER. This average value is calculated by taking a weighted average of domestic prices of traded goods (assumedly, willingness to pay prices stated in rupees) and a weighted average of the border prices of these same goods (stated in dollars). The ratio of these

The shadow exchange rate is a more critical variable in the willingness to pay analysis than in the generic foreign exchange numeraire. The reason is that the foreign exchange impacts of traded goods need to be converted into consumption values based on the willingness to pay for the good. The rate at which the conversion is made is critical to the resulting value of the good.

two weighted averages gives the SER.

However, there are two serious practical problems associated with the use of simple equations for calculating the weighted average tariff rate:

First, in principle, the weighted average prices used should be for future traded goods at the margin, since the project will provide or use foreign exchange in the future. In practice, the weighted average prices tend to be based on recent historical prices and to be based on averages (usually a five-year average, with adjustments made for the expected effect of new trade policies). This is simply a practical consideration. We might be able to get the data for past trade; we would, of course, have to estimate or guess future values for these same data.

Second, in principle, the willingness to pay prices for the traded goods should be based upon actual, observed willingness to pay in domestic markets for the traded goods. However, in practice, the weighted average of domestic prices tend to be derived by estimating them rather than by observing market behavior; they are estimated by calculating the weighted average tariff and subsidy rate (WATR) on traded goods and raising border prices by the percentage indicated by WATR.

Again, this is simply a practical procedure that is required by the fact that we do not have an unlimited budget to use in sampling prices of traded goods in the market. This practice is based on the logic that the tariffs on imports will tend to raise their domestic market prices by the amount of the tariff, while the subsidies on exports will tend to increase their local market prices by the amount of the subsidy. Obviously, this practice—while clearly convenient—tends to ignore the domestic price effects of nontariff barriers (see Technical Note 18).

Domestic Price and Border Price Level Denominations

In practice, the SER tends not to be calculated by equation 4.1, but rather by using the following formula:

$$SER = (1 + WATR) \times OER \qquad (6.1)$$

where:

SER   = Shadow exchange rate;

WATR = Weighted average tariff and subsidy rate; and

OER   = Official exchange rate

The willingess to pay approach to shadow pricing is much easier to understand and interpret when it is done by using a domestic price calculation (rather than border price equivalents—i.e, using SER = Rs 12.5 : $1, rather than SER = Rs 10 : $0.80). It is much easier to relate the domestic price calculation to the idea of measuring how much people would be willing to pay for each good and service, since everyone is accustomed to paying prices that are comparable to the domestic price level calculation than to the border price level calculation. Thus, willingness to pay analysis is much easier to explain in SER terms than it is in SCF terms—even though the SCF is just another way of expressing the SER.

It is relatively easy to see that an exchange rate of Rs 12.5 = $1 is exactly the same as one of Rs 10 = $0.80. This can also be seen in the implicit relationships between the SER and SCF:

$$\text{SER} = \frac{\text{OER}}{\text{SCF}} \qquad (6.2)$$

$$\text{SCF} = \frac{\text{OER}}{\text{SER}} \qquad (6.3)$$

$$\text{PREM} = \frac{\text{SER}}{\text{OER}} \qquad (6.4)$$

$$\text{SCF} = \frac{1}{1 + \text{PREM}} \qquad (6.5)$$

where:
PREM = (1 + WATR).

From the above equations, it follows that:

If WATR = 25 percent, then PREM = 1.25, and SCF = 0.80.
If OER = Rs 10 : $1, then SER = Rs 12.5 : $1; or
SER = Rs 10 : $0.80.

A domestic price level calculation in the willingness to pay numeraire uses the SER = Rs 12.5 : $1 approach, while the border price level calculation uses the SER = Rs 10 : $0.80 approach. The problem in explaining the border price level calculation to policymakers is that they will naturally tend to think of "scarce" foreign exchange translating into a SER of Rs 12.5 = $1, while the border price level calculation uses the SER of Rs 10 = $0.80.

Weighted Average Tariff Rate (WATR).
The average of all tariffs paid on imported goods and all subsidies paid on exported goods, each weighted by the proportion that the good represents in the value of total trade of the country. In practice, it is usually calculated by adding together customs data on the total value of all imports and exports and on total net tariff collections and subsidy payments, so that the weighting occurs automatically.

A willingness to pay price calculated at the border price level is difficult even for economists to grasp. Thus, willingness to pay analysis is easiest to explain and to intrepret when it is done in domestic prices—i.e., using a SER like the Rs 12.5: $1 rate, rather than by hiding the SER of Rs 10 : $0.80 behind the SCF of 0.80 in the so-called "conversion factors" approach to willingness to pay. If you are an instructor, this is one of the issues that you will have to grapple with in teaching from Gittinger (1982), if you choose to use the willingness to pay approach in combination with a border price level calculation.

If you use the willingness to pay method and decide to denominate it in border price equivalents, you may find it easier in some cases to explain the SER approach first and to use that as a way of achieving an understanding of the SCF approach. Alternatively, you may use the generic foreign exchange numeraire and avoid altogether trying to explain the willingness to pay. Note, however, that should you use a foreign exchange numeraire, you may well have equal difficulty (though a completely different set of difficulties) when it comes time to deal with nontraded outputs in the foreign exchange numeraire.

Instructors of project economic analysis (and practitioners who must explain their calculations to others) should keep two factors in mind when deciding whether to use the willingness to pay or the foreign exchange numeraire:

First, in explaining the willingness to pay numeraire, there are two points at which difficulty is often encountered, depending upon whether this numeraire is denominated in domestic price terms or in border price terms:

- *Domestic Price Approach.* This approach is very confusing to noneconomists. Specifically, it involves removing specific taxes and subsidies on traded goods, then adding back the effect of weighted-average taxes and subsidies. (This has been discussed previously.)

- *Border Price Approach.* The logic of reducing to the border price level the willingness to pay prices of nontraded goods is also confusing, since noneconomists tend to be accustomed to applying the "foreign exchange premium" by multiplying both sides of the OER equation by one plus the premium, rather than by dividing both sides of the equation by one plus the premium.

Second, in explaining the foreign exchange numeraire, the biggest problems occur in developing the logic of converting nontraded outputs into foreign exchange impacts. Nontraded inputs, in contrast, are not difficult to explain in the generic foreign exchange numeraire, because we can easily see the logic of tracing the direct and indirect foreign exchange impacts.

The foreign exchange impacts of nontraded outputs are less obvious, since they affect foreign exchange only by substituting domestically for traded goods. Thus, traded goods which are close substitutes for these nontraded outputs must be found, and the border prices of those substitutes must then be used in place of the domestic prices of the nontraded outputs in the economic analysis. This process too may be confusing to noneconomists.

The Exchange Rate in a Generic Foreign Exchange Numeraire

The exchange rate is not as critical a variable in the generic foreign exchange numeraire, particularly when used for projects in the industrial and agricultural sectors where substitutes can be found for most nontraded outputs. This is one of the advantages of the foreign exchange numeraire compared with the willingness to pay numeraire. Because all inputs and all outputs of the project are ultimately converted into foreign exchange impacts in the foreign exchange numeraire, the relative value of the objective function will be unaffected by the exchange rate. This point will become more obvious to us the more we work with the foreign exchange numeraire.

Because it often does not matter what exchange rate is used in the foreign exchange numeraire, we may find it convenient to use the official exchange rate where it is deemed desirable to convert between currencies. This is simply a convention, however; it is not mandatory. Any exchange rate could be used, including any of the three SERs discussed in Chapter 4. This attribute of the foreign exchange numeraire makes it particularly convenient in appraising projects in countries with multiple exchange rates and with "tiered" foreign exchange markets (such as the "two-tier" or "Window I" and "Window II" market announced by the Bank of Ghana in 1986).

In fact, it is not absolutely necessary to use an exchange rate in applying the foreign exchange numeraire in the agricultural sector. In the face of problems, such as multiple exchange rates, the decision has often been made to denominate the foreign exchange impacts in units of foreign currency (such as the British pound sterling, the French franc, the Japanese yen, or whatever is the currency of the country's major trading partner), rather than worrying about what exchange rate to use in converting the foreign exchange impacts into units of the local currency.

The exchange rate is not as critical in the generic foreign exchange numeraire because all inputs and outputs of a project (whether they are traded or nontraded goods) are ultimately converted into foreign exchange impacts. Consequently, the relative values of the good will be unaffected by the exchange rate.

7. Comparing the Two Economic Efficiency Numeraires

Summary. *The decision on whether to use a willingness to pay (WTP) numeraire, or a foreign exchange numeraire, to conduct project economic efficiency analysis rests as much on convenience as on anything else. The WTP numeraire is most convenient when projects involve mostly nontraded goods, while the foreign exchange numeraire is more convenient when most inputs and outputs are traded. The conversion of nontraded goods impacts into the foreign exchange numeraire may be difficult in countries that have few traded goods—a topic discussed more fully in Chapter 13. Similarly, the absence of a good estimate of the shadow exchange rate will impede the application of the WTP approach.*

The foreign exchange numeraire was popularized by the OECD Manual (1968), which also originally argued that all goods and services should be shadow priced in terms of their prices under "first best" policies. The WTP numeraire has been around much longer, though it was formalized in the UNIDO Guidelines (1972), which countered the OECD argument by suggesting that accounting prices should take into account elements of government failure that were likely to remain during the life of the project. The OECD approach came to be called "first best" shadow pricing, while the UNIDO approach represented "second best" shadow pricing. The distinction between, and the importance of, these two definitions is the subject of Chapter 7.

There are several possible ways to define a numeraire for use in the economic efficiency analysis of projects. Two numeraires that have become prominent in recent years are the willingness to pay numeraire and the generic foreign exchange numeraire. Both of these numeraires are used in the Squire-van der Tak method, which has become the standard method of project economic analysis in the World Bank. There are advantages and disadvantages in applying and in teaching each of these numeraires; these will become apparent as we go along in this volume.

The willingness to pay (WTP) numeraire is most easily applied in valuing nontraded goods. Explaining the economic valuation process for traded goods is a bit more circuitous, but can be accomplished by taking advantage of the noneconomists' natural inclination toward taking a "commodity" view of foreign exchange. By converting the "commodity" of foreign exchange into willingness to pay values for an average of all traded goods, the foreign exchange impacts can be converted into units of consumption equivalent in terms with the units of consumption indicated by the nontraded goods.

The foreign exchange numeraire was popularized by the OECD Manual in 1968, while the willingness to pay numeraire was formalized in the UNIDO Guidelines in 1972.

The generic foreign exchange numeraire is most easily applied in valuing traded goods. The valuation of traded project inputs can be made fairly straight forward by viewing the process as one of tracing the direct and indirect foreign exchange impacts implied by using these inputs in the project. The most difficult valuation problem in the generic foreign exchange numeraire relates to nontraded project outputs, where traded substitutes must be found before the foreign exchange impacts can be estimated. So long as traded substitutes can be found for the nontraded outputs, the project outputs can be readily valued in foreign exchange terms. However, in the few cases—mostly found in the urban sector—in which traded substitutes cannot be found for nontraded project outputs, the foreign exchange numeraire loses some of its appeal.

Obviously, the foreign exchange numeraire is most appropriate in cases in which a majority of the project inputs and outputs are traded. In such cases, the majority of the project's impacts will occur directly in units that are expressed in the numeraire; and we will not have to go through a complicated process of converting nontraded goods into foreign exchange impacts. By the same token, the willingness to pay numeraire is most appropriate in cases involving largely nontraded goods; then, the issue of the "correct" calculation of the SER is not so critical to the analysis. Unfortunately, there will be some of both kinds of projects in the agricultural sector investment program. Thus, we must end up selecting a numeraire which is more appropriate in some cases than in other cases.

In countries in which traded goods play an important role in the economy, the foreign exchange numeraire may provide a convenient method for conducting project economic analysis. Presumably, in this case a majority of the project inputs would involve traded goods. Expressing the impacts of these goods in the foreign exchange numeraire would be relatively straight forward. In general, we may say that the foreign exchange numeraire is the most straight forward and easiest to apply in cases in which traded goods are particularly important in the project and in the economy. By the same token, we may generalize that the WTP numeraire may be most appropriate and easiest to apply in cases in which a majority of the goods and services involved are nontraded goods.

However, these generalized statements must be accompanied by caveats such as "other things being equal," or the economists' *ceteris paribus*. (Consider the case of subsistence farming in Uganda in Case 12 of Part V. Here, commodities which are tradable in principle are valued at their domestic market prices because the production, which is not exchanged within the economy, does not affect foreign exchange directly or indirectly.)

The foreign exchange numeraire is the easiest to apply in cases in which traded goods are particularly important in the project and in the economy. The willingness to pay is the easiest to apply in cases in which a majority of the goods are nontraded goods.

From the preceding paragraph we might conclude that, in countries with essentially closed borders, the foreign exchange numeraire might not make much sense. If there is little in the way of traded goods in the total basket of goods and services in that country, then the choice of foreign exchange as the numeraire may be inappropriate (see Chapter 13).

However, if the country is also plagued by a wide range of distortions in internal markets, it may be difficult to estimate willingness to pay values as well. In a case like this—and there are numerous such cases around the world—any method of economic analysis has difficulty.

There is a set of truisms that we may state regarding project economic analysis:

  a. The more distorted the markets for traded and nontraded goods in an economy, the more we need to use economic analysis or shadow pricing in project planning.

  b. The more we need to use economic analysis in project planning, the more difficult it is to estimate the accounting prices, since (following the preceding truism) we shall be working from sets of highly distorted prices and will have no point of reference from which to work.

  c. Countries which exhibit major trade distortions (and, thus, major distortions in the markets for traded goods) also tend to exhibit major distortions in the markets for nontraded goods; as a result, it is difficult to apply either the willingness to pay approach, or the foreign exchange numeraire, to project economic analysis.

The more distorted the market for traded and nontraded goods, the more we need economic analysis in projects. The more we need to use economic analysis in project planning, the more difficult it is to estimate accounting prices.

One of the factors that motivated the writing of the OECD Manual (1969) was the importance of "thoroughly distorted" countries. Trying to find some reference point from which an appropriate set of shadow or accounting prices might be derived, the authors of the OECD Manual finally settled on international prices or "border prices." Border prices (i.e., CIF and FOB prices at the border of the country being analyzed) represented a ready source from which consistent accounting prices could be derived for the country.

The OECD Manual took the position that, whether or not the government chose to use the alternatives afforded by international trade, the CIF and FOB prices for tradable goods represented options for the country; and these options could be used in deriving accounting prices for use in project economic analysis.

One of the factors that motivated the writing of the UNIDO Guidelines was the authors' opposition to the use of border prices in project economic analysis in cases in which trade options would not be pursued by the government either "with" or "without" the project. The UNIDO Guidelines argued that border prices should not be used for all goods and services impacted by the project, as had been proposed in the original version of the OECD Manual.

Instead, the UNIDO Guidelines suggested that project economic impacts be measured in "more realistic" terms by taking into account the true alternatives likely to exist and by considering governments' tendencies not to follow the advice of economists only. The willingness to pay numeraire focused not just on what the government "ought" to do, but also on what it was likely to do. (Of course, the prescription applied equally as well to the use of the foreign exchange numeraire. See Case 8 on Colombia in Part V.)

Unfortunately, neither the UNIDO Guidelines approach to project economic analysis, nor their numeraire, was able to solve the practical problem of estimating consistent accounting prices in the "thoroughly distorted" economies. In those cases, the method of presenting the results was and is not the real problem. The real problem is one of having the time, the budgetary resources, the ingenuity, and the motivation to determine the real resource flows that are hidden behind the distorted financial prices that are paid and received by the project.

❖

8. Project Analysis versus Policy Analysis

Summary. *We should begin project appraisal by asking what aspect of market failure is occurring and how the project is going to correct for it. Some projects are occasioned by market failure, while others arise as partial corrections for government failure. Project appraisal should not be separated from sectoral policy analysis. Often, project economists will develop during project planning a level of subsector knowledge which exceeds that of others in potential policymaking positions and, thus, will be in the best position to recommend policy changes.*

Generally, good policies have more impact than do good projects, because policies affect entire sectors. Project economists cannot estimate accounting prices for project planning until they know whether or not advice on policy reform will be followed. Accounting prices may be calculated in terms of a totally reformed environment— the so-called "first best" situation, or they may be calculated in terms of continued distortions—the so-called "second best" situation. Sectors in which project and subsector policy decisions tend to be made simultaneously—such as industry—may be best served by some form of "first best" approach; while sectors such as agriculture, where projects represent small additions to the subsector, might be justified in using a "second best" approach. No matter which approach is used, it may sometimes turn out to be wrong.

This chapter deals with the policy aspects of project analysis. It is important for practitioners and trainers to understand project appraisal in the context of sectoral and macroeconomic policies. Practicing economists should also understand the following policy-related points:

a. Project analysts learn things in the process of conducting project analysis that gives them a comparative advantage in arguing for policy reform to increase efficiency in the subsector in which the project is located, and in some of the backward-linked (i.e., input supplying) and the forward-linked (i.e., output purchasing) sectors.

b. Policy reform will often do more to increase national economic efficiency than will one more good project.

c. It is important for project economists to understand the difference between and the implications of "first-best" versus "second best" shadow pricing systems, and the way they relate to the policy environment.

d. Projects which are economically viable when appraised using second-best shadow pricing may not be viable under first-best shadow pricing, and may create vested interests against improving the policy environment.

Project appraisal should not be separated from sectoral policy analysis.

e. Project analysts should always ask the following basic policy-related questions before they get deeply into appraising any proposed project:

- What is the market failure that this government intervention is designed to correct for?

  - Is it market failure?
  - Is it government failure?

- Through what mechanism is this project going to restore optimality and correct for the market failure that the planner has identified?

- Is there a better way to achieve this objective which is less costly, less disruptive, or more specific to the problem as it has been identified?

The Project Analyst's Subsector Expertise

Project analysts can learn a great deal about a subsector in the process of doing a project appraisal. If they do their job well, they should be able to recognize the good and bad impacts that government policies have on the subsector within which their project falls (see Box on Nigerian Beverage Sweeteners, page 52). Project analysts would do their country a disservice if they do not look beyond the project appraisal to ask deeper questions about the policy framework affecting the project.

In the Nigerian example, project analysts could see that producer incentives were severely distorted by the government's policies on the exchange rate, and that efforts to rationalize trade and exchange rate policies were really the first order of business. As we shall discuss later in this chapter, making project investments in such an environment might not represent the best thing for the country, and it might make it more difficult later to do the things that are best for the country.

Project analysts often know more about the firm-level implications of subsectoral policies than anyone else in the government. They also know a great deal about the effects of macroeconomic policies on that sector. This is often true, because—in the process of collecting detailed information on the subsector and of analyzing that information—analysts learn a great deal about the financial and economic impacts that government policies have on that subsector. In fact, it is not unreasonable to argue that—if project analysts are not able to provide such an analysis—they should not be advising society on how to spend its money in the first place (see Technical Note 19).

Project analysts often know more about the firm-level implications of subsectoral policies and about the effects of macroeconomic policies on the sector they work in than anyone else in the government. They would do their country a disservice by not looking beyond project appraisal to ask deeper questions about the policy framework affecting the project.

Looking for Policy Implications during Project Appraisal: The Case of Nigerian Beverage Sweeteners

While appraising a project to produce maize for processing into beverage sweetener in Nigeria, project analysts were able to discover several policy-related issues regarding the maize sweetener subsector in that country. Three of the issues are mentioned below:

First, the overvalued exchange rate (Nigerian naira 0.80 = US$ 1) that existed prior to September 1986 made it difficult for Nigeria to produce any tradable good domestically without substantial protection. It introduced several disrupting influences in the economy which led to economically costly "rent-seeking" behavior by producers, rather than inducing them to focus on production and marketing of products. [For a good discussion of rent-seeking behavior, see Bhagwati and Srinivasan (1983), pages 317-34, and the references.] Investments were often pursued not for productive purposes, but rather as a means of getting access to scarce and rationed foreign exchange, and to get the foreign exchange at naira prices which substantially undervalued the foreign currency.

The "second tier" auction market, introduced late in 1986, allowed the freed-up market for foreign exchange to raise the rate to more than 3 naira = US$ 1. At the new exchange rate, tradable goods production made much more financial and economic sense in Nigeria, and many of the disruptive policies that had been used to maintain the overvalued exchange rate could be removed.

Second, the demand for sweetener production capability in Nigeria was partly caused by import licensing, occasioned by the overvalued exchange rate. This had two disruptive impacts on the Nigerian economy:

• Because of the uncertainty regarding their ability to get import licenses as needed to import raw materials, many firms were investing in local production capacity as an insurance mechanism rather than as an efficient primary source of raw materials; and

• Because of the rationing of foreign exchange, the production plant and equipment for processing maize sweeteners could be acquired at an exchange rate of naira 0.80 = US$ 1 by those who had the political connections required to get an import license. The plant and equipment could be sold later in the local market at a price more closely reflecting the real scarcity of the foreign exchange that was used to import the equipment—i.e., at a price more than three times higher. This motivated investors to pursue investments because of the privileged access to the "quasi-rents" on foreign exchange rather than because of the real productivity of the investments.

Third, there are many alternatives to maize-based sweeteners, including sugars made from cane or from beets. Many countries subsidize production of those commodities, making CIF prices for imported sweeteners very attractive. It is questionable whether it makes economic sense for Nigeria to use land to produce a product for which numerous inexpensive substitutes exist. The land could be used for other purposes.

Good Policies versus Good Projects

It is an often-stated truism among economists that "a good policy beats a good project any day." What economists mean by this simple statement is that a good policy will affect the whole subsector, while a project will affect only a part of the subsector. For example, by pricing rice at an economically efficient level, all farmers will be induced to produce the "right" quantities of rice; however, providing irrigation water below cost to compensate for the distorted price of rice will affect only those farms which receive the subsidized water (see Technical Note 20).

Another reason for good policies being better than good projects relates to what economists call "the specificity rule." What the rule says is that the intervention that is chosen should be directed as specifically to the target problem as is possible. In the rice example, if the problem is that there are poor people who cannot afford as much rice as the government would like them to have, the specificity rule would say that it is more efficient to buy rice and give it to the poor (or simply to give them money) than it is to control the price of rice at a low level and to try to make up for the production disincentive by providing subsidized irrigation water via a project investment.

In our earlier discussion of strategic planning and government intervention to achieve national planning objectives, we discussed policies and projects as the two major forms of intervention. In dealing with a wide range of planning objectives, we find that policies and projects are to some extent substitutable and to some extent complementary to each other. For example, we often find countries with policies which provide for initial subsidies for fertilizer during the period when farmers are learning to use chemical fertilizers (see Technical Note 6).

Beyond some learning period, the fertilizer subsidies are to be removed. However, we find that the benefits of fertilizer are also tied to the availability of irrigation as a complementary input. Thus, projects to provide irrigation water may be pursued in combination with policies designed to induce the use of chemical fertilizers (e.g., initial subsidies on fertilizer use to be removed after the learning period). This fertilizer pricing/irrigation project combination provides an example of a complementary relationship between policies and projects. An example of a substitutable relationship between projects and policies relates to flood control. Flood control projects and floodplane zoning policies may be used in some cases as alternatives which achieve the same objectives of minimizing property damage and minimizing the loss of life.

A good policy beats a good project any day. A good policy will affect the whole subsector; while a project will affect only a part of the subsector.

We sometimes find that projects are pursued as a means of making up for a bad policy—i.e., as a mechanism to correct for government failure. In the agricultural sector, projects often are used as mechanisms for supplying rationed inputs to farmers to make up for output prices that are held at low levels. Or we find projects which are intended to supply potentially tradable products that are in short supply in local markets because of foreign exchange rationing, or other trade restrictions. We also find projects which are intended to supply what are essentially private goods, because the government's policy has destroyed the private suppliers of those goods. In many of these examples, the country would be better served by forgoing the project investment and reforming the policies that are discouraging nonproject production. This issue will be discussed further in a later section.

First-Best versus Second-Best Shadow Prices

The issue of policies versus projects is at the heart of the long-standing debate over first-best and second-best shadow prices. The debate revolves around several interrelated and sometimes subtle economic issues which have to do with the government's trade and other policies, economists' policy advice, and the way economists derive shadow prices for use in the economic appraisal of projects.

Many developing countries impose trade and exchange-rate barriers that reduce the economic efficiency at which their economies are able to operate. Economists constantly advise governments of developing countries to reform their trade, exchange rate, and other policies in order to reduce these inefficiencies. [See, for example, Zeitz and Valdes (1986). Refer also to the comments about Yugoslavia in Technical Note 7.]

First-Best Shadow Prices. *Accounting prices which represent the prices that would exist under optimal policies. When used in project cost-benefit analysis, these prices would—in theory—yield a set of projects that would be optimal in the reformed economic environment that the economists' policy advice is directed toward achieving. The "first best" situation from a social welfare perspective would be to have no distortions and to have projects which were designed using first-best accounting prices.*

Whether governments heed the economists' advice is not always clear. One factor which makes governments hesitate in heeding the economists' advice is the number and importance of the citizens who make money off of the trade and price distortions at the expense of the country and its other citizens. The longer the distorted policies exist, the greater the number and the richer will be those citizens who benefit at other people's expense; and the more politically powerful these beneficiaries will become.

The original Little-Mirrlees (OECD, 1969) approach to shadow pricing supported the use of border prices for all project inputs and outputs. Their argument for using border prices was appealing on several grounds. First, they argued that if free trade policies were pursued by the government, all local prices would be determined by border prices. This would occur because (as we have said elsewhere in this text) all goods and services produced and consumed in the economy use tradable inputs in their production, or substitute for tradable goods in consumption, or both. Thus, trade policies will affect the prices of all goods and services, whether those goods and services are tradable or nontradable.

Second, the economists' policy advice and their shadow pricing system should be mutually consistent. It made no sense, Little and Mirrlees argued, to advise the pursuit of freer trade while using shadow prices which assumed the continuation of trade barriers. Thus, to be consistent with their policy advice, economists should derive their shadow prices based on an assumption of free trade. That way, when the country's trade barriers were removed, the projects that had been built would be appropriate to the prices that prevailed under the new policies.

The first-best thing for the country to do would be to pursue good policies, including free trade (except, of course, possibly imposing "optimal" tariffs and subsidies in exceptional cases). Shadow prices derived under such conditions are usually referred to as "first best" shadow prices, indicating that they are the opportunity costs which would prevail in the presence of correct policies. Under first-best conditions involving free trade, all opportunity costs could be measured in border prices. (Note that we are including under "free" trade the use of socially optimal taxes and subsidies. See Case 11 in Part V.)

One point of contention between the authors of the UNIDO Guidelines and those of the OECD Manual was the realism of the first-best shadow pricing approach. The UNIDO authors argued that experience had shown that many countries were not likely to pursue efficient policies during the life of the projects. Thus, by designing projects based on first-best shadow prices, economists would not be designing the optimal set of projects for the environment that was likely to exist.

Analysts should instead derive shadow prices in a way that would assure the best set of projects under the distorted conditions that were expected to exist during the life of the project, argued the UNIDO authors. The first-best thing for a country to do, of course, would be to alter its trade and other policies to make them more efficient; but the country was not likely to do that. So, the second-best thing to do was to build the best projects possible within the distorted environment.

The objective of the shadow pricing exercise was to help the analysts determine which project designs would have the greatest positive impacts on national economic efficiency in the distorted environment that was expected to continue. In other words, the objective was to help analysts find the second-best option. Thus,

Second-Best Shadow Prices.
Accounting prices which measure the marginal social value of project inputs and outputs when projects are carried out in a distorted environment that is expected to continue during the life of the project. When used in project cost-benefit analysis, these prices would yield a set of projects that would be optimal in the distorted environment that is expected to continue to exist. If the policy distortions cannot be removed, then the best welfare option is to have projects which are designed according to second-best accounting prices rather than the distorted financial prices which exist.

these shadow prices came to be called "second-best shadow prices."

Tradable versus Traded Goods. The essential difference between first-best and second-best shadow prices is that the former views all goods and services as tradable directly or indirectly and, thus, views all inputs and outputs as having opportunity costs which are defined by CIF and FOB prices. The second-best approach to shadow pricing, in contrast, uses the terms "traded" and "nontraded" rather than the terms "tradable" and "nontradable" and takes the position that not all economic values can be measured in border price terms.

Tradable and Nontradable Goods. The terms tradable and nontradable deal with the issue of tradability in principle— i.e., taking into account comparative advantage and transport costs only. A good which is nontradable (in principle) would be subject to the following inequality:

$$\text{CIF} > \text{Local cost} > \text{FOB} \qquad (8.1)$$

where:

CIF = cost, insurance, and freight on imported goods; and
FOB = free on board cost of exported goods.

A tradable good, in contrast, would be subject to one of the following mathematical relationships:

$$\text{Importable good: Local cost} > \text{CIF} \qquad (8.2)$$

$$\text{Exportable good: FOB} > \text{Local cost} \qquad (8.3)$$

Textbooks on international trade and payments often define three groups of nontradables:

    a. labor;
    b. land; and
    c. services.

The definitions in equations 8.1-8.3 are generally in keeping with the textbook definition, except that the nontradable goods in equation 8.1 would also include bulky or heavy goods which have a high freight-to-value ratio.

Traded and Nontraded Goods. The terms traded and nontraded take into account not only comparative advantage and transport costs, but also the expected government policies on trade barriers. Thus, a good which is tradable in principle may be nontraded in practice because there is expected to be an import ban on the good

First-best shadow prices view all goods and services as tradable directly or indirectly. The second-best approach uses the terms "traded" and "nontraded," and takes the position that not all economic values can be measured in border price terms.

during the life of the project. In the second-best shadow pricing system such a good would be treated as nontraded and would be shadow priced accordingly. In the first-best shadow pricing system, the banned import would nevertheless be treated as tradable and would be valued at its CIF price (see Technical Note 21).

Because first-best shadow pricing treats all goods and services as tradable directly or indirectly, it is also consistent with the foreign exchange numeraire. This was one of the factors which led Little and Mirrlees (OECD, 1969) to adopt the foreign exchange numeraire. However, the willingness to pay numeraire would be appropriate where substantial trade barriers exist and where many goods are nontraded in practice—whether or not they should have been tradable in principle. Thus, the UNIDO (1972) authors chose a willingness to pay numeraire. Of course, it is possible to use either numeraire in a first-best or a second-best shadow pricing approach. Nevertheless, the foreign exchange numeraire and first-best shadow pricing have remained linked together in the thinking of many economists; the willingness to pay numeraire has had a similar fate with second-best shadow pricing.

After much debate on the realism of first-best shadow pricing, Little and Mirrlees compromised somewhat in the second edition of their book, *Project Appraisal and Planning in Developing Countries* (1974). [See the February 1972 issue of the *Oxford Bulletin of Economics and Statistics*, particularly the contributions of Vijay Joshi, pages 3-32, and Partha Dasgupta, pages 33-52. Little and Mirrlees reply to criticisms to their methodology in the same issue.] This compromised position was adopted by Squire and van der Tak (1975) and was also reflected in the system of shadow pricing discussed in Gittinger (1982). The decision on whether to treat a questionable good as tradable or as nontraded in the economic analysis has been left open. In fact, this compromised approach puts analysts in a position of having to decide upon which edge of the two-edged sword they will cut.

The two-edged sword of shadow pricing is a subtle one, but it can be very important in some subsectors. The problem is this: first-best shadow pricing will be a better approach in some cases, while the second-best approach will be more appropriate in others. But it is not always easy to determine *ex ante* which approach to take.

At the project planning stage, we have a choice of designing a project based on first-best shadow prices (i.e., border prices), or second-best shadow prices (i.e., taking into account government policies). Those are two different project designs, in principle. One

Traded Good.
A good which is internationally traded:
a. in fact, and
b. at the margin
by the country in whose behalf the project or policy analysis is being conducted. The trade may occur either because the good is tradable in principle and no government failure is present, or because the good is nontradable in principle and government intervention of some form leads to international trade in that good by the country. In project and policy analyses, the terms tradable, nontradable, traded, and nontraded always refer to trade at the margin.

Nontraded Good.
A good which is not internationally traded by the country. The failure to trade in the good at the margin may arise either from the good being nontradable in principle, or from it being subject to intervention which leads to it being nontraded in practice.

design will be appropriate in one environment, while the other will be appropriate in the other environment. If we choose the second-best shadow price design, and the government retains its inefficient policies, then we have built the best project for the country under the circumstances that actually exist. But, because the project was "appropriate" in the distorted environment, we may have also added another vested interest in keeping in place the distorted policies that exist. That is one edge of the sword.

On the other hand, we could use first-best shadow prices in designing the project. We would thus be consistent with the policy advice. And if the government actually heeded the advice, we would have both a good policy and a project that is appropriate within that policy environment. However, if the government continued to pursue distortionist policies, the country would be worse off with this first-best designed project than it would have been with the alternative project that was designed on the basis of the second-best shadow prices. That is the other edge of the sword.

Both shadow pricing approaches can be wrong in every application. However, the probabilities are greater in some cases than in others. For example, we find that in the industrial sector, policies tend to get formulated at the same time the investment decisions are made. This occurs because of the tendency of industrial subsectors in developing countries to have only one firm or a few firms, and because of the juxtaposition of scale economies and relatively small domestic markets for industrial products.

Thus, in industrial project appraisal, we usually cannot separate project analysis from sectoral policy analysis. For example, a proposal will be made to invest in a spinning plant to make yarn from imported cotton to substitute for imported yarn. Along with the appraisal of the investment will be a policy decision on whether to ban yarn imports in order to protect the new industry from foreign competitors.

First-Best Analysis of Industrial Projects. Because policy decisions and investment decisions tend to go hand in hand in the industrial sector, industrial economists usually argue in favor of using first-best shadow pricing. In other words, they refuse to consider the yarn, in the earlier example, as nontraded for purposes of valuing the output of the spinning project. The first-best shadow pricing approach imposes on industrial projects the requirement that they be competitive with imports in the local market, or that their exports be competitive in other national markets, or both.

In the industrial sector, policy and investment decisions tend to go hand in hand. Hence, industrial economists tend to favor first-best shadow pricing.

Second-Best Analysis of Agricultural Projects. In the agricultural sector, policies tend to be made separate from investment decisions. This occurs because of the large size of most agricultural subsectors and because of the minor importance of each new investment decision relative to the size of existing production capacity. In agriculture, it is closer to the truth to assume that the project analyst will be unable to change the policies affecting the project's subsector. Thus, agricultural project analysts tend to favor using second-best assumptions in deriving the shadow prices to be used in their sector.

The problem with second-best shadow pricing is not so much a theoretical one as it is a behavioral one. If you teach this shadow pricing approach to a practitioner, the shadow pricing assumptions tend to reinforce the line agency staff's existing tendency to act helpless in suggesting policy changes, while arguing for expanded investments into their distorted sector. In other words, the second-best assumptions make it easier for some practitioners to justify accepting many policies that are just plain awful—indeed, may even support their natural tendencies in this direction.

There is a great need to get planners in line agencies to be more activist in terms of policy issues rather than being so active in trying to justify additional investments in their sector—channeled, of course, through the good offices of their own agency. A basic problem which stretches the integrity of the agency staff of agricultural and industrial sectors is the impact that distortions can have in justifying additional investments in their sector. (The industrial and agricultural sectors are mentioned because many of the projects in these sectors are occasioned by government failure rather than market failure. This problem is addressed in the next section.)

When we take into account all of these issues, a good case can be made for returning to Little and Mirrlees' original recomendation of complete border pricing—i.e., treating everything as tradable directly or indirectly, and border pricing everything. That approach imposes a discipline that will force us to ask why certain projects look so awful when calculated in border prices. Unless we look realistically at economic values, in the way that border pricing forces us to look, it is difficult to use the economic analysis effectively to consider policy implications as well.

Policy Analysis and The Theory of Market Failure

Even experienced project economists have a tendency to forget, in the heat of the project planning experience, that the project represents an alternative "intervention" for helping to restore optimality after some aspect of market failure has occurred. It is

In the agricultural sector, policies tend to be made separate from investment decisions because the importance of each new investment is minor relative to the size of production capacity in the sector. Hence, agricultural economists favor second-best shadow pricing.

useful for us to remember that the model that is being applied in economic efficiency analysis is based on the presumption that some aspect of market failure is occurring and that the government is fulfilling its role of a regulator to undertake interventions to restore optimality to make up for the failure that is manifesting itself elsewhere in the economy.

Scarcity of Intervention Capacity. There is a very simple reason for addressing the issue of market failure in every project that is to be appraised. The reason has nothing to do with ideology. It has to do with practicality and resource scarcity. Among the scarcest resources in developing countries are those that are required to regulate and to manage. These resources, being scarce, must be used carefully and efficiently. In the public sector, there is often not enough regulatory and management expertise to manage the entire economy.

Thus, in the interests of national economic efficiency, those resources should be applied where they will have the greatest impact and where other management and regulatory resources are not already fulfilling a substantial part of the need. The least need for public sector management is in those sectors where the market works fairly well. These sectors, as well as those where the market does not work very well, were briefly described in the preceding chapters.

Rationing of Intervention Capacity. The greatest need for, and the highest productivity of, public sector management capability exists in those areas where the market does not work well, or does not work at all. The "theory of market failure" is meant to help us identify exactly where those scarce public sector regulatory and management resources are most needed. In appraising a proposed project, the first act of economizing is to ask: How is the market failing to do the thing that I am asking the government to use its scarce resources to do?

The second question that we should ask should be obvious from the first question: How is the proposed project intervention going to correct for that failure? Again, the intervention should be limited to the failure that has been identified, and it should be as specific to the problem as is feasible.

Among the scarcest resources in developing countries are those that are required to regulate and to manage. Those resources should therefore be applied where they will have the greatest impact.

If we ask these questions every time we begin the appraisal process, we will find that our answers will fall into two groups:

   a. some project objectives will be related to market failure; and

   b. some project objectives will be related to government failure.

Recall from our previous discussions that, in principle, projects (like policies) should be designed to correct for distortions introduced by market failure. [Alternatively, we could think of the project as a perturbation in the economy, undertaken to enhance the incomes of targeted groups. See Diewert (1986).] And both forms of government intervention—projects and policies—should, in principle, aim at restoring optimality. Recall also that we have said previously that projects often result from attempts to correct for distortions introduced by other government policies—i.e., from government failure. An example from Bangladesh should help to illustrate the problem (see Box on page 62).

The case of the Bangladesh hand tubewell project is not unusual. Many projects are undertaken not because of some aspect of market failure occurring in that sector, but as additions to or corrections for government failure occurring in that or in other sectors. For this reason, project economists must take a deeper and a broader look at the policy context of the projects they are appraising. It is not sufficient to apply shadow prices to the financial accounts, run an economic rate of return, and write up a report recommending funding. The economist's real value in the project planning process is in reshaping projects to make them more consistent with economic objectives and in looking beyond the project at the policies that shape the sector. Often, the effect of shaping sectoral policies will be much more productive than the effect that the project will have in continuing in a distorted environment.

Project economists must take a broader look at the policy context of projects. It is not enough that they apply shadow prices to financial accounts, calculate an economic rate of return, and recommend funding.

An Application of The Theory of Market Failure: The Bangladesh Hand Tubewell Project

In 1980, the World Bank appraised its first hand tubewell (HTW) project in Bangladesh. The project supplied several hundred thousand cast iron pumps to small farmers for purposes of drinking water and small-scale irrigation. The pumps were produced under government contracts with several dozens of foundries throughout the country. A small research and testing component was included in the project.

The Bank's Bangladesh Hand Tubewell Project appraisal mission asked the first question at the outset of the appraisal: What aspect of market failure is leading to government intervention to procure and distribute HTW and to conduct research and testing of HTW? The question was a relevant one. The foundry sector in Bangladesh comprised upward of one hundred firms—sufficiently large to qualify as competitive. The product in question was clearly a "private good" in that there were no major externalities associated with HTW production or use, the HTW were titleable and transferrable, and bore no significant social benefits that were not captured by the family that purchased them. In terms of market failure, only the research and testing component and the information function could be viewed as cause for government intervention.

Research and testing had the attributes of a public good because it was impossible for developers of improvements in technology to retain the financial benefits to themselves. Any improvements were quickly picked up by other foundries, and—in the Bangladesh context—the developers had no way to control the loss of their technology. Thus, research by private producers would not be undertaken, at least not to the level of expenditure that seemed justified.

There was also an "information" function that the project could perform. That is, the project—by distributing and popularizing the HTW—could take the risk out of producing and marketing the product by the private sector. But it was questionable whether this was needed. Several hundred thousand tubewells had already been distributed by UNICEF and by the Bangladesh government with the help of the United States Agency for International Development.

Furthermore, during project implementation, the government insisted on supplying HTW at a subsidized price, effectively driving private suppliers out of the market. During the appraisal and, particularly during implementation, members of the appraisal mission began to question whether—in terms of the theory of market failure—there was any legitimate role to be played by the public sector in HTW production and distribution in Bangladesh.

In fact, the driving force behind the HTW project lay in two factors that were present in the Bangladesh economy at the time the project was planned and appraised:

a. The foreign exchange needed for importing the pig iron and coke to make cast iron products was not freely available. Pig iron and coke could only be imported through a government agency at the time the project was appraised. Thus, the private sector was unable to get the raw materials it needed to produce what was essentially a private good.

b. Officials in the Government of Bangladesh, either for ideological or for personal reasons, exhibited strong preference for public sector control of HTW production and distribution. In short, the driving force behind the HTW project was government failure.

continued ➡

Tubewell Project (continued)

In 1986, a second Bangladesh HTW project was proposed to the World Bank. By then, the Bangladesh government had instituted a wage earners scheme (WES) under which foreign exchange earned by Bangladeshi citizens working abroad could be repatriated through official channels. Under the WES, repatriated foreign exchange was made available for a list of items that could be imported under the scheme. Pig iron and coke were on the approved list. By then, the particular government failure that had been the driving force behind the first project was no longer present.

In addition, the monitoring and evaluation of the first HTW project had led the World Bank to think more seriously about the impact on private producers resulting from the first project. The appraisal of the second HTW project scheduled for January 1987 was postponed while these and other issues relating to the project were further discussed between the World Bank and the government.

PART II

Calculating and Interpreting Conversion Factors

9. Cash Flows and "Real" Resource Flows

Summary. *Economic efficiency deals with the maximization of society's consumption over time. Financial prices which lie behind financial cash flows may not accurately reflect the value to society of the real resource flows that are involved. Likewise, certain reporting formats—such as income statements—may not accurately reflect the timing of those flows. To analyze economic efficiency of projects, a special cash flow format is used; adjustments are made to the financial flows to make the cash flow statement better reflect real resource flows. The adjustments include deleting financial flows that do not reflect resource flows, incorporating implicit costs, and removing "sunk" costs while retaining "incremental" costs.*

We have said that to an economist the function of economic activity is to generate consumption. We have also said that society's consumption is affected by the amount of final goods and services that are available; and that one widely accepted way to measure the value of those goods and services to society is to estimate it's willingness to pay for them.

An economic activity that has not created a final good, or provided a final service, for consumption by society cannot be said to have generated an economic benefit to society. (Note, however, that we will normally take the willingness to pay for an intermediate good as a measure of the consumption value of the final goods that the intermediate good will eventually be used to produce.) Similarly, any economic activity that uses a resource, which otherwise might have been used for consumption, has created a cost to society.

Ideally, we should be able to value all project outputs in willingness to pay terms, and account for these outputs at the time the consumption takes place.

Likewise, project inputs should be cost in terms of willingness to pay for the alternative final goods they would have produced, and account for the inputs at the time the forgone consumption would have taken place.

Ideally, in conducting project economic analysis, we would like to value all project outputs in willingness to pay values, and account for these outputs at the time the consumption takes place. Likewise, we would like to cost all project *inputs* in terms of willingness to pay for the alternative final goods they would have produced, and account for the inputs at the time the forgone consumption would have taken place.

The Cash Flow Format. The formats that we use in project economic analysis—as well as the valuation conventions that we apply—are meant to achieve the two objectives mentioned in the preceding paragraph. To accomplish the latter objective (i.e., the timing of the accounting), we set up the project accounts in a cash flow format. The cash flow format allows us to reflect the actual resource flows much more accurately (in terms of the objectives mentioned earlier) than would an income statement format. [The process of building up and using a financial cash flow for a farm is discussed in Gittinger (1982), pages 127-140, under the heading of "Farm Budget." The farm budget is a form of financial cash flow statement.]

Weaknesses of The Income Statement Format. The issues addressed in this section are most problematic in traditional financial accounting as used in processing industries. Some of the issues arise in farming activities, however. Let us review briefly the drawbacks to using traditional financial statements in appraising projects [see Gittinger (1982), Chapter 5]. The income statement misrepresents actual resource flows in several ways:

First, several expense items in the income statement show costs at a time other than the point in time at which resources were actually taken away from their alternative uses. These expense items include:

- *Depreciation expense.* An accounting convention which accounts for fixed asset costs over a number of years rather than reflecting the costs when the resources are tied up.

- *Amortization expense.* An accounting convention which accounts for intangible fixed assets—such as patents, licenses, and preoperating expenses—over a number of years, rather than reflecting their costs at the time they are incurred.

- *Resource depletion allowance.* An accounting convention which shows the decrease in the value of land as the resources are extracted, rather than showing the decrease by taking a lower salvage value for the land at the end of the project when the land is returned to nonproject use.

Second, in calculating the "cost of goods sold," the inventories of finished goods and inventories of goods in process are valued at cost (including an allocation for overhead costs, if absorption costing is used) or at market value—whichever is lower at the time the income statement is prepared.

Inventories are then subtracted from operating expenses to determine the cost of goods sold. This procedure is equivalent to putting a value on the inventories. However, this accounting approach misrepresents real resource flows since:

- **a.** producing inventories ties up resources just as does producing goods for consumption (therefore, these costs should be reflected in the financial accounts); and

- **b.** inventories have no value to society until they are consumed.

The cash flow format in project economic analysis allows us to reflect the actual resource flows much more accurately than does an income statement format.

The cash flow format should be set up to fully cost all production, but to value the production only when it is actually sold. It should show no economic value for any inventory, and it should cost all resources when they are taken away from other uses. (Inventories of raw materials should be cost in full at the time these inventories are built up.) In farm accounting, this problem is dealt with, in part, by using the "time-adjusted cash flow" approach [Schaefer-Kehnert (1978)].

Third, income statement expenses show only what economists call "explicit" or financial costs. They do not include the "implicit" or oportunity costs of resources already owned. In project cash flow analysis, we should set up financial cash flows "with" and "without" a project; then, we should subtract the "without project" cash flow from the "with project" cash flow in deriving the "incremental cash flow." This procedure implicitly costs the resources which have not already been cost explicitly in setting up the "with project" cash flow. [Forecasts of the state of the economy without the project are necessary for properly shadow pricing the benefit and cost streams—particularly when a country is at the margin of self-sufficiency in a commodity. See Cases 8, 9, and 10 in Part V.]

Point of First Sale Valuation

The convention of valuing all outputs at the point of first sale has two objectives:

a. to avoid having the project take credit for the value-added that occurs at later stages in the processing; and

b. to account for the timing of consumption as closely as possible.

For project outputs that are processed further, this practice tends to overvalue them slightly. (Since these outputs will be recorded earlier in the accounts than the point at which they are actually consumed, they will not be discounted heavily when the accounts are finally subjected to discounted cash flow analysis. Except for such economic activities as producing steel for shipbuilding, this distortion in timing is generally not worth worrying about.)

We need to note that in the point-of-first-sale convention, project output which goes into finished goods inventory has no economic value; this is because economic value does not occur until the item is actually consumed. In economic analysis, as a matter of convenience, consumption is assumed to take place when the output is sold.

Cash versus Credit Sales

In economic analysis, there is no need to differentiate between cash and credit sales, and it is irrelevant when, or even whether, payment was made. The difference between cash and credit sales is taken care of in the financial cash flow statement by placing all credit

The cash flow format should be set up to fully cost all production, but to value the production only when it is actually sold. It should show no economic value for any inventory, and it should cost all resources when they are taken away from other uses.

transactions at the bottom of the cash flow table (i.e., short-term credit transactions, such as financing of accounts receivable, etc.) so that the top part of the financial cash flow statement (or the farm budget) shows all transactions as though they were cash transactions. In making the economic cash flow statement from the financial cash flow statement, we normally ignore the credit transactions at the bottom of the statement. We work only with the top part of the financial cash flow statement.

The convention of ignoring credit transactions may be altered for projects in which:

 a. the financing is obtained from sources external to the country; and

 b. the financing is "tied" to that particular project.

Generally, these conditions hold true only for projects involving foreign private financiers (e.g., in the natural resources sector these would include timber growing and/or harvesting, mining projects, some agroindustrial exports activities, etc.). We normally assume that bilateral and multilateral project finance is part of a programmed package of assistance which would be available for alternative projects in the event that a project in the programmed set was found unacceptable upon appraisal.

However, most of the agricultural projects that would be appraised by agricultural line agencies would not be of the tied-financing type. Thus, it is a common practice to ignore these cases in regular agricultural projects, and to ignore all credit transactions.

Normally, cases involving tied financing should be appraised by a joint team comprising staff from both the agricultural line agency and from one of the central economics agencies in the country, such as the Planning Office and the Ministry of Finance. [In the projects financed by the International Finance Corporation, an affiliate of the World Bank that focuses on the private sector, the analysis of financial flows is routinely included in the process of completing the economic analysis. This contrasts with agricultural projects funded by the Bank's other affiliates that work primarily with the public sector.]

Cash versus Real Transactions

A Common Denominator of Resource Flows. We have said that we are interested in real resource flows. This interest is not changed by the fact that we use currency units counted in willingness to pay terms to measure resource flows. This practice easily misleads noneconomists to think that it is the money flows that are important in project economic analysis. (Note that the

In economic analysis, there is no need to differentiate between cash and credit sales, and it is irrelevant when, or whether, payment was made.

funds flow analysis is critical in financial planning for the project, but it is a financial analysis concern for the project and for each farmer: it is not a concern of the economic analysis, except in the way in which funds flows affect individual behavior, and thus the expected real outcomes of the project. The financial analysis problems are important, and they must be addressed in parallel to the economic analysis issues. Obviously, both sets of issues must be dealt with in planning viable projects.)

That misunderstanding among noneconomists is an unfortunate side-effect of our need for a common denominator for measuring the resource flows. Perhaps, we could avoid this misunderstanding by instead measuring all resource flows in equivalents of one ton of wheat and using a decimal version of "wheat-tons" as our common denominator; but, this would add another tedious—and probably equally confusing—conversion problem to our calculations. [Energy planners often use a ton of coal equivalent (TCE) as a common denominator.]

Resource Flows versus Transfer Payments. The use of currency units in measuring relative resource flows in the project economic analysis is simply a convenience: The currency unit gives us a convenient common denominator for adding and subtracting the sums of the resource flows. In some cases, the currency flow represented by the financial price will be the same as the number of currency units that represent the resource flow. In other cases, the financial flow will not be the same as our common denominator measure of the resource flow.

One good example of the latter case is the payment of a "head tax," which governments have charged every citizen, on occasion, as a way of collecting revenue. In that case, currency clearly does flow from the taxpayer to the government; but, there is no underlying resource flow that we need to use currency units to measure. In this case, we would simply ignore the financial flow in the economic analysis, since it does not represent any real resource flow.

The use of currency units to measure resource flows in project economic analysis is simply a convenience. We could use "wheat-tons" as a common denominator instead of rupees or dollars, except that it would create many conversion problems.

When the currency flow is different from the actual resource flow, we define the difference between the two as a transfer payment. The term "transfer payment" indicates that the financial price that is being paid does not represent the actual values of the resources involved; thus, the distorted price has the effect of transferring purchasing power in one direction or the other—i.e., away from the purchasers if the financial price is higher than the real resources involved, and toward the purchasers if the financial price is unduly low.

Explicit and Implicit Costs

Explicit or Financial Costs. Costs which occur "out of pocket" are termed explicit costs. These costs are recorded in traditional financial statements as expenses incurred by the enterprise in carrying out its business. Explicit costs are associated with purchased inputs, hired labor, borrowed capital, and so forth. Payments for inputs made directly to the supplier cause the enterprise to incur explicit costs.

Implicit or Opportunity Costs. "Opportunity costs" represent the benefits forgone. These costs also are real costs, for they represent something that is given up as a result of deciding to take one course of action instead of another. For example, a farmer may withdraw his savings from the cooperative saving bank, where the money was earning 6-percent interest per year, to invest the money in a new sprayer. The cost of the new sprayer, then, would include both explicit and implicit cost elements. The explicit cost element would be represented by the purchase price of the sprayer, while the implicit cost element would be represented by the annual interest that would be lost as a result of withdrawing the savings from the bank.

Traditional financial accounts include only explicit costs. However, good financial decisionmaking should take into account both implicit and explicit costs associated with the decision. Economic analysis always takes into account both explicit and implicit costs. In agricultural project analysis, both the financial and the economic accounts are normally set up in such a way that all items that have not been cost explicitly will be cost implicitly. The implicit costing is done by subtracting the "without project" cash flow from the "with project" cash flow to derive the incremental cash flow (see Table 9.1).

All of the purchased inputs that are used in producing the farm's output in Table 9.1 are cost explicitly—in both the "with" and the "without" project cases. However, the nonpurchased inputs are not cost explicitly because there are no "out of pocket" costs associated with providing family labor, the farmer's land, and the hand tools and other implements that the farm family already owns.

Opportunity Costs.
These costs represent the benefits forgone. These costs are "real" in that they represent something that is given up as a result of deciding to take one course of action instead of another.

However, we must note that without the project, the farm family would have had a net cash flow of Rs 523. This Rs 523 would have been left over after the purchased inputs had been paid for, and it would represent the total of the net inflows that would be available to compensate for the family's labor, land, capital, and the other factors of production.

If the farm represented in Table 9.1 participates in the proposed project, then the farm family will forgo the "without project" returns of Rs 523 in favor of whatever it can earn for its land, labor, and capital by using these in the project. The implicit cost of using these factors in the project will be the income forgone by not using them outside the project; this is shown in the table as the "without project" net cash flow of Rs 523. By subtracting the Rs 523 in deriving the incremental net cash flow attributable to this farm's participation in the project, we have implicitly cost the factors of production owned by the farm family.

Note that we can implicitly cost nonpurchased inputs only if the "without project" column in Table 9.1 includes all family income without the project. For example, off-farm income with and without the project must be included as inflows for this subtraction to implicitly cost family labor correctly.

Note also that the table will impute a zero cost for family leisure. In other words, if family labor input without the project is 600 person-days per year, while family labor input with the project increases to 700 person-days per year, Table 9.1 will show an implicit cost of zero for the 100 extra days of labor. The reason is that there will have been no without-project income attributed to that extra labor.

Table 9.1 will not be able to count implicitly the "psychic cost" of having to work more days per year. The costing of incremental family labor (other than the cost attributable to foregoing compensated off-farm work) will have to be handled in side calculations deriving from the labor budget calculations.

Opportunity Costs and Shadow Prices of Inputs. In project economic analysis, the economic cost of project inputs will be derived from their opportunity costs. The opportunity cost will be measured in terms of the impacts that those inputs would have had in their nonproject alternative use (i.e., "without the project" use). We have used the term "impacts" rather than "income" or "benefits," because the measure of the cost of the inputs will depend upon the numeraire being used in the economic analysis.

In project economic analysis, the economic cost of project inputs will be derived from their opportunity costs. The opportunity cost will be measured in terms of the impacts that those inputs would have had in their alternative without-the-project use.

Incremental and Sunk Costs

The analysis of a project (in contrast to that of a company) is based on the analysis of "decision-related" impacts—i.e., the decision of whether or not to implement the project. Those impacts can be divided into two groups:

   a. positive impacts called "benefits;" and

   b. negative impacts called "costs."

Table 9.1. Implicit and Explicit Costing in Cash Flows

Example. Cash Flow for Model Farm. Year Four. In Rupees		
	Without project	With project
Inflows		
Beans	200	280
Maize	300	350
Lettuce	80	120
Outflows		
Purchased seed	5	15
Fertilizer	10	25
Pesticides	2	20
Plowing services	5	10
Hired labor	25	40
Other inputs	10	10
Net cash flow	523	630
Without project		-523
Incremental net cash flow		107

Note: The farmer's land, labor, and the inputs already owned are cost implicitly by subtracting the "without project" net cash flow from the "with project" net cash flow. All purchased inputs are cost explicitly by showing their costs explicitly in the table.

By "decision related" we mean that the impacts will not occur if we make one decision, while they will occur if we make the alternate decision. This is the same issue as the "incremental" analysis discussed in Gittinger (1982) on page 315; and it is the same as the issue of "with project" versus "without project" analysis. "Incrementality" is a critical issue in assessing project benefits and costs.

Traditional financial accounts, designed for the analysis of companies rather than of projects, do not differentiate between sunk costs and incremental costs. While it is possible in some accounting systems to make a delineation of costs which are related to production as opposed to those which are not, the basic financial accounts are not set up for that purpose. For example, a simple analysis of sunk and incremental costs using the economist's distinction between short-run fixed and variable costs can be carried out by using the financial statements. But unless "direct

The decision of whether or not to implement a project depends on benefits and costs. "Incrementality" —the difference between "with project" and "without project" cash flow—is a critical issue in assessing project benefits and costs.

cost accounting" is used rather than the traditional "absorption costing," it can be difficult to rearrange the information for such a purpose.

In fact, two sets of accounts are normally set up in project planning:

    a. one set of "incremental" accounts for the project analysis itself; and

    b. a second set of accounts for the analysis of the company that implements the project.

The second set uses the approach of traditional financial statements, or of farm enterprise accounts, in the case of agricultural projects.

The issue of sunk and incremental costs arises at several points in project analysis. Gittinger (1982) discusses one such application on page 55. We are concerned here with the use of these cost concepts in calculating "supply-price conversion factors," which will be dealt with in following chapters. In that application, the concept of sunk and incremental costs will affect the way overheads and profits are dealt with in calculating the incremental economic costs of supplying project inputs, assuming that we work from the kinds of cost data that normally are provided by traditional financial accounts.

In "absorption costing," overhead costs are absorbed in the cost of goods sold and in the costing of inventories. In "direct costing," overheads are not absorbed into these calculations. This is more of an issue in agro-industries than in farm accounting.

10. The Meaning of Conversion Factors

Summary. *After a financial cash flow for a project is derived and initial adjustments are made, then other values in the cash flow must be adjusted for the remaining distortions in "border" and "domestic" prices. These adjustments may be made by multiplying the financial values by appropriate "accounting ratios," "conversion factors," or "shadow price factors"—all of which refer to the ratio of the economic value to the financial value of items in the project cash flow. The denominator of the ratio will be the same no matter which method is used for analyzing economic efficiency.*

However, the numerator will vary depending upon the numeraire used—whether the values are denominated in border or domestic prices, and whether first-best or second-best shadow pricing is being used. The ratios may be calculated for both traded and nontraded goods. In calculating the ratio for a specific good or service, both the border distortion and the domestic distortion will be corrected in estimating the numerator. Conversion factors generally refer to economic valuation done in border price terms, while shadow price factors usually refer to valuation in domestic price terms.

Either denomination may be used regardless of whether we conduct "partial border pricing" or "complete border pricing." The former refers to border pricing which makes extensive use of the standard conversion factor (SCF), while the latter refers to border price calculations involving detailed tracing of the impacts that nontraded goods have on traded goods.

Accounting Prices, Financial Prices, and Accounting Ratios

The terms "shadow price," "accounting price," and "economic value" are often used interchangeably in project economic analysis. Though each term tends to have historical linkages with one system of appraisal or another, each term means basically the same thing.

Our objectives in deriving these economic values, or accounting prices, are to:

a. develop a measure of real resource flows which excludes financial flows that do not represent real resource flows; and

b. show the measure of resource flows in units of our numeraire.

We would expect the set of economic values to be different for each possible definition of the numeraire.

The terms "shadow price," "accounting price," and "economic value" basically have the same meaning in project economic analysis.

In conducting project economic analysis, we would like to have an economic accounting price for each particular input and output. Gittinger (1982) goes into some detail regarding the derivation of economic values, based on the willingness to pay calculation at both the domestic price level and at the border price level (pages 243-284). Thus, Gittinger discusses the steps involved in deriving two sets of economic accounting prices for a project. However, we must bear in mind that these two sets of economic accounting prices are closely related to each other; they differ only in the aggregate adjustment that takes place between the domestic price level and the border price level.

Thus, each of these two sets of economic values may be derived from the other set simply by dividing or multiplying by PREM, the "premium" on foreign exchange, discussed in Part I:

a. The set of border price level (i.e., the SCF approach) economic values discussed in Gittinger (1982) may be derived from the domestic price level (i.e., the SER approach) economic values by dividing each of the SER-approach economic values by PREM (see equation 6.5).

b. Alternatively, the SER-approach (i.e., domestic price level) economic values may be derived by multiplying each of the SCF-approach (i.e., border price level) economic values by PREM.

Once a set of economic accounting prices has been derived to fit the numeraire that has been defined, each economic price can be compared directly with the corresponding financial price for each item in the project cash flow. In some cases, the economic values will be lower than the financial values; in other cases they will be higher. The interpretation of this difference will depend to some extent upon what numeraire is used and the price level at which the numeraire is denominated (e.g., the domestic price level versus the border price level). In each case, however, the difference between the financial price and the economic accounting price will indicate the price distortions affecting that particular good or service.

Often, we will find it convenient to make a set of ratios from the sets of accounting and financial prices—i.e., to divide each economic accounting price by the financial price of the cash flow item. This practice can be helpful because once these ratios are known, they may be used to convert other financial values into economic values. This capability greatly facilitates the process of converting the project financial cash flow into a project economic cash flow.

The ratio of economic value to the financial value is known by several names: accounting ratios, accounting price ratios, conversion factors, or shadow price factors. Each name means basically the same thing (though some of these ratios have been developed using specific shadow pricing approaches, and thus continue to be associated with those approaches).

The term "conversion factor" has come to be associated with a shadow pricing process in which financial prices are converted to border price calculation in either the willingness to pay numeraire or in the foreign exchange numeraire. The conversion factors were popularized by the OECD Manual; thus, the term tends to have a somewhat stronger association with border price calculations done in the foreign exchange numeraire than with border price calculations done in the willingness to pay numeraire [the approach discussed in Gittinger (1982)].

Nevertheless, the term "conversion factor" has tended to be used in applying both the foreign exchange and the willingness to pay numeraires in border prices. In these applications, the conversion factor will sometimes be referred to as the ratio of the economic value over the financial value of the item, and sometimes it will be referred to as the ratio of the border value over the financial value of the item. (We will clarify the latter definition of the ratio in the sections that follow.)

The term "shadow price factor" is associated with the conversion of financial values into economic values in a willingness to pay numeraire calculated at the domestic price level. We are not defining hard and fast rules for these particular terms: rather, we are reporting on observed tendencies to associate particular terms with particular numeraire denominations. We point out these tendencies because of the analytical advantages provided by clear communication. The substance of this discussion is that it is generally best to use economic analysis terms in a way in which others are accustomed to using them.

The Concept of Border Prices

"Border price" and "border pricing" are important terms in project economic analysis and in the analysis of pricing and trade policies. "Border price" is a more accurate term than "international price" that is sometimes used as an alternative. Border prices are specific to a particular country, whereas it is not clear what the basing point is for quotations in international prices. But even the term border price needs to be made more specific to be used in a practical context.

There are two border prices for each product at each port in the world. One is the CIF (cost, insurance, and freight) price, which relates to products imported through that port; the other is the FOB (free on board) price, which relates to products exported through

Conversion factors generally refer to economic valuation done in border prices, while shadow price factors usually refer to valuation done in domestic prices.

that port. [CIF and FOB prices are discussed in Gittinger (1982), pages 78-83.] In countries having more than one major port, it may not be sufficiently specific to use the CIF price without saying which port, or what part of the country, you are talking about. This is particularly true in a country such as Saudi Arabia, for example, which has major ports fronting on two seas, or in a country such as Brazil with distances totaling hundreds of kilometers between ports.

While the terms "CIF price at Mombassa" or "FOB price at Karachi" are more specific than the border price, in project appraisal we find it useful to get even more specific than that. Import and export parity prices represent more specificity, because they allow us to calculate border-price-related prices at various points within the country—e.g., at the project gate, at the farm gate, at the market, and so forth. [Gittinger (1982) uses the parity-price approach to deal with border prices, pages 269-271.] These parity prices usually are calculated at the project gate, or at the farm gate.

In common usage, the term "border pricing" may refer to one of the following two applications:

a. the process of deriving a border price for a particular good or service (i.e., the CIF, FOB, or the good's equivalent parity price); or

b. the process of conducting project economic analysis by using either the foreign exchange numeraire or using the willingness to pay numeraire denominated in border prices.

[We know from Gittinger (1982) that parity prices may be derived in either financial or in economic terms. The financial parity price calculation is used largely in market analysis, while the economic parity price calculation is used in project economic analysis and in policy analysis—particularly in applications involving sectoral pricing policies.]

Because of the importance given to border prices in the OECD Manual, the terms "border price" and "border pricing" have come to be closely associated with the methods of analysis presented in the original and in the revised versions of the OECD Manual. Economists commonly use border prices and border pricing in referring to the application of Little and Mirrlees' method of analysis—i.e., economic analysis done in border prices using a foreign exchange numeraire. (Let us note also that, since the initial presentation by Little and Mirrlees was based on first-best shadow pricing, it is often assumed that the term "border pricing" refers to applications using first-best shadow prices. In later editions of their work—published by Heinemann Books—Little and Mirrlees took a position similar to that of Squire and van der Tak: the decision was

There are two border prices for each product at each port in the world:
1. CIF price for imports; and
2. FOB price for exports.

left to the project appraiser in deciding whether to use first-best or second-best shadow prices.) Many economists will be prone to assume that anyone else's use of these terms also implies that the OECD method of economic analysis is being used.

Conversion Factor in the Willingness to Pay Analysis

In the preceding paragraphs, we defined a conversion factor (CF) as a ratio of economic value to financial value of a particular item. We indicated that each item in a project cash flow, in principle, has its own conversion factor. Thus, we may define a "set" of conversion factors as a group which includes conversion factors for every good and service in the country. There would be a different set of CFs for every numeraire; and every item in that set would represent the ratio of the economic value to the financial value of a particular good or service in the numeraire that was being used.

In comparing the two sets of CFs calculated in two different numeraires, the conversion factor for the same item in the two sets would have a different absolute value. But we also showed that any two sets of CFs will be related to each other through the relationship between the numeraires of each of the sets that we are comparing. For example, in the two willingness to pay numeraires presented in Gittinger (1982), the sets of conversion factors for the domestic price level and the border price level will be related by PREM, the premium on foreign exchange. (Previously, we had used the term "accounting ratios." Conversion factors and accounting ratios are simply two different terms for the same thing.)

In using the willingness to pay numeraire, foreign exchange may be treated as a "commodity" which has the capability to generate domestic consumption value. That capability may be expressed by the weighted average value of the consumption basket of traded goods that the foreign exchange represents. (Note that the basket may be made up of different aggregations of goods, depending upon how the calculation is being used. This point will be discussed further in later sections.) This notion of a basket of goods is the normal sense in which the premium on foreign exchange (PREM) is calculated and used. In project appraisal applications, PREM is used to adjust for the distortions between relative consumption values of traded and nontraded goods. In other words, PREM represents an adjustment to the financial prices that we must make in dealing with the distortions caused by trade policies of the government (i.e., border distortions as opposed to domestic distortions). It is not the only adjustment that will have to be made, since distortions resulting from trade policies are not the only distortions that exist in the economy.

In converting financial prices to economic values, there will generally be two sets of adjustments that need to be made. The first is an adjustment to border distortions. This adjustment would be to the financial prices to correct for systematic distortions between traded and nontraded goods (sometimes treated as distortions in the exchange rate). These distortions occur at the border of the country and are caused by the country's trade policies (such as those relating to import tariffs and subsidies, export subsidies and taxes, and import and export quotas). It is this set of distortions that the PREM calculation is designed to capture in the approach discussed in Gittinger (1982).

This set of adjustments is made in either of the following two ways in the willingness to pay numeraire:

   a. *The SER approach*. By applying the shadow exchange rate (SER) to all border prices of traded goods, while using domestic shadow prices (willingness to pay values) for the nontraded goods. This procedure will be followed if the results are denominated at the domestic price level [i.e., using the SER, in the terminology used by Gittinger (1982)].

   b. *The SCF approach*. By applying the shadow conversion factor (SCF) to the shadow priced values of nontraded goods, while applying the official exchange rate to the border prices of traded goods. This procedure would be followed if the results are to be denominated in border prices [i.e., using the SCF, in the terminology used by Gittinger (1982)].

The second is an adjustment to domestic distortions. This adjustment would be made to the financial prices to correct for distortions that occur within the country. The internal distortions could include, for example, the effects of minimum-wage laws on the price of labor and of monopoly elements on the price of locally made machinery. These prices will be adjusted in the economic analysis by applying the valuation principles discussed in Gittinger (1982). For example, in the case of unskilled labor, a shadow price might be derived based on the marginal value produce (MVP) of labor in the alternative use to which that resource would be put "without" the project (see Cases 2 and 3 in Part V).

In converting financial prices to economic values, two sets of adjustments need to be made:
1. adjustment to border distortions; and
2. adjustment to domestic distortions.

If we use accounting ratios or conversion factors in project economic analysis, they should assist in converting financial prices to economic values. Our conversion factors may be calculated so that they incorporate both steps—adjusting for distortions between traded and nontraded goods and adjusting for distortions among nontraded goods—into one conversion factor; or, they may be calculated so that border distortions are handled separately from domestic distortions.

Generally, in applying the foreign exchange numeraire and the willingness to pay numeraire in border prices, the conversion factors will be calculated to include corrections for both the border distortions and the domestic distortions at the same time. For example, in developing a conversion factor for unskilled labor, we might find the following kind of calculation performed:

Assume: MVP of unskilled labor in alternative work = Rs 10/day

Project wage for unskilled labor = Rs 15/day

PREM = 1.25; and

OER: Rs 10 = $ 1.

Since: SER = PREM x OER

Then: SER: Rs 12.5 = $ 1.

(or the same SER may be written as)

SER: Rs 10 = $ 0.80; and

$$SCF = \frac{1}{PREM} = \frac{OER}{SER} = 0.80$$

Further: Shadow wage rate (SWR) = MVP = Rs 10/day
Economic border value of unskilled labor = SWR x SCF
Economic border value of unskilled labor = Rs 10 x 0.8
$$= Rs\ 8/day;\ and$$

Conversion factor for unskilled labor = CFul.

$$CFul = \frac{Economic\ value}{Financial\ value}\ ;\ then:$$

$$CFul = \frac{Rs\ 8/day}{Rs\ 15/day} = 0.56$$

These steps may be shown in more general terms as follows:

$$NB = [(To - Ti) \times OER] + (s.a.NTo - s.b.NTi) \qquad (10.1)$$

Where:

NB = Net benefits from project for year n

To = FOB value of exported project output for year n
(assumed to be only one output)

Ti = CIF value of imported project inputs for year n
(assumed to have only one traded input)

NTo = Financial value of nontraded project output for year n
(assumed to have only one nontraded output)

NTi = Financial value of nontraded project input for year n
(assumed to have only one nontraded input)

s = SCF

a = Shadow price factor for NTo

b = Shadow price factor for NTi

Shadow Price Factors versus Conversion Factors. The shadow price factor is defined as the item's shadow price in domestic terms, without having been corrected for border distortions (e.g., the MVP of unskilled labor in the preceding example). The shadow wage rate (SWR), for example, is the shadow price of labor defined in domestic price terms, without having corrected for border distortions. The ratio of the SWR to the financial wage would give the shadow price factor for labor. To get the conversion factor for labor, we would have to multiply the shadow price factor for labor by the SCF (or by the conversion factor for the output that labor would have produced in its alternative employment without the project, in the "complete border pricing" approach discussed below).

We may thus define conversion factors for each of the inputs and each of the outputs as follows:

$$CFTo = \frac{\text{Border price of To}}{\text{Financial price of To}} = \frac{To}{To + e} \qquad (10.2)$$

Where CFTo = Conversion factor for To

e = Export subsidy on To

(already excluded with other direct transfers)

$$CFTi = \frac{\text{Border price of Ti}}{\text{Financial price of Ti}} = \frac{Ti}{Ti + t} \qquad (10.3)$$

Where CFTi = Conversion factor for Ti

t = Import tariff on Ti

(already excluded with other direct transfers)

$$CFNTo = \frac{\text{Economic value of NTo}}{\text{Financial value of NTo}} = \frac{s.a.NTo}{NTo} = s.a \qquad (10.4)$$

Where CFNTo = Conversion factor for NTo

$$CFNTi = \frac{\text{Economic value of NTi}}{\text{Financial value of NTi}} = \frac{s.b.NTi}{NTi} = s.b \qquad (10.5)$$

Where CFNTi = Conversion factor for NTi

Shadow Price Factor. *Defined as an item's shadow price in domestic terms without having been corrected for border distortions. A good example is the shadow wage rate.*

We can note from the preceding paragraphs that—in the border price version of the willingness to pay numeraire—the conversion factors for the nontraded goods will be their domestic shadow price ratios multiplied by the SCF; while the conversion factors for the traded goods will be their CIF and FOB values divided by their financial prices.

The annual net benefit equation can be rewritten as follows:

$$NB = [(To - Ti) \times OER] + [(a.NTo - b.NTi) \times s] \qquad (10.6)$$

and we would get the same absolute value for net benefits (NB). This is true mathematically; however, in practice, we would have to be extremely careful that we reflected all the indirect foreign exchange that is involved in producing the nontraded input (NTi). Otherwise, these two methods would not correspond to each other. For this and other reasons, it is a general practice to deal with both the domestic and the border distortions in the same calculation in estimating conversion factors.

Conversion Factor in the Foreign Exchange Numeraire

In applying the foreign exchange numeraire, our objective is to determine the foreign exchange impacts of all project inputs and outputs. This process is possible because economics teaches us that:

> **a.** all markets are interrelated; and
>
> **b.** all inputs and all outputs, in principle, have substitutes.

Note that this statement may not apply to projects in the urban sector where the project's nontraded outputs might not have substitutes (e.g., urban water supply). Directly or indirectly, some of these substitutes are traded goods; thus, nontraded goods have an impact on the country's foreign exchange availability. In addition, production processes for all nontraded goods use traded goods as inputs, either directly or indirectly.

In the foreign exchange numeraire, the conversion factor would be defined as the ratio of border values to financial values, where the border value of each item would represent the impact that the good or service has had on foreign exchange. Generally, for project inputs, the foreign exchange impact would be negative; while, for outputs, it would be positive.

If the foreign exchange numeraire were denominated in local currency (i.e., in units of foreign exchange which had been converted into local currency at the OER), then each conversion factor would be a ratio of two local currency values (i.e., the ratio of the economic value in local currency divided by the financial price in local currency). However, if the foreign exchange numeraire were denominated in foreign currency (i.e., in units of foreign exchange which had not been converted into local currency), then each conversion factor would be the equivalent of a specific exchange rate

In the foreign exchange numeraire, the conversion factor would be the ratio of border price values to financial values, where the border value of each item would represent the impact that the good has had on the foreign exchange.

for the item whose economic value (i.e., foreign exchange value) was being determined (i.e., the ratio of the economic value in foreign currency divided by the financial value in local currency).

Some proponents of the foreign exchange numeraire argue that this numeraire is superior to the willingness to pay numeraire. They take the position that it is more accurate to use several shadow exchange rates (SER) than to use only one. This perceived increase in accuracy provided by the foreign exchange numeraire is a misperception on their part, however. The issue is not between using one SER or using several factor-specific SERs; rather, it is an issue of how far we are prepared to trace the direct and indirect impacts that each project has on the economy. In other words, the issue is whether we work under the assumption that all impacts on nontraded goods can be traced to impacts on traded goods.

If we are equally diligent in applying the willingness to pay numeraire (and if we make the same assumptions about the interrelationships between markets), then the same number of specific SERs will be generated in applying the willingness to pay numeraire as will be generated in applying a foreign exchange numeraire. By denominating either of these numeraires in foreign currency rather than in local currency, we make the accounting ratios for project inputs and outputs into specific SERs for each of those inputs and outputs. It does not matter which of these two numeraires we choose to state those impacts in, so long as we make the same assumptions about market interactions.

The point in the analysis at which the issue of diligence and the assumptions of the appraiser and the accuracy of the two economic efficiency numeraires become critical occurs in dealing with non-traded inputs and—in particular—nontraded outputs for which demand-price conversion factors would be obligatory in the foreign exchange numeraire (see the next section for details).

In the application of the willingness to pay numeraire denominated in border prices, the typical practice is to use the SCF in place of demand-price conversion factors for inputs and to use the SCF in place of demand-price CFs for outputs. In the foreign exchange numeraire, the need for tracing the indirect impact on traded goods is a bit more obvious and, perhaps, a bit more likely to be undertaken as a result. Thus, in practice, the comparative accuracy of the two numeraires comes down to a question of whether we use the SCF to derive the demand-price conversion factors rather than using the CFs for the traded goods that are expected to be affected by the project's use of nontraded inputs which are not supply responsive, or which are used in the production of nontraded outputs.

Partial and Complete Border Pricing

No matter what numeraire is used, the terms "conversion factor" and "accounting ratio" refer to the ratio of economic values divided by financial values. The conversion factors that you as the project appraiser will be applying will do basically the same thing: they will convert the project financial prices into project economic prices in terms of whatever numeraire is being used in the economic analysis—whether that numeraire be an economic efficiency numeraire in willingness to pay terms or in foreign exchange terms, or whether it be some altogether different numeraire (see Part III for a discussion of other numeraires).

In the willingness to pay numeraire, there are two different ways in which economic efficiency analysis is applied, depending upon what assumptions we make about the interrelations between markets for traded and nontraded goods and services:

  a. complete border pricing; and

  b. partial border pricing.

In complete border pricing, the same assumptions are made about market interrelationships as those made in the foreign exchange numeraire. In other words, all markets are interrelated, such that impacts on nontraded goods can be traced to impacts on traded goods and vice versa. Since all goods are assumed to be traded goods—directly or indirectly—in this approach the calculation of PREM is not quite so critical. The reason is that all values will end up being adjusted by the same border distortion adjustment factor that is derived from PREM (i.e., the SER or the SCF).

In partial border pricing—this approach is often applied in practice—we work under the largely implicit assumption that traded goods have an impact on foreign exchange, while nontraded goods may not necessarily have such an impact. In this approach, border prices for traded goods are converted to foreign exchange impacts, and the foreign exchange is expressed in willingness to pay values. The willingness to pay values for nontraded goods are then compared with willingness to pay values for foreign exchange in conducting the project economic analysis.

In the partial border pricing method the calculation of PREM is very important, since it will be used to adjust the values between traded and nontraded goods. In this method, we compare the willingness to pay for the foreign exchange represented by the traded goods and the willingness to pay for the nontraded goods themselves. Note that this comparison may be made either at the border price level or at the domestic price level—the two approaches to economic analysis (the SER method and the SCF method) presented in Gittinger (1982).

In complete border pricing, all markets are considered interrelated, such that impacts on nontraded goods can be traced to impacts on traded goods and vice versa.

In partial border pricing, we assume traded goods have an impact on foreign exchange, while nontraded goods may not.

If we eliminate the possibility of having truly nontraded goods (i.e., assuming that all goods are either directly or indirectly traded), then the willingness to pay issue really comes down to a question of willingness to pay for foreign exchange (since every impact really involves foreign exchange directly or indirectly). In that case, the foreign exchange numeraire and the willingness to pay numeraire are applied in the same way, and the question in the willingness to pay application of the economic efficiency numeraire is whether we have the "right" values for the PREM and the SCF (which is the same as asking whether we have the right SER).

If all goods are traded either directly or indirectly in the foreign exchange numeraire, then exchange rate values become unimportant, because they will only be used at the last moment when all of the foreign exchange is moved from one currency denomination into the other; and since all values would be multiplied by whatever exchange rate is chosen, the final comparison will be unaffected. If we do not get too lazy and make unduly liberal use of the SCF in the analysis (i.e., if we use CFi's instead), then the estimate of the SCF will not constitute a serious issue—though the accuracy of the estimates of the CFi's will be important (see Case 1 in Part V). Note that we can only make the forgoing statements in regard to applications which involve complete border pricing; they would not be true if we are talking about partial border pricing.

If the country has limited international trade and has no intention of changing those policies, then there is a good reason to question whether it makes sense to use a complete border pricing approach to project analysis, if we are not going to use the analysis as a bridge into policy-related discussions with policymakers. Such an environment would be most suited to the use of partial border pricing methods—in particular, partial border pricing using the SER approach. This may be viewed as the classic case for which the willingness to pay numeraire denominated in domestic prices makes the most sense. In this case, most inputs and outputs would be *de facto* nontraded goods; the SER would not be used much in the project analysis (and, thus, any slight errors in its calculation would not much matter); and the most relevant measure of economic value would be the willingness to pay for the project's nontraded inputs and outputs. [This is the approach proposed by the UNIDO Guidelines (1972)]. Because of the issue of the sensitivity of the border prices discussed previously, the domestic price version of the willingness to pay numeraire would likely be a more appropriate method than any of the border pricing methods under these circumstances.

If a country has limited trade and is characterized by severe domestic distortions, then no method of economic analysis will be easy to apply.

If the country has limited trade and is characterized by severe domestic distortions, then no method of economic analysis will be easy to apply, though any reasonable method could greatly assist the process of project planning, if applied diligently and if extended to include policy analysis. In particular, it will be practically impossible for noneconomists to conduct any form of meaningful project economic analysis in a highly distorted economy. And even the economists who might attempt to conduct project economic analysis will have to expend a great deal of effort (as well as other resources) to gather the information needed to generate meaningful shadow prices. And yet, this is just the case in which the potential positive impacts from good economic analysis are the greatest—both project analysis and policy analysis. In all likelihood, such a country would be helped considerably by good economic policy analysis— if the analysis could have an impact on the country's conduct of economic policy.

In the current international environment, it is doubtful whether international aid agencies would provide stand-alone project financing for projects in such a highly distorted economy. More likely, the aid agency would not be willing to finance projects at all unless major policy reform was undertaken. If project financing were undertaken, it would likely be done as part of a "sectoral," or "structural," reform package. Because of the increasing number of countries entering the category of the "thoroughly distorted," this kind of package is becoming increasingly important as a mode of project financing by the international aid agencies. These same factors also make it increasingly important that policy analysis be more routinely conducted as a counterpart of project analysis.

11. Categories of Conversion Factors

Summary. *Conversion factors (CFs) are used to convert financial values to economic values in the project cash flow. CFs may be either "specific" CFs (abbreviated as CFi), or they may be "general" CFs (abbreviated as GCF). The CFi is specific to particular goods or services, while the GCF is an average of groups of goods and services. The group from which the average is calculated may be very broad (as in the case of the SCF), or it may be narrow (as in the case of a GCF for local transport services). Generally, the CFi, or the more narrowly defined GCF, is preferred over more broadly defined GCFs because the former should more accurately reflect actual resource flows.*

CFs may be either "centrally calculated," or they may be "project-related" CFs. The former may include both CFi's and GCFs. Generally, project-related CFs are presumed more accurate than centrally calculated ones—particularly CFi; and we recommend that project-related CFi be calculated for project costs or benefits exceeding 10 percent of the project total. CFs can be divided into "demand-price" CFs and "supply-price" CFs. The former are calculated when the primary project impact is manifest through an effect on the demand side of the market for the good, while the latter is calculated when the project impact is on the supply of the good. Much information regarding the government's taxation and sectoral policies is contained in CFs. We can gain valuable policy insights by simply comparing particular CFs with each other and with unity (1.0).

Specific versus General Conversion Factors

Gittinger (1982) provides guidance on calculating what economists call "specific conversion factors." However, the derivation of a second group of conversion factors called "general conversion factors" (sometimes also called "average conversion factors") is left to the Planning Office. General conversion factors are nothing more than weighted averages of particular groupings of specific conversion factors. The way the grouping is made depends upon the use to which the GCF is to be put. In general, the broadest of these groupings will take place in calculating some form of the standard conversion factor (SCF). Thus, the SCF is a form of general conversion factor.

Conversion factors may be "specific" to particular goods and services, or they may be "general" in that they are an average of groups of goods and services.

General conversion factors (GCFs) have a number of uses in project economic analysis. The most prominent use is the conversion to border prices of project inputs or outputs that are too minor by themselves to warrant detailed analytical work. Examples would include local transportation services involved in moving a relatively minor imported project input from the port to the project gate. Rather than spending time to determine the mode of transport and finding the correct economic value for the transport, it may be wiser to just use an average conversion factor calculated for the modes of transport that historically have been involved in moving goods of that type. The modes that might be included for calculating this particular local transport GCF might include contract trucking services, rail service, and perhaps even rickshaw service.

In the following section we discuss some of these GCFs and their relationship to certain specific conversion factors. (Specific conversion factors will be indicated by the letters **CFi**, where **i** refers to the item for which the specific conversion factor is being calculated—e.g., **CFul**, where **ul** refers to unskilled labor and **CFul** means "the specific conversion factor for unskilled labor." The term "conversion factor" will be indicated by the abbreviation **CF**; CFs may, of course, be either CFi's or GCFs.)

Deriving and Using CFs

We have said previously that conversion factors are nothing more than the ratios of border values over financial values of the item whose economic value is being estimated. In economic analysis, when an item is "border priced" all of the transfer payments are deleted in the shadow pricing process before determining the border values. The transfer payments result from the domestic and the border distortions.

We have also said previously that, as a matter of convenience, CFs may be calculated for traded goods as well as for nontraded goods. In any event, conversion factors are really nothing more than a convenience for us—a convenience that can lead to errors in project analysis, if they are not calculated and used carefully.

Whether the CF being dealt with is for a traded or for a nontraded good, the CFs used in project economic analysis fall basically into two groups:

    a. *Project-related conversion factors.* These are calculated by the project appraisal team, where the item being border priced is a major item in the project cash flow (generally, more than 10 percent of project costs or project benefits).

    b. *Centrally calculated conversion factors.* These usually are provided by the Planning Office (or by some other central institution) to be used in cases where the item being border priced is a minor item in the project cash flow (generally, less than 10 percent of the project costs or project benefits).

In general, more specific CFs (e.g., those for rickshaw transport) are preferred to more aggregated CFs (e.g., those for domestic local

General Conversion Factor.

GCF is a weighted average of particular groupings of specific conversion factors. The way the grouping is made depends upon the use to which the GCF is to be put.

transport). By the same token, project-related CFs that are calculated by the project analyst are preferable to centrally calculated CFs (except for CFs relating to so-called "national parameters" such as the SCF, the consumption conversion factor, and the discount rate). This is true, in particular, for specific conversion factors. Specific conversion factors that are centrally calculated will have two weaknesses compared to those calculated by the project analyst:

First, the centrally calculated CFi's will be more aggregated, or more "average," in the following ways:

a. the local transport component of the cost will have to be an average for all sites in the country and will not be project related; and

b. the cost structure for the project inputs will reflect the average producer of that product in the country rather than that of the actual source of the input to the project.

Second, the centrally calculated CFi's are likely to be less current than those estimated by the appraisal team. (They can be no more current than the data upon which they were based. Centrally calculated CFi's tend to rely heavily upon secondary data which may have been collected for some other purpose, such as building input-output models, for instance.)

These weaknesses of centrally calculated CFi's place trainers in project appraisal and managers of line agencies in a difficult position. On the one hand, noneconomists need to understand and be able to use techniques of project economic analysis because in many cases they are the only people involved in planning locally financed agricultural projects, and because agriculturists usually understand the possibilities for substituting technical inputs and outputs better than do economists; therefore, they are usually better suited to reshape agricultural projects to improve their economic impact. On the other hand, it has long been realized that CFs that are correctly calculated by the project appraisal team are generally more accurate than comparable centrally calculated CFs (except the "national economic parameters").

In general, more specific conversion factors (CFs) are preferred to more aggregated CFs; and project-related CFs calculated by project analysts are preferred to centrally calculated CFs.

Every trainer and every line agency manager should recognize this conflict and should keep in mind the compromises that are involved in teaching noneconomists in the line agencies to carry out project economic analysis. Underlying the development of Gittinger (1982) was the recognition that, in a number of countries and agencies, project economic analysis will not be undertaken for locally financed agricultural projects if agriculturists are not taught techniques in project economic analysis and are not motivated to use them.

Forms of General Conversion Factors

Standard Conversion Factor. The SCF is the broadest of the CFs that are discussed in this section. It should normally be calculated as a weighted average of the other CFs, with the weights calculated from marginal proportions that each good represents in the national production of the country. Because it is the broadest of the CFs, it should not be used except when there is no other CF available. There are two different ways of calculating the SCF: the trade data approach and the weighted average CF approach (see Case 1 in Part V for details).

Consumption Conversion Factor. This too is a broad or aggregate CF, though not as broad as the SCF. It too is a weighted average CF, with the weights based on the average propensity to spend and on income elasticities of demand for the various goods and services represented in the consumption basket of the country. This GCF is used in converting nontraded consumption goods into border prices, where we do not have a CFi, or where the item is so minor in the project cash flow that calculating a CFi is not warranted (see Technical Note 22).

Construction Conversion Factor. This is a GCF for use in border pricing general construction activity where it is not practical to break down the components and border price them separately. In deriving this GCF, the weights are usually based on the average expenditure patterns experienced in construction activities that are representative of project construction in the country. It would be useful if the Planning Office would provide different construction conversion factors for different areas of the country. [For a numerical example, see Ahmed (1984).]

Local Transport Conversion Factor. This is a GCF which converts to border prices the average cost of internal transport within the country. It is usually calculated by border pricing the traded inputs (e.g., vehicle costs, spare parts, and petrol, oil, and lubrication) and using the most specific conversion factors that are available on the nontraded inputs (e.g., vehicle maintenance, labor for driving and loading/unloading, and overheads). The local transport conversion factor may be calculated as an average CF for all modes of transport, or different versions may be developed based on different aggregations of modes. For example, a GCF may be calculated for water-borne transport in which barge transport and other forms are combined and averaged together; or a GCF may be calculated in which water-borne and surface transport are combined into one average GCF for transport.

If we know that the goods would move by water, then the CF that is calculated most specifically related to that mode will be the most

Standard Conversion Factor.

It should be a weighted average of the other conversion factors, with the weights calculated from marginal proportions that each good represents in the national production of the country. Because it is the broadest of the CFs, it should not be used except when no other CF is available.

accurate in removing the distortions that affect the price of that particular mode. For example, if we know that the goods will be moved by barge, then our preference for a CF would be in the following order:

   a. a CFi for barge transport;

   b. a GCF for water-borne transport;

   c. a GCF for local transport; and

   d. the SCF.

[For an example of a derivation with a detailed cost breakdown of a supply-price conversion factor for transport services, see Anand (1975). Ahmed (1984) provides an example using input-output data.]

Electricity Conversion Factor. This GCF would be calculated based on the long-run incremental economic cost of supplying electric power for the kinds of projects likely to be included in the government's investment portfolio. When these GCFs are calculated by the World Bank for use by its staff, the calculation is greatly facilitated by the existence of a rational plan which describes expected future expansion of the electricity supply system (see Case 1 in Part V).

In addition, several other GCFs may also be calculated, including: GCFs for manufactured goods that are used as inputs to production processes, civil works conversion factors for the kind of civil works involved in typical government projects, water supply and other public utilities which appear as costs in a large number of projects, and so forth. [See, for example, Page (1982) in addition to the derivations in Mashayekhi (1980) and Ahmed (1984) for the conversion factors of capital goods, intermediate goods, and wages.]

Categories of Specific Conversion Factors

In Chapter 7 of Gittinger (1982), a "decision tree" is presented which categorizes the major types of economic valuation issues that are expected to arise in the economic appraisal of agricultural projects. We have reproduced the decision tree and expanded upon the various categories of valuation issues (see pages 94 and 95).

We separate all project inputs and outputs into traded goods and services, and nontraded goods and services. This will provide us, initially, with four categories of items to be valued in the project economic analysis:

   Traded goods and services
   1. Project outputs
   2. Project inputs

Nontraded goods and services
   3. Project outputs
   4. Project inputs

"Conversion factors for traded goods" (and services) are calculated by dividing the "parity price" of each traded good by its respective financial price. The derivation of import and export parity prices is discussed in Gittinger (1982), pages 269-277. Conceptually, it is easy to understand the derivation of CFs for traded goods. However, it may be a bit more difficult in practice, as is illustrated in some of the examples in Part V. Because there tends not to be as much confusion regarding the economic valuation of traded goods, we shall focus in this section on the nontraded goods.

The following are the major categories of nontraded goods for which we can derive economic values (or the CFs from which we can calculate those economic values):

Nontraded project outputs
   (Demand-price conversion factor)

Nontraded project inputs
   1. Nonreproducible inputs
      a. Land (Demand-price conversion factor)
      b. Labor (Demand-price conversion factor)

   2. Reproducible inputs
      a. Excess capacity exists in the industry that is producing the input (Supply price conversion factor)

      b. No excess capacity exists in the industry that is producing the input
         i. Industry will add capacity to accomodate project demand (Supply-price conversion factor)

         ii. Industry will not add capacity to accomodate project demand (Demand-price conversion factor)

"Nonreproducible inputs" are those whose supply is presumably not directly related to economic phenomena. Land, for example, is assumed to be in fixed supply in absolute terms. Similarly, the absolute quantity of nontraded labor is presumably fixed at any point in time (though the "supply" of labor may adjust to wage increases by increasing the labor force participation rate in the short run). Obviously, such a definition is only useful as a heuristic device in understanding the supply constraints that may be expected to affect these inputs. In recent decades, the development

Conversion factors for traded goods are calculated by dividing the "parity price" of each traded good by its respective financial price.

Figure 11.1, Part A. Decision Tree for Determining Economic Values: Major Steps

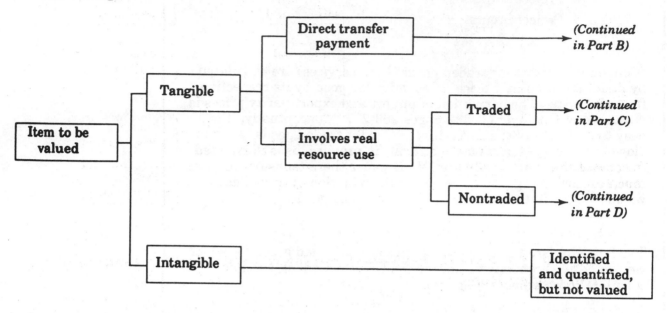

Figure 11.1, Part B. Decision Tree for Determining Economic Values: Direct Transfer Payments

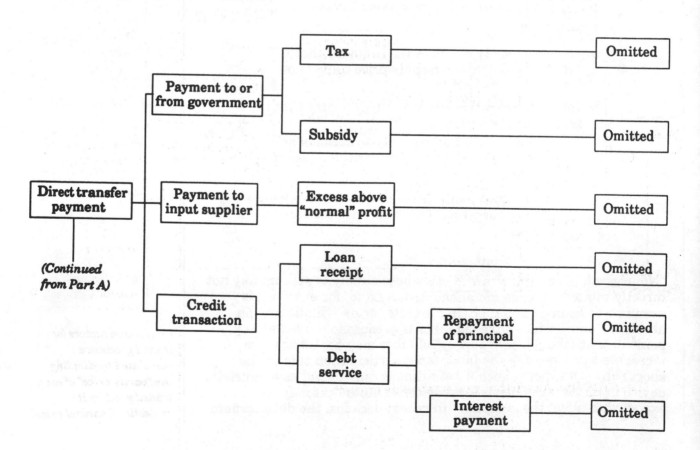

Figure 11.1, Part C. Decision Tree for Determining Economic Values: Traded Items

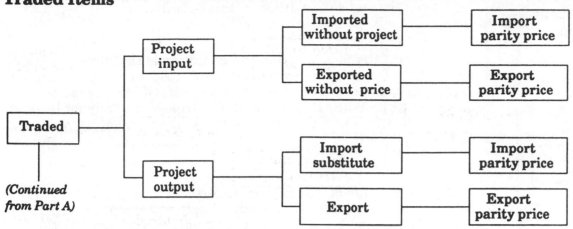

Figure 11.1, Part D. Decision Tree for Determining Economic Values: Nontraded Items

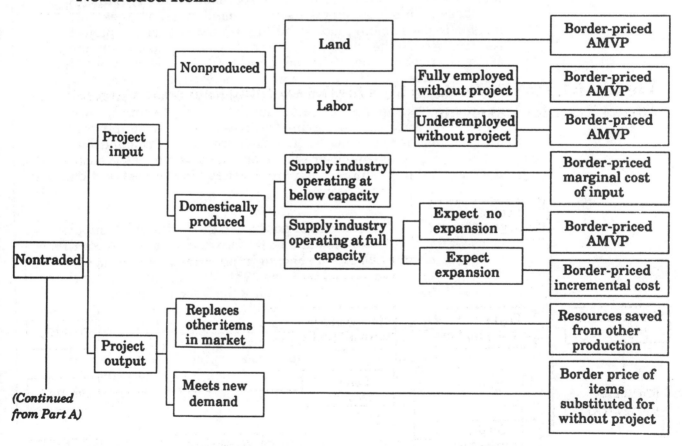

Note: AMVP = Alternative marginal value product.

of international trade in various categories of labor have had a significant impact on the utility of this definition.

The utility of the "nonreproducible" definition is that it implies that the supply of those inputs is inelastic with respect to price. In other words, their total quantity cannot be augmented in response to a price increase. While this is not strictly true—especially for labor—nevertheless, it is useful to us in deciding what kind of conversion factor to calculate.

Analysts generally divide conversion factors for project inputs into two groups, based upon whether the supply of the input is expected to increase to accomodate an increase in demand imposed by the project. Nontraded inputs whose supply will expand to meet project demand will be dealt with by using "supply-price conversion factors." Nontraded inputs whose supply will not expand to meet project demand will be dealt with by using "demand-price conversion factors." For example, we might be appraising a project which will purchase from a local supplier several small diesel engines that are needed to power small, mobile milling equipment for the project. If the engines are the one-cylinder type that are not found any more and would not be among the countries' traded goods, we would have to value these project inputs as nontraded inputs. Immediately, we encounter the question of whether the supply of the engines will expand in order to meet project demand; or will the supply not respond for some reason, forcing the project users to simply bid them away from other purchasers. The different ways of calculating supply-price and demand-price conversion factors in cases such as the one cited in this paragraph are discussed in the next section.

We can define the categories of nontraded goods for which supply price CFs will be calculated and those for which demand-price CFs will be calculated. These are shown in parentheses after each category of nontraded good (see page 93). We can see that, for the inputs, a distinction is made regarding the issue of whether production of the nontraded good will increase in order to supply the project. If it will increase, then the economic cost of the good will be calculated from the incremental inputs required to produce the incremental units needed to supply the project. This case, as we shall see, falls under the heading of a "supply-price conversion factor."

If the supply is not expected to increase, then it makes no sense to cost project inputs in terms of their incremental production cost, for there will be no incremental production of the item. Instead, the project input must be cost in terms of the impacts on the economy that are caused by taking the item away from its alternative use. This latter case falls under the heading of a "demand-price conversion factor." Gittinger (1982) speaks of valuing these inputs in terms of their opportunity costs, and that is just what the demand-price conversion factor for a project input is designed to do. This point is discussed further in the next section.

The way we deal with nontraded outputs will differ depending upon whether complete or partial border pricing is practiced. The partial border pricing approach discussed in Gittinger (1982) advises us to:

    a. determine the demand price for the output; and

    b. multiply that price by the SCF when using the SCF approach.

In applying complete border pricing in the foreign exchange numeraire, we should try to determine the traded goods for which the project's nontraded output would substitute in the market; and we should use the border prices of those goods in estimating the foreign exchange saved by the producing the project's "nontraded" outputs. The ratio of the foreign exchange savings over the financial price of the nontraded output would be the demand price conversion factor for the nontraded output.

Supply-Price and Demand-Price Conversion Factors

"Conversion factors for nontraded project inputs" fall into two groups, depending upon the extent to which supply of the input is able to expand to meet the increase in demand that is imposed by the project. The two groups are:

    a. supply-price conversion factors; and

    b. demand-price conversion factors.

The "supply-price conversion factors" are used in cases in which the supply of the project input being border priced expands to meet the additional demand imposed by the project. Because supply expands, the incremental cost imposed on the economy by the use of this input by the project will be the cost of the incremental resources that are used in meeting the required supply expansion. Supply-price CFs are calculated only for project inputs.

The demand-price conversion factors are used in cases in which the supply of the project input will not expand to meet the additional demand imposed by the project. They are called demand-price CFs because the project inputs will have to be taken away from someone else's use, indicating that the costs will be imposed in the form of unmet demand borne by the alternative user of the input.

Demand-price CFs are relevent in cases in which supply cannot, or will not, increase to accomodate the project. The most prominent examples of inputs for which demand-price CFs are normally

Conversion factors for nontraded project inputs fall into two groups:
1. supply-price CF; or
2. demand-price CF.

Their use would depend upon the extent to which the supply of the input is able to expand to meet the increase in the demand imposed by the project.

calculated are land and labor. (We say "normally" here because certain types of labor in certain countries are viewed increasingly as a traded input—whose supply to the economy can be increased by importing more foreign workers or by exporting fewer domestic workers—rather than being a nontraded input whose supply is fixed in the short run.)

"Specific conversion factors for project inputs" will be either a demand-price or a supply-price conversion factor. GCFs for project inputs, of course, will be an average of several CFi's. In principle, that average may include a combination of CFi's, some of which are demand-price and some of which are supply-price CFi's. However, in practice, GCFs for project inputs will often consist of averages of a set of supply-price CFi's. This is because they will often be calculated from data (such as that for an input-output model) which relate inputs to outputs and which assume that output will expand to meet demand increases. In economist's jargon, such economic models normally assume that supply is "elastic."

"Demand-price CFs for nontraded project outputs" will also need to be calculated. These demand-price CFs will be derived from the ratio of the border price to the financial price, as with all CFs. If it is possible to find substitutes for the nontraded project output, then the border price in the ratio will be that of the traded good for which the project output will substitute, while the financial price in the ratio will be that of the project output (see Technical Note 23). In Gittinger (1982), we are advised to use the SCF as the CF for nontraded project outputs. This approach is probably sufficient in most cases—in particular if the appraisal is being done by someone with limited understanding of economics, or if the output is a minor part (less than 10 percent) of project benefits.

As discussed previously, the use of the SCF in such cases may be based upon either of the following assumptions:

The first assumption is that the items that are being substituted for by the project output have CFi which are close to the SCF. This will be sufficient, if the item represents a small part of project costs, or of project benefits.

To derive economic values for nontraded project outputs, the demand-price conversion factor should be used. If the nontraded output could be substituted by a traded output, then the border price should be that of a traded good, while the financial price should be that of the nontraded output.

The second assumption is that the nontraded good for which the CF is being calculated will not have traded goods substitutes, and thus the border distortion adjustment is being made in terms of the distortion between traded and nontraded goods in general. This would be the case, for example, in dealing with the truly non-tradable goods discussed in Chapter 10.

An Example of Demand-Price Conversion Factor

A "demand-price conversion factor" for a project input is calculated by comparing the financial value of that project input with its economic value, where the economic value is calculated in terms of the losses borne in the alternative use of that same input as a result of the input being transferred to project use. The losses borne by the alternative user of the input can be measured from the marginal value product (MVP) of the input in its alternative use. Since the demand for an input is represented by the input's MVP function, the CFs derived in this way are termed demand-price CFs.

Let us look at unskilled labor as an example of the calculation of a demand-price CF for a project input. First we shall look at a case in which there are no domestic distortions to be dealt with. Then we shall look at a case in which both domestic and border distortions affect the price of unskilled labor. [Case 3 in Part V provides another example of the shadow pricing of labor. See also Tower and Pursell (1986).]

The market for unskilled labor is usually competitive in rural areas, where wages are largely determined by competitive forces and are not controlled effectively by minimum-wage laws, government employee wage structures, multinational wage practices, and other factors which tend to fragment urban wage structures. In such a case, domestic distortions affecting the price of unskilled labor may be minimal. The presence of regional and seasonal differences in wage rates and the presence of labor migration will usually imply competitive unskilled labor markets in rural areas.

The competitiveness of the market for unskilled labor implies that workers tend to be paid their MVP in domestic price terms. The MVP of labor measures the addition to the value of the product that is brought about by adding one more labor input at the margin of production. In competitive markets, workers will usually be paid wages that reflect the MVP of labor. This MVP will depond upon two things:

   a. the marginal physical product (MPP) of labor; and

   b. the price of the output that the labor is being used to produce.

The MPP is the amount that one more laborer adds to output in physical terms (e.g., in kilograms) at the margin.

The MVP of any input is estimated as follows:

$$MVPi = MPPi \times Po \qquad (11.1)$$

The market for unskilled labor is usually competitive in rural areas, where wages are largely determined by competitive forces. In competitive markets, workers will usually be paid wages that reflect their marginal value product.

where:

MVPi = Marginal value product of the input;

MPPi = Marginal physical product of the input; and

Po = The price of the output being produced.

If the rural unskilled labor market is, in fact, a competitive market, then we would expect the MVP of labor to be roughly the same between crops on the same farm, as well as among different farms in the same labor market area. And, if the project that is being appraised is not so large as to greatly alter the demand for labor relative to the supply of labor, then the price of unskilled labor in rural areas should not change drastically as a result of the project. Under those circumstances, we may use the market wage rate as the estimate of the MVP of labor in the nonproject alternative use of that labor. And the market wage rate would be our estimate of the shadow wage rate (SWR).

$$SWR = MVPlabor \qquad (11.2)$$

Note that the SWR represents the opportunity cost of labor stated in domestic price terms. If we use border pricing, we need to state our SWR in border price terms.   There are two ways to convert the SWR to border prices:

If we use the partial border pricing method, we simply multiply the SWR by the SCF.

$$BPl = SWR \times SCF \qquad (11.3)$$

where:

BPl = Border price of labor

If we use the complete border pricing method, we substitute for Po in equation (11.1), the border price equivalent of Po in place of the financial price Po. If the output that the labor would be used to produce in its nonproject alternative employment were rice, then we would substitute the border price of rice for the financial price in the equation on the MVP of labor.

$$BPl = MPPl \times BPo \qquad (11.4)$$

or, alternatively

$$BPl = SWR \times BPo/DPo \qquad (11.5)$$

where:

BPo = Border price of output; and

DPo = Domestic price of output.

If the project being appraised is not so large as to greatly alter the demand for labor relative to supply, then the price of unskilled labor should not change drastically as a result of the project.

In this illustration, we will use the complete border pricing approach. For example, let us say that we are estimating the conversion factor for unskilled labor (CFul) in Bangladesh, where rice production is indeed the likely alternative use for rural unskilled labor. The MVP of unskilled labor and the rural wage rate in Bangladesh would be heavily dependent upon the MPP of labor and the domestic price of rice. Bangladesh is a net importer of rice. For purposes of our calculation, let us assume that there is some minor distortion between the border and domestic prices of rice. Let us also say that the CIF price of rice in Bangladesh (converted to taka at the OER and ignoring, for the time being, the issue of local transport) is Tk 5,000/ton, while the domestic price of rice is Tk 5,500/ton.

Assume that MPP = 0.01 tonnes of rice produced per day,

then MVP = 0.01 x Tk 5500 = Tk 55/day, and

SWR = Tk 55/day

But the SWR of Tk 55/day is stated in domestic prices. We want to get the economic cost of unskilled labor stated in border prices, if we are using the border price level version of the numeraire (as our use of the term "conversion factor" implies). To do so, we revalue the rice in border prices by taking its CIF price, and we recalculate the economic cost of unskilled labor as follows:

BVul = MPP x CIF

= 0.01 x Tk 5000 = Tk 50/day

where:

BVul = Border value of unskilled labor, and

CIF = the CIF price for rice.

The border price for unskilled labor, then, would be Tk 50/day. To get the CFul, we would divide Tk 50 by the financial price of unskilled labor. In a competitive market such as the one we have discussed, the financial price would be Tk 55/day, giving us the CFul, as follows:

CFul = Tk 50/Tk 55 = 0.909

In the Bangladesh example, the conversion factor for unskilled labor (CFul) would be the same as the conversion factor for rice (CFrice). This is true because there is no domestic distortion for unskilled rural labor, per se, in the case just cited. In this example, the only correction so far is for distortions which occur at the border and which occur indirectly through the impact on the domestic price of rice. Note that we could have used the SCF to correct for the border distortion; but the use of such an aggregated CF would have involved correcting for the average distortion affecting all commodities that were weighted into the SCF calculation. If we know that it is the border distortion for rice specifically that is having the major impact on the domestic price of rural unskilled labor, then we will achieve a more accurate correction by using the CFrice rather than the SCF.

What if the majority of rural unskilled laborers were not engaged in rice production and, thus, the wage rate was not primarily distorted by border distortions for rice? What if, in fact, rural unskilled laborers were producing a wide range of crops, each of which had its own specific set of distortions? Well, in that case, we would need to substitute a GCF calculated for the "basket" of crops that they would actually be engaged in producing in the place of the CFrice (see Technical Note 24). The closest GCF that we have to that particular basket of production would be the best one to use. If we had one for "crop products," that would probably be the best one. Or, if we had one for "agricultural outputs," that would be the second best one. And, if we had none of these, then the consumption conversion factor (CCF) would likely be our next best choice. Certainly, in a case like Bangladesh (where a large proportion of total consumption expenditure is accounted for by food), it would be better that we to use the CCF than the SCF in estimating CFul.

What if the rural labor market were not competitive for one reason or another? Then there would be a second element in the above calculation. That element would arise from the fact that the SWR and the financial price were different (i.e., that there was a domestic distortion present, in addition to the border distortion, affecting the price of unskilled labor). In that case, we could not use the market wage as the estimate of the MVP of unskilled labor. We would have to undertake specific studies to determine the MPP or the MVP of unskilled labor, and we would use those data in calculating the shadow wage rate and the CFul. Our border priced economic cost of unskilled labor would still be calculated as MPP x CIF. But the CFul value would be different, since the financial price of unskilled labor would be different from the financial price that was used in the preceding calculation of CFul.

If the rural labor market were not competitive, we would not be able to use market wage as the estimate of the MVP of unskilled labor. Specific studies would have to be undertaken to determine the MVP of unskilled labor.

Let us assume that an agricultural minimum wage of Tk 80/day exists, and that government enforcement was effective so that farmers actually did pay wages of Tk 80/day for unskilled labor, thus causing the project wage (i.e., the financial price of unskilled project labor) to be Tk 80/day. In this latter case, if the border price of unskilled labor were Tk 50/day, as previously estimated, then the CFul would be

$$\text{CFul} = \frac{\text{BVul}}{\text{Min. wage}} = \frac{\text{Tk 50}}{\text{Tk 80}} = 0.625$$

The difference between the previously calculated CFul of 0.909 and the just calculated CFul of 0.625 lies in the domestic distortion that is implied by the minimum wage law. Because of this distortion, the ratio of the SWR in domestic price terms divided by the financial price of unskilled labor is Tk 55/Tk 80 = 0.69. If we were using the SER approach to economic analysis (i.e., a domestic price level-denominated numeraire), then our shadow price factor would be 0.69.

However, we wish to use a numeraire denominated in border price (i.e., the SCF approach), so we must show the economic cost of unskilled labor in border price terms. We do so by multiplying the shadow price factor (which adjusts for the domestic distortion for labor) by the conversion factor for rice (which adjusts for the border distortion affecting unskilled labor), as follows:

$$CFi = DDF \times BDF \qquad (11.1)$$

where:

DDF = Domestic distortion factor; and

BDF = Border distortion factor.

$$CFul = \frac{SWR}{Min.\ wage} \times \frac{Border\ price\ of\ rice}{Financial\ price\ of\ rice}$$

$$CFul = \frac{550}{800} \times \frac{500}{550}$$

$$CFul = 0.69 \times 0.909 = 0.625$$

We can see that in using the complete border pricing approach, we shall always try to use a CFi as the border distortion factor. The SCF would only be used when the project laborers who were being border priced were engaged in producing a wide range of goods and services—a range which was too wide to use a narrower CF. In the partial border pricing approach, in contrast, we could use the SCF because we did not expect that a relationship of any substance existed between the nonproject use of labor and the availability of traded goods.

Conversion Factors for Traded Labor

In today's world, some labor may be valued as a "directly traded" project input. Bangladesh, Korea, the Philippines, and Yemen, for example, all have exported labor to the oil-producing countries of the Middle East at one time or another. Similarly, many African countries have imported skilled and managerial labor to assist in project management functions.

In appraising projects in the labor-exporting countries, any project laborer who would have worked abroad in the absence of the project may be treated as a diverted export [see Gittinger (1982), page 253]. The foreign exchange cost of that worker to the project would be the forgone foreign exchange repatriations— i.e., the opportunity cost in foreign exchange terms of bringing the worker home to work on the project instead of allowing him or her to continue to work in the Middle East. The conversion factor, then, would be calculated by taking the ratio of the forgone foreign exchange divided by the actual financial wages to be paid.

For a project in one of the labor-importing countries, incremental labor imports would be treated as a traded input. The labor's economic cost in foreign exchange terms would be the sum of its foreign exchange repatriations, plus the border priced cost of the labor's subsistence in the country. The conversion factor, then, would be the ratio of this sum divided by the financial wages to be paid.

An Example of Supply-Price Conversion Factor

We may envision three cases in calculating conversion factors for nontraded, reproducible project inputs:

    a. *Excess capacity in the input supplying industry.* In this case, we calculate a supply price CF, in which we consider overheads and profits to be "sunk" elements.

    b. *No excess capacity, but capacity expands.* There is no excess capacity in the supplying industry, but the suppliers agree to increase production capacity to meet the project's demand. In this case, we calculate a supply-price conversion factor in which we consider overheads and profits to represent incremental costs of supplying the input.

    c. *No excess capacity and supply does not increase.* There is no excess capacity in the supplying industry, and the suppliers will not increase production capacity to meet the project's demand. In this case, the project's input will come from the goods that would otherwise have gone to other users; thus, we calculate a demand-price conversion factor for the project input, similar to the CFs that would be calculated in the normal case of land or labor (which are usually considered to be "nonreproducible" inputs).

In the case of project inputs that are not traded and are produced locally under conditions of excess capacity, we need to calculate a supply-price conversion factor. To calculate this factor, we must convert the financial cost to economic costs (via the border pricing approach) by:

    a. deleting taxes and subsidies;

    b. border pricing the incremental traded inputs used in producing the project's input; and

    c. repeating steps **a** and **b** over and over until, in theory, all the incremental nontraded inputs that are used in producing the project's input are reduced to a combination of directly and indirectly traded inputs, land, and labor.

The ratio of the resulting economic value divided by the financial value for the input will be the supply-price conversion factor for this input.

Each specific conversion factor represents the product of a "tracing" exercise, in which each nontraded input is broken down into its inputs—round after round, until the remaining nontraded factors become insignificant. In practice, the point of insignificance is usually defined to occur when the resulting item becomes less than 10 percent of total capital costs (if it is a capital cost item), or of operating costs (if it is an operating cost item).

The following paragraphs illustrate the methods that are often used in calculating supply-price conversion factors. We use the example of a locally made and nontraded one-cylinder engine that is to be used as a project input. In calculating supply-price conversion factors, a distinction is sometimes made between suppliers having excess capacity and suppliers having no excess capacity. Both cases are illustrated below.

In calculating a supply-price conversion factor where the supplying firm (or sector) will have excess capacity sufficient to supply the project input, the "overhead and profits" element of the product cost structure is treated as "sunk" in the short run and is not included in the economic cost of supplying the input. Table 11.1 illustrates calculation of a supply-price conversion factor for engines to be used as project inputs in the case in which excess capacity exists. The excess capacity is expected to last during the period in which the project will be purchasing engines and is expected to be sufficient for the project demand to be met without fully using existing capacity.

Because there is excess capacity, the suppliers will not have to expand to meet the project demand. Thus, the fixed elements of production cost will not be "incremental." Since in economic analysis, we only include incremental costs, the fixed elements will be considered to be "sunk" and will not be included in the calculation of economic costs of the engine. This is indicated by the use of a CF of zero for the "overheads and profits" element of costs in Table 11.1.

Table 11.1. Cost Breakdown: Locally Made Engine
(Excess capacity in engine industry)

	Financial cost (Rs)	Conversion factor	Economic cost (Rs)
Raw materials (RM)			
Imported			
CIF	300	1.0	300
Duties	60	0	0
Local transport	40	0.7	30
Local RM	150	0.6	90
Unskilled labor	200	0.4	80
Skilled labor	50	0.8	40
Misc. materials	20	0.8	16
Utilities	20	0.9	18
Other costs	35	0.8	26
Taxes	100	0	0
Overheads and profits	125	0	0
Total cost	1000		600

CF for motor = Rs 600/Rs 1000 = 0.60

In the case of project inputs that are not traded and are produced locally under conditions of no excess capacity (and the suppliers will expand to meet the project demand), the supply-price conversion factor is calculated exactly the same as the one calculated in the previous paragraph—but with one change. In the present case, the fixed costs are not treated as "sunk costs." Rather, they are also considered incremental costs, since the input-supplying firm will have to expand its capacity in order to supply the inputs that will be demanded by the project.

If you look closely, you will see that the difference between the economic prices and the financial prices will be determined by direct and indirect "transfer payments." In Table 11.2 ("no excess capacity" case), all of the transfers involved government transfers—i.e., they involved taxes and subsidies, and thus were induced by government policies. In the excess capacity case, transfers also went to the firm that was supplying the inputs to the project. These latter transfers had to be due to monopoly elements in the input-supplying industry; in the absence of monopoly elements, competition between suppliers would have forced the supplying firm to reduce the price.

Table 11.2. Cost Breakdown: Locally Made Engine
(No excess capacity in engine industry)

	Financial cost (Rs)	Conversion factors	Economic cost (Rs)
Raw materials (RM)			
Imported			
CIF	300	1.0	300
Duties	60	0	0
Local transport	40	0.7	30
Local RM	150	0.6	90
Unskilled labor	200	0.4	80
Skilled labor	50	0.8	40
Misc. materials	20	0.8	16
Utilities	20	0.9	18
Other costs	35	0.8	26
Taxes	100	0	0
Overheads and profits	125	0.8	100
Total cost	1000		700

CF for motor = Rs 700/Rs 1000 = 0.70

In the face of excess capacity, competition should have forced the price down to a level just sufficient to cover the variable costs. In other words, if the input-supplying industry had been competitive, the financial price actually paid for the project input (one engine) should have been Rs 875, rather than Rs 1,000. The difference between Rs 1,000 and Rs 875 in this case was defined an "excess profit" (In the context of shadow pricing, the excess profits would be called a "transfer payment." Economists use the terms "transfer payment" and "economic rent" when speaking of payments for which there are no real resource costs.) Then in the latter calculation in which the CF for motors was calculated to be 0.70, we must have been assuming that there were no excess profits; otherwise, we would have had to adjust the Rs 125 of "overheads and profits" downward to reflect the "normal profit." Let us recall that in economic analysis a normal profit (the opportunity cost of capital provides a reasonable estimate of what the normal profit should be) is assumed to be part of the opportunity cost of management and entrepreneurship.

In our supply-price conversion factor calculations, when we

included overheads and profits in the incremental costs we used a conversion factor for them of 0.8. In that example, we were assuming a standard conversion factor of 0.8. Let us recall that we said that the specific conversion factors that we used in making the calculations represented the product of having traced that particular input round after round until we had traced all of its inputs back to border prices (i.e., to foreign exchange). For those items that are so small as to not warrant a detailed tracing, we may use average conversion factors—such as the SCF, which is the most aggregated and averaged of all the conversion factors. This is understandable for the overheads. But what about for the profits element?

The (normal) profit represents a cost in the sense that the "entrepreneur" (or the owner) would have applied his entrepreneurship elsewhere and would have earned a comparable profit in the forgone activity. The profit would have related to the production of some other product that society would have consumed instead. And that alternative product had a financial price; it also had a border price. The ratio of those two would have been its CF. Since we did not know what that product would have been, we simply used the average of all the CFs in the country—i.e., the SCF. Here is where we might find it useful to differentiate between two versions of the SCF: one calculated from the total goods and services *produced* in the country, and one calculated from the total goods and services *used* in the country. The former would be the appropriate version for use in this application.

Accounting Issues in Calculating Supply-Price CFs

The format of cost data for the engines, used in Tables 11.1 and 11.2, is laid out to account for two competing considerations:

    a. to obtain incremental cost information in a cash flow format; and

    b. to develop cost information for purposes of profit-and-loss accounting.

This format of the tables could help us conduct interviews to develop the supply-price conversion factors for major project inputs in a way that would accomodate both of these considerations.

Few firms will be willing to disclose their actual profit margin on the product being supplied to the project. We may, therefore, have to lump "overheads and profits" together in one line in the cost table.

An important point to note in preparing for the interview is that few firms will be willing to disclose their actual profit margin on the product being supplied to the project. Thus, to ensure that the interviewee will provide the cost data, we may wish to lump together "overheads and profits" in one line in the table. This will allow the company to argue that all of this item is "overheads" and that profits are low. For purposes of calculating supply-price conversion factors, there is no need to know the profit margin anyway.

Let us recall that in economics a "normal profit" is considered to be the opportunity cost of entrepreneurship. Thus, profit rates roughly equivalent to the opportunity cost of entrepreneurship would be included in the real costs of supplying the product. Profits in excess of the expected normal profit—called "pure" profits by economists and "excess" profits by politicians—may or may not represent "transfer payments" when it comes time to calculate supply-price conversion factors for project inputs.

The existence of pure profits among input suppliers should be assessed in terms of the expected duration of these profits. Are the pure profits simply short-run profits that exist because the industry is in the process of adjustment? Or are they long-run profits that are attributable to some aspect of market failure, such as imperfect competition? In the case of short-run profits, some economists would argue that they are not in "excess," because that is the mechanism by which markets draw additional investment into the production of that product. If the profits are long-run pure profits, then we may have found another case in which the project analysis identifies a need for a more complete policy analysis of the input-supplying sector.

Here again we illustrate our earlier point that the project appraisal team should be expected to learn a great deal about the effects that policies in other sectors of the economy have on the agricultural sector. Most economists would consider such long-run profits to represent transfer payments, and therefore would delete them from the column of real economic costs in calculating the supply-price conversion factors for inputs supplied by such industries. But we should keep in mind the point made in Part I that if the item needs shadow pricing, its supply may also need to be analyzed in terms of policy changes to deal with an existing aspect of market failure.

Let us return now to the issue of getting incremental cost data from accounting data. The cost breakdown in the preceding tables used a "quasi-income statement" format. The overheads that are allocated to the input being supplied to the project will be of two types:

  a. direct overheads; and

  b. indirect overheads.

The existence of "pure" (or "excess") profits among input suppliers should be assessed in terms of their duration. If they are long-run pure profits could they be attributed to some aspect of market failure? If they could be, then we might need a more complete analysis of the input-supplying sector.

"Direct overheads" are that portion of the overhead costs of the company that can be directly attributed to the product that the project will use. "Indirect overheads" are that portion of the company's overhead costs that cannot be allocated among products. Economists consider any method of allocating indirect overheads among products to be arbitrary. [For example, see Backer and Jacobsen (1964), pp. 115-135.]

The practical problem that project analysts have—or the researcher has in developing the models from which CFs might be calculated—is the same as that faced by regulatory commissions and agencies. To some extent, we are at the mercy of the company supplying the cost data. If the company's financial manager chooses to allocate a large portion of indirect overheads to that product, we will find it extremely difficult to go back and recalculate the cost accounts. This problem becomes more acute if the company manufactures a large number of products.

While cost allocation presents a difficulty in calculating supply-price conversion factors, the real issue is "incrementality." Will the demand posed by the project cause an element of cost to increase? That is the issue. Of course, it is generally easier to answer that question for direct costs than it is for indirect costs; and it is clearer in the case of truly variable costs (as opposed to fixed costs or "semi-fixed" costs—such as insurance premiums, for example). We could consult an engineer who knows that production process well and a cost accountant who knows the sector, but in the end it will be our own common sense that we will have to depend upon to fill the table with cost data that represent the incremental impacts caused by the demand posed by the project.

Interpreting Conversion Factors

Using CFs to Interpret Sector Policies.
We have said previously that conversion factors are used to convert a project's financial prices to economic prices in "border price" terms. Because they are applied to the prices used in the project financial cash flow, the value of the CF can be used to compare financial prices to economic values, and thus can be interpreted to yield information regarding government policies affecting those prices. Because of their potential use in making quick judgments on pricing policies, it will be helpful to understand certain generalizations that can be made by comparing the CF for an item with the SCF and with unity.

CFs and Unity.
In general, the closer a CF is to unity (or 1), the smaller are the net distortions of the price for the item. We talk about "net distortions," because there may be more than one distortion affecting the price of an item: some distortions may increase the price, while at the same time other distortions operating on that same item may have the effect of decreasing its financial price. Where the CF = 1, the border price and the financial price for the good are the same. The further the CF is from 1, the greater are the net distortions.

The closer a conversion factor is to unity (or 1), the smaller are the net distortions of the price for the item.

The net distortions for a particular border priced item is a combination of all the domestic distortions and all of the border distortions that affect the item. The net distortions may be dominated by either domestic or border distortions. Or the net distortions for a particular item may be equally affected by each of these two types of distortion. (For a greater appreciation of these "net" impacts on domestic prices, see the CF calculations in Part V.)

CFs Above and Below Unity. If the CF for any good exceeds 1, then the border price exceeds the financial price of the item. In this case, the net effect of the distortions in the economy would be to reduce the financial price of the item relative to comparable international prices. Some analysts choose to say that such an item is "subsidized" in local markets.

CFs for Exported Goods. If the good in question is an exported good, then the domestic price might be lower as a result of a tax on the exports of the good. In equilibrium, the local price of the exported good will be determined by the FOB price and the export tax on the good, as follows:

$$\text{Local price} = \text{FOB} - \text{export tax} \qquad (11.6)$$

In contrast, an export subsidy would raise the local price of a good relative to its border price and would make its CF less than 1:

$$\text{Local price} = \text{FOB} + \text{export subsidy} \qquad (11.7)$$

CFs for Imported Goods. For an imported good, a CF less than 1 implies that net taxes between the border and the final market for the good tend to increase its financial price over its border price, as follows:

$$\text{Local price} = \text{CIF} + \text{import tax} \qquad (11.8)$$

CFs for Nontraded Goods. For a nontraded good, a CF greater than unity (i.e., the economic price exceeds the financial price) indicates that there are net distortions in the economy which reduce that item's financial price below its border price. This would be the case, for example, if there were subsidies on the inputs used in producing the item. Generally, we expect the CF for a nontraded good to be less than unity, since the net effect of a developing country's trade policy is usually to "overvalue" local currency. (Actually, it is more correct to say that the trade policy is part of a set of policies which allow the country to maintain an overvalued currency.)

The trade policies that maintain an overvalued local currency tend to have a net effect of raising the domestic prices of traded goods. Since traded goods will be used as inputs in producing nontraded goods, the border distortions that occur through the trade policies

Trade policies that maintain an overvalued local currency tend to have a net effect of raising the domestic prices of traded goods.

will also tend to increase the prices of nontraded goods relative to border prices.

CFs for Traded Goods. We can see the effect that trade policies have on the prices of traded goods by observing equations 11.6, 11.7, and 11.8. Import tariffs and export subsidies are often used to support overvalued local currencies. As mentioned before, these two policies tend to increase the local prices of traded goods. However, an export tax does the opposite: it makes it more difficult to maintain an overvalued local currency. In fact, a preponderance of export taxes could lead to an undervalued local currency, as would a preponderance of import subsidies—a policy, incidentally, which was related to a slightly undervalued Saudi rial in the mid-1970s.

CFs in Developing Countries. We generally find that in developing countries a majority of nontraded goods must have their financial prices reduced to get them to the border price level. Thus, we normally expect nontraded goods to have CFs less than unity. We expect this, but we find that some of these goods will have CFs greater than unity, while the majority of goods presumably will have CFs less than unity. The average of these CFs, however, will usually be less than unity, indicating the tendency for the trade policy to have the net effect of increasing domestic prices relative to border prices. This net effect would be reflected if we calculated an average of all the CFs. That is what the SCF does.

In practice, we find that SCFs for developing countries tend to range between 0.75 and 0.9. However, a particular country may have a SCF of 0.82; and it may have CFi ranging between 0.2 and 5.0, or even wider. (See the example of Egypt in Part V, where the SCF is calculated to be near unity and yet the CFi ranges from below 0.25 to above 5).

In developing countries, the conversion factors of nontraded goods tend to be less than unity— with SCFs ranging between 0.75 and 0.9.

12. Conversion Factors in Application

Summary. *In calculating conversion factors (CF) and economic values we face several identifiable categories of traded and nontraded goods. Among the traded goods are: exported outputs, for which export parity values may be calculated; import substitutes, for which import parity values may be calculated; imported inputs, for which import parity values may be calculated; and diverted exports, for which export parity values may be calculated. The ratios of each parity value to the financial price will give the CF for that traded good.*

Among the nontraded goods are: project inputs produced under conditions of excess capacity, for which the CF is based on incremental costs only; project inputs for which there is insufficient production capacity and for which the CF will include fixed asset costs among the incremental costs; project inputs (including land, labor, and certain other inputs) whose supply will not increase and for which demand-price CFs will be calculated; and project outputs, for which traded substitutes will have to be identified. In addition, in the second-best shadow pricing model, there may be some tradable goods which will be valued as nontraded goods.

Valuing Directly Traded Goods

Valuing traded goods in the foreign exchange numeraire is fairly easy: just take their CIF and FOB values as the foreign exchange impact (of course, their local cost components—i.e., local transport and marketing charges—will have to be treated as indirectly traded inputs and will have to be converted to foreign exchange impacts). In the foreign exchange numeraire, the foreign exchange impact may be expressed either in dollars, or in rupees converted at the official exchange rate (OER). The normal practice is to express the impacts in local currency at the OER, though for several countries the entire analysis is conducted in units of foreign currency. These are mostly countries with very high inflation rates, where currencies such as the dollar are expected to hold their value much better than the local currency. For example, using dollars rather than cruzeiros (now cruzados) in Brazil would solve a lot of practical problems for us. To make a financing plan in current prices would require extremely wide columns in our worksheets if we work in local currency.

In valuing the foreign exchange impacts of traded goods, we will have to deal with four different categories of traded goods. These four categories are listed on page 114.

To value traded goods in the foreign exchange numeraire, take their CIF and FOB values as the foreign exchange impact. The foreign exchange impact can be expressed in dollars or in rupees converted into dollars at the official exchange rate.

Outputs

a. *Exported outputs.* The foreign exchange impact will be based upon the FOB value (or the marginal export revenue, if the country is a major exporter of the good. See the Egyptian cotton example in Part V.) In addition, the foreign exchange implications of all local transport and marketing charges must be taken into account by applying appropriate conversion factors to these elements.

b. *Import substitutes.* The foreign exchange impact will be based upon the CIF value. In addition, the foreign exchange implications of all local transport and marketing charges must be taken into account by applying appropriate conversion factors to these elements.

Inputs

c. *Imported inputs.* The foreign exchange impacts will be based upon the CIF value. In addition, the foreign exchange implications of local transport and marketing charges must be taken into account by applying appropriate conversion factors to these elements.

d. *Diverted exports.* The foreign exchange impacts will be based upon the FOB value of the input, had it been exported instead of being used by the project (minus any effects on the FOB price of remaining exports of the product, if the country were a major exporter of the input in question). In addition, the foreign exchange implications of all local transport and marketing charges must be taken into account by applying appropriate conversion factors to these elements (see box below).

In the foreign exchange numeraire, there are no truly "nontraded" goods. All goods and services are either directly traded, or indirectly traded. If they are indirectly traded, they can be placed in the traded goods category as:

1. exported outputs;
2. import substitutes;
3. imported inputs; or
4. diverted exports.

Two Bases for FOB Price Statements

FOB on Cost Basis. Includes all costs of producing, transporting, and loading the good for export—including all taxes. Used in contracts which are written on a cost-of-supply basis and in the reporting of many 'basing-point' statements of international prices (e.g., rice FOB Bangkok).

FOB on Net-Back Basis. Calculated by 'netting back' from the market price in the importing country. This is an estimate of the amount of (net) foreign exchange revenues that will be earned by the export parity prices in economic analysis. The chain of calculations should be roughly as follows:

Market price in importing country - local marketing and local transport = net-back CIF price.

Net-back CIF price - international freight and insurance = net-back FOB price.

[There are instances when the status of a traded good changes from being mainly exported to imported, or vice versa, because of natural shocks to production, artificial market distortions, and the evolution of domestic consumption demands and supply capabilities. See Cases 4, 7, 8, 9, 10, and 11 in Part V.]

Valuing Indirectly Traded Goods

Let us recall that in the foreign exchange numeraire there are no truly "nontraded" goods. All goods and services are either directly traded, or indirectly traded. Thus, in principle, all goods and services can be placed under the four headings for traded goods listed on this page. In the foreign exchange numeraire, we assume that all project inputs will reduce the amount of foreign exchange that is available to the country, and that all project outputs will increase the amount of foreign exchange that is available.

Let us recall also that the economic values derived by using the foreign exchange numeraire will bear a particular relationship to those derived by using a willingness to pay numeraire, if "complete border pricing" is followed in both cases. What matters is not the numeraire that is used; but, rather, the assumptions that are made regarding the government's policies and the interrelations among the markets for different goods and services. As we shall see in Chapter 13, the differences in economic valuation, in practice, will come principally in the way we deal with nontraded project outputs and the extent to which we develop and use specific conversion factors for the nontraded project inputs (rather than simply using the SCF for all nontraded goods).

Supply-Price CFs for Indirectly Traded Inputs

We described the process of calculating supply-price conversion factors for reproducible project inputs using the foreign exchange numeraire in Chapter 11. To calculate a supply-price conversion factor, we must break the indirectly traded input down into its own inputs. Then we must identify which of these "second round" inputs are traded and which are indirectly traded. The traded second-round inputs would be border priced immediately using their CIF or FOB prices (or parity prices), while the indirectly traded second-round inputs would be broken down again into traded and indirectly traded third-round inputs, with the traded third-round inputs being border priced and the indirectly traded third-round inputs broken down again. In principle, this tracing process would be carried out, round after round, *ad infinitum*.

To calculate a supply-price conversion factor, we must break the indirectly traded input down into its own inputs consisting of traded inputs, indirectly traded inputs, land, and labor. The indirectly traded second-round inputs would be broken down, round after round, ad infinitum.

Each indirectly traded input in each round can be broken down into inputs consisting of traded inputs, indirectly traded inputs, land, and labor. If the tracing process continues to its logical conclusion, we will be left with directly and indirectly traded goods, land, and labor when the process is completed. The traded goods will, of course, have already been valued in foreign exchange using their border prices (with all taxes and subsidies deleted). The remaining problem will be to value land and labor in foreign exchange. The process of calculating conversion factors for land and labor was discussed in Chapter 11 in the section, "Demand-Price Conversion Factors." We shall take this up again.

Demand-Price CFs for Indirectly Traded Outputs

Valuing project outputs which are not directly traded requires that, in applying the foreign exchange numeraire, we trace their impacts to traded goods for which the outputs substitute. In some cases, the foreign exchange implications may not be immediately obvious, because the implications depend upon how those substitutions are to occur—or, at least, how we think they will occur.

It is important for noneconomists to understand that one characteristic of an economist's thinking is to assume that all goods and services have substitutes. The substitutes need not always be "perfect" substitutes, but economists tend to characterize substitutes by the degree of substitutability, using cross-price elasticities as the quantitative statement of that degree.

A cross-price elasticity which is positive and approaches infinity marks the two goods as perfect substitutes; a positive and high (but not infinity) cross-price elasticity would mark the two goods as close substitutes; while positive but lower cross-price elasticities would indicate that the two goods are only partial substitutes (and, of course, a negative cross-price elasticity would mark the two goods as complements—meaning that they tend to be used together, rather than substituting for each other). For example, in a particular market, wheat bread and maize bread may both be partial substitutes for rice. And if rice is not available to a traditional rice consumer, the consumer may react by substituting in his or her diet either one or both of these partial substitutes for the rice.

Noneconomists should understand that economists tend to assume that all goods and services have substitutes. The degree of substitutability is determined by cross-price elasticities.

We often find in appraising import substitution projects that the project output will be an imperfect substitute for the alternative imported item. This was certainly the case for the teff that was to be produced in the Ethiopia Minimum Package Project, where the World Bank appraisal team valued the teff as a domestic substitute for imported wheat. It is equally true for many other products that must be valued by agricultural project analysts.

Rice production projects often will provide the country with increased outputs of local varieties of rice—20- or 25-percent broken grains, complete with bits of stone and sand picked up from drying the rice on rural roadbeds, or on imperfectly paved drying beds.

This production is expected to "substitute" for imported Thai rice, which is 5-percent broken and perhaps of the high-yielding variety. Obviously, the two types of rice are not the same products. But, the issue is not simply one of whether the products are the same. That would be too narrow an approach from the economist's viewpoint. Rather, the issue is whether the products will, in fact, substitute for each other in consumption.

Similarly, fresh milk to be produced by a dairy project is certainly not the same product as reconstituted milk made from imported milk powder. In fact, with fresh milk production, the analysis is more complicated than with projects producing local varieties of rice. In the case of fresh milk, there is the problem of different byproducts between reconstituted and fresh milk (see the examples in Part V).

When we use a foreign exchange numeraire, we must be careful about the substitutions that can and do take place between products. We must think through each nontraded project output, rather than simply multiplying its price by the SCF. Because we assume that even nontraded goods have traded substitutes, we must think through the interrelationships that exist in the economy to identify what those traded goods impacts are. Sometimes, this process can be complicated.

Take, for example, the case of a forestry project whose major output is fuelwood—obviously a nontraded output in most countries. If we were using a willingness to pay approach with the numeraire denominated in domestic prices rather than in border prices, the marginal demand price of the fuelwood might be taken to be the shadow price for the fuelwood. [This is the approach in the "partial border pricing" method discussed in Gittinger (1982).]

In applying the foreign exchange numeraire, we must find a foreign exchange equivalent for fuelwood produced by a forestry project. To do this, we must ask: "What would those consumers have done had the project not increased the supply of fuelwood?" In other words, we must look for substitutes for fuelwood—substitutes that would be used if we had not built the project. Ultimately, we would like to trace the substitution process to traded goods. Since, in applying the foreign exchange numeraire, we work under the presumption that the markets for all goods and services in the economy are interrelated, we also presume that we can find traded goods which will be impacted by an increase in the supply of nontraded goods.

In using a foreign exchange numeraire, we must be careful about substitutions that can take place between products. We must think through each nontraded project output, rather than simply multiplying its price by the SCF.

The fuelwood valuation problem has been faced by analysts in several World Bank projects in recent years as the Bank has tried to assist countries in reforestation efforts. (See Part V for examples of fuelwood valuation in World Bank projects.) In many countries, the alternative to burning fuelwood in rural areas is to burn animal dung—another nontraded item. Building a project which provides fuelwood to households will often result in the families forgoing the burning of animal dung; and, indirectly, saving animal dung will save fertilizer or rice or some other agricultural good. This is certainly the case in Bangladesh and in India.

Thus, to value the fuelwood in foreign exchange terms, we should calculate the foodgrain imports that would be necessary as a result of the reduced yields that resulted from burning animal dung rather than using it for enriching the soil. It seems a circuitous process to get the appropriate value in the foreign exchange numeraire for the fuelwood that is produced by the project. But it can be a realistic process, if we have good estimates of the technical coefficients involved—i.e., the heat values of fuelwood and animal dung, the yield impacts of animal dung and fertilizer, and so forth.

A second alternative foreign exchange valuation route can also be pursued. This arises if we believe that, instead of substituting for foodgrain imports, the increased fuelwood output will actually substitute for fertilizer imports. This would be the case if we believed that the reaction of the government (or of producers, depending upon the country) would be to import fertilizer rather than allowing foodgrain production to decrease as a result of burning animal dung. In this case, we would use technical coefficients relating animal dung to fertilizer nutrients to calculate the CIF value of fertilizer imports that would be equivalent to the fuelwood that is produced.

What is interesting about these calculations is that—if they are done seriously and with relatively good data—the rice price, the fertilizer price, and the fuelwood price would be very closely correlated. In fact, in countries in which the markets for all three items are fairly free and competitive, we can calculate fairly accurately the actual market price of fuelwood from the other prices by using the technical coefficients that link the three.

Practitioners and trainers may wish to attempt this calculation for their own country. What the exercise will demonstrate is the extent to which all prices in the economy are interrelated in general equilibrium fashion. The extent to which such sets of prices that ought—in principle—to be related to each other are indeed related will provide some measure of the extent to which the assumptions underlying complete border pricing (and the foreign exchange numeraire) are realistic.

Table 12.1. Malawi Second Wood Energy Project: Economic Valuation of Fuelwood

(Based on imported kerosene alternative)

Landed cost of kerosene (MK/liter)	0.38
Retailing cost (MK per liter) [a]	0.22
Economic cost of kerosene at urban market (MK/liter)	0.60
Calorific value of kerosene (MJ/liter)	36.0
Thermal efficiency of kerosene (percent) [b]	30.0
Calorific value of wood at 20-percent moisture (MJ/kg)	4.4
Thermal efficiency of wood (percent) [b]	13.0
Conversion (kg wood/solid meter^3)	700
Value of fuelwood at urban market in terms of kerosene alternative (MK/ solid meter^3) [c]	72.8
Processing and marketing costs (MK/solid meter^3) [d]	6.7
Falling, cross cutting, and extraction to roadside (MK/solid meter^3)	1.0
Value of standing timber in terms of kerosene alternative at periphery of urban area (MK/solid meter^3)	65.1
Transport cost from 50 km (MK/solid meter^3) [e]	6.8
Value of standing timber in terms of kerosene alternative at 50 km from urban area (MK/solid meter^3) [f]	58.3

Source: Annex 14, Table 2. "Malawi Second Wood Energy Project," Staff Appraisal Report 5914-MAI. Washington, D. C.: The World Bank, February 26, 1986. (This is an internal document with restricted circulation.)

a. Kerosene retailed at MK 0.94/liter, of which MK 0.22 are taxes, and MK 0.34 are handling costs and profit of which two-thirds (MK 0.22/liter) are assumed to be marketing costs.

b. With aluminum pots.

c. Wood equivalent = 0.60 x 14.4 x.13 x 700/36 x 0.30 = MK 72.8/solid cubic meter.

d. From Annex 2, Table 9 (World Bank, February 26, 1986), processing costs (market fees, labor for chopping, loading and unloading) amount to MK 4.7/stacked cubic meter or MK 6.7/solid cubic meter.

e. Basic assumption of 22 stacked cubic meters (15.4 solid cubic meters) on a 14-15 ton truck at the rate of MK 1.05/km on asphalt roads. This implies a cost of MK 105 for the roundtrip, or MK 6.8/solid cubic meter. Roundtrip costs are used because there is unlikely to be much freight for the haul from the urban area to the plantation.

f. Lilongwe plantation is on the urban periphery, while Mulanje is 80-100 km from Blantyre. Hence, on average, transport costs from 50 km apply to the government plantation component of the project.

In the World Bank's Bangladesh Mangrove Afforestation Project, the appraisal team explored each of these methods to value the fuelwood to be produced by the project. The team finally settled on the simple solution of using the forecast market price for the fuelwood, multiplied by the SCF. What was the team's reason for finally settling on this simple approach? They found that the answers that they got from each of these methods were not sufficiently different to justify the added difficulty of explaining and defending the more circuitous approaches.

Another possibility is that the fuelwood will simply substitute for kerosene imports. This was the conclusion of the World Bank mission which appraised the Second Wood Energy Project in Malawi (World Bank, February 26, 1986). In this case, the fuelwood was valued as an import substitute for kerosene. Table 12.1 reproduces the mission's calculations (see page 119). In the table, MK denotes kwacha, the Malawi currency.

Truly Nontradable Outputs

In using a foreign exchange numeraire, we would like to calculate the foreign exchange impacts by finding traded substitutes for all nontraded project outputs. This is generally possible in the sectors that produce primarily goods as opposed to services. For certain services, such as hair cuts, massages, janitorial services, garbage collection, and domestic water supply, it may be difficult to find traded substitutes. Domestic water supply provides a relevant case in point, since it will be a project output for public water supply projects.

If there are no truly nontradable outputs in the project cash flow, there is no need to worry about the exchange rate (or the SCF). The problem of the exchange rate can be dealt with by undertaking detailed tracing of foreign exchange impacts of all inputs and outputs.

If there are no truly nontradable outputs in the project cash flow, then there is no need to worry about the exchange rate or the SCF. The problem of the exchange rate can be dealt with by undertaking detailed tracing of the foreign exchange impacts of all inputs and outputs. In this case, the SCF would not be seen as an adjustment for the rate at which traded and nontraded goods exchange for each other, since all of the project inputs and outputs would be considered traded either directly or indirectly. The SCF, instead, would be seen as a rough substitute for a more specific CF.

Where truly nontradable goods are involved as outputs in the project cash flow, the SCF has a different meaning: it becomes the mechanism by which we compare the values of traded and non-traded goods. In this case, the SCF is in fact an adjustment to the exchange rate between traded and nontraded goods.

Demand-Price Conversion Factors for Inputs

Demand-price conversion factors for project inputs become relevant when dealing with a project input whose supply will not expand to meet the project demand. This would be the case in the following circumstances:

    a. a locally produced good which is not imported or exported (i.e., a nontraded good) and for which insufficient productive capacity will exist to meet the demand imposed by the project;

    b. an importable good for which an import quota is expected to be in force such that imports will not be allowed to increase to meet project demand; or

    c. a nonreproducible, nontraded input such as land or labor.

In each case, the project will get these inputs from other users of the good; and we measure the cost of the item in terms of the value of the production that is forgone by those other users of the input. If we work in a foreign exchange numeraire, then the value of the forgone output will be measured in foreign exchange terms. This is the same kind of calculation that was made in Chapter 11 in calculating the CF for unskilled labor in the complete border pricing approach.

The critical issue here lies in the presumption that supply will not expand—i.e., that the input will have to be taken away from other producers who would have been able to use the input, if the project were not undertaken. Usually the input will be "taken away" from them through some market process—i.e., by bidding it away through the market. Sometimes this bidding will cause the price of the input to go up noticeably; sometimes it will not. Usually, we will use this market price as the first lead in measuring the foreign exchange cost of diverting the input from the nonproject use to the project use.

When we say "market" price in the context of these nontraded inputs, we mean the price that exists in a "free" market—perhaps, a secondary market, in some cases—where the primary market may itself be distorted (e.g., the secondary market for the fertilizer that is imported by the government in limited quantities and sold to farmers at a subsidized price). That free market will often give us a clearer lead in tracing the foreign exchange impact than will the official price of many of these inputs. The reason is that, in using such demand-price conversion factors, we assume that supply cannot respond for some reason.

Demand-price conversion factors for project inputs become relevant when dealing with an input whose supply will not expand to meet the project demand.

Sometimes the lack of supply response will be due to policy distortions—e.g., the case of importable inputs which cannot be imported at the margin because of an import quota. Other times, the lack of supply response will be attributable to the fact that the input is "nonreproducible"—a term that is often applied to land and labor inputs (thus, leading some analysts to view land and labor as the only nontradable goods). And sometimes the government's justification for creating policy distortions will derive from a perceived lack of supply response. Intervention in the markets for many locally produced agricultural inputs, for example, is often justified on these grounds. Similarly, the markets for nonreproducible inputs of land and labor are subject to government's action to control prices. Whether the government's action is the cause or the result, the effect will be that in many of these cases, the official price may not provide us with a reliable lead to the economic cost of the input.

Calculating demand-price conversion factors for nontraded project inputs involves the following steps:

a. Determine the marginal value product (MVP) of the input in its alternative use without the project. The "market price" discussed on the preceding page is designed to help us determine the MVP. (Let us recall that enterprise-level demand for an input is represented by the MVP of that input in that particular enterprise; market demand for an input is derived by summing all of the enterprise-level demand functions for the input. Thus, the market demand will be the sum of the enterprise-level MVPs for the input.)

b. Determine the products that the input would have been used to produce in the absence of the project and the approximate marginal percentage weights of the forgone outputs represented in the MVP function.

c. Determine the financial prices and the economic prices (border prices) of the forgone outputs. From this information, develop conversion factors for the forgone outputs.

d. Use the information from **c** to develop a weighted-average conversion factor for the forgone outputs.

e. Multiply the weighted-average conversion factor from **d** by the MVP (which should be the same as the "market price" previously discussed) to determine the border priced opportunity cost of the nontraded project input. To get a conversion factor for the input, divide the project financial price into this border priced opportunity cost.

A simple approach to calculating demand-price conversion factors for a nontraded input is to use the market price to estimate the marginal value product of the input in its alternative use and then to multiply that price by SCF. We will get as a result the border priced opportunity cost of the input in the willingness to pay numeraire.

Gittinger (1982) provides a simpler approach to calculating demand-price conversion factors for inputs. In that approach, we use the market price as an estimate of the MVP in the alternative use and then multiply that price by the SCF to get the border priced economic cost of the input in the willingness to pay numeraire. If that approach is used in applying a foreign exchange numeraire, the practice is equivalent to assuming that the weighted-average conversion factor will work out to be the same as the SCF—which may be satisfactory in many cases, particularly those involving minor inputs (where "minor" is interpreted to mean those representing less than 10 percent of costs).

Demand-price conversion factors for nontraded project inputs are calculated in the foreign exchange numeraire by working through the border priced MVP of the input. As an example, let us look at a pesticide that is a minor on-farm input in a particular project. In this case, we shall assume that the pesticide amounts are so minor that the project itself will not provide the pesticide, but rather the farmers will be left to buy the product in the market. Though the input is minor, we shall need to estimate its economic costs so that we can convert the farm budgets from financial to economic terms. We shall further assume that the pesticide is imported under a quota which is set at 5,000 liters per year; the quota is expected to be fully utilized with or without the project; and it is not expected to be altered during the life of the project. These assumptions are critical to the analysis in that, in this case, these restrictions convert the input from being tradable to being nontraded and change the basis upon which we calculate the marginal economic cost of the input. (Note that the approach being followed in this example is "second best" shadow pricing.)

The pesticide in question is used in protecting both rice and wheat from in-field pests. Rice and wheat, then, will be the forgone outputs. We shall assume that rice is imported at the margin by the country, while wheat is exported at the margin; further, we shall assume that approximately one-fourth of the pesticide used in the country is used on rice, while three-fourths is used on wheat. These, then, are the "marginal percentage weights" discussed earlier. Our project, in contrast, will produce fruits and vegetables for the export market, but our project's output is of no immediate concern to us in the present example. (Note that the percentage weights used here assume that pesticides are not used on fruits and vegetables without the project.)

What we are trying to establish in this example is the calculation of the economic cost of the pesticide, using a foreign exchange numeraire. We cannot use the border price (CIF) of the pesticide, since the pesticide is not traded at the margin. At the same time, in this example, the CIF plus local costs will represent the "official price" mentioned earlier. Because the input is not traded at the margin, the CIF price will not represent the marginal foreign exchange cost; and the CIF-related offical price may not represent

Table 12.2. Calculation of Economic Cost of Pesticide in Presence of an Import Quota: Demand-Price Conversion Factor

MPP of pesticide (on rice)	5 quintal/liter
MPP of pesticide (on wheat)	10 quintal/liter
Domestic price of rice	40 Rs/quintal
Domestic price of wheat	20 Rs/quintal
MVP of pesticide (on rice)	200 Rs/liter
MVP of pesticide (on wheat)	200 Rs/liter
Border price of rice	30 Rs/quintal
Border price of wheat	20 Rs/quintal
CF for rice	0.75
CF for wheat	1.00
CIF price of pesticide	120 Rs/liter
Market price of pesticide	200 Rs/liter

Economic cost of pesticide (in Rs/liter):

EC = (.25 x MVPrice x CFrice) + (.75 x MVPwheat x CFwheat)

EC = (.25 x 5 x Rs 40 x .75) + (.75 x 10 x Rs 20 x 1.00)

EC = 187.5 Rs/liter

CF of pesticide = 0.9375 [a]

1.5625 [b]

---

a. Based on market price of pesticide.

b. Based on CIF price of pesticide.

---

the marginal demand price—depending upon how much of a shortage of the pesticide the quota is expected to cause during the life of the project. (Let us assume that the project is "marginal" in size, so that the pesticide price with and without the project will be basically the same—which will greatly simplify the analysis.)

Thus, we must use some other route to find the indirect foreign exchange impact of having the farmers in the project take the pesticide away from other users. To do so, we need to know the reduction in the output of traded goods (or of nontraded goods which substitute for traded goods in the market) that will result on farms outside of the project.

The foreign exchange costs of the pesticide in question will depend upon three factors. These factors are:

> **a.** the MVP of a liter of pesticide in wheat production and in rice production;
>
> **b.** the border prices of wheat and rice; and
>
> **c.** the marginal percentage shares of wheat and rice in the use of the pesticide.

For purposes of the present example, let us use the additional data from Table 12.2.

Note from the table that the MVP of pesticides is the same on both rice and on wheat. This is as one would normally expect, since microeconomic theory suggests that producers will tend to move an input from one crop to another when the MVP of the input is higher when applied to the receiving crop than when applied to the other crop. But note also that the MVP is measured in financial prices, since these are the prices that producers will be directly affected by. If there were no distortions (neither domestic nor border) affecting the prices of the forgone outputs, then we could simply use the MVP as the economic cost of the input. And if there were no distortions affecting the price of the input, then we could simply use its financial price as the measure of the input's MVP. But this was not the case in the example in Table 12.2. Thus, there were three levels of price distortions that were traced through in determining the economic cost of pesticide:

> **a.** distortions in the price of the pesticide input caused by the import quota;
>
> **b.** domestic price distortions in the prices of the input and of the two outputs; and
>
> **c.** border distortions affecting the input and the two outputs.

Conversion Factors in the Willingness to Pay Numeraire

No matter what numeraire we choose to use, the definition of a conversion factor remains the same: the ratio of the economic value divided by the financial value. The difference lies in the procedures used in determining the economic value that goes in the numerator of the CF ratio.

We have discussed previously the differences between a foreign exchange numeraire and a willingness to pay numeraire, and we have looked at these differences in terms of complete border pricing and partial border pricing. Let us briefly review this point.

No matter what numeraire is chosen, the definition of a conversion factor (CF) remains the same. The difference between foreign exchange and willingness to pay numeraires lies in the procedures used in determining the economic value that goes in the numerator of the CF ratio.

The major differences between the foreign exchange numeraire and the willingness to pay numeraire, in practice, can be related to the following economic values:

     a. the value of foreign exchange;

     b. the value of nontraded inputs; and

     c. the value of nontraded outputs.

In our discussion of the foreign exchange numeraire, we made the point that it did not matter what exchange rate was used, since—in most agricultural projects—all impacts normally could be measured in units of foreign currency. Thus, in that numeraire, the exchange rate issue boiled down to a question of what price level we wished to use in presenting the results:

     a. the border price level (implied by using CFs calculated from foreign exchange values converted using the OER);

     b. the domestic price level (implied by using CFs calculated from foreign exchange values converted using the SER); or

     c. some other price level (implied by using CFs calculated from foreign exchange values converted using some other exchange rate than the OER or SER).

The Exchange Rate in the Willingness to Pay Numeraire

In the willingness to pay numeraire (or in any numeraire in the case of projects producing truly nontradable outputs), the exchange rate does matter. In the standard application, traded goods are valued in the willingness to pay numeraire by applying a willingness to pay value of foreign exchange to the CIF and FOB prices of the traded goods.

There are two possible options for measuring the value of traded goods in willingness to pay terms. The first option is to use the domestic demand prices for the traded goods. These prices will be affected by both the border and domestic distortions that apply to these goods. The second option is to convert the CIF and FOB prices for the traded goods to local currency at some exchange rate which reflects the willingness to pay for the foreign exchange that is gained or lost by the transaction involving traded goods. Starting with the CIF and FOB prices will remove the domestic distortion element from the traded goods values and will leave the border distortion to be dealt with by the exchange rate that is chosen.

In the standard application, traded goods are valued in the willingness to pay numeraire by applying a willingness to pay value of foreign exchange to the CIF and FOB prices of the goods.

Uusually, the second option is chosen, leaving the exchange rate as the major issue to be addressed in valuing the traded goods in the willingness to pay numeraire [see Tower and Pursell (1986)]. The exchange rate issue may then be viewed in any number of ways. It may be viewed as a "commodity" whose willingness to pay value is determined in the market for foreign exchange; or it may be viewed as a medium of exchange whose value is reflected in the willingness to pay values of all of the goods and services which the foreign exchange can be used to buy.

The latter approach is usually taken, and—in principle—the willingness to pay value for foreign exchange is measured by the weighted-average domestic values of the incremental bundle of goods and services that will be made available as a result of earning, or saving an incremental unit of foreign exchange. In practice, the weighted-average value is usually based on the basket of traded goods over the previous five years; and the domestic value of those goods is approximated by the border values plus tariff distortions implied by the tariff revenue collections and subsidy payouts. Generally, we end up with some form of weighted-average tariff calculation on existing trade as the measure of the incremental value of foreign exchange earned, saved, or spent.

Once the shadow exchange rate that is to be used is determined, we must decide whether we wish to express it so as to adjust for the border distortions by reducing domestic willingness to pay values to the border price level or by increasing border values to the domestic price level. The authors of the UNIDO Guidelines (1972) chose to denominate the values at the domestic price level. Gittinger (1982) presents both methods, with the presumption that—in keeping with current World Bank practice—values will normally be denominated at the border price level. Again, let us recall the basic issue regarding which of the following two formulations should be used in expressing the SER:

If we assume that:

> OER = Rs 10/\$1,
>
> WATR = 0.25 percent, and PREM = 1.25

> Then:
>
> Formulation A: SER = Rs 12.5/\$1
>
> Formulation B: SER = Rs 10/\$0.80

Obviously, this is nothing more than a restatement of the SCF versus the SER approach. If Formulation A is chosen, then the CIF and FOB values will be converted at the exchange rate of Rs 12.5 to the dollar, and the domestic prices of nontraded goods will be adjusted for domestic distortions. If Formulation B is used, then the CIF and FOB values will be converted at the exchange rate of Rs 10 to the dollar, and the domestic prices of the nontraded goods will be adjusted for both domestic and border distortions.

The complete versus partial border pricing issue then arises over whether to adjust for the border distortion by using an aggregated CF, such as the SCF, on the domestic-distortion adjusted nontraded goods, or whether to trace them to specific traded goods and apply CFs specific to those particular goods. Many experienced practitioners believe that in most cases the added precision presumably gained in the complete border pricing approach is unwarranted by the basic data that one is working with.

Nontraded Goods in the Willingness to Pay Numeraire

Nontraded goods are treated the same way in the willingness to pay and in the foreign exchange numeraires. The real issue is whether we use a complete border pricing or a partial border pricing approach. In the complete border pricing method, we assume that all markets are related directly and indirectly, such that full tracing can be practiced. The partial border pricing approach truncates that tracing process for some (or all) nontraded goods and simply uses the SCF or the SER to adjust for border distortions, after adjusting the nontraded goods for domestic distortions.

The discussion in Gittinger (1982) essentially recommends the partial border pricing approach. This arises from the fact that the book was written primarily for agricultural practitioners; and the partial border pricing approach is much simpler to apply.

13. Choosing Numeraires and Decision Criteria: Practicality and Sensitivity

Summary. *In a real world characterized by uncertainty and information scarcity, some approaches to making decisions on projects will exhibit sensitivity to certain key parameters. The problems lie in the mathematics of ratio-based measures and of mathematically underidentified and overidentified systems of equations. Problems exist with the foreign exchange numeraire when the number of traded goods is very small; and the foreign exchange values of nontraded goods will exhibit exaggerated sensitivity to changes in the number or prices of traded goods.*

Likewise, internal rates of return for projects involving little capital investment (such as many agricultural projects) will exhibit exaggerated sensitivity to changes in the quantities or values of variable inputs, or in the value of outputs. The choice of numeraire and of decision criteria should take into account the convenience factors discussed in Chapter 6, the policy factors discussed in Chapter 8, and the sensitivity factors discussed in Chapter 13.

Most of the books and articles that deal with the theory of economic cost-benefit analysis use mathematical proofs to demonstrate the many complex interrelationships that exist between different numeraires and among different decision criteria. These are generally helpful to the economist as a device for understanding techniques of cost-benefit analysis. However, there are other considerations which must be added before a practising economist uses these mathematical treatments as justifications for choosing a technique of analysis. These considerations include the sensitivity of the analysis to the choice of numeraire and decision criteria; and the degree of indirection and tedium involved in using these.

One simple rule of thumb should be followed in choosing a numeraire and a decision criterion. Whenever possible, we should base the analysis on the most important element in the project. Or, in the broader investment planning context, the analysis of projects should be based upon the most important element in the country's investment planning. To illustrate this point, let us look at the familiar capital-based decision criteria that emerged from the capital budgeting literature and from private sector investment planning practices.

The capital-based decision criterion arises from the presumption that capital is scarce relative to other factors of production; thus, it

One simple rule of thumb should be followed in choosing a numeraire and a decision criterion. Whenever possible, we should base the analysis on the most important element in the project.

must be budgeted carefully. Capital budgeting techniques—such as those in Chapters 9 and 10 of Gittinger (1982)—are designed to help us choose projects that use scarce capital most effectively. For capital budgeting techniques to be the best way to choose among projects, three conditions must be present:

First, among the factors of production (land, labor, capital, and entrepreneurship—and let us add foreign exchange to this list), capital must be the sufficiently scarce factor to be the focus of the analysis. If capital is not scarce, then some other factor should be used as the basis of the decision criterion: water in arid regions; or skilled labor or managerial capacity in some countries; or foreign exchange.

Second, explicit pricing of the other factors of production must be feasible, since the factor that is used in the decision criterion will often be implicitly priced (e.g., in the internal rate of return criterion).

Third, the factor upon which the analysis is based must be an important item in the project cash flows. For example, if the internal rate of return (IRR) on capital is used as the decision criterion, or if the net benefit-investment ratio is used, then all projects that are being appraised must involve substantial use of capital. Otherwise, the IRR will be extremely sensitive. Small changes in items of cost or benefit will make the IRR jump from, say, 10 percent up to 80 percent or, say, from 30 percent down to -20 percent.

The third condition—of capital being an important element in cash flows—is an important consideration in agricultural projects, since these projects often involve very little capital investment. This is particularly true of IRR calculations at the enterprise level. Financial rates of return in agricultural projects are often extremely high simply because there is little capital involved in the cash flows at that level of the project. These high IRRs will also be very sensitive to changes in output or input prices—i.e., to anything that affects, what accountants would call, the "contribution margin."

For capital budgeting techniques to be used properly, capital must be an important element in cash flows. Financial rates of return in agricultural projects are often extremely high simply because little capital is involved in the cash flows. Thus, we should be wary of financial statements that use capital as the decision criterion for agricultural projects.

What the rule of thumb tells us is that we must be wary of numeraire, or decision criterion, based on items that are relatively insignificant. Mathematical models that show interrelationships between these insignificant factors and other factors in the analysis will not demonstrate the sensitivity that will exist when the factor used in the decision criterion or in the numeraire is insignificant relative to other factors. Thus, we should be wary of capital-based criterion in many agricultural projects and in all enterprise-level calculations. And we should be wary of the foreign exchange numeraire in countries in which traded goods and services are not prominent in the total basket of goods and services used and produced by the projects that are being appraised.

Foreign Exchange Numeraire When Trade is Limited

The critical assumption in comparing these two versions of the economic efficiency numeraire is the assumption that there are few truly nontradable goods and services. In other words, the increased availability of local goods usually decreases the need for traded goods, and conversely the decrease in the availability of local goods usually increases the need for traded goods. The interaction among markets in the country (and the existence of sufficient trade so that we can generally find some relatively close traded substitute for all nontraded goods) is critical to the use of the foreign exchange numeraire.

But what if the country has little involvement in international trade? With few traded goods in the economy, we may find that only a handful of the nontraded goods have close substitutes among the few traded goods that are available; and the direct production costs of most nontraded goods that are used as inputs will be composed mostly of other nontraded goods, as will the inputs of the inputs. Under these circumstances, can we still say that the impacts on nontraded goods will translate into impacts on traded goods, and thus on foreign exchange? The answer still is "yes;" but now it is a qualified yes. Economic modelers have shown that—in general equilibrium models in which all markets are related to each other—impacts on nontraded goods can be traced to impacts on traded goods.

But all of these statements regarding the derivation of border prices relate to "deterministic" mathematical models; and they relate to models in which all markets are assumed to be related to each other on the demand side, or on the supply side, or both. Such declarations ignore the increasing sensitivity of border price estimates as the number of traded goods in the economy (and in the model) decreases; and they ignore the tediously indirect route that we must take in converting all prices to border prices in such cases.

It can be demonstrated mathematically that the shadow prices for nontraded goods can be translated into border price equivalents—so long as the country has one or more traded goods. But the sensitivity of those shadow price estimates will begin to overwhelm

An increase in the availability of local goods usually decreases the need for traded goods. Conversely, a decrease in the availability of local goods usually increases the need for traded goods. The interaction among markets is critical to the use of the foreign exchange numeraire.

this mathematical truth, once we get to a relatively small number, or to a relatively small range of truly traded goods in that economy. As a result, the foreign exchange numeraire becomes an increasingly undesirable numeraire as the importance of traded goods in the economy decreases, because the shadow prices (i.e., the border prices) that are estimated become increasingly unstable. [Under the assumption of constant returns to scale, no joint products, and perfect competition, shadow pricing in terms of a set of traded goods depends upon the number of traded goods relative to the number of factors of production. For a discussion, see Tower and Pursell (1986), Chapter III.]

To illustrate the sensitivity mentioned earlier, let us imagine an economy comprising one thousand goods and services, all of which are traded goods (ignoring, for the moment, the real problem posed by land and labor). In this case, the foreign exchange numeraire is a simple and appropriate numeraire: it is relatively easy to use; and the results of the calculations will not exhibit the sensitivity that will characterize that numeraire when there are few traded goods. Let us recall that the process of border pricing a traded good is straightforward. Remove taxes and subsidies, leaving the CIF or FOB values (or calculate the import and export parity prices, if we take into account market-associated costs). We can see that in this case, there is little room to make calculating errors, which reduces the scope for sensitivity to be a problem for the analysis.

Now let us imagine that the same economy still has one thousand goods and services, half of which are traded goods and the other half are nontraded goods. For the traded goods, the border pricing process is still straightforward. However, for the nontraded goods, the process will be more indirect, more round-about. We will have to border price these goods (i.e., find their foreign exchange impacts) by:

    a. breaking them down into their direct and indirect inputs, if they are project inputs whose supply will increase with the project;

    b. finding their MVP and the border prices of their forgone outputs, if they are inputs whose supply will not increase; or

    c. finding the border prices of their likely substitutes, if they are project outputs.

The sensitivity arises in the tracing process and in the chain of calculations that we must go through when border prices and financial prices are not closely related to each other. When a good is traded, the two prices will be closely related and easy to discern, because the basic thing separating them will be the border distortions; and the border distortions are largely taken care of by deleting the tariffs and subsidies when we deal with traded goods. With nontraded goods, in contrast, the process of converting the financial prices into border prices may be fairly direct and straightforward, very indirect and circuitous, or something in between—depending upon the prominence of traded goods in the economy.

In an economy having an equally large number of traded and nontraded goods, increasing the production of one nontraded good will lead to a reduction in the importation of one or more traded goods which are partial or close substitutes for that nontraded good. For example, if a project produces a local variety of rice which is nontraded, the increased production of rice would lead to a decrease in imports of a completely different variety of rice from the United States, Thailand, or from some other major rice producer.

Where there exists a large and diverse group of traded goods in the economy, we will—more often than not—be able to find a traded good which is a close substitute for nontraded outputs, and the border pricing will be fairly straightforward. Or, when we trace down the direct and indirect inputs used in producing a project input when we calculate a supply-price conversion factor, we will encounter largely traded indirect inputs in the first round or two of tracing; and even that inherently circuitous process will lead fairly directly to traded goods whose border prices we may use in calculating the foreign exchange impact of using nontraded inputs in the project.

And when we must calculate demand-price conversion factors for nontraded project inputs, we will usually find that they would have been used to produce traded outputs without the project; and, thus, the border pricing process will take only a step or two to get us to an indirect impact on some traded good. The process of getting to an impact on traded goods is short and relatively easy, so long as traded goods are numerous and prominent in the economy.

Now imagine an economy comprising one thousand goods and services, nine hundred of which are nontraded and one hundred of which are traded goods. As we decrease the number of traded goods, a close substitute for rice among the traded goods may not exist. In this case, the border pricing of any of the nine hundred nontraded goods must be derived from the border prices of the one hundred traded goods. The increased rice production might even be traced to a reduction in wheat imports, in which case the CIF price

When a large and diverse group of traded goods exists in the economy, we will be able to find a traded good that is a close substitute for nontraded outputs. The shadow pricing thus will be fairly straightforward.

of the wheat imports forgone would become the border price of the local variety of rice.

The sensitivity of the results increases, because now we must go through (in theory) a cross-price elasticity calculation to link the border price of the wheat to an equivalent value for the new rice production, stated in border price terms. Here is where we start to see analysts using "quality adjustments" to account for the fact that rice and wheat are not the same thing. The chain of calculations that is used to establish "equivalence" between rice and wheat (or among fuelwood, cow dung, fertilizer, and rice production, in the case of the fuelwood valuation problem) represents an important juncture at which the sensitivity issue is able to creep in.

As the number of traded goods decreases, the tracing process becomes increasingly indirect. Let us decrease the number of traded goods in the economy a bit further—to, say, fifty traded goods. Now an increase in rice production might be traced indirectly to a reduction in imports of tins of beans and tins of orange juice, if we find that neither rice nor wheat are among the fifty remaining traded goods. These are not very close substitutes, and our equivalence calculations will be loaded with places where we can miscalculate the way that the market will link together the values of rice and orange juice.

Let us take our example to its logical extreme and imagine that the government has imposed trade restrictions to the point that the economy has only two traded goods left—exported tins of pineapple and imported petroleum products. By this stage, we have eliminated even tinned beans and orange juice from our list of traded goods. After these adjustments, there are nine hundred and ninety-eight nontraded goods, including the local variety of rice that was previously discussed.

Now if we use a foreign exchange numeraire in valuing the local rice production from an agricultural project, the foreign exchange impacts can occur through only two products:

> **a.** increased exports of tinned pineapples; or

> **b.** reductions in imports of petroleum products.

By the same token, all other projects in the country's investment portfolio would create foreign exchange earnings or savings through impacts on those same two products; and all project costs would be measured in terms of foreign exchange impacts on those two products.

When we trace the direct and indirect inputs used in producing a nontraded project input, we must trace back round after round until all costs can be categorized as direct and indirect inputs, labor, land, and traded goods. Now that we have only two traded goods left, tracing back to the final three "primary factors" of land, labor and traded goods will require not just one or even two rounds of tracing; rather, it may require numerous rounds, because the amount of petroleum that will be used as a direct input in making, say, a hand-held sprayer will be extremely limited; and there will not likely be any tinned pineapples used as direct inputs in that production process.

By the second round of tracing, we will find additional petroleum used in making the inputs for the inputs; and by the third round, we will find the sum of the petroleum used indirectly will increase. We can see that it will take a lot of rounds before everything can be traced to petroleum and tinned pineapples! The larger the number of rounds, the more scope there is for introducing miscalculation into the tracing process. The more important any one traded good is in getting to the numeraire, the more sensitive the results will be.

The process of tracing the impact of nontraded goods on foreign exchange may become very difficult or even dubious in the "thoroughly distorted" economies discussed previously. And in countries in which international trade is severely limited, the general equilibrium process through which nontraded goods and foreign exchange are supposed to be related might occur very indirectly in the case of many nontraded goods. Or, it might not occur at all.

As we have said in the previous sections, it will not only be difficult to derive and to apply conversion factors in these two types of countries, it will also be difficult to teach noneconomists what the process of project economic analysis is all about. For a variety of political and bureaucratic reasons, experience has shown that it also will be difficult to motivate them to apply economic analysis to project planning. The Gittinger (1982) book was designed for use in teaching the fundamentals of project economic analysis to project practitioners—assumed to be primarily noneconomists. The book was intended to deal with appraisal issues that tend to be critical in approximately 80 percent of the agricultural projects that are appraised. The author recognized that the text would not provide sufficient guidance by itself for the analysis of all types of projects (e.g., projects involving tied financing, those involving traded outputs by major producers of that product, or those projects which are so large that they affect shadow prices).

The Gittinger book also recognized that in some countries the set of price distortions might be so great that noneconomists would have difficulty in applying project economic analysis. Fortunately, a sustantial number of developing countries do not fall into the category of thoroughly distorted. However, the country in which you live may be one of those which does fall into this category. If it does, and you are a teacher of project economics, you may wish to seek outside assistance in identifying or in preparing specialized materials to assist in teaching project economic analysis. Such programs of assistance have been undertaken in the past by the regional development banks (such as the Inter-American Development Bank, the Asian Development Bank, and the African Development Bank), the World Bank, the United Nations Development Programme, and various bilateral donors.

Capital-Based Criterion in Agricultural Projects

The sensitivity issue concerning the foreign exchange numeraire applies equally well to the use of internal rate of return as a decision criterion in projects that have a low ratio of capital cost to variable cost. Though a number of agricultural projects can be categorized as capital intensive, a large proportion are variable-cost intensive. Projects involving improved farming practices or input packages, for example, tend to have low capital investment elements and large "running costs."

The problem with projects that do not use much capital is that capital budgeting techniques of analysis can be misleading. Of particular concern is the tendency for such projects to have high IRRs, both in financial and in economic terms. The financial IRRs (after financing) are often high because project planners provide very high leverage to participating farmers so that their with-project farm cash flow will never be much worse than their without-project farm cash flow. This is particularly true in projects affecting small farmers. It is common practice to finance most, or all, on-farm investments so that—after financing is taken into account—the farmers have made little or no investment of their own. As a result, all or most of the "capital" is financed by loans, and the return on farmers' equity approaches infinity. A financial IRR criterion does not have much meaning in these cases.

The problem with the sensitivity of internal rates of return arises anytime there exists a high ratio of variable cost to capital cost—say, when the ratio is above 0.4.

The problem with the sensitivity of IRRs arises anytime there exists a high ratio of variable/capital cost (calculated by taking one year of variable costs at full development divided by total capital costs, where "capital" is defined in the mathematical sense of all annual net cash flows that are negative). The term "high" ratio is somewhat relative, but in general we can expect sensitivity in the IRR to begin to emerge when the ratio is above 0.4 or so. The issue can be

Table 13.1. Sensitivity of Internal Rates of Return: The Base Case

	Project A			Project B		
Year	Costs	Benefits	Net cash flow	Costs	Benefits	Net cash flow
1	1000	0	-1000	100	0	-100
2	100	250	150	100	115	15
3	100	250	150	100	115	15
4	100	250	150	100	115	15
5	100	250	150	100	115	15
6	100	250	150	100	115	15
7	100	250	150	100	115	15
8	100	250	150	100	115	15
9	100	250	150	100	115	15
10	100	250	150	100	115	15
11	100	250	150	100	115	15
12	100	250	150	100	115	15
	IRR:	9.44%		IRR:	9.44%	

Table 13.2. Sensitivity of Internal Rates of Return: With 10-Percent Increase in Operating Costs

	Project A			Project B		
Year	Costs	Benefits	Net cash flow	Costs	Benefits	Net cash flow
1	1000	0	-1000	100	0	-100
2	110	250	140	110	115	5
3	110	250	140	110	115	5
4	110	250	140	110	115	5
5	110	250	140	110	115	5
6	110	250	140	110	115	5
7	110	250	140	110	115	5
8	110	250	140	110	115	5
9	110	250	140	110	115	5
10	110	250	140	110	115	5
11	110	250	140	110	115	5
12	110	250	140	110	115	5
	IRR:	7.99%		IRR:	-8.84%	

illustrated by the two project cash flows shown in Tables 13.1 and 13.2. In the base case, each project has the same IRR.

The IRR of Project B is more sensitive to changes in the price of either the variable inputs, or of the project output. We can see that a minor overstatement of output prices or yields will cause the IRR of Project B to increase to ridiculous levels. For example, an increase of 5 percent in the yield expectations of Project B (compared with the base case in Table 13.1) will cause the calculated IRR to jump from 9.44 percent to 17.09 percent, and a yield increase of 10 percent over the base case will cause the IRR to jump further to 24.02 percent. If operating costs go down by 10 percent from the base case, the IRR will increase more than twofold, to 22.26 percent. You may wish to verify for yourself that these particular changes would not have such a profound effect on the IRR of Project A, because Project A is more capital intensive.

Many agricultural projects will have cost structures similar to that of Project B; and they will often show very high IRRs as a result. Those IRRs will also be much more sensitive to the very factors that are uncertain in agricultural projects:

> **a.** crop yields,
>
> **b.** output prices; and
>
> **c.** input units and prices.

This combination of sensitivity and uncertainty leads many experienced analysts to argue in favor of a more thorough technical analysis rather than more fine-tuning of shadow prices.

PART III

The Strategic Planning Approach to Multi-Objective Project Appraisal

14. From Multi-Objective Planning to Cost-Benefit Analysis

Summary. *When governments and societies prepare their plans, they want to achieve more objectives than the simple one of economic efficiency. In addition, the dynamic efficiency objective may not be met under some circumstances, including those in which failure in the financial market leads to suboptimal saving and investment. Distributional efficiency is not addressed in the standard efficiency objective—except in the restrictive case in which the beginning distribution is judged acceptable.*

The OECD, UNIDO, and Squire-van der Tak social analysis methods address these issues by proposing a multi-objective framework for defining numeraires and for calculating conversion factors. The social analysis methods proposed by these authors appraise projects in terms of four primary objectives: efficiency, distribution, optimal growth, and government income. This goal-oriented approach to project appraisal makes project appraisal, in principle, consistent with the methodology of strategic planning.

Single versus Multiple Objectives in Planning

In Parts I and II, we discussed different versions of economic analysis of projects. We talked about projects in terms of their traditional objectives of static and dynamic efficiency and identified several different methods of defining the economic efficiency numeraires. We also pointed out that there are other methods of cost-benefit analysis. The more prominent among the "multi-objective" methods is the so-called social cost-benefit analysis methods popularized by the Organisation for Economic Co-operation and Development Manual (1969) and United Nations Industrial Development Organization Guidelines (1972) and incorporated into the three-level version—financial analysis, economic analysis, and social analysis—of project appraisal by Squire and van der Tak (1976).

Social analysis methods appraise projects in terms of four objectives: efficiency, distribution, optimal growth, and government income. This goal-oriented approach makes cost-benefit analysis similar to strategic planning.

The analytical methods developed in the OECD and UNIDO books had integrated economic analysis, social analysis, and goverment fiscal analysis into one equation, or "objective function." In addition, they formalized and systematized the discussion of the relationships between the measure of benefits and costs and the discount rate. This represented a major change in the way project appraisal generally had been carried out prior to the publication of these two books. The authors called this method of analysis "social analysis," rather than economic analysis. [We should note that some economists had for years before been using the term "social analysis" to refer to the method now called economic analysis. Because the OECD and UNIDO form of multi-objective analysis has preempted the use of the term "social analysis," traditional methods of project appraisal which focus on only one objective—that of economic efficiency—now tend to be referred to simply as economic analysis.]

But the OECD Manual and UNIDO Guidelines did more than introduce multiple objectives into planning. The importance to planners and to political leaders of setting objectives other than economic efficiency had long been recognized [see Ward (1980), for a review of this history]. What the OECD and UNIDO authors did was to formalize the theoretical link between strategic planning and cost-benefit analysis.

Advisors to governments had long been recommending the use of both national economic planning and cost-benefit analysis for setting multiple objectives. However, prior to the 1960s, few attempts had been made to formally link the two. The OECD Manual accomplished two objectives for economists:

a. it provided a theoretical and methodological link between strategic planning and cost-benefit analysis; and

b. it provided a consistent method of deriving shadow prices that were clearly linked to a nation's actual planning objectives.

While the OECD Manual and UNIDO Guidelines helped to formalize the strategic planning approach to cost-benefit analysis, and thus to crystallize these relationships more clearly in the eyes of theoreticians, in many respects this process tended to further cloud the understanding of many practitioners. Though these approaches made more consistent the process of deriving shadow prices, they also made the process seem more complicated. This perceived complication derived from two sources:

a. the inclusion of multiple objectives in the numeraire, which meant that the analyst had to find some way of valuing impacts on each objective vis-à-vis-the other objectives; and

b. the use of specifically defined numeraires, which meant that the impacts had to be traced to particular categories of citizens and to particular uses of the incomes that were generated by the project.

(The issue of multiple objectives is discussed in this part, while the issue of specifically defined numeraires was discussed in Part II.)

If we could strip the UNIDO and OECD methods back to a single objective—let us say, achieving economic efficiency—we would find each of these methods to be fairly precise in the way that they propose to derive their shadow prices (or "accounting prices," to use

The OECD and UNIDO books helped formalize cost benefit analysis and link it better to strategic planning and national economic management.

their preferred terminology). This is, in essence, what Squire and van der Tak (1976) did when they separated the analysis into three separate steps:

The first step involved conducting the project financial appraisal using existing market prices—prices that the project implementers actually have to pay, including taxes, subsidies, and any other distortions that may affect those prices. This is always a good first step in analyzing any investment, for—regardless of the effect that a project may have on the economy as a whole—there is always the problem of the project implementer's ability to finance the actual flows of funds that are involved.

The second step involved carrying out an economic analysis by converting the financial appraisal prices into economic efficiency prices—without taking into consideration the government income or income distribution objectives that had been formalized in the OECD and UNIDO analyses. The economic analysis methods that are discussed in Gittinger (1982) follow this second part of Squire and van der Tak. [Gittinger's farm modeling discussion follows Squire and van der Tak's first step, the financial analysis.]

The third step of Squire and van der Tak, which is only briefly discussed in Gittinger (1982), involved the use of income weights to accommodate the income distribution objective. Government income was given a weight of unity (1) to accommodate the government income objective, and different values were placed on income that was consumed compared to the income that was saved, in order to accommodate the optimal growth objective. In the OECD and UNIDO methods, the analysis tended to go straight to a full social analysis, without presenting a separate economic analysis.

Squire and van der Tak's method of project analysis involves three steps:

1. use of financial prices;

2. conversion of financial prices into economic prices; and

3. attachment of income weights.

Gittinger (1982) followed the Squire-van der Tak lead by dealing with economic analysis and social analysis separately and focused on the details of applying economic prices to agricultural projects. Gittinger paid limited attention to the issue of "social pricing." At the time Gittinger (1982) was being prepared, the experience in the World Bank was largely limited to financial and economic analyses. However, experiments in using project social analysis had been carried out in the Bank, and decisions had been made to continue with limited application [see Anand (1975); Bruce (1976); Bruce and Kimaro (1978); Squire, Little, and Durdag (1979); Cleaver (1980); Mashayekhi (1980); and Ahmed (1984)]. Social analysis had not become a prominent part of project appraisal in the Bank in spite of the urging by many economists. With the onset of the financial crisis in many developing countries in the early 1980s, the Bank and many of its member countries were forced to pay more attention to economic issues—in particular, policy issues related to national economic management. This was the killing blow from a slow death had begun years earlier for social analysis in the World Bank (see pages 152-154). Social analysis of projects moved further back in the list of topics demanding the attention of the World Bank's staff.

Cost-Benefit Analysis as Strategic Planning

In the pure theory of cost-benefit analysis, we begin by first discussing objectives and numeraires. We cannot derive a shadow price until we know the numeraire that is being used. And ultimately, we cannot interpret the meaning of the project appraisal calculations without understanding the strategic planning objectives for which the numeraire was derived.

The following five points may be useful in understanding the relationships between the techniques and approaches of strategic planning and those of cost-benefit analysis:

a. Projects represent instruments which are available to planners to meet national planning objectives. In principle, the process of project planning and appraisal should aim to meet a society's objectives, as spelled out in the national development plans.

b. The unit of account, or numeraire, in which costs and benefits are measured, is intended to serve as a measure of accomplishment of the nation's planning objectives. The numeraire can be set up in terms of foreign exchange, government income, willingness to pay for consumption, units of investment, and so forth—so long as we are able to convert all of the project's impacts on the plan's objectives into units of the numeraire.

c. Shadow prices for inputs and outputs measure the progress made toward, or away from, achieving the national planning objectives. Benefits represent a movement toward achieving the objective; costs represent a movement away from achieving the objective. These measures of progress—costs and benefits—are denominated in units of the numeraire.

d. The worthiness of different alternatives—as measured by costs and benefits expressed in the numeraire—is compared by selecting the best set of alternatives to help meet the national planning objectives.

e. A "cost" associated with one alternative will be derived from a foregone "benefit" from some other alternative—(an alternative that must be clearly defined as the "without project" alternative, often erroneously assumed to be a "do nothing," or a "no change in the present state" alternative).

We cannot value project benefits and costs until we define our objectives and the numeraire that we are going to use.

This is the so-called opportunity cost approach to deriving shadow prices.

We will continue the discussion of the relationship between strategic planning and cost-benefit analysis in the chapters that follow, and shall end by pointing out the pitfalls of the strategic planning approach as it applies to the appraisal of projects, in practice.

15. The Strategic Planning Approach to Cost-Benefit Analysis

Summary. *Strategic planning involves three elements: a clear definition of goals and objectives, a determination of resources available to accomplish the objectives, and an identification of alternatives for using available resources to meet the stated objectives. Cost-benefit analysis adds a quantitative, optimizing model to the process of evaluating the project alternatives in light of the stated objectives.*

In the multi-objective form of "social analysis," project appraisal includes more of the objectives actually included in planning. The model requires that a numeraire be developed which is consistent with these objectives. It also requires that units of impact on each objective be convertible into equivalent values in terms of other objectives, which implies the presence of a weighting system between objectives and the numeraire. The latter represents a common denominator among the objectives.

As discussed in Chapter 14, cost-benefit analysis has come to be viewed as a form of strategic planning model. All forms of strategic planning have certain elements in common. This is true of national development planning as well as of organizational planning. (The latter is often referred to as "corporate planning." Note that, at least in the abstract, the methods of corporate planning and of national development planning are the same.)

The common elements in strategic planning are:

    a. planning in terms of clearly conceived goals and objectives;

    b. identifying for analysis those sets of alternative interventions (policies and projects) that are intended to have an impact on the strategic planning objectives; and

    c. judging each alternative in terms of its relative impacts on the planning objectives.

Cost-benefit analysis may be thought of as the "highest form" of strategic planning model. It can be described in this way, because it puts the strategic planning process into a format that clarifies the decision criteria and makes the decision process less arbitrary and less ambiguous—objectives which are implicit in all applications of "the scientific method," as defined by scientists from Europe and North America. The technique appears to meet these objectives because it is a quantitative form of a planning model, and because it is directed toward optimizing in terms of the

Strategic Planning.
Involves three elements:
1. definition of goals and objectives;
2. determination of available resources; and
3. identification of alternatives for using available resources to meet stated objectives.

planning objectives that, presumably, have been selected by policymakers and clarified by senior managers. In principle, cost-benefit analysis represents a mathematical statement of the strategic planning approach to decision making.

Objectives and Numeraires

Like other forms of strategic planning model, cost-benefit analysis requires that planners identify alternatives for meeting the planning objectives. As a first step in the planning process, senior management issues a preliminary statement of goals and objectives. As a second step, technical professionals identify the alternatives for meeting those objectives. In principle (as well as in practice), a determination of the resources available and of the technical alternatives for using those resources must be made and presented to senior management.

If the resources and alternatives that exist are insufficient to accomplish the stated objectives, then senior management and technical staff engage in a "plan rationalization" process in which objectives and alternatives are revised until a "consistent planning set" is achieved. This planning set then becomes the basis for a written plan that usually is produced when the planning is similar to national development planning.

In the cost-benefit version of the model, planners attempt to analyze all the alternatives that have been proposed and to select the sets of alternatives that have the highest value in terms of the "numeraire" that has been established in the objective function of the model. In development planning, these alternatives fall broadly into two groups:

a. policy alternatives (e.g., monetary policy, fiscal policy, trade and commercial policies, and sectoral policies, such as input and output pricing policies); and

b. investment alternatives (i.e., projects).

In cost-benefit analysis, planners identify the various alternatives that are available for meeting planning objectives. These alternatives are then ranked and selected on the basis of the highest value yielded in terms of the numeraire.

Cost-benefit analysis can be applied either to project or to policy alternatives. Obviously, when cost-benefit analysis is applied to policy alternatives, it will be much broader in scope than when it is applied to project alternatives. This is true because policies impact entire sectors, while the impact of a project will normally be more limited. Gittinger (1982) notes the possibility of applying economic cost-benefit analysis to policies as well as to projects (pages 271-279), but since that book's primary audience is project planners, the possibility suggested is mainly to remind project planners of the broader context within which the planning of projects should be fitted.

The term "numeraire" refers to the unit of account in terms of which "benefits" and "costs" are counted in cost-benefit analysis. For example, in one form of cost-benefit analysis—enterprise profit-and-loss accounting—the numeraire is "net income" or "profit." In that particular cost-benefit application, costs would be termed "expenses," while benefits would accrue in the form of "revenues."

In cost-benefit analysis, the numeraire is defined so that it represents "quantifiable progress" in meeting one or more of the planning objectives—usually the primary objective, or the most important one. In the enterprise example, cited in the preceding paragraph, the income statement would represent a cost-benefit analysis because it measures progress in terms of the "profitability" or "income" objective of the enterprise. Other objectives that could be analyzed in that enterprise would include "wealth generation" and "security" (or risk minimization). These objectives are dealt with in the financial statement analysis, though they are usually handled in separate calculations through the application of financial ratio analysis (such as profitability ratios, efficiency ratios, liquidity and risk ratios, and the like).

In the financial analysis of projects and enterprises, there is currently no generally accepted analytical model for showing all of a firm's financial objectives in one numeraire. Thus, financial statement analysis, as currently practiced, represents a form of quantitative analysis in terms of selected strategic business objectives (which usually include profitability, liquidity or security, and efficiency); but it does not represent "optimization" in terms of all of the diverse objectives that are being analyzed by the financial analyst. The reason is that there usually are no "conversion weights" available for converting units of other objectives like security into the objective of profitability, and vice versa. [In this respect, financial ratio analysis is similar in approach to the "decision matrix" of the four-account framework proposed by the Water Resources Council in the United States in the late 1960s. For details, see Ward (1980).] Even if a model were available for optimizing all of an enterprise's financial objectives, it would still not include nonfinancial objectives that motivate so many business owners.

In the single-objective forms of the cost-benefit model that were discussed in the preceding parts of this volume, the objective of economic efficiency was taken as the primary objective. Secondary objectives, such as government income and employment, were taken into account only in separate calculations. Many analysts feel that this approach provides a clear presentation of the conflicts among objectives to those in charge of making the final decision about

In the financial analysis of projects, there is no model for showing all of an enterprise's financial objectives in one numeraire. In the income statement, the numeraire could be "net income" or "profit."

projects and policies. In the single-objective approach to cost-benefit analysis, there is a clear delineation between "primary" and "secondary" objectives and benefits, because the primary benefits usually are presumed to be contained in the numeraire.

In the purest form—i.e., the fully-quantified form—of the cost-benefit model, units of the secondary objectives would be converted into units of the primary objective using conversion weights and then would be valued in terms of the numeraire. The numeraire could be defined to measure progress in meeting the primary planning objective, or it could be defined in terms of some aggregated measure of progress in meeting all objectives.

However, it is not always possible to define the numeraire in units of the primary objective. For example, in the OECD (1969) formulation of the national economic planning model, the numeraire of the analysis was defined in terms of "uncommitted foreign exchange available to the government"—foreign exchange that could then be used for investment in development. There was not a single primary objective: rather, there were several high priority objectives, with weights used to convert among the various objectives. The income and consumption weights provided the mechanism through which income impacts on private individuals and on the government could be made comparable.

Intermediate versus Final Objectives in the Numeraire

An intermediate objective—as opposed to a final objective—could represent a means of achieving one or more final objectives. The numeraire in OECD (1969) expressed progress in meeting an intermediate objective. Progress in achieving "uncommitted foreign exchange available to the government" represented progress in meeting the major final objectives in the OECD project appraisal system. The final objectives included:

a. economic efficiency (i.e., the value to society);

b. income distribution (i.e., the distribution of consumption, or "equity");

c. optimal growth (i.e., the value of consumption over time relative to the return on reinvestment of savings); and

d. government income.

Pure cost-benefit analysis requires conversion of all important impacts into units of the numeraire.

Let us recall that a quantitative, optimizing model which has more than one objective must also have a numeraire which measures progress in achieving all of the objectives. The OECD numeraire of "free foreign exchange available to the government" is related to progress in achieving each of their stated objectives. In addition, the

OECD numeraire included two criteria—the generation of foreign exchange and of government income—that often are separated into two by many governments in selecting projects. Both of these criteria are critical to increasing the main form of investment in development over which governments have control: public investment.

The objective of increasing public sector investment was prominent in the development plans of many developing countries at the time the OECD Manual was first written. It continues to be an important objective today, since a substantial part of public sector investment in many countries is financed by foreign capital of some sort—whether in the form of bilateral and multilateral grants and loans, or in the form of commercial bank loans.

But government investment is an intermediate objective; it is not the only planning objective of importance to governments. Other important objectives have included income distribution and increased consumption by all citizens. Thus, it became necessary to develop a weighting or conversion system for converting impacts on these objectives into the numeraire—i.e., putting the impacts on all objectives into the "common denominator" of uncommitted foreign exchange available to the government for investing in development.

In the multi-objective project appraisal system, this meant that income weights would be required for comparing income between the government and individuals at different income levels. It also meant that a measure of the value of consumption, relative to that of investment, had to be developed; the government and each of its citizens needed resources for current consumption as well as for investment. And because current investment represented future consumption, a method of valuing future consumption in relation to present consumption had to be developed. All of these conversions had to be consistent with the numeraire of the analysis.

Differences between OECD and UNIDO Methods. Shortly after the OECD method of project appraisal was presented, UNIDO issued its own "Guidelines for Project Evaluation" (the so-called "UNIDO Guidelines," published in 1972). The guidelines also dealt with multiple objectives. There were several minor differences between the UNIDO Guidelines and the OECD Manual; these differences are well documented in the economics literature. Part of that literature is cited in the annotated bibliography to Gittinger (1982).

Government investment is an intermediate objective. Final objectives that are deemed important by governments include income distribution and optimal growth.

One important difference between the OECD Manual and the UNIDO Guidelines was that the latter used a slightly different numeraire for comparing its four objectives. The guidelines suggested that "aggregate consumption" be the composite objective, and that the "unit of account" (i.e., the numeraire) be "a unit of average present consumption today." Impacts on other objectives (such as government income and optimal growth) then had to be converted into this aggregate consumption-based numeraire, and the shadow prices had to be derived in a way which allowed this conversion among the objectives.

After years of comparing and contrasting the OECD Manual and the UNIDO Guidelines, the economics profession seems to have concluded that the two methods essentially lead to the same results. In other words, projects that are accepted using one method will also be accepted when appraised under the other method, and that both methods will come to the same conclusions on unacceptable projects. If the same assumptions are made about expected future policies and about the relationships between traded and nontraded goods, and if the same conclusions are drawn regarding the relative values of income to different groups, the two methods would be mathematically equivalent. The reason for this consistency lies in a simple mathematical truism.

The mathematical equivalence of the OECD and UNIDO methods can most easily be demonstrated by recalling that the distinction lies simply in the mathematics of how the two "objective functions" are set up. (We are assuming, of course, that the analysts using the two methods work from the same objectives and assumptions.) Let us recall that we simplified the major objectives of both methods into:

> **a.** economic efficiency;
>
> **b.** optimal growth;
>
> **c.** government income; and
>
> **d.** income distribution.

Let the following symbols represent units of impact on each of these variables:

> E = economic efficiency;
>
> O = optimal growth;
>
> G = government income; and
>
> D = income distribution.

UNIDO and OECD methods have been shown to give essentially the same results.

In simple terms, we may define the weights which convert impacts on the other three objectives into equivalent impacts on the economic efficiency objective, as follows:

w1 = value per unit of impact on economic efficiency;

n2 = number of units of **O** that is judged equal to one unit of **E**;

n3 = number of units of **G** that is judged equal to one unit of **E**; and

n4 = number of units of **D** that is judged equal to one unit of **E**.

Once we know the values of **w1**, **n2**, **n3**, and **n4**, we can write our objective function to make any of the four objectives the "primary" objective. In other words, we can define the numeraire in terms of any one of the stated objectives—if we know the value of one of them and the weights to convert the others into it.

In essence, what the UNIDO Guidelines did was to set up the maximizing equation so that units of value were expressed in terms of **E**, while the OECD Manual set up the maximizing equation so that units of value were expressed in terms of **G**. In the former case, **E** represented "aggregate consumption" because it also expressed the optimum growth in consumption over time. In the latter case, **G** was expressed in units of foreign exchange rather than in units of local currency. (Because both methods allow the calculation of an exchange rate that links the two currencies, it does not matter which of the two currencies is used in denominating the numeraire.)

In theory, the ideal numeraire should express progress in meeting all of the strategic planning objectives. The ideal application of cost-benefit analysis would involve converting measurements of the project's impacts on all objectives into a common unit of analysis. This conversion would be more tedious if the numeraire was defined very precisely (e.g., "foreign exchange in the hands of government"—the OECD numeraire) as opposed to cases in which the numeraire was defined less precisely (e.g., "net foreign exchange" as in the so-called "Bruno ratio," or "local cost of saving foreign exchange" numeraire).

The difficulty of conducting a cost-benefit analysis could be reduced by:

a. reducing the number of objectives that are included in the analysis; and

b. selecting a unit of account that is not overly specific in terms of where benefits and costs accrue.

Once we have defined the weights which links the various objectives, we can state our numeraire in terms of any of our planning objectives.

Gittinger (1982) used a numeraire that was sufficiently simple to be quickly understood and applied by noneconomists working in the field. That numeraire was economic efficiency, a single-objective numeraire that did not require specific determination of the location of the impacts of the projects being appraised. In choosing this numeraire, income distribution and savings issues were ignored as part of the economic analysis.

Income Distribution Objective. The inclusion of an income distribution objective, or an optimal growth objective, forces the units of impact to be accounted for in very specific terms. The inclusion of an equity objective—equality of income, or income distribution—by necessity, requires that we trace the impacts of the project to different income groups in the society. This is obviously the case, since we cannot apply different income weights to different groups, unless we know where the income goes and into which income group the recipients fall. For this reason, transport economists in the World Bank made a strong case in the late 1970s that social analysis should not be routinely applied to the appraisal of transport projects. They argued that the impacts would be extremely difficult and costly to trace by income group. As a result, social analysis was not applied to the Bank's transport projects.

In social analysis, our work does not end by simply identifying the recipients of the income. We need to develop different weights for each income group. These income weights are used to convert the income impacts received by different groups into a comparable income unit for some reference group. For example, in the Squire-van der Tak system, the reference group is represented by individuals at the "critical consumption level" (CCL). Income received by individuals at this level is given an income weight of 1. In other words, a rupee of income received by this group is given a weight of one rupee. Individuals having an income lower than those at the CCL would have a weight exceeding 1 placed on their incomes, while those having incomes above the CCL would receive a weight a less than 1. In the Squire-van der Tak system, the government receives an income weight of 1—the same as individuals at the CCL [see Bruce (1976)].

With optimal growth as one of the objectives, we must determine if the increase in incomes resulting from the project will be saved (invested) or "consumed" by the recipients. Furthermore, in the discounted cash flow analysis, we will have to deal with two discount rates: the opportunity cost of capital and the social time preference rate (see Chapter 21). Consumption will be discounted back to the present with the use of the social time preference rate, while income

Social analysis requires that we trace project impacts to different groups in the society.

that is invested will presumably grow at the rate implied by the opportunity cost of capital.

In the single-objective version of the cost-benefit model, these two discounts rates are normally assumed to be the same. If they are the same, then it will not be necessary to differentiate between income that is consumed and income that is invested. It will not be necessary, because the rate at which the invested income will grow will be the same as the rate at which the future consumption will be discounted back to the present. As a result, the present value of the stream resulting from invested income will be the same as the current value of the income would be if it were consumed immediately; and it will be sufficient to simply use the economic opportunity cost of capital as the discount rate.

In the multi-objective version of the model, the two discount rates will be different from each other, because the growth rate will be presumed to be suboptimal. In other words, society values future income at a higher rate than the rate implied by the opportunity cost of capital. Thus, at the margin, the value of total consumption may be increased by forgoing additional present consumption in favor of investment in the future. (The implications of suboptimal growth are discussed further in Chapter 21. In addition, Section 6.4 of the UNIDO Guidelines contains a well-developed discussion of the optimal growth issue.)

In recent years, less attention is being paid to the social analysis part of the Squire-van der Tak method. There are at least four reasons for this development:

First, many analysts view the social parameters—the accounting prices used in the social analysis—to be "arbitrary." Proponents of social analysis argue, however, that the social parameters are no more arbitrary than the practice of applying an income weight of 1 to everyone, as is implicitly done in economic analysis.

Second, politicians often do not like to give official sanction to the social parameters, though they may well agree with them and make decisions based on similar implicit weights. The reason for politicians' reluctance is that the income weights state explicitly the relative trade-offs among competing objectives. To maintain their political base, politicians usually must act as if they believe all objectives can be achieved simultaneously. That is, there are no trade-offs.

Third, agricultural project planners often are disturbed at the

Since the early 1980s less attention has been paid to social analysis.

spurious accuracy that is implied by the social parameters. They are concerned that "fine tuning" is being done based on technical analysis that is subject to wide margins of error. For instance, benefit distributions are based on rice yields that might as easily be 1.5 tons per hectare as 2.5 tons per hectare.

Fourth, in many projects, it is difficult to tell who the beneficiaries are. Let us recall that it is necessary to know the income groups receiving the benefits in order to conduct the income weighting for the social analysis; and it is necessary to know the beneficiaries so that judgments may be made regarding their propensities to save and to consume out of new income. In certain types of projects, it may be costly to conduct the research that is necessary to determine exactly who the beneficiaries really are. As pointed out earlier, transportation economists have argued successfully that social analysis should not be used for projects in their sector because of this difficulty. However, in most types of agricultural projects, it is generally easier to identify the beneficiaries than it is for projects in sectors such as transport.

The Gittinger Numeraire

The approach taken in Gittinger (1982) is consistent with the economic analysis methods discussed in Squire and van der Tak. In Gittinger (1982), the unit of account, or numeraire, is defined as roughly equating to units of national income. But as we work through the book, it becomes clear that it is not "national income" measured in the normal way: rather, contributions to national income are measured in terms of "willingness to pay" market prices. Or, to put it another way, the Gittinger numeraire is really an "economic efficiency" numeraire, stated in willingness to pay terms. It is closely related to the UNIDO numeraire, except for two differences.

First, the Gittinger numeraire is a single-objective numeraire, like that of step two of the Squire-van der Tak approach. In other words, there are no "other objectives" (such as optimal growth, income distribution, or government income) that must be converted into units of aggregate consumption. Thus, there is no need for income weights, investment weights, and other weights to convert these "other objectives" into the primary objective, or into the numeraire. Likewise, in the Gittinger approach, there is only one discount rate to worry about, since the economic analysis does not explicitly address the issue of nonoptimality of the growth rate.

Gittinger Numeraire.

1. Uses an economic efficiency numeraire stated in willingness to pay terms.

2. Calculates shadow prices in border prices, or in domestic prices.

Second, in Gittinger (1982), we are instructed on how to calculate shadow prices in this numeraire. We calculate either in border prices (using economic efficiency conversion factors), or in domestic prices (using traditional shadow prices and a shadow exchange rate). The emphasis, however, is on border pricing in order to be consistent with current practice in the World Bank. The UNIDO Guidelines, generally, recommends using domestic prices rather than border prices.

While the numeraire that is used in Gittinger (1982) is consistent with Squire and van der Tak's approach to economic analysis, it is not the only numeraire that is consistent with their economic analysis method. In fact, a second numeraire is increasingly being used in applications within the World Bank: this is the "generic foreign exchange" numeraire. We have termed it "generic" because, in economic analysis, there is no preference extended to the government, or to anyone else in the society (though there will be preferences when we go the next step and conduct the social analysis). Unlike the OECD numeraire, the single-objective approach followed in this type of economic analysis does not value foreign exchange held by others differently from foreign exchange that accrues to the government. In that regard, it is similar to the Bruno ratio (or local cost of saving foreign exchange). The generic foreign exchange numeraire is similar to the Gittinger numeraire in that respect.

Both of the single-objective numeraires—the generic foreign exchange and the willingness to pay—that are found in practice in the World Bank are relatively simpler to apply in economic analysis than in social analysis.

❖

Both the "consumption numeraire" and the "foreign exchange numeraire" are found in use in the World Bank. Both are consistent with the Squire–van der Tak method.

16. Strategic Planning and Cost-Benefit in Practice

Summary. *The strategic planning model is based on a rational process in which management sets goals and objectives; technical professionals conduct resource assessments that form the basis for them to come together with their management to rationalize objectives and resources; and technical professionals identify technical alternatives to use the resources to achieve identified objectives. The set of alternatives is ranked and selected based on maximizing the value of the numeraire that is derived from the strategic planning model. In reality, the planning process falls short of the model. Failures occur in setting objectives, in conducting resource surveys, in rationalizing resources and objectives, and in identifying and selecting the right numeraire.*

Objectives are not rationally set for a number of reasons. Incongruity of objectives exists among politicians, government officials, and clients. Objectives are too numerous, vaguely defined, and conflicting to be simultaneously met. Adequate resource surveys are not available because of lack of professional skills in project identification and preparation and lack of money. However, in most developing countries, there exists a scarcity of projects rather than of capital; practically any project that gets partly prepared gets funded. Project planning tends to be ad hoc rather than strategic, and appraisal numeraires are selected based on technicians' views of "appropriate" planning objectives.

The Strategic Planning Model in Theory. The model, when applied to corporate planning, presumes that senior management's objectives are consistent with those of the organization [see Galbraith (1967) for a discussion of organizational planning and performance in the face of separation between ownership and management—in this case, in the context of corporate management]. The model also presumes that the organization is well managed. It assumes that senior management will take responsibility for setting reasonable goals and objectives and for surveying the outside environment to identify those factors which can be controlled, those which can be influenced, and those which must simply be "appreciated" [see Smith, Lethem, and Thoolen (1980)]. The model also assumes that senior managers will work responsibly with technical staff to determine the steps that need to be taken in light of each of these categories of outside factors. Owners, managers, and workers are rewarded and managed such that a congruity of objectives exists among each of the actors [see Morrisey (1969)].

Congruity of Planning Objectives. A politicized environment characterizes both an enterprise as well as a government [Hanna

To be effective, strategic planning requires that managers and technical professionals interact honestly and responsibly.

(1985)]. However, our concern here shall be with applications of national-level strategic planning. In national planning, we often find it difficult to achieve clear direction from senior management in terms of goals and objectives. There is the problem of achieving congruity in the objectives of three disparate parties whose interests are involved in the results and in the processes of planning. These three groups are:

    a. politicians, whether or not democratically elected;

    b. government officials in the planning, budgeting, and line agencies; and

    c. diverse groups of citizens who are both the recipients and the financiers of government activity [see Mitchell (1978)].

Identifying Social Welfare. The prescriptions surrounding the "theory of market failure" and the "theory of regulation" [Stigler (1971)] suggest that the government seek to maximize social welfare. However, in the real world we do not have a single, generally agreed upon perception of social welfare. The goals and objectives of even the citizens—our third group of actors—are diverse, conflicting, and not very clearly stated. Democratic voting systems, for all their supposed advantages, do not resolve these conflicts adequately. These problems are discussed in a plethora of works on welfare economics [partially reviewed in Dasgupta and Pearce (1972), Chapter 1].

Optimism and the Organismic View of Government. In national planning, a complex interplay of goals and objectives takes place among politicians, government officials, individual citizens, and groups of citizens having varying degrees of power and influence. One view of this process, sometimes called "the organismic view of government," holds that somehow this process "organismically" results in goals and objectives being identified and social welfare being maximized. Most economists and political scientists find this view difficult to accept.

Excessive Number of Objectives. What typically results from the interplay of the major influence groups is a planning process that identifies "goals and objectives" designed to satisfy all of the influence groups. Little attention is paid to the "optimal control" problem that is posed by having more objectives than control instruments [see Johnsen (1968)]. Managements do not review the first statement of goals and objectives to narrow them down, or to refine them; neither do managements return to the statement of goals after making an inventory of the resources to revise these goals during the "plan rationalization" process [see Mat (1983)].

Political Value of Vaguely Defined Goals. It may not be in a politician's self-interest to state a goal or an objective clearly. In the

In national planning, there is the problem of achieving congruity in the planning objectives of three disparate groups: politicians, government officials, and citizens. Neither democratic systems nor centrally planned economies resolve these conflicts adequately. As a result, the objectives are designed to satisfy all the influence groups; often, the implementation ends up satisfying no one.

face of divergent and conflicting interests, clearly stated objectives also clearly state who in the society counts most. Politicians and staff of government agencies are best served by creating the perception that all citizens count. Thus, vaguely stated objectives are favored more than clearly stated ones. Clear statements allow analysis of gainers and losers. Clear statements also allow the identification of conflicts among objectives, and force politicians to clarify their judgment on which interests are more important.

Reality versus Perception of Impact. Public sector intervention must be perceived to be taking place to meet perceived social needs. Political success is frequently based on perception, rather than on reality. It is more important to a politician that society perceive that government is attempting to meet a social need than it is to actually meet that need. Likewise, it is also important for society to perceive that a need exists. For example, political figures often talk of the "need" to impose tariff protection against imports to counteract actions taken abroad; but does the country really need this?

The attention to perception rather than to reality leads to perverse problems in the application of strategic planning to national development problems. Among the most common impacts of attention to perception are the following:

a. a larger number of projects are identified than can be funded and implemented in a timely fashion;

b. projects are started with great fanfare, including formal television and newspaper coverage of groundbreaking ceremonies, then allowed to lag after attention shifts to other projects; and

c. funding tends to focus on highly visible projects, such as large-scale river diversions and hydroelectric dams, rather than on small-scale, decentralized tubewell development and "software"-oriented projects which involve changes in practices rather than in investment of capital.

Planning Without Objectives. The result of these factors is that it places technical staff in a difficult position when they have to identify alternatives to meet the numerous vaguely stated and unrationalized objectives. Basically, the stated objectives tend to be unachievable, particularly when they are all viewed together. Technical staff quickly learn to identify projects that are highly visible and which create a perception of meeting important social needs.

Politicization of planning often forces line agency staff to formulate their own project objectives.

Conflict Between Technical Knowledge and Political Agenda

In many countries, technical knowledge is not a prerequisite for holding political office—including the positions of minister and secretary. The strategic planning model assumes some capability (and interest) on the part of management to discuss and direct technical alternatives identified by technical staff.

The absence of a technically knowledgeable management leads to further problems in bringing together objectives and alternatives. With the agenda of technical staff and that of management potentially in conflict, management needs to have technical competence to judge the alternatives put forward by its technical staff. In the absence of technical competence in management, the technical staff is likely to pursue its own objectives while reporting to management in terms of management's objectives [see Agarwala (1983), p. 12]. The presence of a management information system does not solve this problem; it simply quickens the pace and increases the volume of imperfect information that flows upward to managers.

Resource Surveys and Project Identification in Practice

Lack of Resources to Do Inventories. The lack of financial and skilled manpower prevents developing countries from carrying out detailed resource inventories that are needed for identifying projects and for rationalizing development plans. In the agricultural and natural resources sector, in particular, not enough is known about soils, numbers of livestock, and presence of mineral resources. The "action orientation" of most developing countries and of the donor agencies has led to a tendency to move ahead with investments in productive areas rather than in the research and survey work needed to identify critical investments. [Of course, important exceptions to this generalization can be found, such as the planning exercise in the Mekong delta, the water development studies in Pakistan, and the activities of the Master Plan Organization and predecessor study groups in Bangladesh.] As a result, the second critical step in the planning process—the survey of resources needed for identifying alternatives and for evaluating the achievability of plan objectives— tends to be missing.

Lack of Skills to Produce Project Alternatives. Project ranking techniques, which plays a prominent part in many texts and articles on project planning, is nonexistent in most developing countries. Ranking of projects presumes that budget scarcity exists—in other words, that there are more well-prepared projects than there is money to finance them. Thus, the problem at budget making time is implied to be one of selecting out of a large set of well-prepared projects the best of the bunch—where "best" is defined in terms of the cost-benefit analysis done with one of the numeraires that we have discussed in previous chapters.

Failure to do adequate resource surveys and failure to rationalize objectives with resources are the two greatest technical weaknesses in national development planning.

But "capital scarcity" is not a project budgeting problem in most developing countries; rather, the problem is one of project scarcity. Another problem is the unavailability of sufficient skilled technical staff (and, to a lesser extent, sufficient project budget for thorough preparation) to identify properly and prepare a number of projects that national governments and donors would like to be able to fund. This problem was exacerbated in the 1970s by an excess supply of investable funds that resulted from attempts to recycle the "petrodollars" [see Dornbusch and Helmers (1988)]. The recycling attempt greatly increased the amount of external funds searching for good investment alternatives, which in turn contributed to subsequent debt problems.

Despite the availability of external funds, weakness in the third step of strategy planning continued to exist: Even if objectives could be clearly stated, resource inventories completed, and plans rationalized, resources did not exist for identifying project interventions that were appropriate to the plan's objectives and to the nation's resources and to be socially and environmentally sustainable. As a result, any project which was prepared to the point that it could be implemented had a good chance of being funded—whether or not it was the "best" alternative for meeting a plan objective, or was even vaguely related to a plan objective.

Intervention by External Funding Agencies

External funding agencies intervene in the planning, budgeting, and implementation of projects in many ways and for many reasons. An important reason is that the capital or development budgets of many developing countries are largely financed by external aid and concessional assistance. Therefore, aid agencies—like bankers—feel that they have a right to have a say in the use of their money. That intervention is characterized by the financing agency's own parallel tripartite set of interests—management, staff, and clients—as is the budgeting and policymaking of the developing country concerned. The goals and objectives of this intervention can become as incongruent as those of the developing country.

External funding agencies intervene in the planning, budgeting, and implementation of projects in many ways. Frequently, the goals and objectives of such intervention can become as incongruent as those of the developing country.

"Political" objectives clearly influence the interventions of the bilateral aid agencies. To some extent, these same influences are brought to bear on the multilateral agencies—officially, through the boards of directors of such institutions as the World Bank and the regional development banks. These objectives also come into the process through the "aid coordination groups" which have gained prominence in dealing with many developing countries (and which, for the most part, have helped to ameliorate part of the problem of conflicting interventions posed by the various aid agencies).

Staff of bilateral and multilateral agencies can wield strong influence on the planning process. Many development professionals now joke that some countries don't have a "plan;" rather, they have "donors." Much of this influence is of a technical and technique-oriented nature; but in practice, it is difficult to separate technique from ideology and the donor's own interest. Aid agency officials—by virtue of their extensive knowledge of the world at large and ability to judge competence in a broader context—are able not only to influence the selection of international consultants, but must do so out of necessity. By virtue of their control over allocation and disbursement of finance, these officials are able to influence the selection of projects and of project designs; and because of their wider experience and their fiduciary responsibility to their employers, they must do so.

The addition of these outside agendas can create great difficulty for even the best-conceived and best-intended national planning process. As a result, much of project planning tends to proceed not according to a rationalized strategic national development plan. Rather, the planning tends to proceed as an assembly of *ad hoc* activities with objectives that are vaguely stated, often in mutual conflict, and certainly not fitting together as integral parts of a grand, finely tuned national development strategy.

Ad Hoc Projects, Ad Hoc Objectives

In practice, the strategic planning model is seldom applied to national development planning in the neat fashion that textbooks describe. Rather, projects are brought forward one at a time. They tend to be identified in terms of the objectives of the person who identifies the project, or in terms of this person's perceptions of what is good for the country. Because of the scarcity of good projects, they also tend to be brought forward before they are sufficiently well prepared and without being adequately analyzed for their possible impacts on the national economy and environment.

Typically, no alternative means for meeting the project's stated objectives are considered. Alternative project designs are given little or no attention, since the time required to prepare an alternative design for optimization purposes can just as well be put into preparing a second project, which too will be readily funded by the government, or more likely from external sources.

Economic parameters—shadow prices—cannot be calculated by using programming solutions, because the projects that will be included in the investment program and in the mathematical program are not known in advance. Likewise, project ranking and selection cannot be carried out in the way the professional publications suggest it should be done—by using present values calculated in terms of the numeraires consistent with the objectives selected in the strategic planning process.

In practice, the strategic planning model is seldom applied to national development planning. Projects tend to be identified in terms of the objectives of the person who identifies the project. The alternative means for meeting the project's objectives are rarely considered, shadow prices are rarely calculated, and project ranking in terms of the numeraire is rarely done.

Most of the projects that are "identified" are often nothing more than a project name with a vaguely identified cost associated with it. Efforts to rationalize and screen from these lists have caused great frustration for the World Bank staff and other analysts who deal with the "public investment program review" component of operations known as structural adjustment lending.

The failure of the development planning process to bring forward well-prepared projects, which are clearly identified in terms of national plan objectives, has led many donors to involve themselves more deeply in the earlier stages of project planning, long before appraisal. External aid agencies increasingly tend to take on the role that planning theory says is the role of senior management.

Two factors indicate that this trend is not likely to end soon. First, many analysts now widely perceive that there has been a *de facto* default by many developing countries in adequately performing these functions. Second, though government officials of developing countries often complain about interference by donors in the development planning process, the call by these governments for outside funding is likely to increase, rather than decrease, the role of external financing agencies in national planning. To deal with a continuing financial crisis will require that a strategic approach to economic management be taken. Coordination of strategic activities by development agencies appears to be the best alternative that is likely to emerge.

Aid agencies play a major role in the "planning" that actually does take place in developing countries. That role is likely to increase in the future.

PART IV

Practical Approaches to Project Dynamics

Changes in Prices, Exchange Rates, and the Value of the Numeraire

17. Inflation and the Financial Accounts

Summary. *Financial accounts involved in project planning may be calculated in either nominal prices, or in real prices. In contrast, all accounts used in project economic analysis are calculated in real prices. Generally, financial accounts of enterprises, and financial plans of projects and enterprises, are done in nominal terms, while financial statements (financial and economic cash flows) used to calculate the internal rates of return (IRRs) are set up in real prices. Because these various accounts are related to each other in practice, some "crosswalking" is required. Different agencies use different methods for providing the crosswalks between financing tables of projects and enterprises, and those used for calculating IRRs of projects. Some agencies—including the World Bank—use different methods for different sectors.*

Real, Constant, Nominal, and Current Prices

Nominal, current, real, and constant prices are defined in the "Glossary-Index" at the end of Gittinger (1982). Generally, the terms "nominal prices" and "current prices" are used interchangeably, as are the terms "real prices" and "constant prices." An element of confusion surrounds the term "real," however, because it is often used in discussing the flows of "real resources" that is the focus of economic analysis.

We may differentiate between the financial analysis and economic analysis use of the term "real" in the following way:

a. When used in financial analysis, the term "real" implies:

- resource flows (consistently valued at uninflated financial prices); plus
- money flows (deflated by some index of inflation) that may be unrelated to resource flows.

b. When used in economic analysis, the term "real" implies resource flows (valued at uninflated economic prices).

Because it is possible to confuse the term "real" in the financial and economic analyses, and because we can as readily use the term "constant prices" in referring to financial analysis done in "real prices," project economists often use this term in reference to economic analysis. This is the approach taken in Gittinger (1982); we shall follow that same convention in the present discussion.

To avoid confusion, real prices in the financial analysis are referred to as "constant prices;" in economic analysis, they are known as "real prices."

The constant-prices approach to financial analysis has three major advantages:

a. it allows the uninflated financial IRR to be calculated

directly from the financial cash flow;

b. it eases the transition from the project financial account to the project economic account, since the financial cash flow (by being in constant prices rather than in nominal prices) is already part of the way there; and

c. it facilitates the calculation of break-even values and the conduct of switching value analysis.

Note that we can conduct project financial analysis in either current prices, or in constant prices. The difference between the two will be found in the rate of inflation which links the current prices to the constant prices; and the financial IRRs that are calculated from those cash flows are also linked by that same inflation rate [see Gittinger (1982), pages 400-401]. Thus, we will have to make a choice as to which set of prices to use in conducting the project financial analysis.

Current and Constant Prices and the Project Accounts

A major problem posed by inflation is the fact that the relationship among the "basic project accounts" will be affected. In the absence of inflation, it would be possible to derive the forecast "with project" enterprise viability accounts—i.e., the whole-farm budget with the project, in the case of agricultural projects—by simply adding the following accounts together:

a. the enterprise viability accounts without the project;

b. the enterprise investment analysis account; and

c. the financing plan for the project-related investment of the enterprise.

By the same token, if all of the accounts were set up in current prices, or were in constant prices, we could directly add them together to get the "with project" enterprise viability accounts. Mathematically, we could derive any one of these four accounts from the other three. We may refer to the relationship among these three sets of accounts as the project accounting identity:

$$EWP = EWOP + PCFbf + PFP \qquad (17.1)$$

where:

EWP = Enterprise cash flow with project;

EWOP = Enterprise cash flow without project;

PCFbf = Project (incremental) cash flow before financing; and

PFP = Project financing plan.

In theory, identity 17.2 allows us to derive the project account—i.e., the incremental cash flow—by subtracting the "without project" enterprise accounts from the "with project" enterprise accounts:

We can conduct project financial analysis in either current prices, or in constant prices. The difference between the two is the rate of inflation.

$$PCFbf + PFP = PCFaf = EWP - EWOP \qquad (17.2)$$

$$PCFbf = PCFaf - PFP \qquad (17.3)$$

where:

PCFaf = Project cash flow after financing.

However, inflation drives a wedge through these identity equations: financing plans (including PFP) are usually drawn in current prices; enterprise accounts (EWP and EWOP) often are drawn in current prices in sectors other than agriculture; and project cash flows (PCFbf and PCFaf) are usually drawn in constant prices. In the presence of inflation, a number of different methods are used to set up and relate the basic project accounts to each other. For instance, within the World Bank and its subsidiary, the International Finance Corporation (IFC), three identifiable approaches are followed to deal with inflation in the financial accounts.

First, agricultural project analysts in the World Bank set up enterprise accounts in constant prices so that incremental project accounts may be derived directly from them (as in Equation 17.3). The financing requirements are derived in constant terms and then inflated for financial planning purposes.

Second, industrial project analysts set up enterprise accounts in either current or constant prices. The practice varies, depending largely upon the rate of inflation in the country. The project cash flow may be derived by subtracting the without-project cash flow from the with-project cash flow (with the project cash flow then adjusted to constant prices, if the enterprise accounts were in current prices). A common practice is to derive the incremental project cash flow from the "project budgets"—particularly in "green field" and "pure expansion" projects—rather than from the EWP and EWOP accounts. ("Green field investments" and "pure enterprise expansion" are discussed in the next section.)

Third, IFC analysts usually set up enterprise accounts in current prices during the project implementation period and in constant prices after the implementation period.

Financing plans are usually drawn in current prices; enterprise accounts are often drawn in current prices in nonagricultural sectors; and project cash flows are usually prepared in constant prices.

While the approaches used within the World Bank certainly are not the only ways to handle the problems posed by inflation, they are indicative of the range of options that exist. Gittinger (1982) discusses financial accounting both for agricultural projects and for agroindustrial projects; agricultural project planners may well have to deal with analysts representing each of the three approaches mentioned in the preceding paragraphs. [A good reference on the financial analysis of agroindustrial projects is Brown with Deloitte and Touche (forthcoming).]

The first step in understanding when to use constant prices and when to use current prices is to recall a three-part rule of thumb that is commonly used by project practitioners.

First, constant prices are preferred when making cash flows that will be used in calculating internal rates of return. The reason is that the IRR will then not be influenced by the inflation rate. [For a discussion of the mathematical effect of inflation on the IRR, see Gittinger (1982), pages 400-401.] Thus, constant prices are usually used in setting up investment analysis accounts—both for the project-implementing enterprises and for the project as a whole. Constant prices are always used in economic analysis.

Second, current prices are preferred when making a financing plan, or in making any accounts that are directly related to financing. The reason for this preference is that purchases of project materials, disbursements of loans, and debt service are all money flows and occur in current terms. Thus, enterprise financing plans and project financing plans must, at some stage in the analysis, be converted into current prices so that planners can make certain that enough money is made available in current terms when it is required for making the investments. The exception is in high-inflation countries such as Yugoslavia, where—by law—loan repayment terms include both a real interest charge and a "revaluation" (inflation) adjustment for the principal.

Third, either constant or current prices may be used in constructing and analyzing enterprise viability accounts. The financial statements that are used in analyzing the viability of industrial and other enterprises normally are drawn in current prices. In part, this is because the analysis of financial liquidity is an important element of enterprise viability analysis; and in other part, it is because the accounting standards applied in most countries are based upon historical-cost accounting.

In contrast, in agricultural projects, small-farm enterprise viability is typically analyzed by using whole-farm cash flow accounts in constant prices. This practice allows the enterprise's investment analysis accounts to be derived directly from its viability accounts. However, it puts the enterprise viability accounts and the investment financing plan in different price bases, and thus complicates the problem of merging the investment financing plan into the enterprise viability accounts. [This is the reason for the development of the "declining real debt burden" calculation discussed in Gittinger, (1982), beginning on page 158.]

In agricultural projects, small-farm enterprise viability is typically analyzed by using whole-farm cash flow accounts in constant prices.

The analysis of enterprise financial viability usually involves the use of traditional financial analysis techniques, based on standard enterprise financial accounts. If the enterprise is a farm, then this analysis may take the form of farm income analysis, or of farm budgeting. ["Farm income analysis" is discussed briefly in Gittinger (1982), pages 88-90.] Usually, farm budgets will be used in assessing smaller farms in a project. If the enterprise is not a farm, the financial analysis is called "analysis of financial statements." For larger farms, these traditional financial statements may be used in place of farm budgets.

The traditional financial statements will consist of at least an "income statement" and a "balance sheet." Increasingly we find a third statement present, a "sources and uses of funds statement" (sometimes also called a "funds flow statement"), or its equivalent (particularly if the enterprise has outstanding loans, since many lenders now require that such a statement be prepared). [See Gittinger (1982), Chapter 5, for funds flow statements.] Enterprise cash flows can be derived from the income statement and the "project budgets"—the basic accounts that are the foundation for developing the project plan (typically consisting of a capital budget, operating budget, working capital budget, and a sales budget). The project cash flow may be derived by subtracting the enterprise cash flow without the project from that with the project; or the project cash flow may by derived directly from the project budgets, in the case of green field or pure enterprise expansion projects.

Preparing the With-Project and Without-Project Accounts

In agricultural project appraisal, both a with-project enterprise account and a without-project enterprise account tend to be prepared and presented. These are calculated in constant prices and in a cash flow format so that the investment analysis account can be derived as the difference between the "with project" and the "without-project" enterprise accounts. [This process is discussed in Gittinger (1982) in Chapter 4.] Deriving both a with-project and a without-project set of enterprise accounts is much more logical, and reduces the likelihood of errors being made in deriving the incremental cash flow.

To make this point clear, let us look at the seven major categories of investment that might be made at the enterprise level (the "on-farm investment," in agricultural projects):

Green field investments. These are investments which create new enterprises. In this case, the project cash flow after financing (PCFaf) and the enterprise cash flow with the project (EWP) represent the same accounts. This is the simplest case for deriving the project cash flow from the enterprise accounts. Here the project budgets may be used directly in deriving the project and the enterprise cash flows.

Green Field Investments.

These are investments which create new enterprises. In such investments, the project cash flow after financing, and the enterprise cash flow with the project, represent the same accounts.

Pure enterprise expansion. Investments in this category enlarge the scale of operations of the enterprise without affecting the existing activities of the enterprise. In the industrial sector, adding a third manufacturing plant—unrelated to existing plants—would be an example of this type of project. This is the second easiest case for deriving the project cash flow from the enterprise accounts. In this case, subtracting EWP from EWOP will, in effect, "partialize" plants one and two out of the analysis, so that the analysis of the third plant will be analogous to that of a green field investment. In cases in which the project will have no impact, or limited impact, on the rest of the enterprise, the project cash flow may be derived from the project budgets.

Pure replacement of existing capital stock. Investments in this category replace the enterprise's fixed assets, either because of the assets being worn out, or because of economic obsolescence. Deriving the project cash flow can become difficult in these cases, because the without-project cash flow of the enterprise may be difficult to identify. Several alternative without-project scenarios exist, including:

   a. closing down the enterprise;

   b. incurring high maintenance costs and continuing operations as previously done; and

   c. producing lower levels of output with higher raw materials and energy wastage, or some combination of the above.

Replacement with higher volume of output. Replacing the equipment will often increase operating efficiencies more than will maintaining the older equipment. Simple replacement often will not be an option. This case is similar to the pure replacement case in that the without-project enterprise scenario will be similarly derived.

Replacement with quality improvement. Often, replacing the capital stock will also imply an improvement in the quality of the output. Now, we must combine a complicated market analysis on the with-project side, keeping in mind the difficulties of developing the without-project scenario with the old equipment.

Replacement with greater product flexibility. This option is similar to the quality improvement case, but it usually comes with additional uncertainty on the with-project side. The new equipment available to manufacturers may allow greater flexibility in tailoring products to demand and may not be oriented to high-volume, standardized product. In this case, the project design often is geared to an uncertain future, and both the with-project and the without-project scenarios will be difficult to derive.

Pure Enterprise Expansion.
Investments in this category enlarge the scale of operations without affecting the existing activities of the enterprise.

Rehabilitation of assets. This option is meant to rebuild, rework, or repair an enterprise's assets in order to be able to continue to achieve the benefits of the original project or enterprise. In the "pure" rehabilitation case, the objective of the new project is to reestablish the capability to achieve the original project objectives. Rehabilitation projects may reasonably be considered to be subsets of the various "replacement" types previously discussed. The rehabilitation category of projects has become very important in recent years (see Box on "The Special Case of Rehabilitation Projects," page 171).

In only the first two of the seven cases discussed in the preceding paragraphs can we derive an incremental cash flow without preparing a without-project enterprise cash flow. The remaining four cases require that we make some explicit assumptions about what will happen to the enterprise without the project and to subtract the without-project scenario from the with-project scenario.

Enterprise Analysis of Associated Enterprises

"Associated enterprises" can be defined as enterprises which are critical to the success of the project that is being appraised. The recommended practice in the appraisal of World Bank projects is to conduct an analysis of all enterprises that are important to the implementation of the project. This would include:

a. the enterprises responsible for implementing the project (including the numerous farms, in a typical agricultural project, or the electric power company in a power project);

b. enterprises that are expected to provide critical inputs to the project (government agencies or parastatal corporations, in many cases, in agricultural projects—particularly in Africa);

c. enterprises that buy or market a large part of the production of a project (e.g., a marketing agency in the case of export commodities, such as cotton in the Sudan); and

d. financial institutions that are expected to provide financing to project-related enterprises (farmers' credit cooperatives, production credit agencies, banks that make term loans to farmers to finance investments, and the like).

Any entity that is critical to the success of the project should be analyzed. The analysis should be designed to determine whether the enterprise has the financial, technical, and managerial capability to perform as the project plan says the enterprise will perform. In the World Bank's staff appraisal reports—the internal documents which summarize the project appraisal of Bank-assisted projects—the annexes typically present a summary of these enterprise analyses.

Associated Enterprises.
These enterprises are critical to the success of the project that is being appraised.

The Special Case of Rehabilitation Projects

In the early 1970s, rehabilitation projects were considered a special case. Rehabilitation was expected to occur following unexpected damage to project works (e.g., the Tarbella dam in Pakistan), to repair neglected and worn out equipment after a change of economic environment (e.g., in Uganda after Idi Amin's departure), or in rebuilding from old projects (e.g., the current draining and desalinating of lands irrigated under the works originally built by the British in South Asia in the 1800s). In the late 1970s and throughout the 1980s, rehabilitation projects became much more than a special case. By the late 1980s, much of the project portfolio in many countries consisted of "rehab" projects. There are many complex and interrelated reasons for the increased importance of "rehabs."

First, a large pool of projects built in the 1960s and 1970s now exists; many of these are at a stage in their lifecycle at which they must either be abandoned, replaced, or rehabilitated. Many of these projects are prematurely old because they were not adequately maintained, while others have simply reached the end of their asset lives as expected.

Second, the financial crisis that gripped many developing countries during the 1980s has meant that many enterprises have faced a foreign exchange shortage which has prevented them from adequately maintaining, updating, and replacing their equipment. The "export push" accompanying many of the structural adjustment programs in these countries has required them to rehabilitate those sectors having a latent capability to contribute to export earnings. Many adjustment-related projects being financed by the bilateral and multilateral agencies (e.g., the World Bank's Yugoslavia Export Industries Project of 1988) are aimed toward rehabilitating sectors with export capabilities.

Third, the import-substitution strategies followed by many developing countries in recent years (and related, in many cases, to their financial crisis) changed the structure of domestic prices in a way that adversely affected exporters. Many of the traditional export producers either chose not to—or could not afford to—maintain and update their productive assets during this period. With the push toward a more outward orientation (often led by the International Monetary Fund and the World Bank), many of these countries are attempting to rehabilitate their long-neglected export sectors.

Fourth, the (explicit) industrialization strategies and (*de facto*) urbanization policies pursued by many governments during the past three decades have led to neglect and to the taxation of the agricultural sector. As a result, resources have been transferred out of the agricultural sector, particularly in Africa, where such policies—combined with other errors and environmental disasters—led to a situation that required the agricultural sector, as a whole, to be badly in need of rehabilitation by 1988.

Fifth, high interest rates make rehabs more attractive than "new" projects built from the ground up. The reason is that much of the investment nets out as "sunk" costs in the with-project and without-project comparison for the rehabilitation projects. The high interest rates of the late 1970s and the high economic cost of capital in many countries affected by the financial crisis, has meant that—in many of these countries—few projects other than rehabs can meet the rate-of-return criteria necessary for their inclusion in the country's investment program.

Sixth, budgeting systems in most developing countries and the aid financing practices of external aid agencies make it more convenient to finance "deferred maintenance" projects—rehabilitation of projects that were not adequately maintained—than to provide for adequate maintenance of existing projects. Rural roads are simply rebuilt every five to seven years, rather than being built once and maintained annually. Irrigation channels are

continued ➡

Special Case of Rehabs (continued)

"maintained" through externally aided projects implemented every few years, rather than being maintained through the annual budget appropriations. There are numerous reasons for these practices, but they go far beyond the objectives of this "box." However, their impact clearly has been to contribute to the increased importance of rehabilitation projects in the total mix of projects in recent years.

Most rehabilitation projects can be considered to be subsets of the project types previously listed, in particular, the "asset replacement" types (see pages 166-168). The major difference in the project accounts is that—in many of the rehabs—the incremental investment required to rehabilitate the assets is small compared to the "sunk" costs that are involved in producing the expected rehab project outputs. It is this element which tends to give the rehabs high rates of return on the incremental capital invested.

The financial and economic analyses of the incremental investment required for rehab projects are a bit more difficult than those involved in simpler projects, such as green field investments, but they are not insurmountable. The real difficulties with rehabs are encountered in two related areas which should be thoroughly analyzed before the decision is made to go forward with a rehab project:

  a. financial viability of the participating enterprises; and

  b. policy implications surrounding the rehab projects.

Financial Viability of Participating Enterprises. There tends to be a high correlation between the need for rehabilitation and the financial weakness of participating enterprises. In conducting the analysis of the viability of a rehab project, it will be useful to establish the link of causation between these two phenomena. In some cases, the financial weakness of participating enterprises will derive from the need to rehabilitate, while the need to rehabilitate may arise from outside forces (e.g., foreign exchange shortages, spare parts shortages, and so forth). The factors which caused the need to rehabilitate should be identified before agreeing on a project plan; and the appropriate project plan should assure that those same factors do not curtail the life of the postrehab enterprises. In other cases, the need to rehabilitate will derive from financial weaknesses of participating enterprises. An irrigation management agency may have neglected the maintenance of irrigation works because of a shortage of funds; or the Ministry of Transport may have allowed ferry boats—critical to agricultural marketing in countries like Bangladesh—to deteriorate because of lack of funds. In such cases, the project plan should also address the solution of the enterprise's financial problems.

Sometimes, additional equity infusions will resolve the problem of shortage of funds. This has been proposed in the case of many parastatals, such as irrigation authorities, agricultural marketing corporations, and input supply agencies owned by government. At other times, revisions in pricing policies will be required. Water supply authorities (both municipal and irrigation) frequently are plagued by financial weaknesses derived from tariffs that are set below actual costs of supply. The enterprise financial issues and the policy questions that must often be addressed in rehabs are very much tied together. In some cases, mismanagement and inefficiency are the causes of financial problems faced by enterprises, so a more broadly defined approach may need to be taken, including the revision of policies and procedures for appointing and controlling the management of such enterprises.

Policy Implications of Rehabs. Pricing and other policies will often be a causal factor in financially weak enterprises; and financially weak enterprises often need to be rehabilitated. However, this is not the only policy issue that must be faced in assessing rehab projects.

Incremental versus Whole-Investment Analysis. Analysts will often encounter projects in which the benefits from rehabilitating will justify the incremental investment involved, but the benefits will not be sufficient to cover the "sunk" plus incremental costs. There are many facets to the problem posed by this situation; some of these are mentioned in this box.

The financial policy implications. Economists think in terms of resource flows in the future. However, the financial obligations of an enterprise may be unrelated to resource flows, and they can relate to not only incremental flows but also to recovering previously "sunk" costs. This should be taken into account in the enterprise analysis, which should accompany the project analysis. Analysts must also keep in mind that decisions made in dealing with the financial implications of "sunk" costs in one rehab project will set precedents which will affect not only other rehab projects, but also overall financial policies—particularly in countries undergoing structural adjustment.

In many developing countries, development banks made loans in the 1970s and 1980s to agricultural and industrial enterprises for investments which have proven to be unviable in the current environment. In fact, many of the investments were unviable in the then-current environment. Often, these debt-laden enterprises form the nucleus of the productive sector of the country, and of the rehabilitation project being considered. In such cases, decisions made on the financing of the project and the enterprise have serious implications for the future functioning of the country's financial system; and they should not be taken lightly.

Rehabilitating "White Elephants." It is possible to justify rehabs that made no sense based on their full costs—through using incremental benefit and incremental cost analysis. It is a standard practice within the World Bank to undertake two analyses in such cases—in addition to the normal enterprise analysis, technical analysis, and so forth.

The first analysis calculates the rate of return based on the incremental costs and benefits of the rehab. The second analysis calculates the rate of return based on sunk costs plus incremental costs and benefits. If both analyses do not yield IRRs exceeding the cut-off rate, then lengthy discussions may take place regarding the efficacy of financing the rehabilitation project. These discussions may focus upon one or both of the following issues:

a. By rehabilitating the project, will the World Bank send a message to the government that it can "sneak" nonviable investments by the Bank by starting the project, abandoning it, and then putting it forward as a rehab?

b. Will rehabilitating such an enterprise have an impact on the structure of prices in the economy, thus, adversely affecting otherwise viable competitors, or will it send wrong signals to other producers?

Partializing and Issues of Second-Best. In an abstract way, issues of "second best" and incremental analysis are related. In the incremental analysis, we ask: "what impacts are incremental to the decision currently being made?" The "decision" we choose to focus upon determines which other factors get partialized out of the analysis as "sunk." To put it another way: it is a question of where we draw the boundary around the decision that is being made. In more concrete terms, we will be determining how much of the world's problems we will take on when we design an intervention. Rehabilitation projects—more so than green field or pure expansion projects—force us to look more realistically, at broader issues affecting the project.

Project Accounts for Small Farming Enterprises

In projects involving small farms, the enterprise analysis often is conducted differently from that in industrial projects, or public utility projects, or from the analysis of associated nonfarm enterprises in agricultural projects. One reason is that small farming enterprises usually are not expected to prepare financial statements for use in tax reporting and everyday management; so, these accounts are not normally assumed to be readily available to the analyst.

Gittinger (1982) discusses two approaches to enterprise analysis that are sometimes used in agricultural project appraisal:

> **a.** partial budgets; and
>
> **b.** whole-farm budgets.

The "partial budgeting" approach to appraising projects is generally limited to cases in which the project will have minor impact on the farms to be involved. The enterprise viability with and without the project is assumed to be the same. The use of a partial budgeting approach implies that the financial analysis of the farm is limited to the "incremental analysis" that grows directly out of the investment analysis—i.e., to an analysis of the financial implications of the investment. [Refer to Gittinger (1982), Chapter 4, for a review of the differences between income analysis and investment analysis.]

This type of enterprise viability analysis makes the implicit assumption that the nonproject activities of the model farm are sufficiently viable. The analysis also assumes that these activities will not overwhelm the net benefits from the project-related activity of the farm, and thus make the farm as a whole unviable even with the project-related activity (whose viability already will have been determined by the investment analysis). Gittinger (1982) discusses some of the dangers of this type of analysis and makes clear that, for projects that are expected to have a "significant" impact on the participating farms, partial budgets are not recommended.

In the "whole-farm budgeting" approach discussed in Gittinger (1982), the analysis would typically proceed according to the following steps:

First, "project cost table" is developed in constant prices. This table includes the administrative and off-farm costs involved in implementing and managing the project. The costs in the table consist of the "base costs" and any "physical contingencies." Typically, the local currency and foreign exchange costs are shown separately in the table, and all costs are shown year-by-year over the period of project implementation.

In projects involving small farms, the enterprise analysis is often conducted by following two approaches:
1. partial budgets; and
2. whole-farm budgets.

Second, price contingencies are calculated in a worksheet that is not normally included with the appraisal report. The price contingencies are added to the project cost table to arrive at the "total project financing requirements" (off-farm only). This table indicates the amounts that will have to be provided by the government, or by other project financiers, during the project years indicated. It does not include the provision of any credit that may be required to finance project-related on-farm expenditures. These must be calculated in a separate step (see ninth step). The price contingencies are sometimes divided into two categories:

> **a.** money required to finance the price changes caused by general inflation during the project implementation period; and
>
> **b.** money required to finance unanticipated relative price changes in specific items of project cost.

(An alternative approach to **b** is to insist that relative price changes, in principal, belong in the forecast base costs. However, in practice, it may be difficult to forecast such relative price changes; and we may have to provide for these exigencies by augmenting the price contingencies to safeguard the project from financing shortfalls. These shortfalls might be caused by our inability to forecast relative price increases in some items of cost, which are uncompensated by the relative price decreases in other items of cost.)

Third, develop "pattern farm plans" with and without the project. The farm plans are used in deriving the enterprise cash flows in constant prices with and without the project, as described in Chapter 4 of Gittinger (1982).

Fourth, the enterprise cash flows with and without the project (i.e., whole-farm budgets) are used to determine the incremental enterprise cash flow by subtracting the without-project enterprise cash flow from the with-project enterprise cash flow. The differences between the enterprise cash flows with and without the project are attributable to two impacts on the enterprise: the project and the financing plan for the project. These two impacts are separated for analytical purposes by putting the "real" impacts in the top part of the cash flow table and by putting the financing impacts in the bottom of the cash flow table.

Fifth, the incremental enterprise cash flow is used in determining the on-farm financing requirements and in developing the financing plan for the enterprise [see Gittinger, (1982), pages 127-140]. Because many analysts work from the enterprise cash flows in constant prices up to this stage, mistakes are often made in developing the financing plan. The surest way to correctly derive

Moving from on-farm financial analysis to whole-project economic analysis involves eight distinct steps. Aggregating the whole-project financing plan requires a ninth step.

the on-farm financing plans for the pattern farms (and so that the on-farm financial requirements can be correctly aggregated in estimating the agricultural credit requirements associated with the project) is to use the following steps:

a. The inflation rates that have been forecast are used to convert the enterprise cash flow of the pattern farms into current prices for purposes of developing the on-farm financing plans. This is also the best way to see the subtle differences in the way that inflation affects the short-term loan calculations compared to the long-term loan calculations, a difference which often leads to errors in calculating the financing plan and in providing appropriate liquidity in agricultural credit institutions associated with the project.

b. The cash flows in current prices (in item **a**) are used to estimate the short-term and long-term loan requirements of the farms and the debt service on these loans. The financing plan is placed at the bottom of the enterprise cash flow table, so that the top of the table is "before financing" and the bottom of the table is "after financing" [see Gittinger (1982), page 133 and Table 4-19]. This provides an enterprise cash flow before and after financing in current prices. In Gittinger (1982), this table is presented in constant terms, while here we are suggesting that it be initially developed in current terms. To maintain consistency with the constant-prices approach in Gittinger (1982), this current-prices table may be treated only as a worksheet in getting to the constant-prices enterprise cash flow table and in estimating the liquidity requirements of agricultural credit institutions.

c. The enterprise cash flows before and after financing are converted back into constant prices using the inflation rates that have been forecast. This will automatically calculate the "declining real debt burden" on the long-term loan and will correctly calculate the real burden of the short-term loans. It will also correctly show the real short-term financing requirements.

Sixth, the enterprise cash flow before and after financing (derived in **c**) and the analysis leading to this table (e.g., the labor budgets) are used to conduct the analyses discussed in Gittinger (1982) on pages 86 and 87 (i.e., financial impact, incentives, efficiency, and the like.)

Seventh, the procedures in Chapter 7 of Gittinger (1982) and in this volume are used to convert the on-farm and off-farm project accounts into economic values.

Eighth, the procedures in Chapter 8 of Gittinger (1982) are used to aggregate the various economic-value accounts that were developed in the previous step and to calculate the economic rate of return or other measures, conduct sensitivity analysis, and so forth.

Ninth, the information regarding current-price, on-farm financing requirements derived for pattern farms (step five) and the information on the numbers of participating pattern farms used in the preceding step are used to aggregate (in current-price terms) the expected credit requirements of the participating farms and to make certain that adequate arrangements are made for liquidity and loan administration to accommodate the expected level of credit requirements that grow out of the project plan.

Before we can complete the forecasts of the financial accounts, we must discuss several associated forecasts that have to be made. These forecasts include the following:

  a. the domestic inflation rate;

  b. the inflation rate among the country's major trading partners;

  c. the nominal official exchange rate;

  d. the real official exchange rate; and

  e. the shadow exchange rate and standard conversion factor.

These forecasts are dealt with in Chapter 18.

Completing the nine steps requires several associated economic forecasts.

18. Forecasting Exchange Rates, in Practice: The Purchasing Power Parity Calculation

Summary. Forecasting project cash flows requires making three exchange rate forecasts: the nominal official exchange rate (OER), the real OER, and the shadow exchange rate (SER). These forecasts may be made either explicitly or implicitly. A multitude of assumptions may be made in making the forecasts. The most commonly used assumption involves the purchasing power parity adjustment, which presumes that the nominal exchange rate will adjust according to the rate of domestic inflation in relation to foreign inflation, while the real exchange rate remains the same. These conditions are shown to hold, so long as commercial and financial policies are ignored, or are left unchanged.

The model may be adjusted by considering changes in the weighted average tariff rate (WATR), which would affect the relationship between the SER and OER. When the WATR is allowed to change, the real SER may stay the same, while the real OER adjusts according to the change in the WATR. Forecasting this latter set of relationships becomes important in two environments. The first is an environment in which worsening domestic inflation leads to changes in commercial and financial policy. The second is structural adjustment environment, in which commercial and financial policy changes are planned as part of the adjustment.

Forecasting exchange rates requires much more economic understanding—and luck—than can be delivered in this volume. However, we implicitly forecast exchange rates every time we appraise a project. In fact, sometimes we implicitly make forecasts of future exchange rates that would surprise us, if we realized what our forecasts implied.

Three Exchange Rate Forecasts. Project planning requires forecasts of three exchange rates:

a. the nominal official exchange rate (OER), which is needed in making the project financing plan;

b. the real OER, which is needed in making the project financial cash flow in constant prices; and

c. the shadow exchange rate (SER), which is needed in forecasting the OER and in conducting the project economic analysis.

(An alternative to SER is the standard conversion factor, abbreviated as SCF.)

Project planning requires forecasts of three exchange rates:
1. the nominal official exchange rate;
2. the real official exchange rate; and
3. the shadow exchange rate.

Implicit versus Explicit Forecasts of Exchange Rates. The project analyst is not necessarily the one who must make these forecasts; but, it is a fact of life that someone must. If the forecast is not made explicitly, then it will be implicit in the calculations made. One way of making these forecasts is to use the "purchasing power parity" assumption [Lindert, (1986)]. We show the calculation using this assumption because of an important point: if the exchange rate does not change according to the purchasing power parity theorem, then we would expect that the SCF and other conversion factors would have to change during the life of the project.

The normal approach involves an assumption of constant conversion factors; it also involves the assumption of a constant, real official exchange rate. These assumptions are consistent with purchasing power adjustments in the nominal official exchange rate. However, these assumptions may not be consistent with commercial and financial policy reforms scheduled under a World Bank's structural adjustment loan, or an International Monetary Fund's extended fund facility, or some other agreement. In the case of projects implemented during ongoing structural reform, year-to-year real OER changes and changes in the country's conversion factors should be expected.

The Purchasing Power Parity Assumption. "Purchasing power parity" (PPP) implies that the exchange rate will adjust to maintain "parity" in the purchasing power of local and foreign currencies, when the rate of inflation in the home country is different from the rate of inflation among the country's major trading partners. For example, let us assume that local inflation is expected to occur at a rate of 10 percent per year over the next five years, while inflation in the country's trading partners is expected to average only 5 percent per year. The most direct way that parity in purchasing power can be maintained between the two currencies is for the local currency to depreciate at the following annual rate:

$$\text{Rate of depreciation} = \frac{(1 + 0.10)}{(1 + 0.05)} - 1 \qquad (18.1)$$

$$= 4.76 \text{ per cent per year}$$

If the OER were Rs 10 = $ 1 at the beginning of the five year period, the OER would be expected to change as indicated in Table 18.1.

Purchasing Power Parity Assumption.
Implies that the exchange rate will adjust to maintain "parity" in the purchasing power of local and foreign currencies, when the domestic inflation rate is different from the inflation rate of the country's main trading partners.

Table 18.1. Forecast of Nominal Exchange Rate Using Purchasing Power Parity Calculation

Year	OER at beginning of year (Rs/$)	OER at end of year (Rs/$)
1	10.00	10.48
2	10.48	10.98
3	10.98	11.50
4	11.50	12.05
5	12.05	12.62

Note: We assume domestic inflation at 10 per cent per year and foreign inflation at 5 per cent per year.

PPP without Trade Barriers. The calculation in Table 18.1 implicitly assumes that there are no trade or exchange barriers. Among other things, this assumption implies that the SER and OER are the same. We have said nothing of the "real" exchange rate in relation to the "nominal" exchange rate. Clearly, what was calculated in Table 18.1 was the nominal exchange rate. Let us now look at the calculation of the real exchange rate (again making the simplifying assumption that there are no trade and balance of payments distortions, which means that the SER and OER will continue to be the same).

Nominal and Real Exchange Rates. The nominal exchange rate after one year has devalued to Rs 10.48 = $ 1 in Table 18.1. Thus, it now takes Rs 10.48 to import a good costing $ 1 at our border. If we define "real" to mean constant prices (with a base period set at the beginning of year one), then to put the current rupee price of one dollar into base period rupees, we should divide Rs 10.48 by one plus the local inflation rate as follows:

$$\frac{\text{Nominal Rs } 10.48}{1 + 0.10} = \text{Real Rs } 9.524 \tag{18.2}$$

From this calculation, we can see that the real price of a dollar of foreign currency has decreased during the year. But because inflation in the foreign country has occurred at a rate of 5 percent during the past year, the foreign good that we could have bought a year ago for $ 1 in foreign exchange, now costs $1.05 in foreign exchange. What implication does that fact have for our real exchange rate calculation?

The nominal and real exchange rates are related by the ratio of domestic to foreign inflation.

Since we are working in real terms, we are interested in the exchange rate between foreign and local goods. In currency terms, that means that we will need an additional 5 percent in local currency to pay for the inflation in the dollar price of the foreign good that has occurred during the year. Let us multiply, then, the real rupees by the actual number of dollars required to get the real rate of exchange between local and foreign goods after one year— where "real" is defined in terms of a base period, such as the beginning of year one:

$$\text{Real Rs } 9.524 \times 1.05 = \text{Rs } 10 \qquad (18.3)$$

Thus, the "real" exchange rate is still Rs 10 = $ 1. We can see from Table 18.2 that this will be the case for each of the five years for which we have forecast the nominal OER in Table 18.1.

Table 18.2.   Forecast of Real Exchange Rate Using Purchasing Power Parity Calculation

1	2	3	4	5	6
Year	Nominal OER at end of year (Rs/$)	Local price index at end of year	Foreign price index at end of year	Ratio of price indexes	Real OER at end of year (Rs/$)
1	10.48	110.00	105.00	1.048	10.00
2	10.98	121.00	110.25	1.098	10.00
3	11.50	133.10	115.76	1.150	10.00
4	12.05	146.41	121.55	1.205	10.00
5	12.62	161.05	127.63	1.262	10.00

Note: We assume domestic inflation at 10 percent per year and foreign inflation at 5 percent per year.

The result in Column 6 can be obtained by dividing Column 2 by Column 5.

By comparing Table 18.2 with Table 18.1, we can see just what the simple application of PPP theory says about the nominal exchange rate: it says that the nominal exchange rate will adjust in the face of differing domestic and foreign inflation rates so as to maintain the same real exchange rate over time, other things being equal.

Now we come to the point where some analysts will be surprised. Note that we normally conduct investment analysis using constant prices; and note also that a preponderance of appraisals assume a

Purchasing Power Parity adjustment of the nominal exchange rate implies that the real exchange rate stays unchanged.

constant exchange rate during the life of the investment. By using constant prices as the typical practice, we implicitly assume that the nominal exchange rate will devalue each year (see Tables 18.1 and 18.2). We also know the rate at which the the nominal exchange rate will devalue. It will devalue by the ratio of one plus the respective inflation rates at home and abroad.

The preceding point regarding the implicit assumption of a devaluing exchange rate leads us to the politically sensitive issue of prices, such as the exchange rate. It is often possible to use "realistic" price forecasts, even for politically sensitive prices, without having to advertise their use and without incurring the wrath of the political hierarchy. These forecasts can be used implicitly in the worksheets without presenting them explicitly in the published project reports. Even sophisticated readers of the report will need the help of the report preparer to sort their way back to the price forecasts which underlay the final numbers. We shall return to this point in Chapter 20 when we discuss the presentation of project costs and price contingencies in local and foreign currencies.

PPP Adjustment with Trade Barriers. Let us move to the case in which there are trade and balance of payments barriers such that the SER and OER are not the same. From Part II we know that a weighted average tariff rate (WATR) of 25 percent would allow the OER to differ from the SER used in project appraisal by a factor of 1:1.25. Let us assume that the only border distortion affecting the prices of goods and services occurs in the form of tariffs and subsidies (all of which are accounted for in the WATR calculation). Let us also assume that there is no capital flight and that the demand and supply of foreign exchange is totally related to trade. This will allow us to work for the moment with only one SER.

When we use constant prices with a constant exchange rate, we implicitly assume PPP adjustment of the nominal exchange rate.

If the WATR is 25 percent, then our SER used in project appraisal would be related to the OER as follows:

$$SER = OER \times (1 + WATR) \tag{18.4}$$
$$OER = Rs\ 10/\$\ 1$$

It is possible to use realistic price forecasts, even for politically sensitive prices. These forecasts can be used implicitly in the worksheets without presenting them explicitly in the published reports.

Therefore:
$$SER = (Rs\ 10/\$\ 1) \times (1 + 0.25)$$
$$SER = Rs\ 12.5/\$\ 1$$

In forecasting the nominal and real OERs, we would first forecast the SER, as was done in Tables 18.1 and 18.2. Then we would have to forecast the WATR to determine the changes in the OER (see Table 18.3).

Table 18.3. Forecast of SER and Nominal OER: Purchasing Power Parity Calculation

1	2	3	4	5
Year	Ratio of domestic over foreign price indexes	Nominal SER at beginning of year (Rs/$)	Weighted average tariff rate at beginning of year	Nominal OER at end of year (Rs/$)[a]
1	1.048	12.50	0.25	10.00
2	1.098	13.72	0.25	10.98
3	1.150	14.37	0.25	11.50
4	1.205	15.06	0.25	12.05
5	1.262	15.77	0.25	12.62

Note: We assume a domestic inflation at 10 per cent per year and foreign inflation at 5 per cent per year.

    a. Column 5 = Column 3 divided by one plus Column 4.

PPP and the SER. In the real world, it is the SER that moves according to the ratios of domestic and foreign inflation. The OER is then related to the trade (and payments) policies that separate the SER and OER. Assuming that the WATR calculation has captured all of those effects, we estimate the OER by dividing the forecast SER by one plus the forecast WATR, as indicated in footnote **a** to Table 18.3. We could have forecast the nominal OER directly from the ratio of the inflation rates, as we did in Tables 18.1 and 18.2; but, to do so would have assumed that the WATR was unchanged during the five-year period over which the OER was being forecast.

Because the SCF is derived from the WATR, we can say that the forecast nominal OER is derived from the forecast SER and the forecast SCF. Recall that the SCF is related to the WATR as follows:

$$SCF = \frac{1}{1 + WATR} \qquad (18.5)$$

In the real world, it is the SER that moves according to the ratio of domestic to foreign inflation.

If the WATR is 0.25, as in Table 18.3, then the SCF is 0.80. Thus, the SCF has been forecast to remain constant in Table 18.3.

Now let us see what would happen to the OER if the government were to change the trade policy during the five-year forecast period. Table 18.4 recalculates Table 18.3 by using a different WATR assumption.

The WATR, the SCF and OER Adjustments. We can see the two impacts of the change in trade policy in Table 18.4. First, the increase in the average tariff and subsidy rate (WATR), from 25 percent in year 2 to 33 percent in year 3, causes the SCF to decrease from 0.80 to 0.75. Second, the change in trade policy causes the nominal OER to decrease, because the change in tariff rate overwhelms the effect of the continued high domestic inflation compared to foreign inflation. We can see the effect of the WATR change by comparing the entries in Column 6 of Table 18.4 with their counterparts in Column 5 of Table 18.3.

Table 18.4. Forecast of SER and Nominal OER: Purchasing Power Parity Calculation

1	2	3	4	5	6
Year	Ratio of domestic over foreign price indexes	Nominal SER at beginning of year (Rs/$)	Weighted average tariff rate at beginning of year	SCF	Nominal OER at beginning of year (Rs/$)
1	1.048	12.50	0.25	0.80	10.00
2	1.098	13.72	0.25	0.80	10.98
3	1.150	14.37	0.33	0.75	10.81
4	1.205	15.06	0.33	0.75	11.32
5	1.262	15.77	0.33	0.75	11.86

Note: We assume domestic inflation at 10 percent per year and foreign inflation at 5 percent per year.

Column 6 = Column 3 divided by one plus Column 4
         = Column 3 multiplied by Column 5.

Changes in the pattern of trade distortion will affect movements in the OER, after accounting for the effects of inflation.

Note that if the SCF changes, it does so because of policy changes that will affect the ratio of domestic prices to border price of one or more goods or services. Thus, the change in SCF normally implies a change in specific conversion factors also. That means a change in relative prices is occurring in the economy. How realistic is it to expect a change in the SCF? Given the changes in the nominal OER that are shown in Table 18.3, trade policy changes might well be expected to occur, either as the cause of the changes in the OER, or in reaction to the factors that are causing the OER to change.

Changing the SCF Changes the Real OER. What can we say about the real OER compared to the nominal OER? We can say that the real OER can be expected to change in response to a change in the SCF. Differing domestic and foreign inflation rates will not, by themselves, cause the real OER to change over time (though the differing inflation rates would likely be associated with changes in the nominal OER). Rather, it is the changes in the commercial or financial policy that the government undertakes in response to inflation, or to the devaluing exchange rate, that will cause the SCF to change.

Forecasting changes in these commercial and financial policies is difficult and is seldom done in the context of project appraisal. (There are exceptions to this generalization. For example, the Korea Economic Planning Board in the late 1970s made forecasts of the SCF that were based on the government's stated policy of rationalizing the country's tariff and subsidy system.) Because these forecasts are difficult to make, and because such forecasts are feared for their potential to destabilize the economy, they usually are not made in the context of project planning. Instead, certain standard assumptions tend to be made, which include:

   a. the real OER stays constant over the life of the project;

   b. consistent with **a**, the nominal OER makes purchasing power parity adjustments based on the difference between domestic and foreign inflation rates; and

   c. no major changes in domestic economic policy, or in trade policy, will be undertaken; thus, border and domestic distortions are expected to remain unchanged; and specific and average conversion factors—including the SCF—will remain unchanged during the life of the project.

These three assumptions are often made implicitly, without the analyst realizing the implications of the method of calculation that is being applied. Usually these assumptions are made for one or more of the following three reasons:

   a. these assumptions greatly simplify the calculations;

   b. the analyst often will have no basis for making any other assumptions; and

Differing domestic and foreign inflation rates will not, by themselves, cause the real official exchange rate to change over time. Rather, it is the changes in the government's commercial or financial policy that will cause the real OER, and therefore the standard conversion factor, to change.

c. political factors and the fear of destabilizing financial and foreign exchange markets may prohibit the analyst from using any other assumptions than the ones cited earlier.

Standard PPP Assumptions and the SAL Environment. The "standard" three assumptions cited in the preceding paragraph may appear to be unrealistic when the project that is being appraised is to take place within a "structural adjustment" environment. The structural adjustment program may change many of the economic parameters the project assumes to be constant. Indeed, the particular project that is being appraised may well be part of a set of interventions designed to bring about structural reform and changes in prevailing price relationships. In that case, we have the classic problem that relates to planning and appraising individual projects in a general equilibrium context.

Politics of Forecasting Inflation and Exchange Rates. The forecast of the domestic inflation rate may pose more of a problem than the forecast of the foreign inflation rate. Government forecasts of domestic inflation may be overly optimistic. Forecasts by external aid agencies may reflect the same bias, for a number of reasons—including the desire not to offend the host government. Because the exchange rate forecasts have links with the various project accounts, it is important that the analyst work with a reasonable estimate of the expected inflation rates. Thus, the analyst may have to work with an "unofficial" estimate and hide that forecast behind the tables that are presented in the reports. Likewise, he or she may have to also hide the forecast nominal OER behind the main tables and to present in the text only those tables that show the real OER. In Chapter 20, we shall demonstrate one method for developing the financing plan without explicitly showing the forecast nominal OER.

But how do we get the estimate of the actual domestic inflation rate? In most countries, it is not all that difficult to get—unofficially—the estimate of actual inflation. We may just to have to talk "off the record" to economists and officials in the agencies responsible for making such forecasts. They usually can tell us the approximate real inflation rate—if they trust us not to attribute the estimate to them, or to publish the estimate anywhere.

The forecast of domestic inflation rate may pose more of a problem than the forecast of the foreign inflation rate. Government forecasts of domestic inflation may be overly optimistic.

Information on Forecasts of International Inflation Rates. The forecast of foreign inflation can be obtained from the World Bank's "price forecasts for major primary commodities," which is mentioned at various points in Gittinger (1982). If there is a World Bank field office in the country, the resident staff of the Bank could be asked what international inflation rates are being used by the Bank for its own analyses. The World Bank staff refer to this rate as the "MUV," which stands for the "manufacturer's unit value index." The index relates to the kinds of goods and services that are used in World Bank-assisted projects, and is based on expected inflation rates in the industrialized countries that are members of the Organisation for Economic Co-operation and Development (OECD). The MUV is useful for estimating price contingencies (see Chapter 20). However, it is less useful as a measure of general inflation among a country's trading partners. First, the MUV is calculated for a group of OECD countries, which might not be representative of our country's trading partners. Second, the MUV represents only a small number of selected categories of traded goods. Other sources of information include bilateral aid agencies, such as the United States Agency for International Development (USAID); or multilateral organizations, such as the United Nations Development Programme (UNDP), the Food and Agricultural Organization of the United Nations (FAO), and the United Nations Industrial Development Organization (UNIDO); or the regional development banks, such as the Asian Development Bank, African Development Bank, Inter-American Development Bank, and others.

19. Point-in-Time and Interval Accounting Conventions

Summary. *Inflation and cost of capital force project planners to make explicit assumptions about the timing of project costs and benefits—not only between years, but also within years. Four different accounting practices are followed: beginning of year (BOY), end of year (EOY), middle of year (MOY), and continuous accounting.*

The World Bank uses EOY accounting for calculating the internal rate of return and other present values, and MOY assumption (approximating continuous accounting) for price contingency calculations. Many other development and government agencies use BOY accounting for discounted present value calculations. In addition, many financial calculators and financial software either use BOY accounting exclusively, or as the default mode. Simple procedures exist for adjusting present value calculations between EOY and BOY accounting to accommodate the needs of different agencies. Some of these are discussed in this chapter.

In both financial and economic accounting, there are certain assumptions that must be made regarding either the point in time, or the interval, over which costs and benefits accrue. Generally, flow concepts relate to intervals of time—such as, for example, one year, while stock or asset concepts relate to a particular point in time. Thus, for example, an income statement records revenues and expenses over an accounting interval, such as one quarter, or one year; similarly, a cash flow statement records cash inflows and outflows over an accounting interval, such as a cropping period, or a year. A balance sheet, in contrast, is drawn for a particular point in time—such as on the last day of the enterprise's fiscal year.

Similarly, discounted cash flow analysis may be conducted by using either continuous discounting methods (by using discounting methods based on discrete intervals), or by using discrete point-in-time assumptions. In most project appraisal applications, the point-in-time method of discounting is normally used for two reasons:

a. it is mathematically simpler; and

b. because of the uncertainty and inaccuracies that are inherent in project forecasts, the added mathematical precision implied by continuous discounting would represent spurious accuracy.

Discounted cash flow analysis may be conducted by using either point-in-time or interval accounting assumptions. In most project appraisals, the point-in-time method is used.

Obviously, the use of point-in-time assumptions in discounting has implications for the way financial accounts are set up and are related to each other.

If we are to discount on the basis of specific points in time, then we must make a decision about what points in time to assume for the cash flows that we will be discounting. Recall that cash flows represent "flows" that take place over intervals of time, rather than at one specific point in time.

There are choices regarding the point-in-time conventions used in cash flow analysis:

> **a.** beginning-of-year (BOY) accounting;
>
> **b.** middle-of-year (MOY) accounting; and
>
> **c.** end-of-year (EOY) accounting.

Some cash flow analysts will use one convention, while other analysts will use another. Also, we may sometimes find that one point-in-time accounting convention is used for one application by an analyst; while, in another application within the same project, the same analyst will use another accounting convention. For example, in calculating present values from cash flows, World Bank staff normally use the EOY accounting assumption; while in calculating price contingencies, the same staff may use MOY accounting assumptions (actually, continuous disbursement is assumed, with MOY chosen as an adequate approximation).

Beginning-of-Year Accounting. The BOY accounting practice assumes that all project expenditures and all project benefits occur on the first day of each year. Thus, for project year three, the costs and benefits that are recorded would be assumed to occur on the first day of the third year; for project year two, the costs and benefits would be assumed to occur on the first day of the second year; for project year one, the costs and benefits would be assumed to occur on the first day of the first year; and so on for the fourth through the final years of the project life. Note that, if the first year costs and benefits occur on the first day of year one, those costs and benefits would occur on the same day that we would normally use for expressing present values in the discounted cash flow analysis. Thus, in the BOY accounting approach, we would not discount the values that we show for the first year of our project's life.

Similarly, the values for the second year of the project's life would be assumed to occur only one year from the time that we use as the base for the present values; thus, we would discount second year values by only one year; and we would discount third year values for only two years, and so on. Table 19.1 shows this calculation and relates it to MOY and EOY accounting alternatives.

Because the BOY accounting method does not discount the first year

Beginning-of-Year Accounting.
Assumes that all project expenditures and all project benefits occur on the first day of each year. In this approach, we do not discount the values shown in the first year.

value, it has become common practice in using this method to simply assign "zero" to the first year. Each succeeding year would be numbered in sequence: the second project year would be identified as year "one," the third year as year "two," and so on. This practice allows us to use consistently the year number as the exponent in calculating the discount factors that are used in computing the present values.

End-of-Year Accounting. The EOY accounting approach assumes that all costs and all benefits occur on the last day of each year. Thus, year one costs and benefits would occur on the last day of year one; year two costs and benefits would occur on the last day of year two; and so on for each year of the project's life. Because the first year's values occur one year away from the date on which present values will be based, the first year values will be discounted by one year in the discounted cash flow calculations; the second year values will be discounted by two years; and so on. We can see that this will result in lower present values when compared with the present values generated by using the BOY accounting approach.

Table 19.1. Accounting Assumptions and Discounting Conventions

Project year		Project cash flow		
Using BOY assumption	Using EOY assumption	Costs	Benefits	Net cash flow
0	1	1000	0	(1000)
1	2	500	0	(500)
2	3	50	300	250
3	4	50	400	350
4	5	50	400	350
5	6	50	400	350
6	7	50	400	350
7	8	50	400	350
8	9	50	400	350
9	10	50	400	350
10	11	50	700	650

	BOY	EOY
NPV at 10 percent	411	374
B/C at 10 percent	1.24	1.24
IRR (percent)	15.25	15.25

End-of-Year Accounting. *Assumes that all project costs and benefits occur on the last day of each year. In this approach, the values of the first year are discounted.*

Decision Criteria and Accounting Conventions. Note that, while the absolute values of the discounted present worths will be lower using EOY accounting, the relative values (i.e., any comparison based on ratios) will be unaffected. This fact is demonstrated in Table 19.1, where the internal rate of return (IRR), net present value (NPV), and benefit-cost (B/C) ratios are calculated for a project based on EOY and BOY accounting conventions. Notice that the IRR and the B/C calculations will be the same no matter which timing assumption is used. This will be true because both are ratio-based measures in which both the numerator and the denominator are multiplied or divided by the same coefficient, leaving the actual ratio unchanged. The NPV, in contrast, is an absolute number; thus, the NPV will be different in absolute terms. Note further that the NPV in the EOY case is equal to the NPV in the BOY case divided by one plus the discount factor. The relationship is indicated by:

$$PV(EOY) = \frac{PV(BOY)}{(1 + r)} \qquad (19.1)$$

where:

PV(EOY) = present value using EOY accounting;

PV(BOY) = present value using BOY accounting; and

r = discount rate used in calculating PV(BOY).

Thus, from Table 19.1, we have:

$$374 = \frac{411}{(1 + 0.10)}$$

Note that, though the *absolute* value of the NPV will be affected by the choice of EOY or BOY accounting, the ranking of projects based on NPVs will not be affected, since the *relative* values will remain the same. This is demonstrated in Table 19.2, where five sample project cash flows are ranked according to NPV, with the NPV calculated using both EOY and BOY accounting. Note that in both calculations, Project E is the top-ranked project, while Project A is ranked at the bottom, and Project C is marginal in both cases. The rankings are unaffected because the NPVs using EOY accounting are in each case equal to the respective MOY-accounting NPVs divided by one plus the discount rate of 10 percent.

The difference between these accounting methods is discussed here because it will be useful for us to understand which agencies use which approaches, and to be able to recognize which computing tool has been programmed to use EOY accounting and which one has been programmed to use BOY. By understanding the difference, we might be able to save time and embarrassment of having our calculations challenged, or sent back to be redone—valuable time

Though the absolute value of the net present value (NPV) will be affected by the EOY or BOY accounting methods, the ranking of projects based on NPVs will not be affected, since the relative values will remain the same.

that could have been better used in making real improvements in the project plan rather than in responding to questions on the calculations.

Table 19.2. Comparing Net Present Worth of Five Projects Using End-of-Year and Beginning-of-Year Accounting

Year	Cash flows of projects				
	A	B	C	D	E
1	(1000)	(1000)	(1000)	(1000)	(1000)
2	80	120	154	170	300
3	80	120	154	170	300
4	80	120	154	170	300
5	80	120	154	170	200
6	80	120	154	170	300
7	80	120	154	170	300
8	80	120	154	170	300
9	80	120	154	170	300
10	80	120	154	170	300
11	80	120	154	170	300
12	80	120	154	170	300

NPV at 10 percent using the accounting method of:

	A	B	C	D	E
BOY	(480)	(221)	0	104	949
EOY	(437)	(201)	0	95	862

Which Agencies Use Which Accounting Conventions? Having said that different organizations and different analysts use different accounting conventions, let us briefly discuss some examples of these differences. The World Bank, from whose projects the examples in Gittinger (1982) and in this volume are taken, normally uses EOY accounting in its present value calculations. Many other organizations—for example, the water resources agencies in the United States to which much of the professional economics literature on project appraisal methods has been oriented—use BOY accounting. Financial software and financial calculators generally are programmed to use BOY accounting. Some calculators will allow us to reset them to use EOY accounting, some will not.

The World Bank uses EOY accounting in its present value conventions. Some other agencies use the BOY method.

Adjusting Calculators and Software for Accounting Conventions. Software on project appraisal written by or for the World Bank will generally use the EOY approach. However, most financial calculators available commercially are programmed to calculate present values using BOY accounting. In addition, much of the financial analysis software commercially written for use on microcomputers, minicomputers, and main frame computers also use the BOY approach in discounted cash flow analysis. Some software programs may allow change in the accounting assumption.

In all cases, two simple methods exist for "tricking" the software into converting the present value calculations from one accounting convention to another. First, for software that uses a BOY approach, to convert the calculations to EOY accounting, we may:

a. put a "dummy" year zero into our cash flow tables, giving a zero value to all benefits and costs for that year; then give the first "real" project year the year number "one," the second project year the number "two," and so on; or

b. divide the present value by one plus the discount rate that was used—after the software has calculated the present values.

Second, for software that uses the EOY approach, to convert the calculations to BOY accounting, we may multiply the present values by one plus the discount rate that was used in calculating the present values.

Table 19.3. Discount Factor Calculations with Different Point-in-Time Accounting Conventions

Year numbers			Related discount factors		
BOY	MOY	EOY	BOY	MOY	EOY
0	0.5	1	1.0000	0.9535	0.9091
1	1.5	2	0.9091	0.8668	0.8264
2	2.5	3	0.8264	0.7880	0.7513
3	3.5	4	0.7513	0.7164	0.6830
4	4.5	5	0.6830	0.6512	0.6209
5	5.5	6	0.6209	0.5920	0.5645
6	6.5	7	0.5645	0.5382	0.5132
7	7.5	8	0.5132	0.4893	0.4665
8	8.5	9	0.4665	0.4448	0.4241
9	9.5	10	0.4241	0.4044	0.3855
10	10.5	11	0.3855	0.3676	0.3505

Note: The discount factors are based on a cost of capital of 10 percent per year. This particular discount rate is chosen for illustrative purposes only.

Most calculators and computer softwares are programmed to use the BOY approach.

MOY for Price Contingency Calculations. The MOY accounting is used mostly as a shortcut to calculating price contingencies. There are two ways in which the MOY approach may be viewed:

a. as an assumption that all costs and benefits occur on the first day of the seventh month of each year; or

b. as an assumption that costs and benefits are spread out evenly during the year, and that MOY accounting is a simple approximation of this occurrence.

Assumption **b** is the one that underlies the use of MOY accounting in price contingency calculations in the World Bank. Using the MOY assumption is usually viewed as a sufficiently accurate reflection of the true expected pattern of cost accrual, considering the uncertainties that are involved in preparing the project implementation plan. This point is discussed further in Chapter 20.

❖

Middle-of-Year Accounting.

Assumes that all costs and benefits:

1. occur on the first day of the seventh month of each year; or

2. are spread out evenly during the year.

This approach is used mostly as a shortcut approximation to continuous project implementation in calculating price contingencies.

20. Calculating Price Contingencies

Summary. Calculating price contingencies is a mundane part of project financial planning, but it is also an extension of the price and exchange rate forecasts which must be made for the purpose of calculating financial and economic returns. Inflation rates, and assumptions regarding the timing of project expenditures, affect the amount of money that needs to be added to the base costs and physical contingencies to implement the project. World Bank staff normally assume "continuous" implementation throughout each year and approximate this with a MOY accounting assumption in calculating price contingencies. Project financing tables may be presented in any of a number of equivalent ways; some of these are discussed in this chapter.

Price Contingencies With One Currency

Starting from Base Costs. In calculating price contingencies, our objective should be to provide additional money in the financing plan to pay for the inflation that occurs between the time a project is started and the date on which purchases for the project are made. The drawing of project implementation charts—such as bar charts, CPM diagrams, or similar schedules, will help us in estimating the years (and even months) in which project expenditures will take place. These charts also will make clear that project implementation and project expenditures will not, in fact, occur only on the first or the last day of each year. Rather, these expenditures will occur throughout each year.

Timing of Expenditures and Effect of Inflation. Some of the money that is shown for year one in the base costs will be spent on day one of year one. For that particular day's expenditure, the base cost, allocated in constant prices is expected to be sufficient at the time of appraisal. The reason is that for that day—and that day only—constant and current prices are the same (if, in fact, that day has been used as the "base" in the calculations. Note that in the following paragraphs, we shall use the term "base costs" to include physical contingencies, unless stated otherwise).

In contrast, for the last day of the first year, we will need to provide a price contingency for that day's expenditure sufficient to cover one year's worth of inflation. For the implementation that takes place on the first day of the seventh month of the project, we will need to provide price contingencies to cover one-half of a year's inflation.

If we assume that implementation occurs continuously during each year, we might calculate the price contingencies by dividing each

In calculating price contingencies, our objective should be to provide additional money in the financing plan to pay for any inflation that occurs between the time a project is started and the date on which purchases are made for the project.

year's base costs by the number of days in the year and then providing each year's price contingency in 365 parts (see Table 20.1). (Note that the calculation shown in Table 20.1 is rarely, if ever, used in practice.)

Table 20.1. Base Costs and Price Contingencies

Year	Base costs	Expected inflation (percent per year)
1	1,000	12
2	1,200	12
3	2,000	12
4	500	12

Total: 4,700

Year one price contingency:

Daily cost: $1,000/365   = $2.7397

Daily inflation: 12 percent / 365 =   0.0329 percent

Days of year one	Day's portion of base cost ($ 000)	Day's cost in current prices ($ 000)	Price contingency ($ 000)
1	$2.7397 \times (1+.000329)^{\wedge}1$	2.7406	0.000900
2	$2.7397 \times (1+.000329)^{\wedge}2$	2.7415	0.001801
3	$2.7397 \times (1+.000329)^{\wedge}3$	2.7424	0.002703
4	$2.7397 \times (1+.000329)^{\wedge}4$	2.7433	0.003604
5	$2.7397 \times (1+.000329)^{\wedge}5$	2.7442	0.004506
6	$2.7397 \times (1+.000329)^{\wedge}6$	2.7451	0.005408
7	$2.7397 \times (1+.000329)^{\wedge}7$	2.7460	0.006311
8	$2.7397 \times (1+.000329)^{\wedge}8$	2.7469	0.007214
9	$2.7397 \times (1+.000329)^{\wedge}9$	2.7478	0.008117
10	$2.7397 \times (1+.000329)^{\wedge}10$	2.7487	0.009020
|	|	|	|
365	$2.7397 \times (1+.000329)^{\wedge}365$	3.0890	0.349245

Total for year: $62.64

Price contingencies are often used in making a financing plan when the project cost tables are originally set up in constant prices. This is the approach used by World Bank analysts.

Note: The "total for year" was calculated in a separate worksheet before being transferred to this table. Because this method is not normally used for calculating price contingencies, no formula is provided for this calculation. The results are presented for purposes of illustration only.

Alternative Assumptions for MOY Accounting. To an experienced analyst, there is implied accuracy in Table 20.1 that is not warranted by the base cost data with which the analyst normally will be working. Therefore, making detailed calculations, as done in Table 20.1, would be a waste of time. Many analysts approximate the calculations in the table by assuming that project expenditures occur :

a. in the middle of each year and reflecting that assumption by using the MOY convention in numbering the years that are reflected in the exponent of the compounding calculation (see Equation 20.1); or

b. in the middle of each year and reflecting that assumption by using one-half of the year's inflation in calculating the price contingency for each year (see Equation 20.2).

We can see the impacts of these alternatives by using these approaches on the base cost data from Table 20.1 and then comparing the price contingencies between these and the preceding method of calculating price contingencies. First, let us compare the calculation, using the MOY year-numbering option, with the price contingency for year one that is calculated at the bottom of Table 20.1.

$$PC(n) = BC(n) \times [(1 + i)^{n - 0.5} - 1] \qquad (20.1)$$

where:
$PC(n)$ = price contingency for the nth year;
$BC(n)$ = base costs for the nth year, and
$\quad i$ = the inflation rate (assumed here to be constant at 12 percent per year throughout)

$$
\begin{aligned}
PC(1) \quad &= 1{,}000 \times [(1+0.12)^{1-0.5} - 1] \\
&= 1{,}000 \times [(1.12)^{0.5} - 1] \\
&= 1{,}000 \times [1.0583 - 1]
\end{aligned}
$$

$$PC(1) \quad = \quad \$58.30$$

Recall that, in this chapter, we use the term "base cost" as an abbreviation for "base cost plus physical contingencies."

Daily Accounting Compared to MOY Short-Cuts. We can see that the short-cut method of using MOY accounting will approximate the price contingency that would result from the daily disbursement assumption of Table 20.1. Generally, such simplifying assumptions tend to reduce the amounts that are allocated for price contingencies. This tendency is also indicated in the second simplification that is often used in which the inflation rate is halved for the last year of each calculation.

Results of using the shortcut method of middle-of-year accounting will approximate the price contingency provided under the daily accounting method. Most analysts use the shortcut method.

$$PC(n) = BC(n) \times [(1 + i)^{n-1} + i/2 - 1] \qquad (20.2)$$

$$PC(1) = 1000 \times [(1.12)^0 + 0.12/2 - 1]$$

$$= 1000 \times [1 + 0.06 - 1] = \$ 60$$

Note that in this very simple calculation, the price contingency is slightly different from that arrived at using the daily calculation shown in Table 20.1; and it is also different from the price contingency that was calculated using Equation 20.1. Table 20.2 shows the price contingencies for the base costs shown at the top of Table 20.1 using three different calculations:

   a. daily calculation of price contingencies as shown in Table 20.1;

   b. the approach of reducing the exponent by one-half year as shown in Equation 20.1; and

   c. the approach of reducing the last year's inflation by one-half as shown in Equation 20.2.

Shortcuts and Direction of Error. We can see from Table 20.2 that the more "detailed" calculations generally provide higher provisions for price contingencies. In other words, if we calculate price contingencies on a daily basis, we will show larger price contingencies than if we do so assuming weekly or annual disbursements. However, the differences will, in most cases, not be major. Thus, analysts will usually choose the easiest method of calculation.

Table 20.2 Price Contingencies Using Different Methods of Calculation

Year	Base costs ($ '000)	Expected inflation (percent per year)	Price contingencies First method	Second method	Third method
			(in dollars)		
1	1,000	12	62.64	58.30	60.00
2	1,200	12	228.19	222.36	216.00
3	2,000	12	665.95	655.06	628.80
4	500	12	246.47	243.42	232.46
Total:	4,700		1,203.25	1,179.14	1,137.26

Note: The "first method" refers to the method of calculation used in Table 20.1. The "second method" is drawn from Equation 20.1, and the "third method" from Equation 20.2.

Underestimates of Price Contingencies. Note that providing appropriate price contingencies can be very difficult in some circumstances. First, because of shortcut calculations, there will be a tendency to underallocate price contingencies (see Table 20.2). Second, this tendency can be compounded when project managers, politically sensitive to governments' desire, show very low official rates of domestic inflation. Third, the process is complicated further by differences in domestic and foreign inflation; but, if these rates can be anticipated (and there are no other effects on the exchange rate), they can be handled. Fourth, the possibility of unanticipated changes in the exchange rate (i.e., those not captured in the purchasing power parity calculation, if that assumption was used in making the project tables) can greatly complicate price contingency calculations.

This fourth problem would exist, for example, in cases in which a seriously overvalued exchange rate has been maintained for some time and in which it is clear that adjustment in the rate is overdue. In those cases, the government will not wish to have project analysts or anyone else forecasting a change in the exchange rate; and the analyst will have great difficulty in allocating the appropriate amounts of local currency equivalents (or of foreign exchange equivalents). In these cases, a change in the exchange rate is "anticipated;" but, it is not allowed to be reflected in the project planning documents.

Unanticipated Exchange Rate Adjustments. When the exchange rate adjusts in a manner different from that which was anticipated (i.e., in most cases, the purchasing power parity adjustment), it can create havoc on the financial management of projects that are under implementation. Unanticipated adjustments in the exchange rate can seriously disrupt the financial plans that have been made and can leave projects with either too little money, or too much money. For example, during the period of rapid appreciation of the U.S. dollar in the early 1980s, many World Bank-assisted projects for which loan assistance had been allocated in U.S. dollars found themselves with large undisbursed balances.

In retrospect, because of the temporary increase in the purchasing power of the U.S. dollar, too much money had been allocated in terms of that currency. Similarly, because of the rapid devaluation of the Philippine peso, locally financed projects under implementation in the Philippines during the early part of the 1980s found themselves with inadequate allocations of the local currency required for the foreign components of those projects. And project of all types that were in implementation in late 1986 and early 1987 in Nigeria, were seriously affected by the more than three-fold change in the naira-to-dollar exchange rate.

Unanticipated exchange rate changes disrupt project financial

The use of shortcut methods sometimes tends to underallocate price contingencies. This can be compounded when analysts, politically sensitive to governments' desires, show low official rates of domestic inflation.

Exchange rate adjustments that are different from purchasing power parity adjustments can create havoc on project financing plans.

planning through two mechanisms: First, changes in the local currency cost of providing the foreign exchange (or vice versa in foreign-financed projects, such as the World Bank-assisted projects discussed earlier) directly affect the ability of the implementing agency to buy the materials and services that must be purchased in the currency other than that in which accounts and allocations are made. Second, because the markets for traded and nontraded goods are interrelated, changes in the local currency equivalent of the foreign exchange prices of traded goods will indirectly affect the local currency prices of nontraded goods, thus reducing the purchasing power of the allocations for the local currency components of the projects.

Table 20.3. Price Contingency Calculations with Two Currencies: Presentation in Local Currency Equivalents

Project year	Base costs Local (Rs 000)	Foreign	Local annual rate of inflation (percent)	Price contingencies[a] Local (Rs 000)	Foreign
1	1,000	2,000	12	58.3	116.6
2	1,200	4,000	12	222.4	741.2
3	2,000	8,000	12	655.1	2,620.3
4	500	4,000	12	243.4	1,947.3
Total:	4,700	18,000		1,179.1	5,425.4
Grand total					29,304.5

Note: The presentation of price contingency in local currency is based on a real official exchange rate of Rs 10 = $ 1, which implies purchasing power parity adjustment of the nominal official exchange rate as follows:

	Rs/$
Beginning of year 1	10.00
Middle of year 1	10.33
Middle of year 2	11.02
Middle of year 3	11.75
Middle of year 4	12.53

a. Both the local and foreign price contingencies are based on the local inflation rate of 12 percent per year.

The purchasing power parity assumption is often considered a politically acceptable way to calculate price contingencies in foreign exchange because it hides inflation-related changes in the nominal exchange rate.

PPP and Price Contingencies. We saw in preceding chapters, how the purchasing power parity assumption is often used in forecasting exchange rate changes and in setting up project tables. This assumption is nothing more than a politically acceptable way of anticipating inflation-driven exchange rate adjustments—partly because it hides the inflation-related changes in the nominal official exchange rate (see Table 20.3). The key to all of these calculations (and to project planning in general) lies in anticipating the changes that are likely to take place during the life of the project. If we can anticipate these changes (note that the word "anticipate" is simply another term for "forecast"), then we may use the mathematical techniques that are discussed in Gittinger (1982) and in this book, in order to analyze the implications of these changes on the project and to present our results in a systematic manner.

Up to this point, we have discussed techniques for calculating price contingencies, and we have discussed exchange rate forecasts using the purchasing power parity calculation. In the next section, we will bring these two sets of techniques together and will introduce three methods of calculating price contingencies when there are two currencies involved—foreign exchange as well as local currency.

Calculating Price Contingencies with Two Currencies

The process of calculating price contingencies requires a bit more thought when we deal with both local currency and foreign exchange. Not only must we anticipate the inflation rate, we must also anticipate changes in the nominal and real official exchange rates. Since most projects in developing countries involve costs in both local and foreign currencies, our discussion will not be complete until we have demonstrated techniques for dealing with two currencies in calculating project cost and project financing tables.

In Chapter 18, we discussed the use of the purchasing power parity assumption in forecasting the exchange rate. In this section, we demonstrate the use of that assumption in making a project financing plan. In the process, we will discuss three prominently used ways of presenting the price contingency and financing plan calculations. The differences among these three ways are basically mechanical. Note that the decision regarding which method to use in making the presentation is independent of the decision on which mathematical method to use in making the calculations of the price contingencies (i.e., whether to use Equation 20.1, Equation 20.2, or some other calculation device).

The two-currency presentation of the project financing table does not require that the exchange rate be shown. Instead, this method uses both the domestic and foreign inflation rates in calculating the local currency and foreign exchange price contingencies, rather than explicitly showing the changes in exchange rate forecast. This approach is demonstrated in Table 20.4. Note that the table that is presented in the appraisal report would not necessarily present columns 4 and 5 of Table 20.4. This method is most suitable to one of two situations:

    a. when allocations of foreign currency and local currency are made separately and are allocated in the individual currencies; or

b. when the exchange rate is being forecast separately—particularly when some other forecast method than the purchasing power parity assumption is to be used in making the exchange rate forecast.

The one-currency presentation in local currency of the project financing table requires that the foreign exchange costs be converted into local currency (or sometimes vice versa). This presentation will require that some assumption be made about changes in the exchange rate over the life of the project. The most commonly used assumption is the purchasing power parity adjustment, which means that the same real OER is used from year one through the final year of project implementation. It also means that we will have to show explicitly only the local inflation rate (if the tables are shown in local currency equivalents), though elsewhere we may have to deal with the foreign inflation rate and any other factors that may cause the exchange rate to change. This method is demonstrated in Table 20.3.

Table 20.4. Price Contingency Calculations with Two Currencies: Presentation in Both Currencies

1	2	3	4	5	6	7
	Base costs		Annual Inflation rates (in percent)		Price contingencies[a]	
Project year	Local (Rs 000)	Foreign ($ 000)	Local	Foreign	Local (Rs 000)	Foreign ($ 000)
1	1,000	200	12	5	58.3	4.9
2	1,200	400	12	5	222.4	30.4
3	2,000	800	12	5	655.1	103.8
4	500	400	12	5	243.4	74.5
Total:	**4,700**	**1,800**			**1,179.1**	**213.6**

Note: In presenting both currencies, we have used Equation 20.1. Note that 12-percent domestic inflation was used to calculate price contingencies for the local cost component, while 5-percent foreign inflation was used to calculate the price contingencies on the foreign component. Because both currencies are shown, there is no need to indicate the exchange rate between the two currencies. See also Tables 20.6 and 20.7.

a. Calculations of local price contingency:
First year: $1,000 \times [(1.12) - 1]^{0.5}$ = 58.3
Second year: $1,200 \times [(1.12) - 1]^{1.5}$ = 222.4
Third year: $2,000 \times [(1.12) - 1]^{2.5}$ = 655.1
Fourth year: $500 \times [(1.12) - 1]^{3.5}$ = 243.4

The two-currency presentation of the project financing table requires the use of both domestic and foreign inflation rates to calculate local currency and foreign exchange price contigencies. The one-currency presentation requires that the foreign exchange costs be converted into local currency, or vice versa.

The one-currency presentation in foreign exchange allows the assumption on the local inflation rate to be implicitly made, but presentationally hidden. This method presents the project financing plan in foreign exchange rather than in local currency, showing foreign currency values for both local currency and foreign exchange and dealing explicitly only with the foreign inflation rate (usually in a footnote, rather than as a column in the table).

This method of calculating the project financing plan allows us to:

a. deal implicitly with the domestic inflation rate, a politically sensitive topic in an inflation-ridden economy; and

b. avoid the increasingly large numbers that occur in later years of project implementation when the financing plan is shown in (a rapidly devaluing) local currency.

This method can be important in inflation-ridden economies, such as Brazil's, where it is common practice to convert all tables into foreign exchange equivalents. Note, however, that the equivalence of the foreign exchange presentation and the local currency presentation of the price contingencies is not obvious from the price contingencies alone. The conversion back into local currency at the nominal OER must include not only the contingencies, but also the base costs. To see that the same nominal amount of financing is provided by the foreign exchange presentation, compare Tables 20.6 and 20.7.

In presenting project tables, it is possible to use combinations of the three methods mentioned in the preceding paragraphs. For example, we may choose to show calculation of local and foreign price contingencies separately—as in Table 20.4—before combining them into a local-currency-equivalent presentation. This would be particularly true in cases in which changes in exchange rate forecast are not those that would be expected under purchasing power parity adjustments.

Whatever method is used in calculating price contingencies, the sum of the base costs (including physical contingencies) and the price contingencies should equal the total project costs stated in nominal terms. Note that, because the price contingencies were calculated using the MOY accounting convention, the sum of base costs and price contingencies will equal nominal project costs stated in middle-of-year terms. In other words, if we were to choose to work in nominal prices, rather than in constant prices, in setting up the cash flows for discounting purposes (assuming that EOY discounting is to be used), we would need to inflate first-year costs and benefits by one-half a year, second year costs and benefits by one and one-half years, and so forth—to be consistent with the methods demonstrated earlier for calculating price contingencies.

The one-currency method of presenting the project financing table in foreign exchange allows the assumption on the local inflation rate to be implicitly made, but presentationally hidden. This method can be important in inflation-ridden economies.

The MOY accounting convention that has become standard practice in calculating price contingencies and project financing plans creates a bit of inconsistency among the various tables in the appraisal report. One inconsistency arises in comparing discounted cash flow (DCF) calculations with price contingency calculations. In the DCF calculations, the standard practice is to use either an EOY accounting assumption (e.g., in the World Bank), or to use the BOY accounting assumption; in contrast, the price contingencies are calculated under the assumption that costs and benefits accrue either at mid-year, or throughout the year.

Traditional financial statements which are used to analyze the project's farm enterprises that are fairly large are also commonly drawn in nominal terms. Consistency with the project financing plan would dictate that the projection of these accounts use the MOY assumption, or that they assume that the enterprise's expenditures and revenues will occur and be recorded in nominal, historical terms evenly throughout the year. Because financial statements *ex post* are based on nominal, historical costs and revenues which occur throughout the year, the previous financial statements of the enterprise will likely come closest to approximating the MOY basis of the price contingency calculations.

The use of MOY accounting in making the project financing plan means that all associated forecasts also should be made as of the middle of each year (or, equivalently, should assume continuous accrual). The most important case in point is the exchange rate forecast that is used in converting from one currency into another in the project financing tables (see footnote **a** in Table 20.3). If this and other forecasts used in making the project cost tables are not calculated on an accounting basis that is consistent with the price contingency calculations, the tables used in making the project financing plan will not add up correctly.

Financial statement projections made using MOY accounting may match up better with historical financial statements based on actual accruals.

If MOY accounting is used for price contingency calculations, then all other forecasts which are used with the financing plan should also be based on MOY assumptions.

Table 20.5. Price Contingency Calculations with Two Currencies: Presentation in Foreign Currency Equivalents

Project year	Base costs Local Foreign ($ 000)		Local annual rate of inflation (percent)	Price contingencies Local Foreign ($ 000)	
1	100	200	5	2.5	4.9
2	120	400	5	9.1	30.4
3	200	800	5	25.9	103.8
4	50	400	5	9.3	74.5
Total:	470	1,800		46.8	213.6
Grand total				**$2,530.4**	

Note: The presentation of price contingency in foreign currency equivalents is based on a real official exchange rate of Rs 10 = $ 1, which implies purchasing power parity adjustment of the nominal official exchange rate as shown in the footnote of Table 20.4.

Table 20.6. Project Costs in Nominal Mid-Year Terms: Presentation in Local Currency Equivalents

Project year	Base costs Local Foreign (Rs 000)		Price contingencies Local Foreign (Rs 000)		Nominal[a] project costs (Rs 000)
1	1,000	2,000	58.3	116.6	3,174.9
2	1,200	4,000	222.4	741.2	6,163.6
3	2,000	8,000	655.1	2,620.3	13,275.4
4	500	4,000	243.4	1,947.3	6,690.7
Total:	4,700	18,000	1,179.1	5,425.4	29,304.6

Note: The presentation of project costs in local currency equivalents is based on a real official exchange rate of Rs 10 = $1, which implies purchasing power parity adjustment of the nominal official exchange rate as follows:

	Rs/$
Beginning of year 1	10.00
Middle of year 1	10.33
Middle of year 2	11.02
Middle of year 3	11.75
Middle of year 4	12.53

a. In prices as of the middle of each respective year.

Table 20.7. Project Costs in Nominal Mid-year Terms: Conversion of Foreign Currency to Local Currency

Project year	Costs Local ($ 000)	Foreign	Price contingencies[a] Local ($ 000)	Foreign	Nominal OER	Nominal total costs (Rs 000)
1	100	200	2.5	4.9	10.33	3,175
2	120	400	9.1	30.4	11.02	6,164
3	200	800	25.9	103.8	11.75	13,275
4	50	400	9.3	74.5	12.53	6,691
Total:	470	1,800	46.8	213.6		29,305
Grand total						**$2,530**

Note: The presentation of price contingency in foreign currency equivalents is based on a real official exchange rate of Rs 10 = $ 1, which implies purchasing power parity adjustment of the nominal official exchange rate as shown in the footnote of Table 20.4. ❖

21. The Discount Rate for Project Appraisal

Summary. *A project's benefits and costs occur over time. These impacts, which occur at different points, must be made comparable at a specific point in time. A discount rate must be defined in terms of the numeraire that is being used, and that rate must then be used to discount these impacts to present values and in a common unit of account. The discount rate is defined in terms of the rate of fall of the numeraire over time. If a consumption numeraire is used, the discount rate may be referred to as the "consumption rate of interest." If a foreign exchange numeraire is used, the discount rate may be referred to as the "accounting rate of interest."*

Eventually, we must identify the stream of incremental net benefits arising from a proposed investment and express those net benefits in the present value of some chosen unit of account—the so-called numeraire. As explained in Chapter 10 of Gittinger (1982), if the present value of the incremental net benefits—expressed in values relative to the numeraire—is positive, then the investment should be undertaken.

The incremental net benefit of each year in the stream of benefits is expressed in terms of the then-current value of the numeraire. Thus, we must somehow compare the value of the numeraire in each succeeding year of the project to the value of the numeraire at the base period. This is normally done by using discount rates, or more commonly, a single discount rate.

The task of the discount rate is to deal with the fall over time in the real value of the numeraire. In the approach used by the World Bank and discussed in this volume, issues of inflation, uncertainty, and time value are dealt with in separate steps. Chapter 17, in particular, has dealt with adjustments for inflation. In Gittinger (1982), Chapter 10 discusses techniques for dealing with risk and uncertainty. The following discussion will treat the issue of pure time-related value of the numeraire, apart from considerations of inflation, or uncertainty.

Once benefits and costs are expressed in constant terms (in terms of purchasing power relative to the present), the next step is to compare total costs and revenues over the life of the project. This can be done by taking into account how the value of the numeraire changes over this time relative to its value at present. For example, let us consider spending Sh 100 on consumers' goods this year and spending the equivalent (in constant prices) on the same goods next year. If we know that our real income (in terms of this

The task of the discount rate is to measure the fall in the real value of the numeraire over time.

year's shillings) will increase next year, we will probably judge that Sh 100 of consumption *then* is not worth as much as Sh 100 of consumption *now*.

If we discount next year's consumption by 10 percent, Sh 100 of income used for consumption next year is worth Sh 90 of consumption now (Sh 100 x 1/1.10 = Sh 90). In other words, the value of our consumption numeraire relative to its present value has declined by 10 percent during the year. In the simplest case, we might consider this to be the constant rate of decline in the value of the numeraire from year to year.

In the literature on discount rates, the rate of decline in the value of the consumption numeraire is known as the consumption rate of interest (CRI). [If a foreign exchange numeraire is used, the discount rate is called the accounting rate of interest (ARI). These rates are sometimes referred to as the "social discount rate."] The CRI is the rate at which some group's consumption now can be substituted for that same group's consumption later.

Another way to look at CRI is to consider that if next year's consumption (Ct+1) is equal to **1+CRI** times present consumption (Ct), then **1+CRI** represents the value of next year's consumption relative to this year's. The reference group would then be indifferent between consuming either **Ct** or **Ct+1**, since the values of the two would be the same. This would be the case, by definition, whenever:

$$\frac{Ct+1}{Ct} = 1 + CRI \qquad\qquad (21.1)$$

[For examples of the mathematical derivation of the CRI in economic models where a single consumption good is the numeraire, see Squire and van der Tak (1975), pp. 130-140; and Dervis, Martin and Wijnbergen (1984), pp. 40-41.]

Note that the choice of a numeraire determines the social discount rate used to compare and add up the returns to a public investment project over time. The acceptability of an investment (a positive NPV at the social discount rate) will not depend upon the choice of a numeraire (although the size of the NPV will likely vary depending upon the numeraire chosen).

The rate of decline in the value of the consumption numeraire is known as the consumption rate of interest. If a foreign exchange numeraire is used, the discount rate is called the accounting rate of interest. Both rates are referred to as the social discount rate.

In the efficiency approach discussed in Gittinger (1982) and in this volume, additions to the incomes of different groups in an economy are considered equally valuable. The force of this approach is to equate also the value of income in private or public hands. In addition, consumption and investment (whether private or public) are treated as equally valuable. This implies that no constraints limit a country's ability to achieve rates of saving and investment necessary to place the economy on some strategically determined optimal path of growth. Consequently, this simple efficiency approach proceeds on the assumption that the discount rate appropriate for the Squire-van der Tak foreign exchange numeraire (the ARI), and for the consumption numeraire (the CRI), are at all times the same. Moreover, the relative value of public and private income is always unity.

The chief advantage for making the assumptions in the preceding paragraph, in spite of their questionable plausibility, is that we can then substitute the ARI (a parameter which can, in principle, be observed) for the CRI (which is a subjective value and not directly observable). In general, the efficiency approach sweeps aside a number of inconveniences of the consumption numeraire procedure; typically, we do not deal with only one CRI when discounting if the incomes of different groups would be affected differently by a project. [For an example using an explicit economic model, see Little and Mirrlees (1974), pp. 297-305.]

We shall not go into an in-depth discussion of the inequality of the ARI and CRI here, but it is worth noting that in countries subject to constraints that limit the economy's capacity to absorb investments efficiently, the ARI will likely exceed the ARI that would otherwise prevail, and the CRI will fall short of the ARI. (The constraints could include human resource constraint, capacity limitations of port facilities and transportation networks, and so forth.)

A CRI short of the ARI would reflect that a relatively greater value is assigned to investment over consumption goods for the period when the economy's low level of accumulated capital stock hampers achievement of desired levels of investment. (We are assuming, of course, that additions to the country's capital stock would gradually reduce the impact of these constraints.) In this instance, the relative value of investment over private consumption exceeds unity. This is significant in estimating the ARI, because a portion of returns to an investment will be diverted to current consumption and not reinvested.

Let **v** denote the value of public investment relative to private consumption. In general, ARI minus CRI would equal the percentage change in **v** over time. For ARI - CRI > 0, the value of **v** will exceed 0, and **v** will be falling over time. As investment steps up and absorptive capacity constraints subside, the ARI gradually declines and the ARI and CRI approach each other. In the long run, assuming a stable growth in the economy, the ARI and CRI remain constant. [This behavior of the ARI and CRI has been

In countries limited by their economy's capacity to absorb investments efficiently, the accounting rate of interest will exceed the consumption rate of interest, which would indicate that greater value is assigned to investment relative to consumption.

explained by economic models; see particularly Dervis, Martin and Wijnbergen's (1984) simulation of the Egyptian economy from the late 1980s into the next century.]

It is the usual practice of the World Bank to estimate the ARI of an economy and to assume that this value will remain the same for some time. Dervis, Martin, and Wijnberben's (1984) work demonstrates that the use of an estimate for the ARI, made when investment is relatively valuable, may unduly skew investible funds toward projects yielding quick results. [Note that with a varying ARI, project selection would depend upon a positive NPV, as it is possible for a project to have a high economic of return and yet have a negative NPV].

Unfortunately, projecting a reasonable time series of a country's ARI requires a rather sophisticated model of the economy and involves solving a dynamic optimization problem. Fully satisfactory models are difficult to construct and solve, and the choice of the objective function itself is likely to be open to debate. Nevertheless, some countries have absorptive capacity constraints which may cause the ARI and CRI to diverge, at least in the short run.

What can we say here for planners in such countries? We can only warn them to be cautious about rejecting all projects with delayed benefits when working with ARI estimates. In these cases, it might be useful to look at how sharply the ARI would need to decline linearly to enable a project to just gain positive NPV. If the decline in ARI seems reasonable—say of less than 0.5 percent per year over twenty years—then the project should probably be reconsidered. (Judgments will have to be made on the decline based on how efficiently the economy is using incremental investments and the results of modeling exercises of different types of economy—modeling such as of Dervis, Martin, and Wijnbergen's.)

Planners in countries that have constraints on absorbing capital need to be cautious about rejecting all projects with delayed benefits when working with the accounting rate of interest (ARI). If the decline in ARI seems reasonable, then the project should be reconsidered.

The simple efficiency approach described in the following paragraphs represents a rough approximation and is better suited for some economies than for others. [Additional material on the choice of the social discount rate, and when the private rate of return to capital would be misleading, can be found in Boadway and Bruce (1984), pp. 314-322; and in Atkinson and Stiglitz (1980), pp. 474-480, although neither reading provides practical guidelines. The latter is the more difficult reading of the two.]

Ideally, the correctly set ARI allocates available public funds (for projects yielding quantifiable benefits) without having an excess supply of, or demand for, resources. With a given a number of projects, few projects will yield a positive NPV if the discount rate applied is higher. Thus, the ARI serves as a regulator of the uses to which public income can be put.

Notice the assumptions we make in our conditions of optimal saving and investment. By assuming a constant ARI, we are saying that we do not expect any serious deviations from a steady growth of public funds. We assume that the balance of trade will remain constant, or that the country will be able to borrow abroad as much as it requires in the event of shortfalls. To the extent that the volume of funds available to the government will fluctuate around desired amounts, the ARI is likely to move around some average value.

The basis for estimating the ARI is the marginal economic return to capital. By this we mean the extra amount of annualized benefits (measured in units of the numeraire) that one more unit of investment would yield after deducting for depreciation. Let us denote the marginal economic return to capital by the letter **q**. [This might also be called the economic opportunity cost of capital. The notation by the letter **q** is also consistent with Squire and van der Tak's notation.] The marginal return to capital, when it is realized, can either be reinvested, or diverted to current consumption. Assuming that a fraction of the marginal return is reinvested and a fraction is consumed, then the estimate of the ARI is represented by:

$$ARI = sq + (1-s)q/B \qquad (21.2)$$

In Equation 21.2, **B** is the conversion factor for the typical basket of goods consumed at the average level of consumption in the economy. The ratio **1/B** converts values expressed in terms of the numeraire into values of consumption at market prices. Since we consider consumption here to be as valuable as foreign exchange income in the hands of government, **sq** and **(1-s)q/B** are simply added together for an estimate of the ARI. [Otherwise, we would add **sq** and **(1-s)q/vB**.] Note that if there is no consumption out of investment income, then ARI = **q**. Moreover, if there are no distortions in the economy, **q** is just the overall return to investment, either public or private. [An example of an ARI estimate using Equation 21.2 can be found in Ahmed (1984).]

The value of **q** might be estimated by using either microeconomic or macroeconomic data. Squire and van der Tak (1975) describe both approaches in pages 110-120. [The microeconomic estimate of **q** is also discussed in Little and Mirlees (1974), pp. 292-296. Note that their **r** corresponds to Squire-van der Tak's **q**.] We shall illustrate both methods here for convenience.

The basis for estimating the accounting rate of interest is the marginal economic return to capital. The latter represents the extra amount of annualized benefits that one more unit of investment would yield after deducting for depreciation.

Using data from national accounts, the macroeconomic estimate of **q** is:

$$ARI = \frac{NP \cdot SCF}{I \cdot KCF} - \frac{W \cdot LCF}{I \cdot KCF} \qquad (21.3)$$

where:

NP = the incremental increase in net national product at constant market prices;

I   = net investment;

SCF = the standard conversion factor;

W   = incremental national wage bill;

LCF = the labor conversion factor; and

KCF = the capital goods conversion factor.

The ratio of the incremental net national product to investment, as well as the ratio of the incremental national wage bill to investment, might be obtained as an average of national account projections at constant prices. Since national account statistics prepare averages, and the marginal economic return to capital is a measure of the return to the next small increment of investment, the **q** estimated from the macroeconomic data is likely to be an upper limit to the value. A better estimate might be obtained for **q** if microeconomic data are available. This involves the inspection of the typical returns to investment of a number of successful or proposed projects.

Consider a project that entails an initial investment cost of Sh 100 up front and yields for a number of years Sh 15 per year in constant terms, at economic prices, after deducting for labor and nonlabor inputs, appropriately valued in the numeraire. Deducting Sh 5 a year from this residual for depreciation, the return to the investment is 10 percent (q = 10/100).

Suppose we are given the pretax profit rate of a project at market value, net of depreciation. If a fraction of the investment was financed through equity, leaving the fraction **1-f** financed by a loan, then we have:

$$q = f[(r - p) \cdot cf] + (1 - f) [(i - p) \cdot cf]$$

where:

r = the pretax profit rate net of depreciation;

p = the domestic rate of inflation;

i = the market interest rate on loan finance; and

cf = the conversion factor corresponding to the project's output.

The value for the marginal economic return to capital can be estimated by using either microeconomic or macroeconomic data. The former are generally preferred.

If the investment costs contained in the expressions (r - p) and (i - p) were not stated in border prices, it would be necessary to divide them by an appropriate conversion factor. (Recall we are concerned here with the value of investment in terms of foreign exchange, since that is the numeraire we are using.) With q's from a number of projects, we may be able to plot the dispersion of the estimates around some central value. This average value would be the best, although crude, estimate for the marginal economic return to capital. Alternatively, we may take a weighted average of the q's, with the weights being the proportion of the total investment used for the projects. This procedure may allow a few, large public utility projects to skew the results.

The skewing may be good and bad. On the bad side, there is a tendency for rates of return on public utility projects to be understated because analysts are prone to use the utility tariffs as the measure of benefits, without either adding consumers' surplus benefits (in the consumption numeraire), or valuing the traded substitutes (in the foreign exchange numeraire). On the positive side, the skewing caused by these projects may prove to be an acceptable way to capture some of the effects of absorptive capacity constraints, if analysts wish to plan for a gradual decline in the ARI in coming years.

[Note that for reasons presented in Little and Mirrlees (1974), pages 282-287, allowing for the gradual decline of the ARI to a point where v, starting out being greater than unity, falls back to unity does not imply that we need to readjust our estimates for the conversion factor for labor. (Let us recall that v is the value of public investment relative to private consumption.) Because of other adjustments going on, the labor conversion factor is likely to change little over time.]

The estimate of 1 - s and of s follow similar procedures to those used in estimating q. Either a macroeconomic or a microeconomic approach may be used.

The value of B is a weighted average of the conversion factors for the goods consumed at the average level of consumption in the economy, the weights being the proportion of the marginal expenditures on these goods. Estimating B requires collecting information on household expenditures. Lacking such information, we might consider using the SCF, although this is not generally recommended. For these purposes, a consumption conversion factor is preferred (CCF). [For examples of the calculation of CCF, see Ahmed (1984) and Mashayekhi (1980). These publications, as well as other general circulation publications of the World Bank, are available through World Bank Publications, 1818 H Street, NW, Washington, D. C. 20433, USA.]

❖

PART V

Examples of Economic Valuation in Projects

Case Studies, Technical Notes, and Annotated Bibliography

Case 1. The Use of the SCF and the Supply Factor in Valuing Nontraded Project Costs

Summary. *Drawing examples from Thailand and Egypt, this case presents the advantages of, and limits to, using specific, rather than aggregated, conversion factors in project appraisal.*

Because disaggregation can make a great difference in the values of conversion factors, project analysts should be wary of applying average conversion factors to important project costs. In practice, the standard conversion factor (SCF) calculated from trade data may not reflect well either the direction or the scale of distortions in the domestic values of specific nontraded items. For example, electricity in many agricultural projects is an insignificant component in incremental production. In such an instance, we could use the SCF to convert, as a first estimate, electricity tariffs into border values; but, this would be a rather poor first approximation if the government is subsidizing petroleum. Typically, petroleum is a major item in the cost of producing electricity in most developing countries. Since the cost of electricity is minor to begin with, the use of the SCF probably would not significantly affect the economic rate of return. However, in large irrigation schemes, where electricity is an important operating expense, the use of the SCF might skew the economic analysis.

Indeed, some project analysts have viewed the SCF calculated by using trade information as a critical indicator of distortions in the economy and have concluded that a value just below 1 would justify acceptance of a project based on its profitability at market prices. In this case study we hope to instill some appreciation of what the SCF does *not* show when viewed in isolation.

The SCF is meant to serve as an average of the conversion factors for individual nontraded goods, which disaggregate into traded cost components and a few nontraded primary factors (such as labor or land). Barring quantitative restrictions on tradables, and assuming that tradable components dominate supply costs, an appropriate average conversion factor for a minor nontraded project input can be calculated from a weighted average of import taxes and export subsidies. This is the trade value approach to deriving the SCF, and follows from the assumption that the differences between domestic and border prices of tradables would largely account for discrepancies between the market prices of these goods and their economic values in a foreign exchange numeraire—assuming that policies do not change. In practice, the proportions of imports and exports in total trade are used as approximations of these weights to yield the formula given on the next page.

The SCF is meant to serve as an average of the conversion factors for individual nontraded goods. These nontraded goods can be disaggregated into traded cost components and nontraded primary factors, such as land and labor.

$$(M + E) / [M (1 + t_m) + E (1 + t_e)]$$

where **M**, **E**, t_m, t_e represent total imports (CIF), total exports (FOB), the average import tariff rate, and the average export subsidy. (Note that if imports are on average subsidized, t_m is a negative number. Likewise, a negative t_e denotes an average export tax.) At best, the trade value SCF is a rough numerical construction for a particular characterization of nontraded goods.

Where information is available, it is preferable to construct countrywide conversion factors for various broad groups of nontraded goods or services, and to limit the use of the trade-value SCF. In many countries, this can be done because statistical departments maintain input-output tables that trace the flows of payments between economic sectors. Under the assumption that all production costs are constant, input-output coefficients can be derived from the accounts by simply dividing a sector's payments by its total value of production. Once the input-output coefficients are known, they are adjusted by previously determined conversion factors and summed to yield the sector's mean conversion factor. Where tradables are involved in the disaggregation of payments between sectors, the conversion factors are generally the ratios of the border to domestic prices. The conversion ratios for nontraded primary factors are not as readily determined. Depending upon the macroeconomic structure, conversion factors for these may require the use of some sort of general equilibrium model (a numerical representation of the interacting behavior of the government, the producers, and consumers of an economy as a whole) to determine their marginal values to an economy. A discussion of such modelling exercises is well beyond the scope of this book. Interested readers may refer to Dervis and Robinson (1978); Dervis, de Melo, and Robinson (1982); and Tower (1984). Understandably, our concern here is to illustrate how we can derive conversion factors pertinent to the characteristic costs (or benefits) of individual projects once a few other important parameters are known.

Consider, for example, the calculation of the conversion factor of electricity in Thailand based on information found in input-output accounts (see Table 1.01 on page 218). The input coefficients at market prices describe the derivation of the conversion factor for electricity in Thailand in 1975. The coefficients represent the portion of a Thai baht's worth of mining and quarrying, textile products, paper products, and others that contribute to a baht's worth of electricity. Each input coefficient is multiplied by an appropriate conversion factor to arrive at a set of input coefficients at efficiency prices. The sum of these coefficients is the sector's average conversion factor, 0.89980. Incidentally, the SCF for Thailand at that time was estimated to be 0.94. The use of the SCF for the electricity conversion factor would thus slightly underestimate the net economic benefits of a project that used electricity as an input.

Where information is available, it is preferable to construct countrywide conversion factors for various groups of non-traded goods or services. This can be done in many countries because their statistical departments maintain input-output tables.

Table 1.01. Thailand: Calculation of the Conversion Factor for Electricity, 1975

Sector	Input coefficient at market prices	Conversion factor	Input coefficient at efficiency prices
Mining and quarrying	0.00394	0.94 [a]	0.00370
Textile products	0.00064	0.75 [a]	0.00048
Paper products	0.00052	0.92 [b]	0.00048
Chemicals	0.00373	0.94 [a]	0.00351
Petroleum	0.37811	0.95 [c]	0.35920
Plastic ware	0.00017	0.94 [a]	0.00016
Machinery	0.06888	0.85 [d]	0.05855
Motor vehicles	0.00145	0.73 [e]	0.00106
Other manufacturing	0.00060	0.92 [f]	0.00055
Public utilities	0.02505	0.92 [f]	0.02305
Construction	0.00294	0.88 [g]	0.00269
Transport and communication	0.01946	0.87 [h]	0.00256
Trade	0.07872	0.92 [f]	0.07242
Services	0.02576	0.92 [f]	0.02370
Unallocatable	0.00466	0.92 [f]	0.00429
Total intermediate inputs	0.61461		0.55630
Wages	0.06167	0.92 [i]	0.05674
Operating surplus	0.25107	0.92 [f]	0.23098
Depreciation	0.06641	0.84 [j]	0.05578
Net indirect tax	0.00624	0.00	0.00000
Total value-added	0.30539		0.34350
Sector total	1.00000		0.89980

a. Intermediate goods conversion factor
b. Intermediate goods conversion factor for imports
c. Petroleum conversion factor for imports
d. Machinery conversion factor
e. Vehicles and parts conversion actor
f. Standard conversion factor (trade value approach)
g. Construction conversion factor
h. Transportation conversion factor
i. Labor conversion factor
j. Capital goods conversion factor

Source: Ahmed (1983).

John Page (1982) performed a similar exercise for Egypt using input-output data (see Table 1.02). Conversion factors were estimated for 130 goods and services, which were divided into six major groups: tradable intermediates, agricultural inputs and outputs, petroleum products, tradable urban consumer goods, tradable rural consumer goods, and nontradables. The coverage of the commodities include all of the major categories in Egypt's external trade statistics, major consumer goods, and all of the nontradable sectors represented in the 1977 input-output accounts.

There is considerable variability in the distribution of conversion factors for Egypt in Table 1.02. The median of the distribution, which would serve as our SCF, is 0.993. The mean conversion factor is 1.549. A number of commodities have rather high conversion factors, revealing the presence of large subsidies to those sectors (e.g., the conversion factor of 15.299 for fuel oil). The results of the study demonstrate how inadequate private profits can be as indicators of the social profitability of investment. In economies where the distribution of conversion factors are close to one another and less than unity and projects propose to produce exports selling at fixed world prices, profitability at domestic market prices would also imply social profitability. Here, despite an SCF of about 1, we cannot confidently say anything about the efficiency of Egyptian export, or of import-substituting production. In particular, consider the implications of electricity pricing in Egypt for investment choices in agriculture. In contrast to the Thai case, the SCF would not have been a good substitute for an estimated electricity conversion factor.

Egypt's electricity sector has used the full capacity of the generating facilities of the Aswan High Dam and is increasingly relying upon thermal power. The marginal social cost of production for thermal generation was estimated to be E£ 0.0464/KwH in 1980 border pounds; this was based on the E£ 0.014 market tariff of a typical marginal user of electricity [Page (1982)]. The total net subsidy coefficient allowing for direct and indirect input requirements was 2.32, which implied that for every E£ 100 that the private sector spent on electricity, the government was forgoing E£ 232 in revenue.

To see the effect this subsidization can have on the economic returns of new investments in Egyptian agriculture, consider the case of the West Nubariya New Land Development Project. This is a World Bank-assisted reclamation project to rehabilitate 24,000 feddans (2.38 feddans equal one hectare) in the Western Delta. About 162,000 feddans had already been reclaimed in the area during the 1960s, and 128,000 feddans were proposed to be reclaimed, including this project, during the 1980s. Investments were scheduled to be made beginning in 1980 and benefits were to flow in 1985.

The Egyptian CFs presented here show a remarkably great variability and range from low to high. The SCF for Egypt would be a misleading average CF.

Table 1.02. Egypt: Accounting Ratios by Category

Tradable goods

1.	Aluminum	1.061
2.	Buses	0.735
3.	Cement	2.185
4.	Chemicals (industrial)	2.158
5.	Chemicals (inorganic)	0.959
6.	Chemicals (organic)	0.942
7.	Electric machinery	0.965
8.	Electrical distribution machinery	0.830
9.	Electrical motors	0.849
10.	Fittings and fixtures	0.852
11.	Glass products	0.949
12.	Iron and steel products	0.937
13.	Iron and steel building materials	2.358
14.	Iron and steel	0.928
15.	Jute yarn	0.846
16.	Jute bags	0.747
17.	Machinery (metal working)	0.965
18.	Machinery (textiles)	0.965
19.	Machinery (office)	0.768
20.	Machinery spare parts	0.965
21.	Metals (ferrous)	0.965
22.	Metals (nonferrous)	0.998
23.	Metal products	0.899
24.	Paints and pigments	0.911
25.	Paper and printing	0.951
26.	Paper (substitutes)	1.769
27.	Paper products	0.768
28.	Packaging materials	0.806
29.	Plastics	0.810
30.	Rubber (crude)	0.975
31.	Rubber products	0.788
32.	Tires and tubes	0.818
33.	Tobacco (unmanufactured)	0.904
34.	Telecommunications equipment	0.780
35	Trucks	0.910
36.	Wood (crude)	0.994
37.	Wood products	0.975
38.	Vehicle spares	0.868

Agricultural inputs and outputs

39.	Agricultural machinery	1.159
40.	Agricultural machinery spares	1.021
41.	Agricultural implements	0.992
42.	Bags	1.280
43.	Fertilizer (weighted average)	1.663
44.	Pesticides	1.976

The CFs for tradable goods range from a low of 0.735 to a high of 2.358.

continued ➡

45.	Seeds	1.149
46.	Maize	1.313
47.	Onions	4.259
48.	Rice	2.043
49.	Soybeans	0.992
50.	Sugar	0.969
51.	Wheat	1.591

Petroleum products

52.	Crude oil	1.010
53.	Diesel	6.751
54.	Fuel oil	15.299
55.	Gas oil	6.265
56.	Kerosene	5.883
57.	Naptha	4.438
58.	Petrol	1.527

Urban consumer goods (tradable)

59.	Beef (rationed)	1.978
60.	Beef (nonrationed)	1.007
61.	Butane gas (LPG)	4.822
62.	Coffee	0.679
63.	Clothing	1.106
64.	Consumer durables	0.501
65.	Edible fats	1.221
66.	Fish	0.969
67.	Fruit	0.658
68.	Footwear	0.973
69.	Lentils	1.666
70.	Maize	1.797
71.	Milk and products	0.968
72.	Medicines and hygiene	0.939
73.	Passenger automobiles	0.571
74.	Rice	5.407
75.	Sesame	0.929
76.	Soap and detergents	0.821
77.	Sugar (rationed)	1.202
78.	Sugar (nonrationed)	0.483
79.	Tea	0.401
80.	Textiles (nonrationed)	0.970

Urban consumer goods (tradable)

81.	Tobacco products	0.383
82.	Vegetables	0.919
83.	Vegetable oil (rationed)	5.229
84.	Vegetable oil (non-rationed)	2.599
85.	Wheat	3.517
86.	Wheat flour	1.250

continued ➡

The border price of fuel oil was more than fifteen times the domestic fuel oil price in Egypt, indicating a large subsidy to consumers.

Note the relationship between the CFs for rationed and nonrationed urban consumer goods.

Rural consumer goods

87.	Lentils	0.971
88.	Maize (nonsubsidized)	0.927
89.	Meat (nonrationed)	1.163
90.	Rice (nonsubsidized)	1.799
91.	Sesame	1.042
92.	Sugar (nonrationed)	0.536
93.	Vegetable oil (nonrationed)	2.487
94.	Wheat (nonsubsidized)	1.520

Nontraded goods

95.	Animal fodder	1.085
96.	Bread baking	1.156
97.	Banking and insurance	0.328
98.	Beverages	0.731
99.	Biscuits and confectionery	1.058
100.	Building and construction	1.669
101.	Building materials	3.773
102.	Cotton cloth (rationed)	2.985
103.	Cigarettes	0.619
104.	Electricity	3.321
105.	Entertainment and culture	0.779
106.	Food packing	0.947
107.	Food distribution	1.237
108.	Garments (subsidized)	1.112
109.	Grain milling	1.592
110.	Housing (rural)	1.626
111.	Housing (urban, low/mid income)	1.569
112.	Housing (urban, high income)	1.535
113.	Milk products	1.266
114.	Meat processing	0.886
115.	Miscellaneous office services	0.862
116.	Personal services	0.958
117.	Port and harbor charges	1.315
118.	Printing and publishing	1.236
119.	Rail transport (passengers)	1.199
120.	Rail Transport (goods)	1.213
121.	Rail Transport (price)	0.000
122.	Retail distribution	0.711
123.	Road maintenance	1.423
124.	Road transport (passenger)	1.270
125.	Road transport (goods)	1.365
126.	Services NES	1.627
127.	Telecommunications	0.972
128.	Transport (wto png)	1.343
129.	Vehicle repair	0.909
130.	Wholesale distribution	0.798

Note the subsidy on electricity to consumers.

Source: Page (1982).

The West Nubariya project drew on the lessons from the previous reclamation effort in the area and was based on the small-settler approach. The project was designed to provide for an integrated reclamation effort, including detailed technical studies, a complete irrigation and drainage system, and a comprehensive institutional and managerial framework which encompassed training and extension, maintenance, and credit. The authorities expected that the project would provide a good indication of the possibilities for the success of further land rehabilitation in the future.

The project's aim was to promote agricultural production with the establishment of cropping and livestock enterprises designed to produce cash income and a considerable proportion of family food requirements [World Bank (1980), p. 44)]. Two cropping patterns had been considered for the project, one with sugar beet production and one without. In both patterns, cropping intensity was expected to double. The two production patterns considered in the project analysis are given in Table 1.03 on page 224.

Except for watermelon, cabbage, cauliflower, milk, and eggs, all output prices were based on international projections for 1985-1990, adjusted to the farm gate to account for handling, freight, and processing costs. A similar basis was used for fertilizers, animal feed concentrate, most seeds, and machinery costs. Economic prices adopted for the three vegetables were based on wholesale prices in local markets over the past five years, suitably adjusted to the farm gate. For milk, the economic price reflected the cost of reconstituting milk from imported skim milk powder and anhydrous milk fat, at 1980 prices. A premium of 20 percent was added to this reconstituted milk price to reflect local preferences for the fresh product. (For a fuller description of pricing fresh milk, see Case 5.) Prices for eggs, and for green berseem and maize for animal fodder, were based on the local market. Agricultural labor was valued at a price of E£ 0.60 per day, which was about 60 percent of the prevailing average wage. Of particular interest here is the energy cost, which was valued at of E£ 0.46/KwH. The prices used in the analysis are summarized in Table 1.04 on page 225.

The project, like most land reclamation projects, was characterized by a relatively slow improvement in reclaimed soils and a slow buildup in agricultural production. It was also a settlement project in that it was to establish twenty new villages, each of which in time was to evolve into a complete local economy with service facilities and a range of nonagricultural activities. In addition, government plans were well advanced to construct a major new city in the region, whose southern boundary would be immediately adjacent to the project area. In calculating the rate of return, no account was taken of the secondary or multiplier effects arising from the establishment of completely new economies.

In the West Nubariya project, some economic values were based on international prices, others on local prices.

Table 1.03. Egypt: Crop and Livestock Production at Full Development; West Nubariya New Land Development Project

Alternatives	Area (feddan)		Yield (t/feddan)		Production (t)	
	A	B	A	B	A	B
Winter crops						
Sugar beet	-	8,000	-	16	-	12,800
Fodder beet	1,000	-	16	-	16,000	-
Berseem	8,000	8,000	25	25	20,000	200,000
Onion	3,000	3,000	10	10	30,000	30,000
Wheat	2,000	1,000	1.8	1.8	3,600	1,800
Favba beans	1,000	1,000	1.5	1.5	1,500	1,500
Potato	3,000	2,000	10	10	30,000	20,000
Peas	2,000	1,000	2	2	4,000	2,000
Cauliflower	2,000	-	-	-	6,000	-
Cabbage	2,000	-	8	-	16,000	-
Subtotal	24,000	24,000				
Summer crop						
Maize (grain)	8,000	8,000	1.8	1.8	14,400	14,400
Maize (fodder)	6,000	6,000	28	28	168,000	168,000
Sunflower	8,000	8,000	1	1	8,000	8,000
Watermelon	2,000	2,000	10	10	20,000	20,000
Subtotal	24,000	24,000				
Total	**48,000**	**48,000**				
Livestock						
Meat					2,200	2,200
Milk					14,600	14,600
Eggs					350	350
Honey					140	140

Note: 1 ha = 2.38 feddans.

Source: World Bank (1980), p.54

Cropping pattern B assumes sugar beet production, while cropping pattern A is without sugar beets.

The estimates of benefits for the project were confined to valuing the incremental output of the crops and livestock products produced from the reclaimed area. The cost estimates were made for two basic cases: for the first case "social costs" were excluded and for the second, they were included. The "social costs" excluded from the first case comprised health facilities, police and fire stations, and post offices; houses for school teachers and health workers; and village water supply, village electricity, communications, and streets.

Table 1.04. Egypt: Prices for Farm Outputs and Inputs in West Nubariya New Land Development Project

Item per ton	Financial E£	Economic E£
Wheat	84	200
Barley	81	140
Maize	97	168
Fava bean	140	275
Potato	93	110
Onion	63	88
Sugar beet	15	28
Sunflower	160	345
Pea	124	154
Watermelon	67	67
Cabbage	102	102
Cauliflower	137	137
Fodder beet	110	110
Berseem	15	15
Fodder maize	10	10
Meat		
Cattle	900	500
Goat	800	450
Poultry	1200	550
Rabbit	1200	550
Milk		
Cow	140	120
Buffalo	200	168
Goat	160	135
Honey	500	500
Eggs (per 1000)	50	50

Source: World Bank (1980), p. 55.

The annual costs of operation and maintenance associated with the investments listed were also excluded. Approximately 50 percent of the investments excluded were for the buildings, 14 percent for the houses for teachers and health workers, and 18 percent for village water supply. The rationale for excluding these "social costs" was that without the project these costs would have to be incurred elsewhere in Egypt over the next decade. An alternative way of looking at the exclusion would be to say that the investments would have "social benefits" at least equal to their costs, which would be the same as dropping them out of the rate-of-return calculations.

Valuing social benefits, such as health care, can be difficult. Often analysts will exclude the separable costs for these social purposes in calculating the economic returns.

By using the economic estimate for energy costs and excluding the social costs, the economic rate of return of the production pattern with sugar beets would approximate 9 percent, which would include settlers' housing. (If the full market wage were used in the calculation, this return would drop by about one-percentage point.) Contrast this result with a calculation using the same economic values, but with energy priced at its market rate (E£ 0.14/KwH). The internal rate of return rises to 11 percent. At the time of the analysis, the opportunity cost of capital in Egypt was estimated at 10 percent [see Page (1982)]. By this criterion alone—notwithstanding some of the conservative assumptions of the analysis—we should be somewhat uneasy about accepting this project. The stream of net economic benefits is low. Had the true economic value of electricity been neglected and energy costs accepted at face value, we would have had a different impression of the profitability of the project.

For a fuller discussion of the economic cost of electricity when energy is not a significant project input, see Little and Mirrlees (1982), pp. 214-216. Schohl (1979) provides another example of shadow pricing on the basis of input-output accounts.

The economic rate of return for the West Nubariya project is very near the estimated opportunity cost of capital (OCC) in Egypt. If financial prices are used for electricity, the rate of return is above the OCC. If economic efficiency prices are used, the rate of return is below the OCC.

Case 2. Valuation of Nontraded Inputs: Demand-Price Conversion Factors

Summary. *In this case, we discuss the issue of "nonproduced" inputs, such as draft animals, by drawing examples from two Indonesian projects: the Kedung Ombo Multipurpose Dam and Irrigation Project and the Smallholder Cattle Development Project. The case involves the calculation of "demand-price" conversion factors; it illustrates the calculation of a conversion factor for "team labor" and then demonstrates the impact of using that conversion factor rather than a less refined conversion factor. The difference between the "refined" and the "unrefined" conversion factors was found to be small in this case.*

The Government of Indonesia wanted to finance a project to supply cattle to resettled smallholder farmers for use as draft animals. A project was proposed to procure 84,100 head of Bali cattle in South Sulawesi, Nusa Tenggara, and East Java and to transport them to Sumatra and other Sulawesi provinces [World Bank (1985)].

The herds of Bali cattle appeared to be large enough to supply the needs of the project and other government cattle programs without creating a scarcity in the areas from which they were drawn. Because there did not appear to be any direct distortions in the markets for cattle and there were no indirect foreign exchange costs in rearing them, which might link trade distortions with their market price, we might feel tempted to accept the market price for bullocks in South Sulawesi, and the other "source area," as a true indicator of their economic value. However, we should consider that the price of a primary input (such as a bullock) in an undistorted factor market will be based on the technical requirement and the value of the good which uses that input and on the availability of that input.

Bullocks are not like other inputs to agriculture which may be supplied at constant costs. They are really a kind of "nonproduced" capital good. If local markets work efficiently, the price of bullock labor will reflect a rent from its alternative uses, either in the source area, or elsewhere if the domestic market price in the source area is based on what the bullocks sell for as exports to other provinces in Indonesia. In the foreign exchange numeraire, the shadow value of the input naturally translates as the sum of its marginal value product at border prices, but we should be aware that this is not restricted to direct production relations.

Draft animals are not like other inputs to agriculture which can be supplied at constant costs. They are a kind of "nonproduced" capital goods.

In the economic valuation of inputs, we must look for distortions both in the input market as well as in the output market.

Another way to look at shadow pricing is to consider the foreign exchange the government must give up when withdrawing a unit of a factor from private production in order to maintain real incomes. If the procurement of bullocks has no effect upon their use in the source area because there are more animals located in these areas than can be used in local agriculture, and because marketing them elsewhere is impractical, the market price for bullocks should be rather low. In fact, if in the absence of the project these surplus bullocks would not be employed and would not be marketed outside the area, their shadow price would be zero. The shadow price is zero because the government would not incur any foreign exchange cost to compensate for the removal of these animals from the area.

To illustrate, let us suppose that bullocks are not marketed outside the source area and let us rule out a zero shadow price because bullock labor is relatively scarce in the short term. In other words, all able bullocks are put to work. We shall consider a simplified account of its foreign exchange value by following the format of Tower and Pursell (1986). For simplicity, let us assume that the economy produces primarily rice, which is consumed locally and exported at fixed world prices, and provides labor services, which are used only in the area. Let us also assume that the production of rice uses a combination of land, bullock labor, and human labor in a value-added aggregate, which is combined in constant proportions with traded intermediate goods, such as fertilizer and other chemicals. The "labor services" are rendered by human labor alone. The supply of land and bullock labor is fixed in the short term and cannot be substituted for labor services. However, human labor in the area can be used to either produce rice, or to provide labor services. With available technologies and these resources, the source area can supply only certain combinations of rice and labor services when employing all resources. In other words, there is a limit to the quantity of rice that the source area can produce if it is already providing a certain amount of labor services. This limit is set by the production possibility frontier in Figure 2.01. Along the frontier, the economy can provide more labor services only if it produces less rice, and vice versa.

If in the absence of a project the surplus draft animals cannot be employed in the region, or marketed elsewhere, their shadow price would be zero.

In Figure 2.01, the economy is producing at point A on the production possibility frontier with Xo units of rice and Yo rupiahs of labor services (where one unit of labor service trades for one unit of the domestic currency). At the given prices for rice and labor services, the economy is consuming at point C within the frontier, which means that all of the production of the nontraded good is consumed and a surplus of rice is exported. The government holds all foreign exchange.

Figure 2.01. Production Possibilities Frontier for Labor Services and Rice

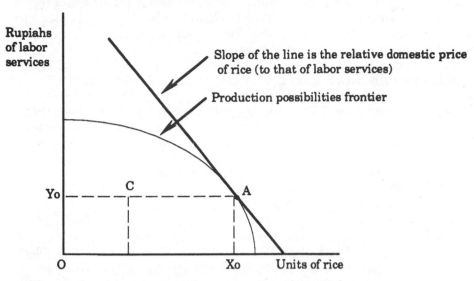

Now let us say the government withdraws a small number of bullocks, while holding the prices for bullocks and labor services constant, by either purchasing the excess supply, or supplying the excess demand that may occur with adjustments in production. Since we have assumed constant costs in production, holding prices constant means that factor incomes and domestic demands for the two goods do not change. With a smaller "capital" stock, the frontier shrinks inward: the economy produces less rice at each level of labor services than before (see Figure 2.02). At all levels of labor services, additional gains in rice production can only be obtained by sacrificing more labor. This reflects decreasing returns to rice production with the smaller quantity of bullocks, but the total quantity of labor in the economy remains unchanged.

Figure 2.02. Production Possibilities Frontier for Labor Services and Rice Before and After Reduction of Capital Stock

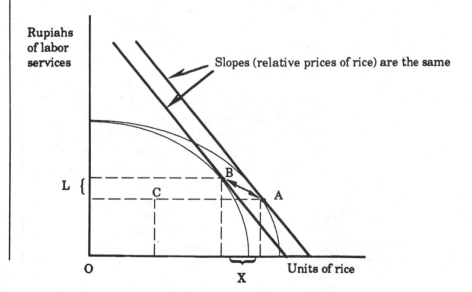

Production in the economy moves from point A to point B in Figure 2.02. Compared with the initial situation in Figure 2.1, the economy is producing L rupiahs more of labor services and X fewer units of rice. This quantity of surplus labor is absorbed by the government to maintain employment at the given wage. Consequently, rice production is scaled back and the amount of surplus exported falls, as domestic demand for rice has not changed. The economic value of the bullocks withdrawn from the economy is the foreign exchange value of the rice production forgone because this is the amount the government must sacrifice to maintain the economy at the same level of real income as before.

Thus, if rice production falls by **x** tons when **z** bullocks are withdrawn from the economy, the conversion factor for the bullocks is **x/z** times the border price for rice. If the domestic market for animals were working efficiently so that the private sector would rent the bullocks based on their marginal value product in terms of the domestic price of rice, then the conversion factor for the bullocks would be the ratio of the border to the domestic price for rice—i.e., rice's conversion factor. Let us ignore the "depreciation" of bullocks and changes in the costs of buying new bullocks over time. Thus, the domestic rental for bullocks is distorted for as long as the domestic price for rice is distorted.

Now suppose the going price for bullocks in the source area is based on a price received for export of the animals to other provinces in Indonesia. As before, the shadow price would be based on the foreign exchange value of the goods the government would need to supply or absorb as a result of production readjustments—to keep prices constant following the withdrawal of some animals from the economy. In the readjustment, some of the labor released from rice production might shift into the production of other export goods, which would reduce the foreign exchange cost of the bullocks.

For many agricultural projects using animals, it is probably best as a first approximation to use crop conversion factors to shadow price animal labor.

The economic value of the bullocks withdrawn from the economy is the foreign exchange value of the rice production foregone.

This basic example should suggest that calculating the marginal social benefit of a nontraded primary input can be rather involved unless we limit, at some risk of error, the analysis to partial effects. In practice, the error probably would not be significant. Here we have shown a special case with animal labor, estimating a demand-side conversion factor based on the input's specific and limited use in the economy and only one other possible use for human labor. In reality, draft animals serve several tasks and there may be a number of conceivable areas of alternative employment. However, for many agricultural projects using animals, it is probably appropriate as a first approximation to use crop conversion factors to shadow price animal labor. In areas characterized by the production of one major export crop, it might often be simpler to seek employment in nontraded rural services than to migrate to other export crop producing areas. For discussions of migration in developing countries and the prominence of nontraded service sectors, see Mazumdar (1975, 1980, 1985).

In general, many of a project's nontraded inputs would be produced items. In these cases, inputs may be supplied with an increase in price by both producing more domestically and by withdrawing some from other uses. Thus, the conversion factors of a produced nontraded input would be a weighted average of its supply-side conversion factor based on the economic costs of the inputs used in producing it, and its demand-side conversion factor would be based on the benefits it produces. In practice, we often assume that the response in the production of an intermediate good to an increase in its price is far greater than its substitution out of other uses. We could ignore the complications of determining the marginal social benefit and base the conversion factor solely on the marginal costs of producing the input. Another approach, which yields the simplest, although perhaps not the most accurate procedure is to assume that the nontraded input can be provided at constant costs, as illustrated in the West Nubariya New Lands Project (see Case 1).

Now consider another project, the Kedung Ombo multipurpose dam in the Jratunseluna River Basin in Central Java. The dam will provide irrigation water for 25,100 hectares in the Klambu Kanana and Sidorejo areas and 34,240 hectares in the Sedadi and Klambu Kiri areas, which get only wet season irrigation. The intensification of agricultural activities would presumably require increases in the level of inputs, including bullock labor. An economic analysis of the agricultural benefits of the dam project noted that there was a shortage of animals in the project area, so a shadow price need not be estimated for bullock labor [World Bank (1985a)]. In deriving the *per diem* economic value of a two-animal-two-person team, the appraisal report shadow priced the human labor component at 50 percent of the market wage. The animal labor was left unadjusted. Thus, the financial price of a team was Rp 4,200, which included two person-days of human labor valued at Rp 2,600. The value of bullock labor per team-day was then Rp 1,600. Thus, the economic price of a team-day was calculated to be:

$$1,600 + 1,300 = Rp\ 2,900$$

The conversion factor for one team-day is therefore:

$$2,900/4,200 = 0.70,\ \text{when rounded.}$$

Now let us consider a conversion factor for bullock labor based on the project area's expected agricultural production without the project. The expected financial and economic values of the crops grown in the area are given in Table 2.01.

Table 2.01. Financial and Economic Values of Crops without the Project

Rice

Economic farm gate price	(Rp/kg)	239
Financial farm gate price	(Rp/kg)	200
Conversion factor		1.20

Maize

Economic farm gate price	(Rp/kg)	139
Financial farm gate price	(Rp/kg)	90
Conversion factor		1.54

Soybean

Economic farm gate price	(Rp/kg)	348
Financial farm gate price	(Rp/kg)	450
Conversion factor		0.77

Mungbean

Economic farm gate price	(Rp/kg)	457
Financial farm gate price	(Rp/kg)	415
Conversion factor		1.10

Sorghum

Economic farm gate price	(Rp/kg)	152
Financial farm gate price	(Rp/kg)	105
Conversion factor		1.45

The cultivation of crops each season requires animal labor for ground preparation. Thus, we shall use the total annual expected value of production without the project to derive weights for an average of these conversion factors. The future production without the project is given in Table 2.02

Thus, assuming that rent for animal labor reflects its marginal value product, the bullock input under this approach would be shadow priced at 19 percent (20 percent, when rounded) more than its market price. The team-day conversion factor would then be recalculated as:

$$1600 \times 1.20 = 1920$$
$$+ 1300$$
$$\overline{3220}$$

$$3200/4200 = 0.77$$
(or 0.8, when rounded)

Adjusting for the animal labor cost gives a team labor CF, which is higher than that used for the Kedung Ombo project appraisal—0.8 versus 0.7.

Table 2.02. Future Crop Production without the Project

Crop production measured in thousand tons:

Rice	248.33
Maize	51.24
Soybean	9.02
Mungbean	3.27
Sorghum	1.68

In financial terms, the values of production in million rupiahs are:

Rice	49,666
Maize	4,612
Soybean	4,059
Mungbean	1,357
Sorghum	176
Total	59,870

The percentages of crop values in the total value of production are:

Rice	0.83
Maize	0.08
Soybean	0.07
Mungbean	0.02
Sorghum	0.00

Multiplying the conversion factors for the crops by these weights we have:

Rice	1.00
Maize	0.12
Soybean	0.05
Mungbean	0.02
Sorghum	0.00
Total	1.19

To see the effect of the higher cost of team labor on the economic analysis of the project, let us note that the new conversion factor would increase the team costs by 14 percent (0.8/0.7 = 1.14). From representative crop budgets it appears that team costs are about two thirds of total farm labor inputs. We would then apply a scaling factor of 1.09 to total labor costs to reflect the 14-percent increase in the team costs:

$$2/3 \times 1.14 + 1/3 = 1.09.$$

We can also see from the crop budgets that labor costs are roughly one-half of total farm costs. Thus, on average, the farm costs in the economic analysis increase about 4.5 percent with a 14-percent increase in the cost of team labor. Equivalently, the net

The higher CF for team labor increases total farm labor costs by a factor of 1.09 in the Kendung Ombo project.

incremental benefits decrease by the same amount.

Table 2.03 shows the net benefit streams of the irrigation component of the dam project using 0.7 and 0.8 to discount team labor. The net benefits in the second stream are obtained by dividing the first stream benefits following the investment period by 1.045. The figures show that benefits are reduced by more than US$ 1 million per year.

Table 2.03. Economic Rate of Return with Specific Conversion Factors for Team Labor Costs
(in million U.S. dollars at January 1985 values)

Year	Net benefits (0.7 Team CF)	Net benefits (0.8 Team CF)
1	(20.56)	(20.56)
2	(39.32)	(39.32)
3	(71.44)	(71.44)
4	(60.81)	(60.81)
5	(0.53)	(0.53)
6	22.19	21.23
7	35.68	34.14
8	39.20	37.51
9	39.50	37.80
10	39.50	37.80
11	39.50	37.80
12	39.50	37.80
13	39.50	37.80
14	39.50	37.80
15	39.50	37.80
16	39.50	37.80
17	38.63	36.97
18	37.78	36.15
19	39.50	37.80
20	39.50	37.80
21	39.50	37.80
22	39.50	37.80
23	39.50	37.80
24	39.50	37.80
25	39.50	37.80
26	39.50	37.80
27	39.50	37.80
28	39.50	37.80
29	39.50	37.80
30	39.50	37.80
ERR (percent)	13.86	13.36

Farm production costs increase by 4.5 percent as a result of adjusting the economic cost of animal labor.

Of course, the results would be further affected if manual labor were not discounted by 50 percent. Nevertheless, we can see that the additional work involved in calculating a conversion factor (CF) for the team is unrewarded by the impact on the economic rate of return (ERR) that has been calculated. We should remind ourselves of the rule of thumb which limits project-related CF calculations to those items comprising more than 10 percent of project costs, or more than 10 percent of project benefits. In this case, the project costs involved amounted to approximately one-third of production costs.

However, the difference between the "refined" and the "unrefined" calculation of the CF that was used for the team labor was small (i.e., 0.8 versus 0.7), leading to a change of approximately 4.5 percent in the incremental net benefit stream and, thus, approximately a 4-percent change in the ERR, from 13.86 percent down to 13.36 percent. (Actually, the difference is approximately 3.6 percent—i.e., 1 - 13.36/13.86 = 3.6 percent).

❖

The economic rate of return decreased by only half a percentage point as a result of the animal labor cost adjustment—from 13.86 percent to 13.36 percent.

Case 3. Valuation of Rural Labor: An Example from Pakistan

Summary. *This case discusses the calculation of conversion factors for rural labor in Pakistan. One interesting aspect of the Pakistan case is that the economic cost of unskilled rural labor exceeds its financial cost, because the prices of the commodities that labor would produce in its nonproject applications are subsidized in the local market.*

To derive a shadow wage rate for an agricultural project we must at first estimate the value of the labor forgone because of employment in the project. This estimation will vary greatly from country to country, and regionally within countries, according to specific circumstances and characteristics of labor markets. If there is widespread unemployment within a country, the shadow wage rate may be effectively zero, as the project would not be diverting labor from other productive activities. This is hardly the case in most developing countries where there are seasonal variations in the demand and employment of rural labor, and where migration between rural and urban areas occurs in response to wage differentials. We should not assume that withdrawal of labor from the so-called informal sector of the urban underemployed and part-time job seekers, or those involved in nonwork activities, comes without an economic cost.

In Pakistan in the 1970s, the response of rural labor supply to increases in the real rural wage (i.e., the nominal rural wage divided by an appropriate price index) was not found to be as sensitive as thought. A small increase in the real wage would not elicit large increase in the supply of labor. Besides, since migrants could apparently find jobs in various sectors of the village or town economy relatively easily, urban-rural wage differentials were thought to reflect the private costs of migration. This characterization of the labor market implied that an expansion in the demand for unskilled labor in the rural sector caused by a large, new project would bring about an increase in the rural wage rate. As a result of a wage increase, some labor would be expected to be drawn from rural and urban employment and nonwork activities.

In estimating a general shadow wage rate for rural unskilled labor in Pakistan, Squire, Little, and Durdag [(1979), pp. 82-90], therefore, considered six factors. These factors are listed on page 237.

To derive a shadow wage rate for an agricultural project, we must estimate the value of the labor forgone because of employment in the project.

236

a. the increased consumption cost resulting from the expansion in employment from the project;

b. the forgone output resulting from the reduction in rural employment;

c. the forgone output resulting from the reduction in urban employment;

d. the reduction in consumption caused by the transfer of urban labor to the rural sector (or by a reduction in the flow of rural-urban migrants);

c. the cost of the income transfer implied by the increase in the rural wage rate (the transfer from rural employers to employees); and

e. the cost of the income transfer implied by possible increase in the urban wage rate.

In calculating the cost of withdrawing labor from rural employment, the authors assumed that labor would be withdrawn from different activities in the same proportion as they are used in those activities. From the calculation in Table 3.01, we can see that as a result of the export taxes levied on rice and cotton and the subsidization of imported wheat, the overall accounting ratio for the value of forgone marginal output of rural unskilled labor is 1.08. In calculating the ratio of the shadow rural wage rate to the financial wage rate, this figure is weighted by the proportion of workers participating in the project who were drawn from rural employment.

It may seen surprising that the economic cost of unskilled labor in Pakistan was calculated to be greater than the financial price of labor (since the labor CF is 1.08). To understand why this could be true, let us look at the conversion factors for the commodities that the labor would have produced in its alternative employment (see Table 3.01). Wheat, rice, and cotton each have conversion factors above 1. The CF for wheat (the commodity having the greatest weight in the calculation) is 1.50, which implies that the price of wheat carries a large subsidy. Thus, labor which is taken away from wheat production carries a cost in economic terms which is 50 percent greater than the apparent financial cost of the forgone output of that labor.

In Pakistan, the economic cost of unskilled labor was calculated to be greater than the financial price of labor.

Table 3.01. Pakistan: Marginal Social Productivity of Unskilled Rural Labor

Activity	Hired labor use/acre (days)[a]	Cropping pattern[b]	Weights[c]	Adjusted weights[d]	Conversion factors[e]	Social cost[f]
Cotton	12.0	0.18	0.18	0.14	1.33	0.19
Wheat	5.4	0.61	0.61	0.27	1.50	0.33
Rice	7.0	0.15	0.09	0.07	1.33	0.09
Sugar	12.5	0.06	0.06	0.05	1.00	0.05
Nonagriculture	-		0.40	0.52	0.80	0.42
Total			1.00	1.00	1.00	1.08

a. Shahrukh Rafi Khan, "An Estimate of the Shadow Wage Rate in Pakistan" (Karachi: *Pakistan Development Review,* Winter 1974).

b. Fiscal year 1974 cropping pattern as reported in "Pakistan: Recent Trends and Development Prospects," (Washington, D.C.: The World Bank, 1976).

c. The weights are calculated from information supplied in J.B. Eckert, "Rural Labor in Punjab," (Government of Punjab, 1972). Eckert reports that annual employment for casual laborers is 136 days, of which 82 are in agricultural activities. Accordingly, the weight, for cotton, for example, is derived as follows: the days of labor required per acre of farmland is the sum of the products of hired labor use and cropping percentage for each crop. For cotton, the labor requirement is 7.25 days/acre. This means that each casual laborer can service 82 days/(7.25 days/acre) = 11.31 acres. Of the 11.31 acres, 2.04 acres would be cropped in cotton (11.31 acres x 0.18 = 2.04.) Each acre of cotton requires 12 days of labor; therefore, 12 days/acre of cotton x 2.04 acres of cotton = 24.48 days devoted to cotton production. This represents 24.28 days/136 days = 0.18 percent of the casual laborer's annual employment. For "nonagriculture" activity, the weight is simply 54 days/136 days = 0.40.

d. Since the conversion factors do not allow for transport and distribution margins, the weights for agricultural activities shown in column 4 are deflated by 20 percent. (In other words, 20 percent is assumed to represent the distribution margin which is then added to nonagricultural activities.)

e. Cotton and rice are exported. We can estimate the average tax on these exports by solving the relation $CF = 1/(1 - tx)$, where tx is the average percentage tax on the export crop in question and CF is the conversion factor for the crop. The conversion factors for cotton and rice are the same (1.33). Both crops are subject to a tax at the rate of about 25 percent [i.e., $(1.33 - 1)/1.33 = 25$ percent]. Wheat is a subsidized import. The size of the

The CFs for agricultural outputs used in calculating the economic cost of rural labor in Pakistan are above unity (1.0), causing the economic cost of labor to exceed its financial cost.

wheat subsidy can be derived in a similar fashion by using its conversion factor and the relation $CFw = 1/(1 + tm)$, where tm is the average percentage tax on imports and CFw is the conversion factor for wheat. A subsidy is considered a negative tax. The subsidy on wheat imports can be estimated to be $(1.50 - 1)/1.50 = 33$ percent. For the nonagricultural product of labor the standard conversion factor for Pakistan at the time, 0.80, was used.

f. Social cost equals the adjusted weight times the corresponding conversion factor.

Case 4. Valuation of Potentially Traded Project Outputs

Summary. *In this case we discuss sugar beet production in Hungary, where a project to improve crop production was designed to increase sugar beet yields and possibly release land for use in producing export crops. A question is raised as to whether to value the project's benefits in terms of the import substitution value of sugar beets, or the export value of the other crops. The project's benefits could have been based on any of a number of different without-project scenarios regarding yield growth and government policy. The text for this case has been adapted from the the appraisal report of the Crop Production Improvement Project [World Bank (1986)].*

The agricultural sector, which includes livestock, is an important branch of Hungary's economy and plays a significant role in trade and employment. In 1984, the agricultural sector provided 18 percent of the gross value-added in the economy, and employed 21 percent of the economically active population. The share of agriculture in GNP has remained stable at 18 percent over the last ten years. The sector's output has generally exceeded the country's food requirements, generated surpluses for export, and provided materials for a number of agriculture-based processing industries. The expansion of agriculture would directly contribute to improving the external balance of the economy.

The Hungarian Seventh Development Plan (1986-90) was introduced in a period when investment in agriculture had been falling and there had been a switch away from agricultural activities and toward industry. By 1985, the level of investment in agriculture, in constant prices, had fallen to about 80 percent of the amount in 1974, and only 64 percent of the amount in 1978. While greater selectivity in investment was certainly warranted, if the level of investment did not rise above that of the most recent past, it would be increasingly difficult for agriculture to grow at adequate rates.

The Hungarian strategy was to rely on profitability at world prices to determine production and investment, rather than on rigid, centralized targets.

To achieve a growth in agricultural output of about 2 percent per year during the Seventh Plan period would probably have required average gross fixed investment at the 1982 level in constant terms. The strategy of relying on profitability in terms of world market prices to determine both the pattern of production and investment, rather than on centralized direction, meant that there would be no rigid official target for either expected output or investment in agriculture during the Seventh Plan period.

The proposed project was meant to improve production efficiency and to increase foreign exchange earnings in convertible currency by expanding the production of agricultural goods either for export, or to substitute for imports. Among other activities, the proposed project was to promote the use of energy-efficient equipment; improve the production potential of selected lands through shaping, drainage, and soil treatment; and produce and spread liquid fertilizer to replace fertilizer of poor quality. To implement the project, loans were to be administered to cooperatives and state-owned farm enterprises.

About 9 percent of the area of farms to benefit from the loans were cropped with sugar beet. Consistent with the government's policy to limit sugar production to meet domestic demand, the improvement of cropping conditions and quality, and the decrease in losses by using improved equipment under the project would have resulted in the reduction of the area under sugar beet by 17 percent, and a corresponding increase in the area planted to export crops. The quantity of sugar produced from sugar beet in the country would not have exceeded the annual levels of domestic consumption, and the area under sugar beet crop would have had to be adjusted annually to maintain sugar production at such levels.

In the economic analysis of the project, the economic prices of the major outputs of the project were based on border prices. These included wheat, maize, and sunflower seeds, which are exported: the relevant prices used were the FOB prices of international equivalents, adjusted for any differences in quality. At the time the project was appraised, Hungary neither imported nor exported sugar. No increase in sugar beet production was proposed under the project, but foreign exchange was to be earned as land was released for the production of other exportable crops. Without the project, a decrease in the land under sugar beet cultivation in favor of export crops would have meant that some imports were necessary to satisfy increased demand for domestic consumption for sugar. As consumption was expected to be satisfied with the project without imports, sugar beet was considered to be an import substitute in the economic analysis of the project. The relevant price is the CIF price, although sugar is not currently traded.

Note that several without-project scenarios are possible, each having a different impact on the valuation of project benefits. They may be divided into two groups of without-project scenarios:

    a. a constant-yield set of scenarios; and

    b. an increasing-yield set of scenarios.

Without the project, a decrease in the land under sugar beet cultivation in favor of export crops would have meant that some imports of sugar would be necessary. As consumption was expected to be satisfied with the project without imports, sugar beet was considered to be an import substitute.

Let us look at the constant-yield scenarios. In the first scenario, sugar demand would be met by increasing the area planted to sugar beet. In this case, the area committed to export crops would have decreased, and export revenues would have been lower. The losses in export revenues would then have represented the project's benefits. In the second scenario, we could assume that all domestic production would remain the same, that demand for sugar would continue to grow, and that without the project the additional demand for sugar would be met through imports. In this second scenario, the benefits would have been calculated from the import parity value of the without-project sugar imports. A third alternative would have involved a combination of the first two.

Let us now look at the increasing-yield set of scenarios. There exists an infinite number of possibilities here, since there is an infinite number of assumptions we could make about future yields without the project. The standard approach is to assume that yields will continue along their long-run average growth path—often increasing at 0.5 percent to 1 percent per year—in the absence of the project. If the domestic demand for sugar is forecast to grow at a faster rate than the without-project yields, then we could draw a set of increasing-yield scenarios which parallel the constant-yield scenarios mentioned in the preceding paragraph.

Setting up the without-project scenario will often be the most perplexing part of the project financial and economic analysis. The project analysts will usually have to build the scenario themselves. In most cases, the project sponsor will focus totally on the with-project planning and will not be interested in building scenarios related to the without-project situation.

The "incremental cash flow" is obtained by subtracting the without-project from the with-project cash flow. Thus, each is equally important in project cash flow analysis.

Several "without project" scenarios are possible for the Hungary project. The "without project" scenario is just as important in project analysis as is the "with project" scenario.

Case 5. Valuation of Nontraded or Infrequently Traded Outputs with Imperfectly Substitutable Traded Alternatives

Summary. *In this case, we discuss the valuation of fresh milk production in Hungary. The case provides examples of typical calculations of import substitution values for beverage milk and its byproducts. Also discussed are some of the issues that are typically faced, in practice, when dealing with import substitutes. This case is drawn from Fitchett (1985).*

A proposed dairy project in Hungary aims to increase foreign exchange earnings in convertible currency by expanding exports of raw and processed animal products. The economic analysis of the project required that an estimate be made of the value of raw milk, which is essentially a nontraded commodity. The way this was approached was to consider the import costs of alternatives for fresh milk. Powdered milk, as a traded commodity, is not a perfect substitute for the locally produced good; therefore, the economic price of milk must take into account the consumers' preferences for the fresh product.

The prices used for the economic analysis of the Hungarian project were based on the border price of powdered milk and butter fat imported from New Zealand. By including the cost of recombining the powdered milk and butter fat to make liquid milk and increasing the cost by 5 percent to adjust for quality and taste difference, the economic price to the producers of raw milk was estimated to be about 18 percent higher than the financial price they actually received. The various steps in estimating the border price equivalent of raw milk are given in Table 5.01 on page 245.

Steps 2 and 3 in Table 5.01 estimate the raw material cost of 1,000 liters of milk. Step 4 estimates the costs of the reconstitution process, of pasteurization, and of packaging and distribution from the factory gate to the retail shelf. The "subtotal" at the end of step 4 represents the total cost of making a liter of reconstituted milk available to the consumer. In Step 5, an adjustment is made for consumers' preferences for the better taste of fresh pasteurized milk. A so-called "freshness premium" of 5 percent is added to the price of the fresh product.

Occasionally, step 5 may run afoul of reality in the face of local

Powdered milk is not a perfect substitute for fresh milk, but it is a close substitute.

The economic value of fresh milk was based on reconstituting powdered milk and imported butter fat. Often a "freshness premium" is added to reflect the lack of perfect substitution.

government regulations. For instance, government regulations may:

    a. fix the price of fresh pasteurized milk below the cost of the reconstituted import; or

    b. not even permit the reconstituted alternative.

In some instances, local regulations may require the blending of imported nonfat dry milk (NFDM) with the local fresh product to "protect" the local producer. In such a case, we may have no credible way of measuring a freshness premium.

In situation **a**, the World Bank's usual practice at appraisal has been to ignore the demonstrably low consumer marginal valuation of milk and instead work with the results of this calculation as shown in Table 5.01. In either case, the persistence of such government practices may impede the long-run development of a viable and vigorous dairy industry and need to be corrected under the proposed project. In the absence of a credible market measure of freshness premium, one alternative would be merely to apply the border price valuation of reconstituted milk (i.e., use zero for the freshness premium) and then undertake a sensitivity analysis at various assumed levels of the freshness premium.

Step 7 in Table 5.01 is an adjustment necessary to compare the processed product with raw milk of a 3.5-percent butter fat content; this step represents the revenues from the pasteurizer's sales of the surplus butter fat. Finally, in step 8 we deduct the costs of collecting, processing, and distributing the local pasteurized product and come up with an estimate—in border prices—of the value of raw fluid milk per liter at the farmgate.

While the procedure described in Table 5.01 is relatively straightforward, we need to review carefully the structure and costs of the local processing and distribution systems. These include relevant trade and foreign exchange policies and the extent of effective protection of some activities. In many cases, there might be important issues in the structure or performance of the collection, processing, and distribution systems—as well as the government regulation of these—which would deserve closer study, and perhaps corrective action under the aegis of a specific project.

In the Hungary case, the Bank's appraisal mission pointed out that while consumers were paying Ft. 6.20 per liter of milk, the government was also providing a subsidy of Ft. 3.52 per liter to processors, and an additional Ft. 2 per liter to dairy farmers. Thus,

The "freshness premium" may be omitted in favor of sensitivity analysis.

Table 5.01. The Farmgate Border Price Equivalent of Fresh Milk in Hungary
(Ft per 1,000 liters)

Step	Nonfat dry milk US$/mt	Nonfat dry milk Ft/mt	Butter fat US$/mt	Butter fat Ft/mt	Liquid milk Ft./1000 liters
1. New Zealand FOB	900		1,900		
Transport to Western Europe	150		150		
Transport to Hungarian border	85		85		
Total	1,135	56,750	2,135	106,750	
2. Kg of dry matter required for 1,000 liters of 2.8 percent butterfat reconstituted milk		100		28	
3. Cost of dry matter		5,675		2,988	8,664
4. Cost of reconstituting dry matter to liquid form (additional to ordinary pasteurizing costs)					866
Pasteurization and distribution costs					3,130
Subtotal					12,630
5. Taste and quality premium for fresh milk (5 percent)					632
6. Estimated retail economic price of 1,000 liters of fresh liquid milk (2.8 percent butterfat)					13,262
7. Pasteurizing plant revenues from butter oil sales					600
Subtotal					13,862
8. Collection, pasteurization, and distribution costs					-3,330
9. Border price equivalent of 1,000 liters of raw milk (3.5 percent butterfat) at the farm gate					10,532
10. Farm gate price (Ft./liter) of raw milk (3.5 percent butterfat)					10.53

Note: An exchange rate of US$1 = Ft. 50 is used in this table.

Source: Adapted from the appraisal documentation of the Hungarian Integrated Livestock Industry Project (internal World Bank documents with restricted circulation).

Table 5.02. Estimating the Border Price of Raw Milk Used in Processed Dairy Products: White Cream Cheese

1.	Cream cheese border price [Ft/kg (FOB)]	84
	Less:	
2.	Collection, processing and distribution costs (including normal profit) [Ft/kg]	28
3.	Residual value [Ft.] of raw milk content [7 liters].	56
4.	Farm gate value per liter of raw milk in terms of border prices [Ft.]	8

Source: Adapted from Table 5.01.

the consumer price covered only 53 percent of the total cost of Ft. 11.72 for a liter of milk; the remainder represented government subsidy to producers and processors. The Bank made specific proposals on phasing out this rather large subsidy. (In a similar project in Tunisia, the government agreed to introduce a retail pricing structure to differentiate fluid milk reconstituted from imported material from pasteurized whole fresh milk; this liberalization of marketing regulations would allow consumers a wider choice of products while improving incentives for domestic producers.)

The production or consumption, or both, of milk is often subsidized in developing countries.

Less attention has been paid to border pricing fluid milk destined for processing plants.

Less attention has been paid to the proper valuation—in terms of border prices—of fluid milk destined for processing into other products. In most markets, milk going into processed products receives a lower price than that going into fresh fluid consumption. Of course, if the product in question is powdered milk, or if the fresh fluid milk input can be easily substituted by nonfat dry milk (NFDM) in the transformation process for the products proposed in the project, the valuation is quite straightforward; the import alternative of NFDM is the pricing basis. In the case of a product to be exported and for which NFDM is not suitable, it would be necessary first to estimate the likely FOB export price of the transformed product and then deduct the total processing and distribution costs (from the farmgate to the border, all in border price terms). In the case of an import substitute, changes must be made in the calculation methodology. The residual represents the farmgate value of the raw milk. A schematic description of the procedure is given in Table 5.02.

Case 6. Valuation of Nontraded or Infrequently Traded Commodities with Imperfectly Substitutable Traded Alternatives

Summary. *Like Case 5, this case is concerned with the border pricing of a nontraded item which has a traded substitute. The item here is buffalo milk in Pakistan. Although there is little or no trade in buffalo milk itself, it can be broken into components that are comparable to commodities that are traded. This case has been adapted from World Bank (1983).*

The first Agricultural Development Bank Project (ADBP) in Pakistan was initiated in 1965; and since then three more ADBP credit projects have been approved by the World Bank. A fifth project has been proposed. Among other components, the project would include three lending schemes for livestock development in the Sind and Baluchistan provinces of the country.

A study of the Pakistan dairy industry concluded that milk production in rural areas is both financially and economically viable on small- and medium-sized farms. However, urban milk production—although financially viable—was considered to be economically inefficient. Under the dairy component of the project, loans would be made to farmers for the purchase of buffalos or cows, construction of dairy sheds, purchase of milking utensils, and for working capital to cover initial fertilizer and concentrate feed costs.

The ADBP would make special efforts to expand the dairy herd and increase production in the areas close to the five new dairy plants under operation, or under construction. Dairy farmers in these areas would receive advice and inputs from dairy plant extension staff and would be assured of a regular outlet for their production. As far as possible, these loans would be made to the landless, or to farmers with small holdings.

The into-factory economic price of milk (which is considered a tradable) was calculated on the basis of import substitutes (see Table 6.01). In their calculations, the analysts did not apply a price for water nor allow for a taste premium. The calculations provide the 6-percent butterfat milk an equivalent value of Rs 2.70 per liter, as the raw material input to a dairy factory at the wholesale level. The farm gate price equivalent to this for buffalo milk, assuming no consumer differentiation between products made from raw milk and reconstituted products, would be Rs 2.3 per liter after allowing for collection charges.

Though buffalo milk is hardly traded internationally, its economic value was calculated based on import substitution. The analysts did not apply a taste premium.

Table 6.01. The Border Price Equivalent of Buffalo Milk in Pakistan

	US$/ton
Butter oil	
US$/ton C&F Pakistan	17,50
Local transport (economic cost)	50
Economic price at factory gate	1,800
Nonfat dry matter (NFDM)	
C&F Pakistan	1,100
Local transport	50
Economic price at factory gate	1,150
Buffalo milk ingredients value	US$/ton of milk
6 percent butter oil	108
9 percent NFDM	103.5
85 percent water	211.5

Most milk in Pakistan, however, is not sold to dairy factories, but is marketed as raw milk. This locally traded milk is considered by the buyer as a retail product and has an equivalent economic price, at the retail level, of about Rs 5 per liter. The price includes adjustments for processing, packaging, and distribution costs. (In most countries, milk retails for over double the farm gate price, and Pakistan is no exception. Farmers sell milk for Rs 3 to Rs 4.5 to local consumers, cafes, or other trade users, after allowing for the costs of local farm milk distribution.)

To estimate the economic price of milk at the farm gate, locally sold milk and milk sold to the processing plants were considered as having different economic values. The proportion that was sold to the dairy industry was considered to have an economic value of Rs 2.3 per liter at the farm gate, while that proportion consumed at the producing farm, or retailed locally, was estimated to have an average farm gate value of Rs 3.5 per liter. Overall, on project farms about two-thirds of the production was expected to be sold to dairies, or wholesalers, while one-third was retailed. This gives an average economic price of Rs 2.7 per liter (i.e., [0.67 x 2.3] + [0.33 x 3.5]). Because world prices of nonfat dry milk and butter oil were not estimated to have either an upward or downward trend, this price was taken to remain constant over the project period and was used in valuing the milk during the life of the project.

❖

Farm gate values for milk sold to processors differed from that of milk sold for fresh consumption.

Case 7. Valuation of Traded Outputs: Uncertainty in the Direction of the Parity Value; The Somalia Case

Summary. *In this case we address the issue of a country at the margin of self-sufficiency in food grains, combined with the uncertainty of rainfed cultivation. A weighted average economic value is calculated for maize in Somalia, where the weights are based on Somalian experience with weather cycles. This case is based on World Bank (1987).*

The Semi-Mechanized Rainfed Agriculture Pilot Project in Somalia is a continuation of the pilot field trials started at Kurtun Waarey and Sablaale sites in the southern part of the country, where herdsmen had been resettled from the North following a drought in the late 1970s. The project aims to put in place a technical and organizational system as part of a larger strategy, which includes irrigation, livestock, health and range development [World Bank (1987)].

The price of maize is a critical factor in the project's success and for wider aspects of Somalia's agricultural development. Until 1982, prices for domestic maize and sorghum—the overwhelmingly dominant local crops—were severely depressed on account of the government procurement policy and ban on private trading. The result was a decline in the domestic production of these cereals for over a decade, massive food aid imports, and destruction of the local marketing system. With liberalized marketing, maize and sorghum prices rose dramatically between 1982 and 1985 (at one point in 1984 the prices rose to twice the import parity levels), which generated a rapid and large production response.

Lately, because of good seasonal conditions, farm prices have settled at or near import parity levels. Somalia is gradually approaching self-sufficiency in the production of maize and in these circumstances, prices should move toward export parity. However, in a poor season, Somalia is likely to import maize, and prices will tend to move toward import parity. Historically, drought has occurred in three seasons out of eight. This probability can be used to calculate a weighted average of import and export parity prices for use in the financial and economic analyses (see Tables 7.01, 7.02, and 7.03).

Table 7.01. Somalia: Semi-Mechanized Rainfed Agriculture Pilot Project Projection of Economic Export Parity and Farm Gate Prices for Maize

(constant 1986 US dollars/ton)

	1986	1990	1995
International price of US No 2 yellow maize Africa destination	123	150	150
Freight and insurance	(40)	(40)	(40)
Value of white maize FOB Mogadishu	83	110	110
At US $1 = 120 Somali shillings			
Value of white maize, FOB Mogadishu	9,900	13,200	13,200
Port clearance, handling, and transport to store	(1,200)	(1,200)	(1,200)
Value of maize in store, Mogadishu	8,700	2,000	12,000
Less: transport from the project area	(1,500)	(1,500)	(1,500)
Farm gate value of maize in project area (export parity)	7,200	10,500	10,500

When weather is good, Somalia may export maize. In those years, the export parity value is the proper economic value of maize produced by the project.

Table 7.02. Somalia: Semi-Mechanized Rainfed Agriculture Pilot Project Projection of Economic Import Parity and Farm Gate Prices for Maize
(constant 1986 US dollars / ton)

	1986	1990	1995
International price, white maize, FOB Gulf	98	120	120
Freight and insurance	70	70	70
Value of white maize, CIF Mogadishu	168	190	190
At US $1 = 120 Somali shillings			
Value of white maize, CIF Mogadishu	20,160	22,800	22,800
Port clearance, handling, and transport to store	1,200	1,200	1,200
Premium for white maize, 25 percent	5,340	6,000	6,000
Value of maize in store, Mogadishu	26,700	30,000	30,000
Less: transport from the project area	(1,500)	(1,500)	(1,500)
Farm gate value of maize in project area (import parity)	25,200	28,500	20,500

When weather is not good, Somalia has to import maize to maintain domestic consumption. In those years, the import parity value is the proper economic value for the project's maize production.

Table 7.03. Somalia: Semi-Mechanized Rainfed Agriculture Pilot Project: Projection of the Weighted Average Farm Gate Price for Maize
(constant 1986 Somalia shillings / ton)

	1986	1990	1995
Farm gate price for maize	13,950	18,750	18,750

Note: The weighted average consists of 3/8 import parity farm gate price + 5/8 export parity farm gate price.

Note the large difference between the export parity values of Table 7.01 and the import parity values of Table 7.02. Remember that the freight costs which protect local producers from imports turn around to penalize them when they try to export. Note that, in this case, international freight costs are higher for imported maize than for exported maize. The analyst assumed that imported maize would come from the United States, whereas exported maize would go to African destinations. Had these assumptions been reversed, both parity prices—as well as the weighted average—would have been lower than indicated.

Because it is not feasible to know in advance which future years will be good and which bad, a weighted average parity value was calculated based on previous experience.

Case 8. Valuation of Traded Outputs: Uncertainty in the Direction of the Parity Value; The Colombia Case

Summary. *Set in Colombia, this case presents a "first-best/ second-best" issue in deciding whether to use the import or export parity price as the basis for calculating project benefits. In Gittinger (1982) and in this book, the issue of "first-best" versus "second-best" shadow pricing was discussed at some length. The issue related to whether we should base the shadow prices in economic efficiency analysis on the prices which would prevail if optimal policies were pursued (i.e., the first-best case), or whether we should base the shadow prices on the opportunity costs which existed, given the fact the government was not likely to pursue optimal policies (i.e., the second-best case) during the life of the project. In the case of Colombia, the issue boiled down to practical terms—i.e., whether to treat rice as an exported output, or as an import substitute, in project economic analysis [see World Bank (1986)].*

Agriculture is the most important sector in the Colombian economy; it presently accounts for about 22 percent of the GDP. Within the sector, crop and livestock products contribute about 52 percent and 43 percent, respectively, to the gross value of production; the remaining 5 percent comes from other rural activities. Agriculture employs two million people, or a quarter of the nation's labor force. The sector's share in Colombia's total registered merchandise exports has fluctuated between 67 percent and 75 percent in recent years.

Of the total value of agricultural exports of US$ 2 billion in 1983, coffee accounted for 73 percent, followed by bananas (7 percent) and flowers (6 percent). Agricultural imports represented 7.5 percent of Colombia's total registered imports for 1983. The main agricultural imports are wheat, soybeans, and fish products. Colombian yields of rice, sugarcane, coffee, cotton, and bananas are comparable with international levels, but for many other commodities, yields are low; and the scope for improvement is substantial. The performance of the livestock subsector has been sluggish over the last decade; only small productivity increases have been achieved.

A project has been proposed to support the rehabilitation of six irrigation districts, covering some 108,000 hectares. The rehabilitation would involve the construction of various irrigation works and the repair of river intakes, weirs, and other control structures. The training of district water users' associations and technical assistance would also be funded.

The chief quantifiable benefit of the project would be the increase in the value of agricultural production as a result of the intensified cultivation of land. For example, the incremental annual production of rice in the six districts is expected to be 72,800 tons, which would be 4.3 percent of national rice production in 1984. In financial prices, the gross value of production would increase from Colombian pesos (Col$) 4,955 million to Col$ 6,775 million at full development.

The economic valuation of the incremental production would depend upon the trade policies the government is expected to pursue. Some of the traded crops whose production is expected to increase under the project may not be tradable in principle. That is to say, Colombia subsidizes the exportation of some crops. In the absence of subsidies, the domestic costs of production may lie somewhere above their FOB prices, which would effectively prohibit their exportation, but below their CIF prices, which would mean that they would be cheaper to produce domestically than to import.

Let us recall that if the domestic costs of production of a commodity are below its FOB price, the economy profits in exporting the good; if the cost is above its CIF price, the economy benefits in importing the item; and if the cost falls in between, the good should not be traded at all. Another possibility is that in the absence of export subsidies, the real costs of production for some commodities may be above their CIF prices, which would signal that the country could be better off importing these items at the margin.

Consider the valuation of rice in the proposed project. Next to coffee, rice is one of Colombia's major crops eligible to receive subsidized export credit from PROEXPORT, the export promotion agency. In addition, the product also receives a tax-reimbursement certificate (CERT) of 25 percent, which is a return of income and land taxes. [Subsidies of this type are common throughout the world. The liberal interpretation of international trade agreements leads many countries to give rebates of domestic taxes on items to be reexported, arguing that the rebates are designed to "return the prices to international levels." Many countries have used this interpretation as a guise for providing export subsidies by calculating generous allowances (including large "wastage allowances") for the taxed inputs as a proportion of the cost of the product that is being exported.]

The economic valuation of the incremental production would depend upon the trade policies the government is expected to pursue.

Such assistance is deemed necessary, particularly in light of an overvalued Colombian peso. The overvalued peso discourages Colombian producers from exporting their products, since the foreign exchange they receive for their exports will be converted into a smaller number of pesos, when the conversion is done at an official exchange rate which overstates the actual value of the peso relative to foreign exchange.

The PROEXPORT subsidy, together with an additional variable export incentive above the CERT, was set to allow Colombian rice to compete on international markets, despite an overvalued exchange rate, whenever production surpluses were expected. [Rice is subject to an export quota, which is determined according to estimated production surpluses over domestic demand. It can be shown that the quota also acts like a tax in terms of the effect that it has on the local price relative to the border price of rice. See Thomas (1986), pp. 62-69.]

However, the domestic competitiveness of Colombian rice production has been eroding since 1975, despite favorable yields. The data in Table 8.01 suggest that domestic production costs may exceed the FOB price for rice even beyond 1982. If this trend continues, the fiscal burden on the government will increase. In view of this prospect, the government may decide to phase out the subsidies. It may also decide to devalue the peso. If this happens, the economic value of rice in the project will depend upon whether the commodity would still be traded—as an import, not as an export (i.e., if its domestic production costs lie above the CIF price)—or not at all (i.e., if the economic production costs fall between the FOB and CIF values).

If the commodity is likely to be imported as a result of foreseen policy changes, then the relevant accounting price to work with in project appraisal is the CIF price (or the import parity price). If, in the absence of subsidies and an overvalued exchange rate, the product would not be traded, then the rice should be priced according to its marginal social benefit. In other words, it should be priced according to the changes that increased production is expected to induce in Colombian incomes and patterns of consumption. In practice, we might have to assume that the production under the project would not affect the level of the domestic price of the project's nontraded output; therefore, the ratio of the marginal social benefit to the domestic price of the commodity (i.e., the commodity's accounting ratio) would be the consumption conversion factor.

Colombia's export subsidy on rice was designed to make up for an overvalued exchange rate.

Table 8.01. Colombia: Index of the Ratio of FOB International Prices in Pesos to Domestic Production Costs of Rice, 1970-1982

Year	Price ratio (1975 = 100)
1970	45.4
1971	60.8
1972	63.6
1973	97.0
1974	146.6
1975	100.0
1976	74.6
1977	75.9
1978	77.3
1979	65.7
1980	61.6
1981	66.3
1982	40.8

Source: Jorge Garcia-Garcia, "Aspects of Agricultural Development in Colombia," cited in Vinod Thomas (1986), p. 235.

The domestic competitiveness of Colombian rice has been eroding since 1975. Domestic production costs may exceed the FOB price for even beyond 1982.

Case 9. Valuation of Traded Outputs: Switching to Export Parity Pricing over the Life of a Project

Summary. *Analysts sometimes overlook the fact that project appraisal involves making two forecasts of the future: one with the project and one without the project. The with-project forecast deals with the effects caused by the project itself. The without-project forecast deals with all of the other things that would happen without the project as well as some things that would happen with or without the project. For example, the without-project forecast must foresee the changes in overall agricultural production that are taking place and which may have nothing to do with the project. These nonproject forecasts are critical in determining the shadow prices that are used for the project. The clearest case of the impact of the nonproject-related factors on project shadow prices is provided by the example of a country at the margin of self-sufficiency in basic foodgrain production. We present such an example from Sri Lanka. The text for this case has been adapted from World Bank (1981).*

Rice production provides an interesting case for observing what happens to the basis for shadow pricing for a country at the margin of self-sufficiency. Many of the world's major rice producers tend to trade rice—i.e., either export it, or import it—on the basis of balance between domestic production and domestic consumption. Countries will move from net importers to net exporters, or vice versa, over a short period of time. And when they make the transition, the basis for calculating border prices will also switch from import substitution to an export.

The basic objectives underlying Sri Lanka's Mahaweli Ganga Development Program, begun in the late 1970s, stem from a need to overcome three major problems facing the country: unemployment, the foreign exchange drain from excessive imports of food and other agricultural products, and a shortage of electric power for industrial development and rural electrification. A third stage of the program, a third irrigated agricultural development project, would provide new irrigation capability for 24,100 hectares and enhanced capability for another 3,620 hectares in other areas already serviced by the program. Most of this will be used for producing rice. The life of the project has been set from 1980 through 2005.

Based on World Bank's projections of population growth, food demand, and rice production, including incremental production attributable to the project, Sri Lanka is expected to become a net exporter of rice in the period 2000-2005. For this period, then, the

Sri Lanka was projected to be a net exporter of rice during the period 2000-2005.

economic price used in valuing rice production is based on the equivalent export parity price for paddy—whether or not the rice that comes from the project area is actually exported, since the net effect of the incremental production will be to make Sri Lanka a net exporter. The rice produced by the project during the period up to the year 2000, was treated as import substituting production and was therefore valued on the basis of import parity prices.

The export parity farm gate price for rice, based on the FOB price, is lower than the import parity price based on the CIF value. By using the export parity price during the period of expected net exporting of rice, the appraisal lowers the value of the net benefit of the project. This simply reflects the fact that more foreign exchange is saved per unit of rice consumed during the stage when domestic production substitutes for imports (1985-1999) than is gained in selling surpluses abroad during the stage of self-sufficiency (2000-2005).

The use of the export parity price after 1990 lowers the price of rice from Rs 4,793 per ton to Rs 4,244 per ton, or by 11 percent. However, because the lower price was used in the later years of the project's forecast life, the reduction did not greatly affect the project economic viability; the economic rate of return still exceeded 17 percent. However, had the export parity price been used to value all rice produced by the project, the 11 percent reduction in project benefits (rice constituted the bulk of project benefits) would have led to a much lower economic rate of return.

Whether the project analyst foresees Sri Lanka making the transition from being an importer to an exporter of rice is extremely important in determining the shadow prices that are used in valuing the project output.

Whether the project analyst foresees the country making the transition from being an importer to being an exporter can be extremely important in determining the shadow prices that are used in valuing the project output. Import prices tend to be higher than export prices, because the same shipping costs that protect local producers from imports turn around to penalize local producers when they become exporters. This problem becomes more acute the farther the country is from the sources of supply and from markets for their output. In this example, we can see the effect that the transition from importer to exporter was expected to have on Sri Lanka. And Sri Lanka is located near to suppliers and to export markets for rice. For African countries, the relative difference between import prices and export prices would be even greater.

❖

Case 10. Valuation of Traded Outputs: Switching to Import Parity Pricing over the Life of a Project

Summary. *As presented in Case 9, the without-project forecast is extremely important because it will be instrumental in determining whether we use import or export prices. If we forecast little progress in nonproject areas, then this will imply that self-sufficiency will be slower in coming. As a result, the higher import-substitution prices will be used for a time period in the project planning process; and projects will look correspondingly more attractive. If we foresee rapid nonproject developments, then self-sufficiency will be attained more quickly; and the lower export prices will be used in the analysis. It is also possible that a country will move from being an exporter to being an importer, as was the case with Côte d'Ivoire in the late 1970s when rising incomes increased the demand for oils and fats at a greater rate than the growth in output of palm and coconut oil. As a result, in the fourth Oil Palm and Coconut Project (presented below), the basis for valuing the project's output can change from one of export to one of import substitution [see World Bank (1977)].*

The Fourth Oil Palm and Coconut Project, supported by the World Bank, was to be implemented in the sparsely populated Southwestern region of Côte d'Ivoire. In this part of the country, oil palm and coconut, together with rubber, had been identified as products with opportunities for development.

When the project was being prepared in 1975, annual palm oil exports had reached 108,000 metric tons. All the production from the project in the Southwest was expected to be exported. Consequently, the economic value of the project's production used in the appraisal was based on the FOB price for palm oil. The production from the project's plantations was expected to reach full maturity in 1985.

Since 1975, the Ivorian population has enjoyed some substantial increases in income. A proportionate increase in the consumption of oils and fats had accompanied this improvement in incomes so that palm oil exports dropped from 68,000 tons in 1980 to 25,000-30,000 tons in 1983/84. Assuming that the per-capita consumption of industrial edible oils remains unchanged, the domestic demand for edible oils is projected to exceed domestic supply by the early 1990s. Unless other action is taken, Côte d'Ivoire will become a net importer of palm oil. This would mean that at the time of the appraisal the project's production from 1993 onward should be

Increases in domestic demand are expected to change Côte d'Ivoire from a net exporter to a net importer of palm oil.

259

based on its import value (the CIF price) rather than its export value (FOB price).

A fifth project has been proposed to assist Côte d'Ivoire to meet the increasing demand for fats and edible oils by both replacement of existing aging oil palm trees and planting new trees in selected areas. The incremental production in oil palm resulting from this activity is expected to maintain the country's status as a net exporter through the year 2000 and some time beyond. The economic analysis of this follow-on project, unlike the appraisal of the fourth project, is appropriately based on the export value of oil palm throughout the life of the investment.

The fifth project is expected to change the country back to a net exporter of palm oil. The economic analysis of this project should be based on the export value of oil palm throughout the life of the investment.

Case 11. The Economic Value of Traded Goods with Variable World Prices

Summary. *When a country is a major producer of a good, we must look not just to an exogenous forecast of the CIF or FOB price; we must also look at the effect that the country's actions have on the CIF or FOB price. We should take into account the price elasticity of demand for the product in international markets. In this case, we address the issue of variable border prices for Egyptian exports of long staple cotton, a commodity which Egypt exports in large volume to the world. Egypt is a large enough producer that—by building additional production capacity—the country may drive down the world price of that commodity. This factor is taken into account in estimating the benefits from producing additional quantities of long-staple cotton.*

Most of the material in Gittinger (1982), and in this book, assumes that a country is not a major importer, or a major exporter, of the traded goods that are involved in the project. In economists' jargon, we would say that we have assumed that the elasticity of supply of imports was infinite at the forecast CIF price; similarly, we also would have assumed that the world demand for the country's exports was infinitely elastic at the forecast FOB price. This is sometimes called the "marginality assumption."

While the assumption made in the preceding paragraph will normally be sufficient, it is not always true that a country's actions will not affect world prices. For example, Bangladesh can affect the world price for jute by increasing its own production and exports, because Bangladesh is a major producer of jute and a major supplier to world markets; Saudia Arabia can clearly affect the world price for crude oil; Brazil cannot assume that its coffee production does not affect world prices; and Zambia cannot ignore the effects that its copper production has on the world price of copper.

When a country is a major producer of a good, we must look not just to an exogenous forecast of the CIF or FOB price, but we must also look at the effect the country's actions have on the CIF or FOB price. In the case of an export by a major producer of the good (e.g., Bangladeshi jute or Thai rice), the benefits would be calculated from the "marginal export revenue," which would be different from the FOB price without the project, since the FOB price would be forced down by the project's output.

The "marginality assumption" is used when the country is a small exporter or importer of a product relative to world trade.

The "nonmarginality assumption" applies when the country is a major exporter or importer of the good.

We should take into account the price elasticity of demand for the product in international markets. [For Bangladesh jute, an estimate of 0.7 is generally used for the price elasticity of exports; Thai rice export revenue is sometimes forecast based on a price elasticity of 4. For details see (Ahmed (1984), p. 9.] We need to calculate a range of values for the marginal export revenue, because of the uncertainty of the other parameters needed to make a precise estimate of the marginal export revenue. In the Egyptian case, the government would be interested in knowing the marginal export revenue associated with various possible outcomes when appraising projects or policies that are likely to affect the level of exports of Egyptian cotton.

The problem here is similar to that faced by an oligopolist or a monopolist in deciding whether to increase output. Because the demand that the producer faces is downward sloping, an increase in output by a major producer will cause the price to drop. Thus, marginal revenue will be below average revenue, and both will decrease as output is increased. The producer, of course, is interested in marginal or incremental revenue in making production decisions. And the question becomes one of whether the incremental export revenue brought about by the project, exceeds the incremental cost imposed by the project. To conduct this kind of analysis, we must estimate the marginal export revenue for different levels of exports from the project.

The marginal export revenue would be used in the project appraisal in place of the fixed FOB price that we had assumed previously in the "normal" case. The normal case is one in which a country is a minor producer of the good and in which marginal export revenue and average export revenue are the same and are unrelated to the level of exports by that minor producer. Obviously, a counterpart problem would exist for a country that is a major importer of a particular commodity. For example, when the Soviet Union imports grains, it has a major impact on world prices, so it takes this impact into account in making import decisions. In this case, the country must look at the "marginal import cost."

Marginal Export Revenue.
The change in export revenue brought about by exporting an additional unit of the good.

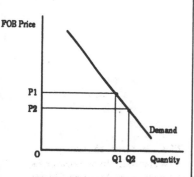

P1 = Price without project

P2 = Price with project

Marginal export revenue
= P1Q1 - P2Q2

Overall, Egypt is a relatively small cotton producer, with only 5 percent of the world's production of all varieties. It is, however, a major exporter of longer staple varieties, accounting for about 30 percent of the world trade in long-staple cotton and about 60 percent in extra-long staple. Considering its large market share in extra-long staple, in particular, it would be inappropriate to assume that Egypt cannot influence the world price of this cotton. The more it brings this cotton to market, the lower the world price will be. The current FOB price, therefore, is likely to overestimate the rate at which additional production can be traded for foreign exchange.

Presuming that Egypt influences the world market price for extra-long staple cotton, the relevant reference for border pricing is the marginal export revenue, which is essentially the focus of a monopolist. Formally, the expression for marginal export revenue is:

$$p(1-1/n)$$

where **n** is the percentage increase in the world quantity demanded over current levels for Egyptian extra-long staple cotton in response to a percentage decrease in its FOB price (the absolute value of the price elasticity of world demand), and **p** is its current FOB price.

The marginal export revenue is the commodity's shadow price for use in the economic analysis, if domestic consumption of the good and the foreign exchange costs of its domestic production would be unaffected by the introduction of the project. Otherwise, we would have to adjust the marginal export revenue by using estimates of the share of imports in the home consumption of the good and the good's domestic price elasticity of demand, price elasticity of supply, marginal social benefit, and marginal social cost. [For a detailed discussion of this far more general case, see Tower and Pursell (1986), pp. 75-92; and Squire and van der Tak (1975), pp. 142-144.] To simplify analysis, we frequently presume that the domestic price elasticity of demand and the price elasticity of demand of supply, or the share of the exported good in domestic consumption, are negligible. These are rather strong assumptions.

Should we have the rather unusual opportunity to appraise a project which would affect the world price of an export commodity, the chances are that we would most likely not have the information or the means for estimating the marginal export revenue. (Let us assume we can ignore the effects on domestic consumption and production costs.) Indeed, we should not expect to construct a statistical model of the global market for the good. This work should be left to institutions such as the World Bank, the International Monetary Fund, the Food and Agricultural Organization of the United Nations, or government trade ministries with resources for such analysis. However, we can perform a few alternative appraisals using different values of **n** to test the sensitivity of the project's economic viability. It may be appropriate to identify a switching value of **n**, below which the project becomes undesirable. If the project is large enough to affect world prices to an extent that the project could fail the selection criterion—the opportunity cost of capital—we should consider delaying the project until information becomes available to suggest whether we should expect the actual value of **n** to be above this switching value.

The marginal export revenue may be the relevant economic price to use for an exported output when "nonmarginality" applies.

Often, we will not have the data needed to calculate the marginal export revenue, or the marginal import cost.

Table 11.01. Extra Long Staple Egyptian Cotton
(Price per ton)

Price component	Market value (E£)	Conversion factor	Economic value (E£)
FOB	800	1.008	800
Marketing	(38)	0.86	(33)
Transport/handling	(60)	1.34	(80)
Ginning	(80)	1.21	(96)
Miscellaneous	(45)	0.32	(14)
Taxes	(167)	0.00	0
Farm gate price	410	-	577
Conversion factor		1.41	

Price component	Market value (E£)	Conversion factor	Economic value (E£)
FOB	600	1.00	600
Marketing	(38)	0.86	(33)
Transport/handling	(60)	1.34	(80)
Ginning	(80)	1.21	(96)
Miscellaneous	(45)	0.32	(14)
Taxes	(167)	0.00	0
Farmgate price	210	-	377
Conversion factor		1.79	

In the case of Egyptian extra-long staple, however, it may be possible to estimate the marginal export revenue without an econometric study by using the world price of a closely related commodity. Although Egypt can influence the price of extra-long staple cotton, it can be considered a price-taker for long staple cotton, whose price would presumably set the floor for the price of extra-long staple.

Page (1982, p. 94) provides an indicative, farm gate economic price estimate for extra-long staple, applicable until 1985, based on the expectation that the FOB price of long staple will be, in constant 1982 terms, between E£ 800 and E£ 600 (see Table 11.01). The conversion factors for the items in the price structure had been previously derived (see Case 1).

In the absence of adequate data on the marginal export revenue, we may choose to augment the switching value analysis.

[For a numerical example of a conversion factor calculation taking into account domestic consumption and production cost changes, see Ahmed (1984), p. 70, which uses the formula from Squire and van der Tak (1975), p. 144.]

❖

Case 12. Valuation of Nontraded Project Outputs: Production of Tradables for Subsistence

Summary. *In this case, we address the issue of tradable products which are nontraded at the margin. The increase in agricultural production in this project in Uganda is expected to be consumed by the domestic producers, with the result they have no marketable surpluses with which to purchase imported commodities. The earnings from the incremental production would have to be valued on the basis of what these rural producers would be willing to pay for imported commodities had the incremental production not been committed to subsistence. The earnings would need to be adjusted by a suitable conversion factor to get the value of nontraded outputs in foreign exchange. This case has been adapted from World Bank (1984).*

A smallholder project has been proposed to increase food production and family incomes in Eastern and Northern Uganda. The main elements of the proposed project include:

a. the procurement of input supplies and the strengthening of the management of input distribution;

b. the provision of civil works, vehicles, equipment, technical assistance, training, and research; and

c. the strengthening of agricultural extension as well as monitoring and evaluation services.

The chief benefit of the project would be the increase in agricultural production of exportable and traditionally nontraded crops. By exportable, we mean the domestic costs of production fall below, or are equivalent to, export parity prices. The domestic prices of the nontraded crops are below the equivalent import parity prices, but lie above the equivalent export parity prices. The rural markets for these goods operate freely without distortionary taxes.

However, the present levels of farm production and consumption in the project area are so low, that a bulk of the increase in agricultural production under the project is expected to be consumed on the farm. Households presently consume whatever they produce: they have not had marketable surpluses with which to purchase imported commodities. The agricultural infrastructure in the area is weak, and the expected impact of the project's provision of inputs on yields is uncertain. In the economic analysis of the project, it is probably best to assume that incremental production will not be traded.

Exportables are goods whose costs of production lie below their export parity prices.

The most important consequence of the project would be the improvement of nutritional levels for the rural population rather than import savings or export earnings. The increases in production would not mean that items that otherwise would have been exported would be consumed domestically, or that surpluses would be exchanged for the consumption of additional imported goods, subject to tariffs or subsidies. It would then be appropriate in this instance to use prevailing financial prices—such as they are for what little is traded internally—for the values of outputs in the project's economic appraisal.

If all of the agricultural commodities involved in the project were nontradables in principle (i.e., domestic production costs fell between equivalent export and import parity prices)—and increased production and income were to imply increased internal trade in the country and consumption of tradables among the rural population, then we would need to take this into account in the economic analysis. The economic prices in the analysis would have to be based on the prices that consumers are willing to pay—as opposed to parity prices—but these would have to be adjusted by a conversion factor. Ideally, it should be the consumption conversion factor for the rural population concerned, or less ideally, the standard conversion factor estimated for the country.

The rationale for using the consumption conversion factor is as follows. Suppose that with every 100 shillings worth of incremental production not committed to subsistence, a household purchases 80 shillings of imported wheat subject to a tariff; 10 shillings worth of exportable maize subject to a duty; and 10 shillings worth of subsidized, imported kerosene. Suppose that the accounting ratios of these commodities are, 0.60, 0.80, and 1.20, respectively. The conversion factor for the value of the project's incremental production would be:

$$(0.80 \times 0.60) + (0.10 \times 0.80) + (0.10 \times 1.20) = 0.68.$$

If there are no tradables affected by the project, then economic values would have to be based on the willingness to pay, converted to foreign exchange impacts using a conversion factor.

In terms of the foreign exchange numeraire, every 100 shillings that the targeted smallholders earn from the incremental production of internationally nontraded outputs is worth 68 shillings of foreign exchange. In contrast, the rather special assumptions we have made regarding the consumption of the proposed project's production in Uganda imply that a hundred shillings of production is worth a hundred shillings of foreign exchange. This follows because, in the consumption of the incremental production, foreign exchange is neither saved nor used.

❖

Case 13. Valuation of Nontraded Project Outputs: Nontradables with Importable Substitutes

Summary. *This case addresses the issue of finding border values for nontraded outputs. In this example, maize is considered a close substitute for sorghum and millet. Maize is traded, while the other two cereals are not. Import parity prices and conversion factors for maize are calculated and used for the nontraded substitutes. The text has been adapted from World Bank (1986).*

The Federal Government of Nigeria requested the World Bank to fund an agricultural development project in Borno State. The proposed project would support the efforts of Borno to provide improved services to the rural population in the better endowed southern third of the state. It would aim to improve the supply of agricultural inputs, strengthen the extension service, and develop small-scale irrigation for the purpose of increasing farm incomes and crop output.

The project would increase the production of sorghum and millet, among other crops. Both of these commodities are nontraded, which would mean that in the economic appraisal of the project we would have to estimate accounting prices based on the marginal social benefits from the increased production of these crops. Unless there is evidence to the contrary, we would ordinarily assume that the elasticity of domestic demand for these two commodities is perfect. What this says is that the project's incremental production would not lower domestic market prices. Under this assumption, the ratio of the marginal social benefit to the market price of one of the commodities is the consumption conversion factor (CCF). The CCF is similar to the standard conversion factor (SCF) in that it is a general conversion factor reflecting the degree of divergence between international and domestic prices in the economy.

Whereas the SCF is based on the total values of imports and exports and the average tax rates on imports and exports, the CCF is based only on those importables and exportables that are a part of a typical household's basket of consumption goods. In practice, the calculation of the CCF is often based on the consumption of a typical household of average income in the country. It would be preferable to calculate separate CCFs for urban and rural households, and possibly for subgroups within these two broad divisions, but usually the information to do a credible job on this is lacking.

While the SCF is based on the total values of imports and exports and the average tax rates on imports and exports, the CCF is based only on those importables and exportables that are a part of a typical household's basket of consumption goods.

If data on household consumption are unavailable, or their collection is too time consuming, the SCF is used as an estimate of the CCF, but this is bound to be a rather crude estimate as the SCF includes items not representative of consumption baskets. Differences in relative distortions between sectors also tend to average out in the SCF by the law of large numbers.

In the appraisal of this project, the World Bank staff estimated a CCF to convert the domestic financial prices of millet and sorghum into their economic equivalents. The appraisal staff noted that millet and sorghum are substitutable staples in the Southern Borno area. Of the total area of farm land, sorghum was to cover roughly 52 percent, millet 41 percent and maize 7 percent. Cowpeas was to be widely interplanted through much of the sorghum and millet crop. Vegetable production, under irrigated conditions, was to take place in small pockets adjacent to rivers and access roads. As close substitutes in consumption, millet and sorghum were expected to command the same price. If the price of millet decreased, the price of sorghum was expected to decrease as well.

The Bank's appraisal staff also assumed maize to be fully substitutable for either millet or sorghum, as Nigeria normally imports maize to make up for shortfalls in the local production of sorghum and millet. Maize is a traded commodity whose price is internationally set. Since maize is substitutable for millet and sorghum, the domestic prices of millet and sorghum would be no less than the import parity price for maize. If the price of maize were less than the price of millet and sorghum—assuming full substitutability—then rural consumers would purchase only maize. Likewise, producers knew that they would capture the entire grain market if their prices were less than the import parity price for maize. It would be to their benefit to have the millet and sorghum price close to the import parity price for maize since this price represented the most that they could obtain for their production.

As the financial prices of millet, sorghum, and maize are considered to be the same under the assumption of full substitutability—their economic prices would be the same as well. The CIF border price for maize, adjusted for distribution and transportation costs—was used as the basis of the economic price for the grains in the project's appraisal. The economic price for the coarse grains is given in Table 13.01. The accounting ratio—the ratio of the economic to the financial price—for coarse gains was 0.53 in 1986.

Prices of substitute products tend to move together.

If the population in the project area is fairly homogeneous, and if maize is the most important tradable commodity that would be a

Table 13.01. Nigeria: Southern Borno Agricultural Development Project; Financial and Economic Farm Gate Prices for Coarse Grains

	Financial prices		Economic prices	
	1986	1990	1986	1990
Cost per ton (FOB US$)[a]	105	111	105	111
Freight and insurance to Nigerian ports ($/ton)	45	45	45	45
CIF Nigerian ports ($/ton)	150	156	150	56
CIF Nigerian ports (N/ton)	150	156	150	156
Port handling and clearance (N/ton)	18	18	6	6[b]
Transport to retail market (N/ton)	75	75	29	29[c]
Reference market price (N/ton)	243	249	185	191
Less:				
Local transport costs (N/ton)	15	15	6	6[c]
Primary marketing costs (N/ton)	24	24	8	8[b]
Add: Value of stalks (N/ton)	60	60	20	20[b]
Farm gate prices (N/ton):	264	270	191	197

Coarse grains CF = 191/264 = 0.53

Source: World Bank, (1986c).

Note: Coarse grains here include sorghum, millet, and maize.

a. Only maize prices are used since there is little international trade in sorghum and millet, and Nigeria would normally import maize to make up for shortfalls in the local production of sorghum and millet.

b. The standard conversion factor (SCF) has been taken to be 0.33. Up to September 1986, the official exchange rate (OER) of the naira was fixed at 0.8 naira per US dollar. After September 1986, an auction market for foreign exchange was established by the Central Bank. By May 1987, the exchange rate in the auction market had devalued the naira to approximately 4 naira per US dollar, which indicated the degree to which the OER had overvalued the naira during 1986. The conversion factors that were used in the appraisals of Nigerian projects during 1986 by the World Bank had to reflect distortions between the prices of traded and nontraded goods. The distortions were caused by the overvaluation of the naira in that period of a fixed and overvalued OER.

c. A transportation conversion factor (TCF) of 0.39 has been applied. See footnote b for an explanation of the low value of all conversion factors for Nigeria in early 1986.

Because of the substitutability in consumption between maize, sorghum, and millet in Nigeria, the analyst used the parity price for maize to value the other two grains.

part of an area household's consumption, 0.53 would constitute an appropriate CCF for the project's output. Note that what this says is that for every 100 naira worth (in financial prices) of millet, sorghum, or maize produced by the project, the economy saves the equivalent of about 53 naira in foreign exchange (at the official exchange rate). The SCF, at the time of the project, was calculated to be 0.33—much below the coarse grains conversion factor of 0.53. Consequently, it would be more appropriate—if the ratio 0.53 represented a consumption conversion factor for the project—to use this figure instead of the SCF to value the production of cowpeas and vegetables in the project.

[In 1986, the Nigerian naira was officially valued at US$ 1.25, a rate which overvalued the currency by 300 percent. In the autumn of 1986, the government instituted an auction system for foreign exchange which, by May 1987, allowed the value of the naira to fall to about 4 naira per US dollar.] Without offsetting changes in the commercial regime—such as tariff and nontariff barriers—the change in the exchange rate should have brought the SCF of 0.33 back toward 1. Similarly, all of the CFs would have been affected and would need to be recalculated since the commercial regime was also being adjusted at the same time. [See the discussion in Part IV concerning the effects of domestic inflation on the nominal and real exchange rates and the political pressures it creates for a country's commercial policy.]

This is an example of how a project appraisal might approach the valuation of a nontraded output in the absence of appropriate CCFs when the output can be considered to have a fully substitutable traded alternative. Note that this assumption of substitutability is less reasonable at some times than at other times—as in the example of fresh milk output (see Case 5).

❖

The low values of the CCF and SCF for Nigeria in 1986 derived from the severe overvaluation of the naira at that time.

The lack of a good CCF estimate led the analyst to use the parity price for maize in valuing the consumption benefits from sorghum and millet production.

Case 14. Valuation of Commodities that are Important as Final Goods and as Intermediate Goods in the Consumption of Different Income Groups

Summary. *This case looks at yellow maize in the Philippines, a commodity that is both a feedgrain and a foodgrain. The issues surrounding foreign exchange and distributional impacts are discussed. The structure of the example's argument follows Little and Mirrlees (1982), pp.167-169.*

Two forms of maize are grown in the Philippines: white and yellow. White maize is consumed as food by low income groups; it is also used as a feedgrain to produce livestock products that are consumed by higher-income Filipinos. (White maize accounts for about 75 percent of the total maize production.) Yellow maize is used exclusively for animal feed.

Because of equity concerns, the Government of the Philippines maintains a monopoly on the importation of yellow maize. Now consider that a project has been proposed to increase the domestic production of yellow maize in some region in the country, as a result of which the market price would be lowered and benefits would accrue to the private sector. How should one value the incremental maize production in terms of foreign exchange in the hands of the government, assuming that the government will maintain its import monopoly?

The relevant price for valuing maize production in this case is not the international CIF price, but rather the price of the commodity based on the willingness to pay. This does not mean that the economic value of incremental maize production is equivalent to its financial value. It is important to note how benefits are distributed as a result of a fall in the price of the intermediate good. Let us suppose that domestic production of yellow maize is insignificant and that the government imports the national supply, say 10,000 metric tons. Let the monopoly price of the maize be normalized to 1 peso per ton. Let us also suppose that the project produces 1,000 tons and that to market the total national supply (the government's 10,000 tons plus the project's 1,000), the domestic price drops from P 1 to P 0.95 per ton.

First note that the total expenditure on the yellow maize increases from P 10,000 to P 10,450 (i.e. 11,000 x 0.95), an increment of P 450.

It is important to note how benefits are distributed as a result of the fall in the price of an intermediate good.

271

Livestock owners spend P 450 more on yellow maize than they did before the project's production. Government revenue falls from P 10,000 to P 9,500, a reduction of P 500. The maize growers, selling the maize to livestock owners, make P 950 in domestic terms. Now, suppose that the revenues of livestock owners increase by P 970 because the better-fed cattle command a better price among the final consumers, or simply because there is more meat on the hoof to sell. We shall assume that any increases in the market price for meat as a result of improved quality does not involve a social cost. In domestic terms, the livestock owners enjoy a benefit of P 970 - 450 = P 520. This may be converted in border terms by multiplying it by the standard conversion factor (SCF), say, 0.80. The livestock sector's benefit is P 520 x 0.80 = P 416. If the livestock sector spends P 450 more on maize, P 450 less is spent on other commodities. Suppose that the P 450 has been diverted from expenditures on some good imported with a 10-percent tariff. Government revenue is further reduced by P 41.

P 450 = border price x (1 + 0.10) x quantity,

which implies that the tax revenue is:

(P 450/ 1.10) x 0.10 = P 41.

The income of the maize growers in border terms is:

P 950 x SCF = P 760.

All together, the social benefit of the incremental production is:

P 416 + P 760 - P 500 (the government's loss of sales)
- P 41 (loss of import tariff revenues) = P 635

The ratio of the social benefit to the domestic value of the incremental maize production is, thus:

P 635/ P 950 = approximately 0.67

In this example, the economic analysis must summarize impacts on the government, maize producers, livestock producers, and consumers.

What this means is that every P 100 spent on the project's incremental production of yellow maize is worth P 67 in foreign exchange (in the hands of the government). If distributional weights were applied to the consumption of those less well off and to that of those who eat the cattle feeding on the maize, this economic price would be lower to reflect equity concerns for the poor. The result of doing this could be to skew the selection of projects away from the production of yellow maize that goes for cattle feed and toward food crops that benefit primarily lower income groups—i.e., if the economic price of white maize is shown to be competitive with the price of yellow maize. In any event, this example shows that the economic value of the incremental production of an intermediate good that is imported under fixed supply is not necessarily the sum that buyers (here, livestock owners who use the good as an input) are willing to pay. The economic valuation depends upon the distribution of the benefits of the production and the nature of the substitute uses of income.

Note that if the project were public, the government would have an increase in revenue of P 450 (P 10,450 - P 10,000). Assuming that all other benefits were the same, the social benefit would be:

P 450 - P 41 + P 416 + = P 825.

The accounting ratio would then be:

P 825/P 950 = 0.89.

This means that every P 100 spent on the project's incremental production of yellow maize is worth P 89 in foreign exchange in the hands of the government.

Now consider the presence of other domestic producers of yellow maize. Their total production is less than the total volume of imports and they cannot expand production in the short term to erode fully the government's import monopoly. (This is actually not true in the Filipino case, but heuristically let us assume it is so.) The prevailing market price is set by demand, and is somewhat less than the price that would accompany a full state monopoly. Since there are other producers, the fall in price as a result of the project—considering all other supplies as being fixed—results in a loss that is divided between the government and the other private producers. That loss is less than the P 500 calculated previously because the revenue of the private producers is likely to be valued less than the loss borne by the government. Let us suppose that the government loses P 400 and the private producers lose P 100. In terms of the foreign exchange numeraire, the government loss is P 400 (the government does not make transfer payments to itself), but the private loss may be estimated as:

P 100 x the SCF, here, 0.80.

The total producers' loss would then be:

P 400 + P 80 (i.e., P 100 x 0.80)= P 480.

If equity concerns are taken into account, the CF would likely be lower.

The CF would be different for maize produced in a public maize production project compared with a private project in this hypothetical example.

This example illustrates some of the complexities that can arise in conducting project economic analysis and the need for the analyst to clearly think through the possible market interactions that may occur. The need to work through these interactions, of course, is most critical for the major inputs and outputs—i.e., the ones that meet Gittinger's (1982) "materiality" criterion. Project outputs (except, perhaps, in projects producing numerous small outputs) will almost always be "material," in this sense, and should normally be analyzed with attention to detail.

Only major items should be subjected to such detailed analysis of market interactions.

Technical Notes

Note 1. Perfect Competition

A considerable part of microeconomics is devoted to describing the "correct" choices of inputs and outputs for producers, under a particular environment in which such decisions are to be made. Here, the term "environment" encompasses such things as the set of existing markets, a producer's degree of influence upon the prices of inputs and outputs, technology, information, government policy, and various forms of risk and uncertainty. When speaking of the "correct" choices for producers, we must keep in mind the assumptions being made about the producer's environment.

If we assume that producers act to maximize profits; have full information; behave competitively without influence upon prices; work with constant returns to scale technology—or at least without increasing returns to the technology—and are unaffected by government actions, then we can readily show that production levels and inputs are chosen such that wages and factor prices are equated with their marginal value products.

In other words, wages and factors are equaled with the value of the extra output produced as a result of employing one more unit of a factor, while holding the employment of all other factors constant. This description of the "optimal" behavior of a producer can change as we vary the assumptions made about the environment.

In addition, there are ways in which the stylized environment just described relates to one of perfect competition, discussed further in Part I. The assumptions for perfect competition underlie much of the so-called neoclassical economics. The perfectly competitive environment may not correspond well with reality in many or most instances, but it nevertheless remains an important benchmark case leading to relatively simple, tractable results. In some circumstances, the assumptions may serve as a rough approximation.

For standard treatments of the theory of the perfectly competitive firm, see Laidler (1981), Henderson and Quandt (1980), Malinvaud (1977), and Varian (1984) to mention a few. These texts, listed in increasing order of difficulty also discuss some of the complications arising from relaxing the assumptions of perfect competition.

In addition, there are a few other useful surveys of the economic consequences of variations in the size of industry, limited access to information, risk, uncertainty, and government policies on taxation. When the number of firms is small enough to influence the market prices of a differentiated product, or for certain inputs, monopolies or oligopolies develop, and "optimizing" behavior differs from that of the purely competitive firm. The behavior of monopolists— being an extreme case at one end of the pole with the extreme conditions of perfect competition being at the opposite end—is well understood. The mechanics of two-firm markets, or duopolies, have also received much attention.

When a market involves several firms, and assumptions about the similarity of firms are relaxed, the description of "correct" behavior becomes much more complicated and enters the realm of game theory. For a survey of oligopoly theory under conditions of full information, see Friedman (1983). In oligopolistic settings, uncertainty or incomplete information regarding, for example, other firms' motivations leads to various types of strategic behavior; see Vickers (1985) for a useful review. [Also consider Varian (1984) for a good, general introduction to the economics of information.] For an introduction to game theory, see Friedman (1986). An extensive and at times mathematically demanding treatment of some of the implications of risk in agricultural production can be found in Newbery and Stiglitz (1981). For an account of the effects of taxation upon production, see Atkinson and Stiglitz (1980), lectures five through seven. All of these documents have extensive references.

Note 2. Consumer Theory

The consumer's problem of choosing a bundle of goods, with given prices and a budget constraint, is similar in form to the problem of a competitive firm. The competitive firm chooses a technically feasible, optimal production plan, with given prices of its output and inputs. Excellent standard texts for consumer theory are Green (1976) and Deaton and Muellbauer (1980). Both works discuss consumer choice under uncertainty, a useful survey to consider is Hey (1984).

Note 3. Keynesian, Classical, and Neoclassical Approaches

How do prices that competitive firms and consumers face come about? The existence and stability of a set of economywide "correct" prices are subjects of a difficult branch of economics called general equilibrium theory. [Those who are interested should refer to the seminal work of Debreu (1959).] We broach the topic here because a fundamental notion behind shadow pricing is the idea that we can imagine a "shadow equilibrium," supported by a set of shadow prices, where supplies are balanced by demands in all markets. The neoclassical macroeconomic perspective takes the view that automatic mechanisms exist in a competitive monetary economy, if there is sufficient flexibility in prices, to ensure that material balances will emerge.

The ability of an economy to rebalance itself

after a disturbance (such as the introduction of a project that may divert some of the economy's resources from other uses) through appropriate readjustment of prices provides the basis for the exercise of shadow pricing. Like general equilibrium theory, macroeconomics can be concerned with the determination of prices and factor incomes—at a somewhat aggregated level of analysis—but we need not presume that prices in force in an economy will necessarily clear markets.

It is common for texts to present Keynesian and classical perspectives as two opposing general approaches to macroeconomic analysis. In the Keynesian approach, aggregate output is demand-determined; it does not guarantee that the economy will operate at full employment unless the government intervenes to maintain an appropriate aggregate level of demand. The inability of the economy, left on its own, to maintain full employment is generally attributed to rigidities in prices and wages. For example, in Keynesian modelling of (Western, industrialized) economies where output is represented by a single homogeneous product, the money wage is given at any point in time [see Sargent (1979)]. The level of price, aggregate output, employment, interest rate, flows of consumption, and investment are determined by the system simultaneously.

In the classical approach, by contrast, the money wage is a variable to be determined by the system. Classical modelling includes a separate condition specifying balance in the labor market. As a result, the model "dichotomizes," or breaks down into two separate parts. In the first part, the "real" or nonmonetary variables of aggregate supply—such as output, employment, and the real wage—are determined. The rest of the model shows that aggregate demand in turn adjusts through variation in money values to achieve overall balance between supply and demand. Full price flexibility in the classical model ensures that the amount of labor supplied is the amount demanded, and not more; with equilibrium in the labor market, the economy is at full employment in the sense that all those who wish to work at the equilibrium wage can do so. Thus, there are workers who voluntarily remove themselves from the workforce. From the classical point of view, if *involuntary* unemployment does exist, it may be attributed to a real wage that is not flexible downward. Whether the high rates of unemployment in Western Europe during the first part of the 1980s were of the Keynesian or the classical type has been an issue of considerable debate because the appropriate policy responses for restoring full employment are quite different in the two cases [see Blanchard, Dornbusch, and Layard (1986)].

For our purposes, we can work with either a Keynesian or a classical framework. However, in the Keynesian model (presuming rigid wages over the pertinent planning period), we assume that the government can manipulate the exchange rate or tax policies to maintain full employment and material balance in the economy [see Tower and Pursell (1986)]. Shadow prices for an economy having automatic adjustment mechanisms, according to the neoclassical view, are likely to differ from those in an economy where the government is playing an active role to keep internal and external balance. The essential difference between the classical and neoclassical models of a competitive monetary economy is the inclusion in the neoclassical model of the real balance effect as an important adjustment mechanism in the short term. The "real balance effect" refers to the short-run influence of prices upon the demand for money, which in turn can affect the real parts of the economy.

In the long run, it can be shown that the behavior of the neoclassical model approaches that of the dichotomizing classical model [Grandmont (1983)]. As pointed out in Tower

and Pursell (1986)—citing recent work by Blitzer, Dasgupta, and Stiglitz (1981); and Bell and Devarajan (1983)—the calculation of shadow prices may depend upon the adjustment mechanisms at work in an economy. This paper adopts a neoclassical perspective to facilitate the discussion, but also to elaborate some practical guidelines for estimating shadow prices. As always, a certain price in rigor is paid for simplifying.

To be honest, there are reasons to doubt that the automatic adjustment mechanisms in the neoclassical models of competitive monetary economies are always strong enough to do the task [see Grandmont (1983)]. Therefore, there are reasons to doubt that some active government intervention will not be necessary. We should bear this in mind, but should not lose sight of the central concept we hope to illustrate here: the shadow price of a factor or good in the foreign exchange numeraire is the amount of foreign exchange that the economy must give up every time one unit of the factor or good is withdrawn from the private sector and diverted to some other use (such as a government project) if full employment is to be maintained through the operation of appropriate adjustment mechanisms, and real income is to remain constant [see Tower and Pursell (1986)]. Examples of "appropriate adjustment mechanisms" include government policies, market mechanisms, or some combination of both.

The alternative to assuming general equilibrium—including the Keynesian case of the rigid wage, but accompanied by compensating government intervention—is to conjecture that, at least in the short run, markets may not clear. Planned or desired demands and supplies may not be realized. In the absence of adjusting prices, quantity rationing may take place. This disequilibrium view of macroeconomics can offer some rather interesting insights into the effects of alternative government policies given, for example, possible adjustment costs in changing prices or the strength of unions in labor negotiations, in the short run.

However, difficulties arise in explaining why prices should fail to adjust in the face of excess supplies and demands as time goes on. We might then be justified in defining shadow prices in terms of hypothetical long-run adjustments restoring desired balances in the economy. Those who are interested in temporary equilibria with quantity rationing should read Barro and Grossman (1974), Muellbauer and Portes (1978), Dixit (1978), Neary (1980), Neary and Roberts (1980), and Benassy (1982). For a review of this literature, see Cuddington, Johansson, and Lofgren (1984). (Soon after the appearance of his 1974 article, Barro abandoned his interest in the disequilibrium perspective and devoted his writing to neoclassical macroeconomics).

Note 4. Economic Efficiency and the Pareto Efficient Equilibrium

Underlying the neoclassical approach, discussed in Technical Note 3, is the notion of equilibrium in a competitive monetary economy. There are actually several concepts of equilibrium to which economists often, if only implicitly, refer. For an excellent discussion of equilibrium concepts in economics, see the first chapter of Dasgupta and Heal (1979). Here, we wish to point out that the neoclassical competitive equilibrium has the attribute of being Pareto efficient. By this we mean that no other equilibrium is possible in which one individual is judged better off without making at least one other person worse off. [For practical measurements of individuals being judged as being better off in terms of consumption-based welfare, see Deaton (1980), Ng (1983), and Varian (1984), among others.]

We should bear in mind that a Pareto-efficient competitive equilibrium is not necessarily equitable from a social point of view. In general, many competitive equilibria may be possible, depending upon the distribution of resources, or of entitlements to the use of resources, in the economy. Moreover, any allocation of resources in an economy which is Pareto-efficient, and at the same time socially desirable, can be supported as a competitive equilibrium through an appropriate redistribution of resources. However, in practical terms, this is a rather difficult task because individuals would have to reveal quite a bit of information about their abilities and preferences when it may not be in their best personal interest to do so.

We might then regard the neoclassical approach as being in a sense neutral on the distribution of income: efficiency is defined primarily on technical grounds as the benefits that may accrue to any one group in the economy which are not valued any differently than those received by any other group. For such comparisons, the shadow pricing would need to partition economic agents by income and by other characteristics, solicit the preferences of the individuals within these groups, and combine these preferences to define the representative, collective choices for each group. Judgments regarding the relative values of the consumption of different groups would appeal to some specified social welfare function (SWF) [see Ng (1983)]. There are problems with each of these steps.

Technically and politically, a government may find the task of gathering information treacherously difficult to carry out. There are many technical problems to aggregation. Moreover, the selection of the SWF is a matter of judgement: it may be impossible to devise a social ranking of preferences which is rationally consistent with the rankings of individuals. [For a discussion of these so-called "impossibility" propositions, see Ng (1983). The efficiency approach described in Gittinger (1982), and discussed in this volume, refers to the problems of collecting information and making valid interpersonal comparisons.

The focus of the analysis, therefore, is a somewhat narrow one: the maximization of income and consumption, where accruals to all individuals, including the government, are valued equally. Note that the force of this position is that all incremental project-generated income contributes equally to growth in the economy whether in the form of additions to consumption, or investment; and that the economy is already saving at the right rate [see Squire and Tak (1975), p. 4 and following]. Moreover, the efficiency approach—since it does not consider distribution effects—also neglects giving special consideration to the value of foreign exchange in the hands of the government.

For governments that are concerned about inequality and willing to parameterize the values of consumption to different groups, the Squire and van der Tak methodology of 1975 sets out a procedure for taking the distribution of income into account. Examples of the application of the Squire-van der Tak method can be found in Cleaver (1980), Mashayekhi (1980), and Ahmed (1984). In practice, many governments have considered the use of any explicit set of distributional weights on consumption to be too provocative.

However, the efficiency approach is not meant to provide shadow pricers with an avenue for conducting politically neutral investment analysis. It simply ignores certain considerations that governments will nevertheless need to contend with. After all, neutrality (on the distribution of income and project benefits) itself is properly subject to ethical judgment. Full noncommitment may

eventually be as politically disruptive as a specific assignment of distributional weights. Note also that neoclassical macroeconomics refers to the operation of particular adjustment mechanisms in an economy. The achievement of a Pareto-efficient equilibrium may not be beyond an activist government trying to respond to genuine market failures or imperfections. This is discussed further in the this volume. For more on the properties of competitive equilibria, see Ng (1983), Boadway and Bruce (1984), and Varian (1984).

Note 5. Growth Theory

Intertemporal decisionmaking and optimal growth are not simple subjects. For introductions to the theory of consumption over time, see Green (1976) and Deaton and Muellbauer (1980). The basic reference for growth theory is Dixit (1976). You may also wish to consult Burmeister (1980), and lecture seven in Atkinson and Stiglitz (1980). For an example of an application of optimal growth theory to shadow pricing foreign exchange, and deriving the discount rate for investment analysis, see Dervis, Martin, and Wijnbergen (1984).

Note 6. Input Subsidies

The level of fertilizer subsidy has been a rather sensitive issue between the World Bank and Nigeria. Generally, it is argued that in certain circumstances a temporary fertilizer subsidy may be justified to assist the adoption of the use of fertilizer in a particular crop region of a country: "The only theoretical case for a permanent fertilizer subsidy is the existence of a nonoptimal tax on output for public revenue purposes. The subsidy is justified primarily for highly fertilizer-responsive crops, such as irrigated rice and maize. The same rationale can be applied to food crops when the goal of the government is to increase food self-sufficiency, despite the fact that the objective is not usually economically efficient. In both cases, using fertilizer subsidies for highly responsive crops will be more effective for the treasury than to use output price support. However, this type of subsidy cannot be effective in the countries of the Sahel because of poor fertilizer response of the crops grown there" [Binswanger and Shalit (1984)].

However, evidence from India suggests that fifteen years of subsidy ought to be long enough for most farmers to have a good acquaintance with that input [see Cheong and D'Silva (1984), p. 27, particularly footnote 1]. See also Timmer (1985 and 1986) on rice production in Indonesia, where crop response has justified temporary use of a fertilizer subsidy.

Note 7. Interest Rate Distortions

For a discussion of these issues see von Pischke, Adams, and Donald (1983 and 1984); also Braverman and Guasch (1987). Yugoslavia is an example of a country which has suffered from gross interest rate distortions and misdirected investment. Interestingly, correcting the interest rate distortions alone would probably not improve Yugoslavia's employment and severe balance of payments problems and may even worsen them [Yagci and Kamin (1987)]. This is an example of one of the propositions of the "theory of the second best," discussed in Technical Note 20. In the case of Yugoslavia, it would appear that an exchange rate devaluation would have to accompany a reform in interest rates. Thus, addressing an artificial distortion, or market failure, in an economy may require a compensatory policy package and not a simple withdrawal of the offending policy. This may be one reason why projects appear attractive as substitutes for policy reforms. See the "policy versus projects" discussion in Chapter 8.

Note 8. Social Choice

As mentioned in Technical Note 3, a basic result in welfare economics is that under certain conditions, a competitive equilibrium is Pareto efficient; however, several Pareto-efficient competitive equilibria are generally possible with appropriate redistribution of resources. The "fair" equilibrium is presumably the one favored by society as a whole, but how is the social choice determined? A serious difficulty lies in determining whether the preferences of individuals over possible outcomes, expressed, say, by a system of majority voting, can be used to construct a meaningful social choice. For a discussion, see Ng (1983), Sen (1970, 1973, 1977, 1984, 1985 and 1987), and Varian (1984).

Note 9. Ranking Policy Choices

As opposed to the earlier utilitarian approach of Bentham, Mill, Sidgwich, and Edgeworth [see Spiegel (1971)], recent work in welfare economics has been concerned with the ranking of alternative economic policies without making assumptions about the comparability of individual welfares. Although the so-called "new welfare economics" has provided some guidelines to ranking policies, it does not [as discussed by Atkinson and Stiglitz (1980), pp. 351-352] allow a complete ranking of all policies. Policymakers may still need to specify alternative social welfare functions (SWF)— even if any one SWF cannot be reliably chosen—to test the sensitivity of a policy's consequences to underlying normative commitments.

Note 10. Market Failures in Agriculture

For a discussion of market failures in agriculture, see Stiglitz (1987). Besides commenting on the complications introduced by the presence of public goods, increasing returns, and externalities, Stiglitz also directs attention to incomplete markets in insurance futures and credit and to imperfect information.

Note 11. Comparing Private and Social Profitability

You might think that the usual rule of deleting taxes and subsidies implies a hypothetical adjustment of the market prices facing producers and consumers. This is incorrect. If this were so, and we imagine the aftermath of the removal of all tax elements from market prices, then any subsequent changes in consumer and producer behavior would alter the supplies and demands the analyst had wished to value. This is why it is worth stressing that shadow pricing is an exercise comparing measures of private and social profitability under a set of policies that are not expected to change. Unlike the objects under study in quantum mechanics, economic activities are not altered by this act of measuring because there is no real, or imagined, interaction between behavior and values. Of course, it might be the case that a government decides to abandon some policies as a result of shadow pricing, but this moves beyond what a set of shadow prices proposes to do. Changes in the prices facing economic agents do alter the rules of the game. As a result, we are not necessarily talking about the same economy in comparison; expected changes in material balances would have to be taken into account. For further discussion about the treatment of taxation in shadow pricing, see Little and Mirrlees (1982), pp. 75-79, pp. 156-161, and pp. 223-228.

Note 12. Monopolistic Pricing

Monopolistic pricing according to the interaction of supplies and demands in a market is Pareto inefficient. Consider a single good, the demand for which increases as its price to consumers decreases. In other words,

the price that consumers are willing to pay for the good varies inversely with the good's availability. Suppose the monopolist produces an arbitrary amount, which could be sold entirely at some price to consumers. Now consider the production of one more unit of the good. At the initial price, the monopolist would receive an increase in revenue equal to that price. However, to sell all of the production, including the extra unit, the selling price must decline by a certain amount. The monopolist then loses some revenue on each unit of the initial quantity of production. The difference between the value of production, including the extra unit, at the initial price and at the new clearing price, as determined by the demand response, is the marginal revenue of the firm at that level of production. In theory, the monopolist (who produces a good or service which can be resold) operates to equate marginal revenue with his marginal production cost (the cost of producing one more unit). The market determines at which level the monopolist will produce, but at this level, the price which the consumer pays is a markup from the marginal cost of production. This contrasts with pricing in the perfectly competitive environment, where the price of production is equated with its marginal cost.

Suppose the monopolist is operating at the level of production where his marginal revenue is equal to his marginal cost. If the monopolist could discriminate in his pricing, then he could produce one more unit of the good and sell it at a price that is, say, a little below the initial price. Since the price of this unit is still above the cost of producing of it—which is the marginal cost of production at the initial level—the monopolist could make an extra profit. Consumers benefit by having an extra unit of the good according to their willingness to pay for it. Moreover, these additional monopoly profits could be distributed between the firm and consumers to make everyone better off. This process of making Pareto improvements by producing additional units and selling them at declining prices could continue as long as the price at which consumers would purchase a unit of production lies above that unit's marginal cost [Varian (1984), pp. 184-185]. The competitive level of output is reached when the price of an extra unit equals its marginal cost.

Note 13. Optimal Prices for the Regulated Monopoly

The basic argument is that economic efficiency can be improved, if the prices of a regulated monopolist were chosen to maximize the sum of consumers' and producers' surpluses. If the regulated monopolist were operating with constant marginal costs and producing goods the demands for which were independent from one another, then the optimal set of prices would be defined by the marginal costs in each of the monopolist's markets. If the monopoly is "natural" with decreasing average costs, and the firm must operate with the constraint of breaking even out of its sales, the set of optimal prices for the regulated monopoly—called the Ramsey prices—becomes more complicated. The calculation of these prices can be simplified if we impose certain conditions upon consumer demands [see Brown and Sibley (1986)].

Note 14. Political and Institutional Pressures

Though politics and political culture are outside the scope of this book, an understanding of the political and institutional pressures which have shaped policies are a real part of the exercise of economic analysis. It is essential to understand how distortions have been introduced into an economy and how these have persisted in order to forecast shadow prices and future policy responses to expected structural changes which might occur. Moreover, it is not enough to identify reforms toward greater efficiency in an economy; we must at the same time assess whether proposed economic reforms are indeed practical and sustainable with benefits

reaching targeted groups. Economic prescriptions are desirable insofar as they are feasible. Of course, owing to the many substantial differences among cultures, political processes, and institutions, it would be unhelpful or even foolish to search for generalizations, but we could draw attention to the imperatives of nation-building—as distinct from state-building—confronting especially the countries of Sub-Saharan Africa. For an interesting case study, see Bienen's (1983) account of investment allocations in Nigeria. For useful theoretical discussion of these issues, see Schmid (1978), Ng (1977 and 1987), and McKee and West (1987).

Note 15. Economic Value of Nontraded Commodities

Consider, for example, the valuation of sorghum and millet in Nigeria (Case 13 in Part V). Here, the nontraded food commodities substitute in consumption for other tradable items. The economic value of these nontraded commodities in a foreign exchange numeraire is then the foreign exchange that can be earned from the release of these goods from domestic consumption (assuming that present nontraded production is relatively unresponsive to domestic price changes).

Note 16. Shadow Price of Foreign Exchange

Another definition of the shadow exchange rate, which is also related to SER1, is the shadow price of foreign exchange in utility numeraire, discussed in Tower and Pursell (1986), pp. 44-46 and p. 94; and in Warr (1980), p. 34. It is the amount of real income which must be given up to earn one unit of foreign exchange. If a project generates an amount of producers' and consumers' surplus at consumers' prices, while using an amount of foreign exchange, the net benefit of the project can be determined only if all the items were expressed in common units of account. This could be done by dividing the value of the producers' and consumers' surplus by the shadow exchange rate. This might be called a "social" shadow exchange rate because its definition depends upon the marginal propensities to consume of those who would be directly affected by the set of taxes and subsidies imposed by the government to convert real income into foreign exchange. The price of foreign exchange will change when the government moves from one system of direct taxes affecting one group of consumers to another system affecting some other group with different marginal propensities to consume.

Note 17. Conversion Factors for Intermediate Goods

The calculation of the conversion factors for intermediate goods is simplified by assuming the provision of supplies at constant costs. (For an example, see Case 1 in Part V.) When an input is in limited supply, and particularly when it is a primary factor of production, we need to look at the social benefits forgone in withdrawing some of the inputs from the private sector for use in a project. Human labor or land usually falls in this category, but animal labor may as well. (See Case 2 in Part V, which considers the value of bullock labor in Indonesia.) In general, the shadow price of a factor is the sum of its marginal net products, each valued at its shadow price, where the marginal net products are calculated under the assumption that the government releases a unit of factor and adjusts purchases and sales of goods to freeze prices, while also adjusting factor-specific income taxes and subsidies so as to leave after-tax wage rates unchanged [Tower and Pursell (1986), p. 53].

Note 18. Demand-Price and Supply-Price Conversion Factors

This describes a demand-price conversion factor for a nontraded good and applies, strictly

speaking, when the supply of the good is unresponsive to changes in its domestic price (perfectly inelastic supply). However, it is frequently assumed that additional supplies can be provided at constant cost (perfectly elastic supply). This greatly simplifies the shadow pricing, for if a nontraded good is supplied at constant costs, its border price is the value at world prices of its traded direct and indirect inputs plus the value at shadow prices of its domestic primary factors. This is the result of Diamond-Mirrlees (1976) and is the rationale behind Case 1 in Part V concerning the pricing of electricity in the West Nubariya New Lands Project. Consequently, a conversion factor derived from the costs of producing a nontraded good is called a supply-price conversion factor. For further comments, see Tower in Tower and Pursell (1986), pp. 110-111.

In general, the supply of a good has an upward-sloping supply curve (imperfectly elastic supply). In other words, the supply of the good is responsive to changes in the producer's price. In this case, the conversion factor is a weighted average of the good's demand-price and supply-price conversion factors, the weights being supply and demand price elasticities [see Squire and van der Tak (1975), pp. 144-145 and Tower's follow-up remarks in Tower and Pursell (1986), pp. 114-116].

Note 19. Macroeconomic Analysis

Policymakers refer, at least implicitly, to some model of the economy. Although it is not always clear when gauging the macroeconomic consequences of policies in some developing countries which principles and theoretical procedures should best be applied in analysis, practically speaking, some assumptions need to be made on a case-by-case basis, unless evidence indicates that they should be abandoned or modified, in the hope of offering some useful information for governing.

Unfortunately, this procedure may encourage an inertia in policy to set in, as the onus may be not so much on policymakers, given their own political and institutional interests, to validate assumptions as it may be on others to discredit them. Yet policymakers may feel bound to discredited policies even when they have lost enthusiasm for the principles (or the model) behind them.

In Africa, for example, import substitution strategies in the 1960s, adopted by many newly independent countries keen on establishing state institutions and demonstrating economic independence, discounted the responsiveness of African agriculture to effective taxation. As governments increasingly relied on agriculture for revenue as public sectors ballooned, fiscal urgencies made it harder to consider changes in tax incidence, regardless of the strength of assumptions [see World Bank (1984), Nellis (1986), and Anderson (1987).] Here, the issue is not simply the capability of economic analysis, or the institutionalization of economic policy reform, but of having the financial means to consider necessary departures from the *status quo* [see World Bank (1986)].

Since the 1960s there have been numerous pathbreaking and controversial developments in macroeconomic theory. Pending empirical studies, the relevance of these developments for developing countries have yet to be firmly established. Much will depend upon the credibility of government behavior and on the nature, availability, and use of economic information in microeconomic decisions. For useful reviews of approaches to modelling developing economies, see Prachowny (1984) and Taylor (1983). See also the work in multimarket analysis by Singh, Squire, and Kirchner (1985); Braverman, Ahn, and Hammer (1983). Corden (1987) is another good reference on macroeconomic analysis for developing countries.

Note 20. The Theorem of Second Best

One of the propositions of the "theorem of second best" is that when one or more of the first order conditions characterizing the ideal of a competitive equilibrium do not hold, then we should not expect that it would be desirable to have any of the other conditions to hold. In other words, if there are a number of distortions in an economy, correcting any one distortion to move toward perfect competition may not enhance welfare; it may even worsen the situation. Of importance here is not simply the efficiency losses resulting from a policy, but also the possible short-run social costs of removing the distortion.

For a concrete example, consider the rice pricing policy in Thailand. Following World War II, rice export taxation amounted to about 35 percent of FOB value. The tax was meant, first, to transfer financial surplus from the farmer to urban employers and the government. Second, it was meant to buffer domestic rice prices from international price shocks. The taxation resulted in lowering the intensity in the use of inputs, which resulted in low paddy yields [O'Mara and Le-Si (1985)]. Apparently, the low use of inputs has not been a concern because surpluses were still being generated from new lands. As O'Mara and Le-Si describe, all suitable land for rice cultivation is now in use.

Moreover, Thailand can no longer afford the efficiency losses from the taxation because rice is no longer a primary source of government revenue. Elimination of the tax, however, is not a simple choice and probably should not be undertaken without other accompanying measures to ease adverse effects on producers and consumers. Rice provides over half of the calories in the Thai diet and is the major determinant of wages and the cost of living. Most Thai farm families grow rice, but because family sizes, farm sizes, and growing conditions vary considerably from region to region, not all are net sellers of rice. If the tax is removed, it is bound to signal changes in production and consumption which will hurt those families which are, or subsequently become, net purchasers of rice. We do not mean to suggest that the desirability of efficiency pricing as the basis for shadow prices in project analysis depends on fragile assumptions. As Little and Mirrlees explain—referring to the formal presentations of Diamond and Mirrlees (1971), Dasgupta and Stiglitz (1972), and Mirrlees (1972)—the basis for border pricing depends on rather weak assumptions, despite the presence of distorting taxes, externalities, public goods, monopolists, price bargaining, and irrational behavior [Little and Mirrlees (1982) pp. 367-373]. This is discussed in this volume.

Note 21. Quantitative Trade Restrictions

Bhagwati and Srinivasan (1981) formally demonstrate why Little-Mirrlees border pricing is not appropriate in the presence of quantitative trade restrictions. They also show that these restrictions can be modified by eliminating, with offsetting subsidies, the changes in consumption distortions that the restrictions generate to preserve the applicability of the Little-Mirrlees prices.

As a rule of thumb, if quantitative restrictions are binding, then the restricted commodity should be treated as a nontraded good because, at the margin, it is not traded [see Tower and Pursell (1986)]. In other cases where the restrictions are not wholly binding, the force of the quantitative restriction may be represented by an implicit tariff rate. A discussion of this may be found in Squire and van der Tak (1975). Also see Dervis and Robinson (1978) and Mashayekhi (1980) for analytical examples.

Note 22. Trade Data and the Consumption Conversion Factor

See Case 13 in Part V for an example of the use of the CCF. For examples of calculating a CCF using trade data, see Mashayekhi (1980) and Ahmed (1984). The Thai case [Ahmed (1984)] is particularly interesting because the value of the CCF, derived from the trade data for the period 1976 through 1980, implied that the average distortion for consumption goods was almost nonexistent, although it was commonly known that the average rate of protection in the imported goods sector had been large. The reason for the overestimation of the CCF was that the average share of consumption goods exports in total trade of consumption goods was 80 percent, and export taxes on rice tended to offset the effect of the average import tax on consumption goods. Separately, conversion factors for imported and exported consumption goods were 0.773 and 1.032 respectively. The trade value approach also overestimated the CCF because it did not take into account Thailand's market influence on the world price for rice. Ahmed (1984) demonstrates that the CCF is sensitive to assumptions about the nature of the world demand for rice.

Note 23. The Economic Value of Fuelwood

The economic value of fuelwood can be similarly derived by using the values of imported fuel substitutes such as kerosene (see Cases 5, 6 and 13). However, the valuation of fuelwood can be peculiar because in addition to the value of imported substitutes, we may also need to consider—in areas where pressing shortages of fuelwood have led to evironmental degradation—the value of incremental production increases and foreign exchange savings on fertilizers when an improvement in the availability of fuelwood would release supplies of animal dung to agriculture (see the discussion on the Bangladesh Mangrove Forest Project in Chapter 12).

Note 24. Farm Labor and the Consumption Conversion Factor

In China's Red Soils Area Development Project [World Bank (1986)], it was determined that local farm labor received in domestic terms twice its true marginal value product (MVP). A farm laborer's MVP is therefore one half of the market wage. Since this labor is used to produce chiefly food commodities consumed in the area—commodities which are tradable, or have traded substitutes—the MVP is in turn adjusted by a rural consumption conversion factor. Note that even if it were felt that the market wage does represent a laborer's MVP because there is no widespread unemployment or underemployment (since wages are not sticky, or factor market distortions are absent), the use of the consumption conversion factor would still be necessary as long as there are distortions in product markets.

Note 25. The Border Pricing Procedure and Optimal Tax Theory

Second-best Taxation and Production Efficiency. The basis for the border pricing procedure can be found in optimal tax theory. In an influential paper, Diamond and Mirrlees (1971) explored the best use of commodity taxes after ruling out (rather, after accepting the reality of not having the choice of) lump-sum taxation. The chief result of this analysis is that public production should be efficient. That is, at the position where the economy is contributing the most to social welfare with optimal commodity taxes in place, the government can decentralize production in the public sector by having managers maximize profits at the level of producer prices associated with the optimal level of public sector production. At this optimum, the marginal rates of transformation throughout public production are the same. Moreover, production in the private sector should also be efficient for those parts of the economy operating competitively under constant returns to scale,

as long as all inputs and outputs are subject to taxation. In this aggregation of production sectors, all marginal rates of transformation are equated. Production in this sum of public and private sectors can be directed by a common set of producer prices. For small, open economies trading at internationally fixed prices, the efficiency result means that the appropriate prices for production involving tradable goods are their world prices. [In the terms used in Bhagwati and Srinivasan's (1983) survey of trade theory, the foreign rate of transformation (FRT) should be equal to the domestic rate of transformation (DRT), but may vary from the domestic rate of substitution (DRS).] There are no tariffs as such; although, imports of final consumption goods may bear a charge as their domestic substitutes carry consumption taxes.

The border pricing rule in cost-benefit analysis is an application of the production efficiency result and as such is an implication of the "theory of second best." Under this theory, in the presence of an irreversible distortion in the economy, social welfare may be improved with the introduction of a second distortion (to offset the first), but welfare will not be as high as would be with the use of a measure that directly neutralizes the source of the problem. Thus, the unavailability of lump-sum taxation means that we cannot dismiss the problems of inappropriate income distribution, as in the fundamental welfare theorem, and the use of instruments should bear as directly as possible on achieving the appropriate distribution. Consumption taxes can be employed because of the income effects they induce, while leaving production efficiency unaffected (as long as production operates under constant returns, or profits can be taxed away).

Piecemeal Policy Reforms. This feature of the targeting of interventions suggests that the violation of the Pareto conditions characterizing the first-best economy (FRT=DRT=DRS) should be minimized by class. If a consumption externality exists, the best response to it is an appropriate intervention directly targeted at the consumption distortion, leaving all other relations intact. If this response is not feasible, then the introduction of an offsetting distortion may improve welfare. Conversely, the removal of an existing consumption tax or subsidy, which does not correspond with the second-best use of commodity taxes, must consider why the distortion exists in the first place. If the situation exists as the best response to another distortion, then the negative admonition of the second-best theory comes into play. If it is a historical accident, there is less cause for alarm in suggesting a remedy.

However, if a distortion exists because of a political lobby, the distortion—depending on strengths of political influence—may be irreversible, which, as we mentioned earlier, modifies how remaining policy instruments are used for a "third-best" result. In short, the second-best theory does not entirely rule out piecemeal policy reform; the theory suggests that for reform to be successful, it should focus on groups of goods strongly related to one another through substitution or complementarity. For further discussion of tax reform in theory and practice, see Newbery and Stern (1987); and Dixit and Kyle (1985), part 4.

The principle of targeting extends to trade policy and domestic production. Domestic production externalities imply corrective taxes on domestic production only: optimal trade policies are not involved. With other things at their second best, only trade distortions—e.g., a country not exploiting its monopoly power in trade—separating the foreign and domestic rates of transformation call for trade policy interventions. [For expositions, see Bhagwati and Srinivasan (1983); and Dixit and Norman (1980), chapter 6.] Tariffs should not have a redistributive or a revenue-raising appropriate distribution. Consumption taxes can be employed because of the income effects they induce, while leaving production efficiency unaffected (as long as production operates under constant returns, or profits can be taxed away).

The targeting principle also pertains to the pursuit of noneconomic objectives by the government. For example, domestic production targets, say, specifying grain production for purposes of food security, should be encouraged not through the protection of an import tariff, but directly through a production subsidy. The argument that a tariff might also raise some amount of government income is not relevant [see Dixit and Kyle (1985)].

Project Appraisal and Trade Theory. Little and Mirrlees are most commonly associated with presenting the implications of optimal tax theory for small, open economies and for the appraisal of projects undertaken in such economies. At the time Little and Mirrlees came out with the first version of their project appraisal manual (the OECD Manual), trade theory, in subjects such as second-best tariff setting [see Corden (1974) for a survey], had also been wrestling with similar issues of optimization, subject to policy-imposed distortions; yet at that time, a treatment of cost-benefit analysis within a fully specified trade model was lacking. Important papers filling this gap included those by Findlay and Wellisz (1981), Srinivasan and Bhagwati (1978), and Bhagwati and Wan (1979). These papers took up the determination of shadow prices for nontraded factor inputs.

There was also some confusion as to whether or not the border pricing approach described by Little and Mirrlees (1969 and 1974) represented a second-best rule when distortionary tariffs and other taxes already existed in the domestic economy [see Weckstein (1972)]. The fundamental premise for the analysis of taxation in Diamond and Mirrlees (1976) was after all the unavailability of lump-sum taxes. The optimization problem that followed then allowed for the free choice of sets of prices for producers and consumers. In other words, the tax problem was not explicitly set up to optimize under given price constraints. Joshi (1972) identified the problem of using the world pricing rule for tradables when quantitative trade restrictions are binding. Lal's (1984) survey and comparison of cost-benefit approaches presented the Little-Mirrlees shadow pricing of traded (in the absence of strict trade quotas) commodities as a procedure applicable in the presence of these distortions, but did not offer a formal demonstration. Diamond and Mirrlees (1976) and Warr (1980) have clarified the principle rigorously; see also Bliss (1987).

Treatment of Nontraded Goods.

The shadow pricing of nontradables by their "foreign exchange equivalent" is a problem. The Little-Mirrlees method converts a non-traded commodity into traded commodities, which are valued at their world prices, by calculating the marginal social costs of its inputs. This method is not generally correct. It is correct when, as a result of a change in public production, or use of a nontraded commodity, adjustments take place in private sector production and not in consumption [see Warr (1980)]. In other words, the nontraded good is not consumed and is used only in the production of consumable goods, which are all tradable; or it is consumed, but its demand is unresponsive to price; or its supply is perfectly elastic. [Findlay and Wellisz (1981) and Srinivasan and Bhagwati (1978) assume the first case—that the nontraded good is not consumed.] This production side adjustment is the assumption underlying the use of input-output tables, as discussed in Case 1 in Part V, for constructing average conversion factors. For many items, such as electricity, it is probably a reasonable approach. Milk may be one example of a nontraded item where consumption adjustments come in. In practice, however, it seems that there would be few such cases to worry about.

We should also note that, strictly speaking, if the special assumption of adjustments only in private production is valid, the technologies involved must be of fixed coefficients for observed estimates to represent the proportions used of inputs after the adjustment takes place. Cost minimizing firms will adjust proportions of inputs used, if possible, in response to input price variations, which are possible in the short run for nontradable inputs with changes in their public sector production or use (as in a project, for example). For small changes in production or use, as compared to the rest of the economy, production coefficients are not likely to change much. In practice, the foreign exchange equivalent method for pricing nontradables may provide a reasonable approximation to the actual shadow value of nontraded goods. For an exposition and assessment of pricing rules for nontradables, see Warr (1982).

The Optimal Tax Problem and Agriculture.

In discussing the meaning and application of second-best theory, some of the general implications of optimal tax theory for cost-benefit analysis have also been noted. However, because national contexts and pertinent constraints vary, these general guidelines will require some modification. Indeed, Heady and Mitra (1984) demonstrate that it might be desirable to tax inputs into near subsistence agriculture, which would imply that the prices of tradable inputs in that sector of the economy might not equal their world prices. In light of what has already been said about second-best theory, this should not appear as too surprising. Some of the aspects of agriculture in developing countries which would bear on tax analysis and the choice of prices for project appraisal have already been noted. Newbery and Stern (1987), Heady and

Mitra (1984), Ahmad, Stern, and Leung (1987), Newbery and Kyle (1985), Newbery (1989), Atkinson (1987), and Sah and Stiglitz (1984) discuss appropriate agricultural taxation at length.

The basic efficiency result from optimal tax theory states that intermediate goods should not be taxed and the incidence of commodity taxation should be shifted entirely to consumers. The economic model underlying these conclusions allows the government to choose which prices consumers and producers should face to guide their decisions. All goods could be subject to taxation (or subsidization) in which case there would be no limitations on which prices the government could alter.

The analysis also makes the assumption that all production takes place under constant returns, so there are no profits; or under diminishing returns, where there are profits, but these are fully taxed away. The force of this feature in the model is that production changes do not transmit changes in consumption through the channel of profit income.

For agriculture in developing countries, neither one of these assumptions is likely to hold. Agricultural land, inelastically supplied, generates rents which are difficult to tax, if they can be taxed at all. A discussion of the availability and effectiveness of various agricultural tax instruments may be found in Newbery and Stiglitz (1987). Also— particularly when subsistence households are involved—it is difficult, if not impossible, to have consumers face prices which differ from the prices they receive as producers. Thus, in this part of the economy, not all transactions can be taxed.

Because of the constraints on taxing rural

profits and the transactions between producers and consumers who are the same individuals, the desirability of taxing production arises. Corlett and Hague (1953-1954) pointed to this possibility in presenting a case involving a numeraire good, which was interpreted as leisure, and two other commodities. The problem was to decide, in the absence of lump-sum taxation, which of the two commodities should be taxed at a higher rate to raise government revenue. The case demonstrated that a commodity which cannot be directly taxed should be indirectly taxed, as the next best measure. In other words, when some tax instruments are not available, the remaining instruments are used in such a way as to simulate as closely as possible the levy of lump-sum taxation [see Sandmo (1987)].

Ordinarily, if the remaining instruments include taxes on consumers' goods, these would be used. In the agricultural producer-consumer case, where profits from agricultural production induce consumption changes and this consumption cannot be directly taxed, the tax theory would suggest that the incidence of taxation fall back upon production. This could be done by taxing inputs—such as fertilizers, pesticides, and tractor services—and by taxing output (preferably gross output instead of net marketed surplus because taxing the former would allow greater use of rural tax instruments). For details, see Newbery and Stiglitz (1987)].

Dasgupta and Stiglitz (1972) discussed such desirability of production inefficiency in relaxing assumptions about the ability of the government to tax profits away. Their analysis is recast in Mirrlees (1972) and Munk (1980), which provide simpler and more elegant presentations of the argument.

Another way to accommodate the special nature of the rural sector in the formulation of the indirect tax problem is to include agricultural production under rural consumption and work with rural net demands. This can be done if rural rents (here profits accruing to land) are not taxed. Inputs into agricultural production then appear as positive net consumption demands, as would normal consumption goods. Net marketed surpluses of agricultural production, after subtractions for household consumption, would be interpreted as negative net consumption demands. The structure of the tax problem is now the same as before, but there is no longer a presumption of efficiency in rural agricultural production as rural consumer prices (also representing agricultural producer prices) may differ from the prices of those goods produced elsewhere in the economy. For example, the shadow prices (equal to world prices) for fertilizers in the commercial production of rice may not be the same as for rice production by smallholders. See Heady and Mitra (1984) for a discussion of the effects that other features in the economy may have on relative shadow prices. The other features refer to equal rates of taxation of some goods in both rural and nonrural sectors, migration, and land tenure.

Efficiency versus Equity in Agriculture.
The trade-offs between efficiency and equity become more obvious when considering the issues which agriculture in a developing country raises for second-best tax policy [see Newbery and Stiglitz's (1987) discussion of the debate on agricultural taxation and the terms of trade]. The taxation of rural production may imply a subsidization of urban consumption; however, rural living standards are not likely to be any higher than those in urban areas. The results of optimal tax theory suggest that taxation should fall more on goods whose demands (here, agricultural net surpluses) are relatively inelastic. There is conflicting evidence as to whether aggregate agricultural production in developing countries is less responsive to price than industrial production; but even if it were true in the aggregate, and

agriculture should be taxed relatively more, the responses of individual crops may be quite high. Moreover, the crops better suited for taxation may be those grown by households at the lower end of the distribution of rural incomes. Besides, a fall in the rural real wage may also induce a fall in the urban real wage, and possibly affect the welfare of that group relatively more.

Strong tax biases against agriculture already exist in many developing countries, particularly in Sub-Saharan Africa [see World Bank (1986)]. The second-best concern that now arises, in relation to an already distorted environment, is whether reforms can be identified on a small scale to improve the situation without making some worse off. The identification of price reforms for the largest set of goods would require information that would be impractical or too costly to collect. The identification of price reforms for a smaller class of agricultural inputs and outputs, which are not consumed, may be possible by using information available from the current distorted equilibrium. For details, see Sah and Stiglitz (1984). These price reform rules might be used to guide the sensitivity analysis of subsistence or smallholder projects being appraised, where time or resources may not permit the derivation of specific shadow prices for tradables in the rural sector and may require the use of world prices as averages.

Note 26. Foreign Exchange Constraints, Shadow Exchange Rates, and Conversion Factors

Use of SERs and Conversion Factors in Project Appraisal.
In practice, two types of parameters have been used to adjust the financial prices of goods and services to their economic values, for purposes of economic cost-benefit analysis: shadow exchange rates (SERs) and conversion factors (see World Bank Central Projects Note 2.03, titled, "Conversion

Factors and Shadow Exchange Rates;" also cleared for distribution outside the World Bank as EDI Course Note CN-350). The shadow exchange rates, although subject to various interpretations, are meant to establish the correct relationship between the prices of nontraded goods and the prices of traded goods. The (single) shadow exchange rate, once calculated, is used to convert the foreign currency prices of traded goods into the domestic currency. Alternatively, individual or average conversion factors for the prices of nontraded goods are used. (A conversion factor is simply the ratio of the shadow price of a good to its domestic price.)

Foreign Exchange Constraints and SERs.

The SER, as used in cost-benefit analysis, does not necessarily imply the presence or lack of foreign exchange constraints within an economy. Whether or not a country is persistently in a position of external debt or surplus, the SER can indicate the same relationship in the prices between traded and nontraded goods. The SER indicates a distortion between border prices and domestic prices which is not adequately reflected in the official exchange rate. A trade balance may coincide with distortions in relative prices and imply a SER that nevertheless diverges from the official, nominal exchange rate.

Suppose that a one-period project's financial account can be described as:

$$e.X - e.M - N = P$$

where e is the official exchange rate (OER); X and M are foreign currency (world market values) amounts for project output, here exported, and imported inputs, respectively; N is the sum, in domestic currency, of a nontraded good used in production; and P is financial profit. In economic terms, using the SER this would become:

$$e^*.X - e^*.M - N = P^*$$

where e^* is the SER and P^* denotes economic profit (or net cash flow). The SER, however, can be written as a ratio:

$$e^* = e/n$$

for some number n. Then,

$$e.X - e.M - n.N = P^{*'}$$

where $P^{*'}$ is of the same sign as P^* (whether a project is acceptable or not depends only upon whether the economic profit is nonnegative). The number n may now be interpreted as the conversion factor relating the domestic and border prices of the nontraded good.

Nonuniqueness in the Definition of SERs.

The use of the SER, defined as the OER divided by the conversion factor of the nontraded good involved, or the use of the conversion factor with the border values of traded goods, lead to the same conclusion. It can be seen that the definition of the SER will vary with the nontraded good used in the project. For several such projects, each using a different nontraded input, there could be as many SERs.

The SER is unique only if there is one type of nontraded good used in projects. As a simplification, we might propose that labor be the sole nontraded good, but this would mean that all labor be the same in the economy. It does not seem very plausible, however, that all activities would draw from a single pool of labor such that should any one activity increase its use of labor the effects on the remaining activities would be the same. By accident, all conversion factors may be close to one another [and well represented by a standard conversion factor (SCF)] to allow the definition of a unique SER in the economy. Again, we would not expect that distortions would naturally tend to be such that conversion factors would cluster tightly together. (See the conversion factors calculated for Egypt in Case 1 in Part V.)

Foreign Exchange Constraints and the SCF. If a country sustains foreign exchange loss because of exogenous changes in its terms of trade, the SCF will change if, in response to this loss, the government adopts trade policies—say, tariffs—which affect the relative prices of various traded and nontraded goods, or which alter the shares of exports and imports in trade in the trade-weighted SCF. Otherwise, foreign exchange concerns are not directly reflected in the SCF. The loss of foreign exchange resources should reduce the expected rate of growth of the economy and render projects, which generate more reinvestible surpluses, more attractive. The suboptimal investment in the economy for this or some other reason would imply that additional investment expenditures should be considered more valuable than additional consumption expenditures. By this ordering, the value of public income equals the value of investments; and additional foreign exchange in the hands of the government should be more valuable than in the hands of the private sector, which, in consuming a part of it, would give rise to an opportunity cost in terms of foreign exchange forgone.

If a project generates private sector income, part of which is consumed while the remainder is saved (i.e., reinvested in the economy), the foreign exchange constraint would be reflected through the use of a consumption conversion factor (CCF) based on some set of distributional weights on income groups. The effect of using the CCF would be to tilt investment decisions toward those projects which generate relatively more savings (in terms of foreign exchange). In conducting economic analysis, investment is generally assumed to be optimal; the complications of reflecting some premium on investment, and of having to state some preference over the distribution of incomes, are glossed over.

Use of the SER versus Conversion Factors in Project Appraisal. In summary, the economywide SER procedure is not generally recommended. Where there are several nontraded commodities and a number of distortions affecting the relative prices of traded and nontraded goods in an economy, the SER as an average measure can only take into account the actual distortions that bear upon a project. SERs can be constructed for individual projects to reflect adequately the appropriate relative prices for the goods actually involved; but, if we go through all this trouble, we would do better to carry the reasoning through and work with conversion factors for the flexibility they would bring to the analysis. Moreover, the use of conversion factors can avoid confusions arising from the use of a SER which has been defined independently of project-specific adjustments in the prices of nontraded commodities. (For a discussion on the use of the SER versus conversion factors, see Annex III to Central Projects Note 2.03/EDI Course Note 350.)

Accounting for Foreign Exchange Effects in Projects. To quantify a project's expected economic benefits, some World Bank staff appraisal reports have described foreign exchange effects, such as net foreign exchange savings, annual discounted inflows, and outflows of foreign exchange, including debt service. Note that the border pricing approach to economic analysis already incorporates a project's foreign exchange effects. The effects are directly accounted for in traded items and indirectly for nontraded goods, which are broken down into traded and nontraded elements. The foreign exchange equivalents of truly nontraded goods are measured on the basis of their effects upon domestic purchases of other traded goods [see Tower and Pursell (1986)]. In any event, measures of foreign exchange flows based on a project's use and production of goods are unlikely to capture the full effect of the project on a country's balance of payments: it would also be necessary to account for the impact upon the balance of payments of changes in expenditures due to project-induced changes in incomes.

It is a normal practice in the World Bank to treat funds as untied in the project economic analysis; therefore, debt service on project funds should not be attributed as a cost. In COMPASS and in PC-COSTAB, the mainframe and microcomputer software packages used by the World Bank and FAO for project planning and analysis, it is possible to separate out the foreign exchange content of a project's costs for purposes of financial planning. This feature is not intended to identify the foreign exchange effects (just described) for the economic justification of a projects; rather, it has been included to meet other presentational objectives.

Annotated Bibliography

Adams, Dale W., Douglas H. Graham, and J. D. von Pishke. 1984. *Undermining Rural Development with Cheap Credit.* Boulder, Colorado: Westview Press, Inc.

Adams, Dale W., Gordon Donald and J. D. von Pishke. 1983. *Rural Financial Markets in Developing Countries: Their Use and Abuse.* Baltimore: Johns Hopkins University Press for the Economic Development Institute of the World Bank.

Agarwala, Ramgopal. 1983. "Planning in Developing Countries: Lessons of Experience." *World Bank Staff Working Paper* no. 576. Management and Development Series no. 3. Washington, D.C.: The World Bank.

Ahmad, E., N. Stern, and H. M. Leung. 1987. "The Demand for Wheat Under Nonlinear Pricing in Pakistan," *Journal of Econometrics*, no. 36, pp. 55-65.

Ahmed, Sadiq. 1983. "Shadow Prices for Economic Appraisal of Projects: An Application to Thailand." *World Bank Staff Working Paper* no. 609. Washington, D.C.: The World Bank.

This is one of the World Bank-sponsored applications of social cost-benefit analysis. Discussed in Case 1 in Part V.

Ahn, Choong Yong, Jeffrey S. Hammer, and Avishay Braverman. 1983. "Alternative Agricultural Pricing Policies in the Republic of Korea: Their Implications for Government Deficits, Income Distribution, and Balance of Payments." *World Bank Staff Working Paper* no. 621. Washington, D. C.: The World Bank.

This paper describes an application of World Bank research in multimarket analysis, which is an approach for examining the real consequences of changes in policy which delivers general equilibrium-like results using essentially partial equilibrium techniques.

Amacher, Ryan C. and Holley H. Ulbrich. 1986. *Principles of Economics.* Third edition. Cincinatti: Southwestern Publishing Company.

An introductory text, the book is noteworthy in three respects. First, it contains a good discussion of the economic role of government. Second, it contains broader ranging discussion of competing viewpoints in macroeconomic theory and policy than found in most introductory texts. Third, it includes an introduction to the theory of public choice. Though written for the American market, this broader orientation makes the text an attractive introduction to economic principles.

Anand, Sudhir. 1975. "Appraisal of a Highway Project in Malaysia: Use of the Little-Mirrlees Procedures." *World Bank Staff Working Paper* no. 213. Washington, D. C.: The World Bank.

Anderson, Dennis. 1987. "The Public Revenue and Economic Policy in African Countries: An Overview of Issues and Policy Options." Washington, D.C.: The World Bank.

The paper outlines the findings of several studies issued by Bank staff on the problems of raising public revenue and financing public services in developing countries, particularly in Africa.

Atkinson, A.B. 1987. "Instrumental and Economic Policy—The Quest for Reasonable Value," *Journal of Economic Issues,* vol. 21, no. 1, pp. 189-202.

Atkinson, A B. and J. E. Stiglitz. 1980. *Lectures on Public Economics.* London: McGraw-Hill.

This book provides an excellent, extensive survey of the positive and normative theories of taxation. A good knowledge of calculus is required to follow the text completely, but this should not discourage you from mining what you can—the authors provide much material. The time you spend in struggling with the text is well worth the effort.

Austin, James E. *Agroindustrial Project Analysis; Critical Design Factors.* 2nd edition. Washington, D.C.: The World Bank. Forthcoming.

Backer, Morton and Lyle E. Jacobsen. 1964. *Cost Accounting: A Managerial Approach.* New York: McGraw-Hill.

A readable and well-illustrated cost accounting text. Suitable for use by both accountants and managers.

Balassa, Bela. 1984. "Prices, Incentives and Economic Growth." *Weltwirtschaftliches Archiv,* vol. 120, no. 4, pp. 611-630. *World Bank Reprint Series* no. 339.

Barro, R. J. and H. I. Grossman. 1971. "A General Disequilibrium Model of Income and Employment." *American Economic Review.* vol. 61, no. 1 (March), pp. 82-98.

Bell, C. and S. Devarajan. 1983. "Shadow Prices for Project Evaluation under Alternative Macroeconomic Specifications." *Quarterly Journal of Economics*, vol. 98. no. 3, (August), pp. 457-477.

This article stresses the need to explain the logical basis for shadow prices according to the adjustment mechanisms assumed to be in place in an economy. Cited in Tower and Pursell (1986), p. 109.

Benassy, J.P. 1982. *The Economics of Market Disequilibrium.* New York: Academic Press.

This is a rather technical, exhaustive exposition by one of the subject's pioneers. It is mentioned here as a reference for those who are interested in a rigorous and formal treatment of the nature, existence, and uniqueness of temporary equilibria with quantity rationing.

Bhagwati, J. N. and T. N. Srinivasan. 1981. "The Evaluation of Projects at World Prices Under Trade Distortions: Quantitative Restrictions, Monopoly Power in Trade and Nontraded Goods." *International Economic Review*, vol. 22, no. 2, (June), pp. 385-399.

Cited in Technical Notes.

Bhagwati, J. N. and T. N. Srinivasan. 1983. *Lectures on International Trade*. Cambridge, Massachusetts: MIT Press.

This text provides a good, compact course on trade, combining topics in the pure theory and normative aspects of trade policy. Terseness, however, was obtained at the cost of some useful exposition in some of the formulations, which may also contain some typographical errors. Another excellent text on trade theory is Caves and Jones (1981).

Bhagwati, J. N. and H. Wan. 1979. "The 'Stationarity' of Shadow Prices of Factors in Project Evaluation, With and Without Distortions." *American Economic Review*, vol. 69, no. 3 (June), pp. 261-273.

Bienen, Henry. 1983. "Oil Revenues and Policy Choice in Nigeria." *World Bank Staff Working Paper* no. 592. Washington, D.C.: The World Bank.

Binswanger, H.P. and Haim Shalit. 1984. "Fertilizer Subsidies: A Review of Policy Issues with Special Emphasis on Western Africa." *World Bank Discussion Paper* no. ARU 27, Washington, D.C.: World Bank.

Blanchard, Olivier, Rudiger Dornbusch, and Richard Layard [editors]. 1986. *Restoring Europe's Prosperity: Macroeconomic Papers from the Centre for European Policy Studies*, Cambridge, Massachusetts: MIT Press.

This is the first annual report produced by the Center for European Studies. The chapters concern macroeconomic prospects and policies for Europe, public debt, employment and growth; and the effects of the U.S. deficit and the value of the U.S. dollar.

Bliss, J.C. 1987. "GATT Dispute Settlement Reform in the Uruguay Round—Problems and Prospects," *Stanford Journal of International Law*, vol. 23, no. 1, pp. 31-55.

Blitzer, Charles, Partha Dasgupta, and Joseph Stiglitz. 1981. "Project Appraisal and Foreign Exchange Constraints," *Economics Journal*, (March), pp. 58-74.

Boadway, Robin W. and Neil Bruce. 1984. *Welfare Economics: Theory and Applications*. Oxford: Basil Blackwell.

This book concisely introduces both theoretical and applied aspects of modern welfare economics for advanced students (senior college and graduate level). The last chapter reviews recent literature on cost-benefit analysis conducted in terms of consumption numeraires.

Brander, James A. and B.J. Spencer. 1984. "Trade Warfare: Tariffs and Cartels." *Journal of International Economics,* vol. 16, nos. 3-4, (May), pp. 227-242.

Traditional trade theory argues that major importers (i.e., those large enough to affect world prices) of a product can improve national welfare by levying an import tariff on the product. This article demonstrates that in dealing with a monopolistic supplier of the product, the country may be better off subsidizing imports of the good. See Jones (1987) for a qualification of this conclusion. Both articles are relevant to Case 11 in Part V.

Braverman, Avishay and Luis Guasch. 1987. "Rural Credit Markets and Institutions in Developing Countries: Lessons for Policy Analysis from Practice and Modern Theory." *World Development.* Forthcoming.

Brown, James G. with Deloitte and Touche (Canada). *Agroindustrial Project Analysis; Investment and Operations.* Washington, D.C.: The World Bank. Forthcoming.

Brown, Steven J. and David S. Sibley. 1986. *The Theory of Public Utility Pricing.* New York: Cambridge University Press.

This is a very useful text introducing and developing basic concepts, including consumer surplus, Ramsey price rules, and Coase's theorem. See Technical Notes.

Brown, Steven J. and Young Kimaro. 1978. "An Economic and Social Analysis of The Chao Phaya Irrigation Improvement Project II." *World Bank Staff Working Paper* no. 299. Washington, D.C.: The World Bank.

This paper describes an early application of social cost-benefit analysis in the World Bank following the Squire-van der Tak adaptation of Little-Mirrlees methodology.

Bruce, Colin. 1976. "Social Cost-Benefit Analysis: A Guide for Country and Project Economists to the Derivation and Application of Economic and Social Accounting Prices." *World Bank Staff Working Paper* no. 239. Washington, D.C.: The World Bank.

Supplements the methodology set forth in Little and Mirrlees (1974 and 1982) and Squire and Tak (1975).

Buchanan, James M. and Robert D. Tollison. 1984. *The Theory of Public Choice - II.* Ann Arbor: University of Michigan Press.

Contains a series of articles related to applications of the public choice theory. Buchanan's writings in this area are largely responsible for his receiving the 1987 Nobel Prize in Economics. The public choice theory goes beyond the simplistic behavioral assumptions of social-welfare optimizing government and applies the behavioral assumptions of the neoclassical theory to analyze the behavior of the public sector. An excellent source which can be used to provide additional perspective on the experience reflected in Chapter 13 of this book.

Burmeister, Edwin. 1980. *Capital Theory and Dynamics*. New York: Cambridge University Press.
Cited in Technical Notes.

Caves, R. E. and R. W. Jones. 1981. *World Trade and Payments*. 3rd edition. Boston: Little, Brown and Company.
This text is essential reading for any serious study of trade and international economics.

Cheong, Kee-Cheok and Emmanuel D'Silva. 1984. "Prices, Terms of Trade, and the Role of Government in Pakistan's Agriculture." *World Banking Staff Working Paper* no. 643. Washington, D.C.: The World Bank.

Cleaver, Kevin M. 1980. "Economic and Social Analysis of Projects and of Price Policy: The Morocco Fourth Agricultural Project." *World Bank Staff Working Paper* no. 369. Washington, D. C.: The World Bank.
An early World Bank-sponsored application of social cost-benefit analysis following the methodology of Squire and van der Tak (1975).

Corden, W. Max. 1974. *Trade Policy and Economic Welfare*. Oxford: Clarendon Press.

Corden, W. Max. 1987. "The Relevance for Developing Countries of Recent Developments in Macroeconomic Theory." *The World Bank Research Observer*, vol. 2, no. 2. pp. 171-188.

Corlett, W.J. and D.C. Hague. 1954. "Complementarity and the Excess Burden of Taxation." *Review of Economic Studies*, vol. 21, pp. 21-30.

Cornes, Richard and Todd Sandler. 1986. *The Theory of Externalities, Public Goods and Club Goods*. New York: Cambridge University Press.
This book is an extremely useful review and synthesis of a diffused literature. It introduces and develops fundamental notions and their implications for applied welfare economics.

Cuddington, John T., Per-Olov Johansson, and Karl-Gustaf Lofgren. 1984. *Disequilibrium Macroeconomics in Open Economies*. Oxford: Basil Blackwell.
This book reviews and integrates existing macroeconomic disequilibrium theory for open economies [essentially Dixit (1978)]. The role of money is highlighted and the existing open economy disequilibrium framework is extended to the case of perfect capital mobility. The

authors examine commercial policies, including those aimed at import substitution, sector output and employment objectives, and the external balance. Analyses of tariffs and quotas are also considered. Cited in Technical Notes.

Dasgupta, Ajit K. and D. W. Pearce. 1972. *Cost-Benefit Analysis: Theory and Practice*. New York: Barnes and Noble.

A good, readable introduction to the theory of cost-benefit analysis. Contains a good introduction to welfare economics as related to cost-benefit analysis.

Dasgupta, Partha. 1972. "A Comparative Analysis of the UNIDO Guidelines and the OECD Manual." *Oxford Bulletin of Economics and Statistics*, vol. 34, no. 1 (February), pp. 33-51.

See the discussion in Chapter 8 of this book.

Dasgupta, Partha and G. M. Heal. 1979. *Economic Theory and Exhaustible Resources*. New York: Cambridge University Press.

Dasgupta, Partha and Joseph Stiglitz. 1972. "On Optimal Taxation and Public Production." *Review of Economic Studies* (January).

Deaton, Angus. 1980. "The Measurement of the Welfare, Theory and Practical Guidelines." *Living Standards Measurement Study Working Paper*, no. 7. Washington, D. C.: The World Bank.

The aim of this paper is to provide a systematic basis for the measurement of welfare, working from the economic theoretical constructs of preferences and utility toward practical implications.

Deaton, Angus and J. Muellbauer. 1980. *Economics and Consumer Behavior*. New York: Cambridge University Press.

Debreu, Gerard. 1959. "Theory of Value: An Axiomatic Analysis of Economic Equilibrium." *Cowles Foundation Monograph*, no. 17. New Haven: Yale University Press.

This is the definitive text on the general equilibrium theory which provides a rigorous basis for fundamental optimality theorems of welfare economics.

Dervis, Kermal and Sherman Robinson. 1978. "The Foreign Exchange Gap, Growth, and Industrial Strategy in Turkey: 1973-83." *World Bank Staff Working Paper* no 306. Washington, D. C.: The World Bank.

This study discusses the implications of a multisector general equilibrium model that endeavors to capture the major features of the Turkish economy, linking economic performance and trade policy. The paper is noteworthy for its practical handling of analytical complications due to the widespread presence in the Turkish economy of quantitative trade restrictions.

Dervis, Kermal, Jaime de Melo, and Sherman Robinson. 1982. *General Equilibrium Models for Development Policy.* New York: Cambridge University Press.

This is a survey of the state of the art on computable general equilibrium modelling. It combines a theoretical discussion of the properties of multisector applied equilibrium models, starting with input-output tables, with numerical applications to particular countries and problems. The market clearing prices that emerge as solutions to the computable models are shadow prices. An alternative way of deriving shadow prices is to start with an initial market equilibrium and then disturb the market clearing relations about their equilibrium values [see Tower (1984) and Diewert (1986)]. The formal, mathematical presentation is clear, but requires a knowledge of matrix algebra.

Dervis, Kermal, Ricardo Martin, and Sweder van Wijnbergen. 1984. "Policy Analysis of Shadow Pricing, Foreign Borrowing, and Resource Extraction in Egypt." *World Bank Staff Working Paper* no. 622. Washington, D.C.: The World Bank.

Diamond, Peter A. and James A. Mirrlees. 1976. "Private Constant Returns and Public Shadow Prices." *Review of Economic Studies*, vol 43, no. 131, (February), pp. 41-47. See Technical Notes.

Diewert, W. E. 1986. "The Measurement of Economic Benefits of Infrastructurel Services." *Lecture Notes in Economics and Mathematical Systems* no. 278. M. Beckmann and W. Krelle [editors]. Berlin: Springer-Verlag.

Dixit, A. K. 1976. *The Theory of Equilibrium Growth.* New York: Oxford University Press.

Dixit, A. K. 1978. "The Balance of Trade in a Model of Temporary Equilibrium and Rationing." *Review of Economic Studies*, vol. 45, no. 141, (October), pp. 393-404.

This article first presented the disequilibrium model of the small, open economy which is the subject of much of Cuddington, Johansson, and Lofgren (1984). See Technical Notes.

Dixit, A. K. and A. S. Kyle. 1985. "The Use of Protection and Subsidies for Entry Promotion and Deterrence," *American Economic Review,* (March), pp. 139-152.

Dixit, Avenish and Victor Norman. 1980. *Theory of International Trade.* Cambridge: Cambridge University Press.

Dornbusch, Rudiger. 1980. *Open Economy Macroeconomics.* New York: Basic Books.

This text compiles a series of macroeconomic models of the open economy, developing the key interplay of relative prices and the determination of income. The book is not easy reading, but it is an extraordinary synthesis of the literature which should aid the understanding of economic models created specifically for developing countries, which combine Keynesian elements of wage and price rigidities and sluggish adjustment.

Dornbusch, Rudiger and F. Leslie C.H. Helmers [editors]. 1988. *The Open Economy: Tools for Policymakers in Developing Countries.* EDI Series in Economic Development. New York: Oxford University Press.

Findlay, R. and S. Wellisz. 1981. "Project Evaluation, Shadow Prices, and Trade Policy." *Journal of Political Economy,* (March), pp. 58-74.

Fitchett, Delbert A. 1985. "The Milk Pricing Maze; A Practical Approach for the SAR." AGR Interim Guidance Note no. 9 (an internal document with restricted circulation). Washington, D.C.: The World Bank. See Case No. 5.

Friedman, James W. 1977. *Oligopoly and the Theory of Games.* Advanced Textbooks in Economics no. 8. New York: North Holland.

Friedman, James W. 1983. "Oligopoly Theory." *Cambridge Surveys of Economic Literature.* New York: Cambridge University Press.

Friedman, James W. 1986. *Game Theory with Application to Economics.* New York: Oxford University Press.

Friedman, Milton. 1966. *Essays in Positive Economics.* Chicago: The University of Chicago Press.

Galbraith, John Kenneth. 1967. *The New Industrial State.* Boston: Houghton Mifflin Company.

Gittinger, J. Price. 1982. *Economic Analysis of Agricultural Projects.* 2nd edition. Baltimore: The Johns Hopkins University Press for the Economic Development Institute of The World Bank.

A revision of the 1972 edition of the book by the same title, which quickly became a classic in the field. The second edition is much expanded and improved and approaches encyclopedic stature in the field of agricultural project planning and appraisal. Both editions were written primarily for agriculturalists in government agencies that prepare projects for the government, or for outside funding. While the second edition contains much more material on project economics than did the first edition, many readers and instructors have suggested that the one chapter (32 pages) devoted to project economics is nevertheless insufficient to meet the needs of agricultural project economists. This book is partly intended to complement Gittinger (1982).

Grandmont, Jean-Michel. 1983. "Money and Value; A Reconsideration of Classical and Neoclassical Monetary Theories." *Oxford Bulletin of Economics and Statistics,* New York: Cambridge University Press.
See Technical Notes.

Green, H. A. 1976. *Consumer Theory.* 2nd edition. London: Macmillan.
This is an excellent, readable exposition of consumer theory (formal presentations are relegated to the appendices), which is all the more remarkable because it is cited in Atkinson and Stiglitz (1980). This is a sophisticated text that tends to be rather technical.

Hanna, Nagy. 1985. "Strategic Planning and Management: A Review of Recent Experience." *World Bank Staff Working Paper* no. 751. Washington, D. C.: The World Bank.

Harberger, Arnold. 1989. "Applications of Real Exchange Rate Analysis." *Contemporary Policy Issues,* vol. 7, no. 2, pp. 1-26.

Heady, Christopher J. and Pradeep K. Mitra. 1984. "Optimum Taxation and Shadow Pricing in a Developing Economy." *World Bank Discussion Paper* no. 83, Washington, D.C.: The World Bank.

Henderson, James M. and Richard E. Quandt. 1980. *Microeconomic Theory: A Mathematical Approach.* 3rd edition. New York: McGraw-Hill.

Hey, John D. 1984. "Decision Under Uncertainty." *Mathematical Methods in Economics.* F. van der Ploeg [editor]. New York: Wiley and Sons.

Johnsen, Erik. 1968. "Studies in Multiobjective Decision Models." *Studentlitteratur.* Monograph no. 1. Lund, Sweden: Economic Research Centre.

Jones, Ronald W. 1987. "Trade Taxes and Subsidies with Imperfect Competition." *Economics Letters,* vol. 23, no. 4, pp. 375-379.
Reconsiders the Brander and Spencer (1984) argument in a general equilibrium framework and shows that their argument is, in general, correct; but specific and ad valorem forms of taxation may yield different results.

Joshi, Vijay. 1972. "The Rationale and Relevance of the Little-Mirrlees Criterion." *Oxford*

Bulletin of Economics and Statistics, vol. 34, no. 1 (February), pp. 1-32.
See the discussion in Chapter 8.

Keynes, John Maynard. 1936. *The General Theory of Employment, Interest, and Money.*
London: MacMillan and Company.

Killick, Tony 1981. *Policy Economics; A Textbook on Applied Economics of Developing
Countries.* London: Heinemann.
An excellent treatment of many of the economic policy issues faced by officials in developing
countries. An intermediate level treatment of the subject, it requires knowledge of basic
economic principles.

Killick, Tony, [editor]. 1982. *Adjustment and Financing in the Developing World: The Role of
the International Monetary Fund.* Washington, D.C.: International Monetary Fund.

Laidler, David. 1981. *Introduction to Microeconomics.* 2nd edition. New York: Wiley and
Sons.

Lal, Deepak. 1974. "Methods of Project Analysis: A Review." *World Bank Occasional Paper*
no. 16. Baltimore: Johns Hopkins University Press for the World Bank.

Lal, Deepak. 1984. "The Real Effects of Stabilization and Structural Adjustment Policies: An
Extension of the Australian Adjustment Model." *World Bank Staff Working Paper* no. 639.
Washington, D.C.: World Bank.

This paper outlines a version of the orthodox trade theoretic treatment of the small, open
economy. This so-called Australian model of balance of payments is used to answer questions
on how to minimize the welfare costs of traditional stabilization and adjustment packages.
The model is similar to the macroeconomic description underlying Tower and Pursell (1986)
and Tower (1984) discussions of shadow prices. Note that Figure 2 following the text appears
to be improperly drawn.

Lamb, Geoffrey. 1987. "Managing Economic Change: Institutional Dimensions." *World Bank
Discussion Paper* no. 14. Washington, D.C.: The World Bank.

This paper is a preliminary effort to bring the issue of institutionalizing policy capacity into
sharper focus, and to suggest ways of improving approaches to adjustment lending, public
sector management asssistance, and economic analysis in support of policy reform. It is
intended to increase awareness of the institutional and political factors in economic reform
and indicate how to deal better with these factors.

Lindert, Peter H. 1986. *International Economics.* 8th edition. Homewood, IL: Richard D.
Irwin, Inc.

Little, I. M. D. and James Mirrlees. 1969. *Manual of Industrial Project Analysis in Developing Countries: Volume II; Social Cost Benefit Analysis.* Paris: Organisation for Economic Co-operation and Development.

This book is the original "Little-Mirrlees Manual" that was both widely heralded in the late 1960s and widely debated in the economics profession in the 1970s. In the OECD Manual, Little and Mirrlees took a stronger position regarding the use of border prices in the face of distortions than in the later version that was issued in 1974 with a revised title (see the next annotated entry).

Little, I.M.D. and J.A. Mirrlees. 1974 and 1982. *Project Appraisal and Planning for Developing Countries.* New York: Basic Books.

This book is essentially the text of the authors' OECD *Manual of Industrial Project Analysis; Volume II; Social Cost-Benefit Analysis*, which they further developed to cover infrastructural, agricultural, and other rural projects. This is the basic reference for the rationale behind the use of the foreign exchange numeraire. The Little-Mirrlees methodology contrasts with that of the UNIDO "Guidelines for Project Evaluation," written by P. S. Dasgupta, S. A. Marglin, and A.K. Sen (New York: United Nations, 1972); see the discussion in Chapter 8 in this book; and the February 1972 issue of the *Oxford Bulletin of Economics and Statistics*.

Little, I.M.D. and James A. Mirrlees. 1972. "A Reply to Some Criticisms of the OECD Manual." *Oxford Bulletin of Economics and Statistics*, vol. 34, no. 1 (February). pp. 153-168.

In this article, Little and Mirrlees reply to the criticisms of their cost-benefit methodology. The criticisms include: First, the criteria proposed are based on the assumption that the government will follow optimal economic policies in all respects. Second, the prescriptions for the estimation of the economic prices for nontraded goods are inadequate, either because they are wrong or because thay are hard to put into practice, especially when most commodities have to be regarded as nontraded. Third, in many developing countries, few commodities can be regarded as traded goods and the proposed use of border prices is of very limited use. Fourth, the methods encourage the project evaluator to ignore income inequalities and their relevance to his or her decisions. Fifth, the evaluator is encouraged to neglect externalities, although these are of great importance in practice. Sixth, the methodology encourages the use of projects to generate savings, which could be better done through taxation. Seventh, strategic considerations, such as independence in the production of various commodities, are not allowed to influence project decisions. See the discussion in Chapter 8.

Malinvaud, Edmond. 1977. *Leçons de Théorie Microéconomique.* 4th edition. Paris: Dunod.

Malinvaud, Edmond 1985. *Lectures on Microeconomic Theory.* Revised edition. Advanced Textbooks in Economics, vol. 2. New York: North Holland.

Marglin, S. A. 1963. *Approaches to Dynamic Investment Planning.* Amsterdam: North Holland Publishing Co.

Marglin, S. A. 1963a. "The Opportunity Costs of Public Investment." *Quarterly Journal of*

Economics, vol. 77, no. 2 (May), pp. 274-289.

Marglin, S. A. 1963b. "The Social Rate of Discount and the Optimal Rate of Investment." *Quarterly Journal of Economics*, vol. 77, no. 1 (February), pp. 95-111.

Marglin, S. A. 1966. "'Comment' on Dale W. Jorgenson: Testing Alternative Theories of the Development of a Dual Economy." *The Theory and Design of Economic Development*. Irma Edelman and Erik Thorbecke [editors]. Baltimore: The Johns Hopkins University Press.

Marglin, S. A. 1967. *Public Investment Criteria, Benefit-Cost Analysis for Planned Economic Growth*. Cambridge: Massachusetts Institute of Technology Press.

Marsden, Keith and Therese Belot. 1987. "Private Enterprise in Africa: Creating a Better Environment." *World Bank Discussion Paper* no. 17. Washington, D.C.: The World Bank.

This paper addresses the main constraints to private enterprise and competitive markets in Africa, how governments might remove these constraints, the role of foreign aid donors in developing an efficient private sector in the future, and the potential impact of private enterprise upon African economic performance. An annex summarizes five cross-country studies which have estimated the impact of government and the private sector on economic growth.

Mashayekhi, Afsaneh. 1980. "Shadow Prices for Project Appraisal in Turkey." *World Bank Staff Working Paper* no. 392. Washington, D. C.: The World Bank.

Quantitative trade restrictions impose serious problems for shadow pricing because these distortions, unlike tariffs, often sever links between a commodity's world price and its price at home. In some instances, it may be appropriate simply to quantify the overall consequences of current policies. For example, in this paper, the exercises deriving average, countrywide parameters account for the effects of a trade regime characterized by numerous nontariff distortions by including, along with an average nominal tariff rate, an implicit regime tariff. The nominal tariff added to the average nominal rate (after netting out domestic handling and transport costs) fills the gap between the CIF prices of imports and their effective, short-run domestic costs. The paper is also useful for describing a procedure for estimating the marginal productivity and opportunity cost of capital.

Mat, Johari bin. 1983. "Regional Development in West Malaysia: A Comparative Effectiveness Study of Jengka, Dara, Kejora, and Ketengah." Monographs of the National Institute of Public Administration. Kuala Lumpur: Institut Tadbiran Awam Negara (INTAN).

Mazumdar, Dipak. 1975. "The Rural-Urban Wage Gap, Migration and the Shadow Wage." *World Bank Staff Working Paper* no. 197. Washington, D. C.: The World Bank.

Mazumdar, Dipak. 1980. *The Urban Labor Market and Income Distribution*. New York: Oxford University Press for the World Bank.

Mazumdar, Dipak and Constantino Lluch. 1985. "Indonesia: Wages and Employment. A World Bank Country Study." Washington, D. C.: The World Bank.

See Case 1 in Part V.

McKee, Michael and Edwin G. West 1987. "Further Perspectives on the Theory of Second Best." *Public Finance*, vol. 42, no. 1, pp. 146-151.

Meier, Gerald M. [editor]. 1983. *Pricing Policy for Development Management*. EDI Series in Economic Development. Baltimore: Johns Hopkins University Press for the Economic Development Institute of The World Bank.

An integrated set of readings covering many of the pricing policy issues facing officials in developing countries. Begins with readings on introductory price theory and progresses through practical applications to such topics as marginal cost pricing and multipart tariffs. Multisectoral in orientation, the book includes several readings on topics of interest to agricultural planners.

Mirrlees, James A. 1972. "On Producer Taxation." *Review of Economic Studies,* vol. 39, no. 117, (January), pp. 105-112.

Referred to in Technical Notes. This article is difficult reading and should only be attempted by those with a good background in economics.

Mishan, E.J. 1971. *Cost-Benefit Analysis: An Informal Introduction*. New York: Praeger Publishers.

A good introduction to the welfare economic theory of cost-benefit analysis. Contains an interesting discussion of the 'multiple roots' problem in the internal rate of return.

Mitchell, William C. 1978. *The Anatomy of Public Failure: A Public Choice Perspective*. Original Paper no. 13. Los Angeles: International Institute for Economic Research.

Morrisey, George L. 1969. *Management by Objectives and Results*. Menlo Park, California: Addison-Wesley Publishing Company.

Muellbauer, John and Richard Portes. 1978. "Macroeconomic Models with Quantity Rationing." *Economic Journal*, vol. 88, no. 352 (December), pp. 788-821.

See Technical Notes.

Munasinghe, Mohan and Jeremy J. Warford. 1982. *Electricity Pricing: Theory and Case Studies*. Baltimore: The Johns Hopkins University Press for the World Bank.

Munk, K.J. 1980. "Optimal Taxation with Some Nontaxable Commodities." *Review of Economic Studies*, (July), vol. 47, no. 4, pp. 753-765.

Musgrave, Richard A. and Peggy B. Musgrave. 1988. *Public Finance in Theory and Practice*. 5th edition. New York: McGraw-Hill.

A classic text in public finance. Encyclopedic in its coverage, it is an excellent introduction to the theory and practice of public sector economics. Used extensively in the preparation of Part I of this book.

Neary, J.P. 1980 "Short Run Capital Specificity and the Pure Theory of International Trade." *Economic Journal*, vol. 88, no. 351, (September) pp. 488-510.

This paper describes a diagrammatic technique to illustrate adjustments in an economy to changes in terms of trade, factor endowments, and levels of factor market distortions when in the short run, capital is sector specific and the only mobile factor of production is labor. This macroeconomic perspective of capital specificity underlies the approach of Tower (1984) and Tower and Pursell (1986) and is thought to capture to some extent the capital constraints characterizing many developing countries.

Neary, J. P. 1980. "Nontraded Goods and the Balance of Trade in a Neo-Keynesian Temporary Equilibrium." *Quarterly Journal of Economics*, vol. 95, no. 3, (November), 403-29.

Neary, J. P. and K.W.S. Roberts. 1980. "The Theory of Household Behaviour Under Rationing." *European Economic Review*, vol. 13, no. 1, (January), pp. 25-42.

Nellis, John R. 1986. "Public Enterprises in Sub-Saharan Africa." *World Bank Discussion Paper* no. 1. Washington, D.C.: The World Bank.

This paper reviews the information currently available on African public enterprises, describing their number, type, sectors of operation, employment patterns, and their financial and economic importance.

Nentjes, Andries and Thijs Zuidema. 1987. "A Determination of the Opportunity Costs of Government Projects: A Neo-Classical Versus Keynesian Approach." *Public Finance*, vol. 42, no. 1, pp. 119-136.

Derives two models for use in estimating EOCC under two sets of assumptions. The first is neoclassical equilibrium with zero excess demand in all markets. The second is Keynesian unemployment arising from a lack of effective demand. No empirical content is provided for either model.

Newbery, David M.G. 1989. "Theory of Food Price Stabilization," *Economic Journal.* vol. 99, pp. 1065-1083.

Newbery, David M.G. and Nicholas Stern [editors]. 1987. *The Theory of Taxation for Developing Countries.* New York: Oxford University Press for the World Bank.
Cited in Technical Note 25.

Newbery, David M.G. and Joseph E. Stiglitz. 1981. *The Theory of Commodity Price Stabilization: A Study in the Economics of Risk.* New York: Oxford University Press.
The text of this paper is rather mathematically sophisticated, but illustrates well the distinctions which should be made between the short- and long-run impacts of policy changes affecting risks facing producers and consumers.

Newbery, David M.G. and Joseph E. Stiglitz. 1987. "Wage Rigidity, Implicit Contracts, Unemployment, and Inefficiency." *Economic Journal,* vol. 97, pp. 416-430.

Ng, Yew-Kwang. 1983. *Welfare Economics: Introduction and Development of Basic Concepts.* London: Macmillan.

Ng, Yew-Kwang. 1977. "Towards a Theory of Third Best." *Public Finance,* vol. 32, no 1, pp. 1-15.

Ng, Yew-Kwang. 1987a. "The Role of Economists and Third-Best Policies." *Public Finance,* vol. 42, no. 1, pp. 152-155.

Ng, Yew-Kwang. 1987b. "'Political Distortions' and the Relevance of Second and Third-Best Policies." *Public Finance,* vol. 42, no. 1, pp. 137-145.
The three articles listed above are part of an exchange between the author and McKee and West (1987) regarding political factors and distortions in the economy. The articles, taken together, are relevant to the discussion of "natural" and "artificial" market failure in Part I of this volume.

O'Mara, Gerald and Vinh Le-Si. 1985. "The Supply and Welfare Effects of Rice-Pricing Policy in Thailand." *World Bank Staff Working Paper* no. 714. Washington, D.C.: The World Bank.
In this paper, models of household production and consumption decisions are used in the analysis of selected farm households in the Northeast and Upper North regions of Thailand. The objective is to assess the effects of variation in land quality, farm, and family size on welfare and on supply response to rice tax policy. The analysis specifies three farm sizes and three family sizes, though these differ between regions, with land quality remaining a regional variable. While the effects on short-run welfare differ among farm sizes, family sizes, price domains, and regions, they are explained by one circumstance: households that become net

purchasers of rice are worse off, while households selling rice are better off. In the longer run, evidence from macroeconomic studies suggests that adjustments in the nominal wage for off-farm employment will offset welare losses by purchasing households.

Page, John M. 1982. "Shadow Prices for Trade Strategies and Investment Planning in Egypt." *World Bank Staff Working Paper* no. 521. Washington, D.C.: The World Bank.

This paper presents estimates of efficiency and social accounting prices for commodities and factors of production in Egypt which were appropriate for the period 1979-1985. The shadow price estimates are based primarily on a modified input-output method which decomposes domestic supply prices into foreign exchange and primary factor content.

Prachowny, Martin F.J. 1984. *Macroeconomic Analysis for Small Open Economies*. New York: Oxford University Press.

Ray, Anandarup. 1984. *Issues in Cost Benefit Analysis*. Baltimore: Johns Hopkins University Press for the World Bank.

This book complements Squire and Tak (1975) and extends some of the discussion there. Much of the text derives from interpretive "Notes" written while Ray served as Economic Advisor in the World Bank's Operational Policy Staff. Tower and Pursell (1986), p. 86, and Tower [in Tower and Pursell (1986), Appendix A] comment on some of the special assumptions implicit in Ray's presentation.

Sah, Raaj Kumar and Joseph E. Stiglitz. 1984. *Taxation and Pricing of Agricultural and Industrial Goods*. Cambridge, Massachusetts: National Bureau of Economic Research.

Samuelson, Paul A. 1989. *Economics*. 13th edition. New York: McGraw-Hill.

Encyclopedic introduction to principles of economics, this is one of the most popular introductory textbooks in history—rivaling even Marshall's classic *Principles of Economics*. The book is noteworthy in that it allows several levels of sophistication to be achieved by the reader. The text is easy to read for beginners, while technical annexes, footnotes, and citations allow interested readers to delve deeper into the subjects that are addressed in the text. Examples are heavily oriented toward American economic issues.

Sandmo, A. and J. H. Dreze. 1971. "Discount Rates for Public Investment in Closed and Open Economies." *Economica,* vol. 38, no. 152,(November), pp. 395-404

Sandmo, A. 1987. "A Reinterpretation of Elasticity Formulae in Optimum Tax Theory." *Economica,* vol. 54, no. 213, (February), pp. 89-96.

Sargent, Thomas J. 1979. *Macroeconomic Theory*. New York: Academic Press.

This is a rather difficult text in terms of its mathematical sophistication. It does, however, provide a useful introduction to the difficult area of stochastic macroeconomics for graduate students.

Saunders, Robert J., Jeremy J. Warford, and Bjorn Wellenius. 1983. *Telecommunications and Economic Development.* Baltimore: The Johns Hopkins University Press for the World Bank.

Scandizzo, Pasquale L. 1980. "Methodologies for Measuring Agricultural Price Intervention Effects." *World Bank Staff Working Paper* no. 394. Washington, D. C.: The World Bank.

Describes the use of microeconomic, informal methodologies in six country case studies (Argentina, Egypt, Kenya, Pakistan, Thailand, and Yugoslavia). Confirms that extensive intervention by governments has turned the domestic terms of trade against agriculture and has had significant efficiency and income distribution effects. The methodologies used include nominal and effective protection coefficients, domestic resource cost and net economic benefit coefficients, producer and consumer subsidy equivalents, and producer and consumer surpluses. These methodologies are relevant to the conduct of the sectoral policy analyses discussed in Part I.

Schaefer-Kehnert, W. 1978. "Review of Time Adjustment Methods in Farm Investment Analysis." *EDI Working Paper* no. 030/027. Washington, D.C.: The World Bank.

Schmid, A. Allan. 1978 and 1987. *Property, Power, and Public Choice: An Inquiry into Law and Economics.* New York: Praeger.

An excellent treatment of the institutional factors that shape the functioning of private and public economic activity. Contains a good discussion of aspects of market failure.

Schohl, Wolfgang W. 1979. "Estimating Shadow Prices for Colombia in an Input-Output Framework." *World Bank Staff Working Paper* no. 357. Washington, D.C.: The World Bank.

Sen, Amartya K. 1970. *Collective Choice and Social Welfare.* Advanced Textbooks in Economics, vol. 11. New York: North-Holland.

Sen, Amartya K. 1973. *On Economic Inequality.* New York: Oxford University Press.

Sen, Amartya K. 1977. "Social Choice Theory: A Re-Examination." *Econometrica*, vol. 45, no. 1, (January), pp. 53-84.

Sen, Amartya K. 1977a. "On Weights and Measures: Informational Constraints in Social Welfare Analysis." *Econometrica*, vol. 45, no. 7 (October), pp. 1539-1572.

Sen, Amartya K. 1984. *Resources, Values and Development*. Oxford: Basil Blackwell.

Sen, Amartya K. 1985. *Commodities and Capabilities*. New York: North-Holland.

Sen, Amartya K. 1987. *On Ethics and Economics*. Cambridge: Harvard University Press.

Silverman, Jerry M. 1984. "Technical Assistance and Aid Agency Staff: Alternative Techniques for Greater Effectiveness." *World Bank Technical Paper* no. 28. Washington, D. C.: The World Bank.

This paper is relevant to the discussion of intervention by donors in Chapter 13 of this volume. Silverman proposes alternatives for making technical assistance more effective.

Singh, Inderjit, Lyn Squire, and James Kirchner. 1985. "Agricultural Pricing and Marketing Policies in an African Context; A Framework for Analysis." *World Staff Working Paper* no. 743. Washington, D.C.: The World Bank.

The paper describes an analytical framework designed to address some of the important agricultural pricing issues that frequently arise in many African countries. It contains a description of producer, consumer, and marketing characteristics common to African countries; presents an analytical framework designed to capture these characteristics; outlines policy uses of the framework; and discusses a series of policy results derived from a prototype application of the framework.

Smith, William, Francis Lethem, and Ben Thoolen. 1980. "The Design of Organizations for Rural Development Projects: A Progress Report." *World Bank Staff Working Paper* no. 375. Washington, D. C.: The World Bank.

A widely cited paper which clarifies the role of senior management in organizations in developing countries and reviews experiences and problems in improving development management.

Spiegel, Henry W. 1971. *The Growth of Economic Thought*. Englewood Cliffs, New Jersey: Prentice Hall.

A good treatment of the evolution of economic thought, including classical, neoclassical, and Keynesian views, with brief synopses of the theories of many of the economists mentioned in this volume.

Squire, Lyn and Herman G. van der Tak. 1975. *Economic Analysis of Projects*. Baltimore: Johns Hopkins University Press for the World Bank.

This book presents a cost-benefit methodology based on the foreign exchange numeraire, but extends the Little-Mirrlees method to illustrate how shadow prices can be altered to account for governmental concerns over the distribution of income in the economy. The authors contrast the derivations of efficiency and social prices. See the discussion in Chapter 8 in this book. Also see Tower on Squire and van der Tak, pp. 144-145, in Tower and Pursell (1986), Appendix B, and other comments in Tower and Pursell, pp. 86 and 92.

Squire, Lyn, I.M.D. Little, and Mete Durdag. 1979. "Application of Shadow Pricing to Country Economic Analysis with an Illustration from Pakistan." *World Bank Staff Working Paper* no. 330. Washington, D.C.: The World Bank.

This paper demonstrates the application of the Squire-van der Tak (1975) methodology.

Srinavasan, T.N. and J. H. Bhagwati. 1978. "Shadow Prices for Project Selection in the Presence of Distortions: Effective Rates of Protection and Domestic Resource Costs," *Journal of Political Economy,* (February), pp. 97-116.

Stigler, George J. 1971. "The Theory of Economic Regulation." *Bell Journal of Economics and Management Science,* vol. 2, no. 1, (Spring), pp. 3-21.

Stiglitz, Joseph E. 1987. "Some Theoretical Aspects of Agricultural Policies." *The World Bank Research Observer,* vol. 2, no. 1 (January), pp. 43-60.

This article provides a systematic framework within which subsidies, taxes, credit, price stabilization, and expenditure policies affecting agricultural markets can be assessed. The article focuses on the consequences of imperfect information, risk, and credit markets and considers the incentive and distributive effects of alternative government programs.

Taylor, Lance. 1983. *Structuralist Macroeconomics: Applicable Models for the Third World.* New York: Basic Books.

Thomas, Vinod. 1986. *Linking Macroeconomic and Agricultural Policies for Adjustment with Growth; The Colombian Experience.* Baltimore: Johns Hopkins University Press for the World Bank.

This book deals with economic policies for growth and adjustment during periods of rapidly changing circumstances and links them to developments at the sectoral level. It is based on the experience of Colombia, which, after a long period of successful performance, has been experiencing a downturn in economic growth and increased deficits in the external and fiscal balances. Used in the preparation of Case 8 in Part V.

Timmer, C. Peter. 1986. *Getting Prices Right; The Scope and Limits of Agricultural Price Policy.* Ithaca: Cornell University Press.

The approach is primarily a partial equilibrium one. Special reference is made to the operation of BULOG, the rice marketing parastatal in Indonesia.

Timmer, C. Peter. 1985. "The Role of Price Policy in Increasing Rice Production in Indonesia,

1968-1982." HIID Development Discussion Paper no. 196. Cambridge, Massachusetts: Harvard Institute for International Development.

This paper discussses some of the unusual circumstances of Indonesia's use of fertilizer subsidies to stimulate rice production.

Tower, Edward. 1984. "Effective Protection, Domestic Resource Costs and Shadow Prices; A General Equilibrium Perspective." *World Bank Staff Working Paper* no. 664. Washington, D.C.: The World Bank.

In this paper, simple general equilibrium models are built, linearized about their initial equilibrium and then used to analyze the economic effects of various changes in policy. In the process, the models are used to elucidate effective protection, shadow prices, and domestic resource cost, and the relationships among them. In particular, the paper discusses applications to simple approaches to second-best tariffs, including second-best optimum tariffs on imported capital goods; alternative definitions of nominal and effective rates of protection; the symmetry between effective protection and value-added subsidies; the relation between effective protection and shadow prices; and the relationship between the effective rate of protection and domestic resource cost.

Tower, Edward and Garry Pursell. 1986. "On Shadow Pricing." *World Bank Staff Working Paper* no. 792. Washington, D.C.: The World Bank.

The principal purpose of the monograph is to use general equilibrium methodology to explain the logical foundations of shadow prices and the techniques for deriving shadow price expressions. The nature and meaning of shadow prices is first discussed. The authors then present a simple model in which each traded good (traded at a fixed world price) is produced with intermediate inputs and a value-added aggregate which is used in fixed proportions and with constant returns to scale, where the value-added aggregate is a variable proportions function of a sector-specific fixed factor and an intersectorally mobile factor of production which is common to all sectors. This fixed factor model is thought to be particularly applicable to developing countries and has been presented in various forms as the so-called "Australian" balance of payment model of the dependent economy [see Neary (1978), Dornbusch (1980), and Lal (1984)]. Using the model, the authors derive shadow prices for labor, traded goods, nontraded goods, and foreign exchange assuming full employment and a flexible real exchange rate, with household welfare being held constant by adjustments in income taxes. The same basic approach is extended to more complex models, including models with alternative adjustment mechanisms (and not necessarily nondistorting taxation). The authors also discuss how to shadow price factors, goods, policy parameters and autonomous parameters in terms of other goods whose shadow prices are known without having to solve a general equilibrium model (although it is assumed that some general equilibrium model had been solved to yield the known shadow prices). The work explains the logical foundations of the formulae used in Squire and van der Tak (1975) and Ray (1984) and generalizes their approaches. The first three appendices comment from a general equilibrium perspective on some of the shadow price expressions proposed in the three books on shadow pricing, while the last two appendices illustrate the kind of analysis that is needed if the models are so complex that they require matrix inversion.

United Nations Industrial Development Organization (UNIDO). 1972. "Guidelines for Project

Evaluation." Prepared by P. S. Dasgupta, Steven A. Marglin, and A. K. Sen. New York: United Nations.

Commonly referred to as the "UNIDO Guidelines." Frequently compared and contrasted with the OECD Manual [Little and Mirrlees (1969). See also Little and Mirrlees (1974 and 1982) during the early and mid-1970s.] Like the OECD Manual, the UNIDO Guidelines used a multi-objective approach (i.e., included objectives other than economic efficiency, such as income distribution and optimal growth). However, there were important differences between the two methods. These are summarized most cogently in Lal (1974).

Varian, Hal. 1984. *Microeconomic Analysis*. 2nd edition. New York: W. W. Norton.

Vickers, John. 1985. "Strategic Competition Among the Few; Some Recent Developments in the Economics of Industry." *Oxford Bulletin of Economics and Statistics,* vol. 1, no. 3 (Autumn), pp. 39-62.

Ward, William A. 1980. "Cost-Benefit Rules for Industrial Incentives: A Proposed Technique for Establishing Criteria for Industrial Grants." WP 8001. Charleston: The Center for Metropolitan Affairs and Public Policy Studies, (January).

Warr, P. 1977a. "On the Shadow Pricing of Traded Commodities," *Journal of Political Economy*. vol. 85, no. 4, pp. 865-875.

Warr, P. 1977b. "Shadow Pricing with Policy Constraints," *Economic Record,* (June-September), pp. 149-166.

Warr, P. 1980. "Properties of Optimal Shadow Prices for a Tax-Distorted Open Economy." *Australian Economic Papers*, no. 19 (June), pp. 31-34.

Weckstein, R.S. 1972. "Shadow Prices and Project Evaluation in Less Developed Countries," *Economic Development and Cultural Change,* vol. 20, no. 3, pp. 31-55.

The World Bank. 1977. "Fourth Oil Palm and Coconut Project, Côte d'Ivoire." Staff Appraisal Report no. 1204-IVC. (This is an internal document with restricted circulation.) Washington, D.C.

Used in the preparation of Case 10.

The World Bank. 1980. "New Land Development Project (West Nubariya), Arab Republic of Egypt." Staff Appraisal Report no. 3010-EGT. (This is an internal document with restricted circulation.) Washington, D.C.

Used in preparation of Case 1.

The World Bank. 1981. "Hand Tubewells Project, Bangladesh." Staff Appraisal Report No 3280-BD. (This is an internal document with restricted circulation.) Washington, D.C.
Referred to in Chapter 8.

The World Bank. 1981. "Mahaweli Ganga Development Project III, Sri Lanka." Staff Appraisal Report no. 3128CE. (This is an internal document with restricted circulation.) Washington D.C.
Used in the preparation of Case 9.

The World Bank. 1983. "Fifth Agricultural Development Project, Pakistan." Staff Appraisal Report no. 4410-PAK. (This is an internal document with restricted circulation.) Washington, D.C.
Used in the preparation of Case 6.

The World Bank. 1984. "Agricultural Development Project, Uganda." Staff Appraisal Report no. 5009-UG. (This is an internal document with restricted circulation.) Washington, D.C.
Used in the preparation of Case 12.

The World Bank. 1985a. "Smallholder Cattle Development Project, Indonesia." Staff Appraisal Report no. 5615-IND. (This is an internal document with restricted circulation.) Washington, D.C.
Used in the preparation of Case 2.

The World Bank. 1985b. "Kedung Ombo Multipurpose Dam and Irrigation Project, Indonesia." Staff Appraisal Report no. 5346a-IND. (This is an internal document with restricted circulation.) Washington, D.C.
Used in the preparation of Case 2.

The World Bank. 1986. "Financing Adjustment with Growth in Sub-Saharan Africa, 1986-90." Washington, D.C.
This is the World Bank's fourth report focusing on development issues and requirements in sub-Saharan Africa.

The World Bank. 1986. "Second Wood Energy Project, Malawi." Staff Appraisal Report no. 5914-MAI. (This is an internal document with restricted circulation.) Washington, D.C.: The World Bank.

The World Bank. 1986a. "Irrigation Rehabilitation II Project, Colombia." Staff Appraisal

Report no. 5954-CO. (This is an internal document with restricted circulation.) Washington, D.C.

Used in the preparation of Case 8.

The World Bank. 1986b. "Crop Production Improvement Project, Hungary." Staff Appraisal Report no. 5899-HU. (This is an internal document with restricted circulation.) Washington, D.C.

Used in the preparation of Case 4.

The World Bank. 1986c. "Southern Borno Agricultural Development Project, Nigeria." Staff Appraisal Report no. 5933-UNI. (This is an internal document with restricted circulation.) Washington, D.C.

Used in the preparation of Case 13.

The World Bank. 1986d. "Red Soils Area Development Project, China." Staff Appraisal Report no. 6072-CNA. (This is an internal document with restricted circulation.) Washington, D.C.

The World Bank. 1987. "Semi-Mechanized Rainfed Agriculture Pilot Project, Somalia." (This is an internal document with restricted circulation.) Washington, D. C.

Used in the preparation of Case 7.

Yagci, Fahrettin and Steven Kamin. 1987. "Macroeconomic Policies and Adjustment in Yugoslavia; Some Counterfactual Simulations." *World Bank Discussion Paper* no. 16. Washington, D.C.: World Bank.

Zeitz, Joachim and Alberto Valdes. 1986. "The Costs of Protectionism to Developing Countries; An Analysis for Selected Agricultural Products." *World Bank Staff Working Paper* no. 769. Washington, D.C.

This study quantifies welfare and foreign exchange costs arising in developing countries as a result of protectionist policies on many agricultural products. A detailed analysis is given for four key commodities. For each commodity, the potential long-run gains to developing countries from a complete removal of tariff and nontariff barriers are analyzed within the framework of a comparative-static world market equilibrium model. The study considers fifty-eight developing countries as well as seventeen developed economies.

❖

Distributors of World Bank Publications

ARGENTINA
Carlos Hirsch, SRL
Galería Guemes
Florida 165, 4th Floor-Ofc. 453/465
1333 Buenos Aires

AUSTRALIA, PAPUA NEW GUINEA,
FIJI, SOLOMON ISLANDS,
VANUATU, AND WESTERN SAMOA
D.A. Books & Journals
648 Whitehorse Road
Mitcham 3132
Victoria

AUSTRIA
Gerold and Co.
Graben 31
A-1011 Wien

BAHRAIN
Bahrain Research and Consultancy
Associates Ltd.
P.O. Box 22103
Manama Town 317

BANGLADESH
Micro Industries Development
Assistance Society (MIDAS)
House 5, Road 16
Dhanmondi R/Area
Dhaka 1209

Branch offices:
156, Nur Ahmed Sarak
Chittagong 4000

76, K.D.A. Avenue
Kulna

BELGIUM
Jean De Lannoy
Av. du Roi 202
1060 Brussels

BRAZIL
Publicacoes Tecnicas Internacionais
Ltda.
Rua Peixoto Gomide, 209
01409 Sao Paulo, SP

CANADA
Le Diffuseur
C.P. 85, 1501 B rue Ampère
Boucherville, Québec
J4B 5E6

CHINA
China Financial & Economic Publishing
House
8, Da Fo Si Dong Jie
Beijing

COLOMBIA
Infoenlace Ltda.
Apartado Aereo 34270
Bogota D.E.

COTE D'IVOIRE
Centre d'Edition et de Diffusion
Africaines (CEDA)
04 B.P. 541
Abidjan 04 Plateau

CYPRUS
MEMRB Information Services
P.O. Box 2098
Nicosia

DENMARK
SamfundsLitteratur
Rosenoerns Allé 11
DK-1970 Frederiksberg C

DOMINICAN REPUBLIC
Editora Taller, C. por A.
Restauración e Isabel la Católica 309
Apartado Postal 2190
Santo Domingo

EL SALVADOR
Fusades
Avenida Manuel Enrique Araujo #3530
Edificio SISA, ler. Piso
San Salvador

EGYPT, ARAB REPUBLIC OF
Al Ahram
Al Galaa Street
Cairo

The Middle East Observer
8 Chawarbi Street
Cairo

FINLAND
Akateeminen Kirjakauppa
P.O. Box 128
SF-00101
Helsinki 10

FRANCE
World Bank Publications
66, avenue d'Iéna
75116 Paris

GERMANY, FEDERAL REPUBLIC OF
UNO-Verlag
Poppelsdorfer Allee 55
D-5300 Bonn 1

GREECE
KEME
24, Ippodamou Street Platia Plastiras
Athens-11635

GUATEMALA
Librerias Piedra Santa
5a. Calle 7-55
Zona 1
Guatemala City

HONG KONG, MACAO
Asia 2000 Ltd.
6 Fl., 146 Prince Edward
Road, W.
Kowloon
Hong Kong

HUNGARY
Kultura
P.O. Box 149
1389 Budapest 62

INDIA
Allied Publishers Private Ltd.
751 Mount Road
Madras - 600 002

Branch offices:
15 J.N. Heredia Marg
Ballard Estate
Bombay - 400 038

13/14 Asaf Ali Road
New Delhi - 110 002

17 Chittaranjan Avenue
Calcutta - 700 072

Jayadeva Hostel Building
5th Main Road Gandhinagar
Bangalore - 560 009

3-5-1129 Kachiguda Cross Road
Hyderabad - 500 027

Prarthana Flats, 2nd Floor
Near Thakore Baug, Navrangpura
Ahmedabad - 380 009

Patiala House
16-A Ashok Marg
Lucknow - 226 001

INDONESIA
Pt. Indira Limited
Jl. Sam Ratulangi 37
P.O. Box 181
Jakarta Pusat

ITALY
Licosa Commissionaria Sansoni SPA
Via Benedetto Fortini, 120/10
Casella Postale 552
50125 Florence

JAPAN
Eastern Book Service
37-3, Hongo 3-Chome, Bunkyo-ku 113
Tokyo

KENYA
Africa Book Service (E.A.) Ltd.
P.O. Box 45245
Nairobi

KOREA, REPUBLIC OF
Pan Korea Book Corporation
P.O. Box 101, Kwangwhamun
Seoul

KUWAIT
MEMRB Information Services
P.O. Box 5465

MALAYSIA
University of Malaya Cooperative
Bookshop, Limited
P.O. Box 1127, Jalan Pantai Baru
Kuala Lumpur

MEXICO
INFOTEC
Apartado Postal 22-860
14060 Tlalpan, Mexico D.F.

MOROCCO
Société d' Etudes Marketing Marocaine
12 rue Mozart, Bd. d'Anfa
Casablanca

NETHERLANDS
InOr-Publikaties b.v.
P.O. Box 14
7240 BA Lochem

NEW ZEALAND
Hills Library and Information Service
Private Bag
New Market
Auckland

NIGERIA
University Press Limited
Three Crowns Building Jericho
Private Mail Bag 5095
Ibadan

NORWAY
Narvesen Information Center
Book Department
P.O. Box 6125 Etterstad
N-0602 Oslo 6

OMAN
MEMRB Information Services
P.O. Box 1613, Seeb Airport
Muscat

PAKISTAN
Mirza Book Agency
65, Shahrah-e-Quaid-e-Azam
P.O. Box No. 729
Lahore 3

PERU
Editorial Desarrollo SA
Apartado 3824
Lima

PHILIPPINES
National Book Store
701 Rizal Avenue
P.O. Box 1934
Metro Manila

International Book Center
Fifth Floor, Filipinas Life Building
Ayala Avenue, Makati
Metro Manila

POLAND
ORPAN
Palac Kultury i Nauki
00-901 Warszawa

PORTUGAL
Livraria Portugal
Rua Do Carmo 70-74
1200 Lisbon

SAUDI ARABIA, QATAR
Jarir Book Store
P.O. Box 3196
Riyadh 11471

MEMRB Information Services
Branch offices:
Al Alsa Street
Al Dahna Center
First Floor
P.O. Box 7188
Riyadh

Haji Abdullah Alireza Building
King Khaled Street
P.O. Box 3969
Dammam

33, Mohammed Hassan Awad Street
P.O. Box 5978
Jeddah

SINGAPORE, TAIWAN, MYANMAR,
BRUNEI
Information Publications
Private, Ltd.
02-06 1st Fl., Pei-Fu Industrial
Bldg.
24 New Industrial Road
Singapore 1953

SOUTH AFRICA, BOTSWANA
For single titles:
Oxford University Press Southern
Africa
P.O. Box 1141
Cape Town 8000

For subscription orders:
International Subscription Service
P.O. Box 41095
Craighall
Johannesburg 2024

SPAIN
Mundi-Prensa Libros, S.A.
Castello 37
28001 Madrid

Librería Internacional AEDOS
Consell de Cent, 391
08009 Barcelona

SRI LANKA AND THE MALDIVES
Lake House Bookshop
P.O. Box 244
100, Sir Chittampalam A. Gardiner
Mawatha
Colombo 2

SWEDEN
For single titles:
Pritzes Fackboksforetaget
Regeringsgatan 12, Box 16356
S-103 27 Stockholm

For subscription orders:
Wennergren-Williams AB
Box 30004
S-104 25 Stockholm

SWITZERLAND
For single titles:
Librairie Payot
6, rue Grenus
Case postale 381
CH 1211 Geneva 11

For subscription orders:
Librairie Payot
Service des Abonnements
Case postale 3312
CH 1002 Lausanne

TANZANIA
Oxford University Press
P.O. Box 5299
Dar es Salaam

THAILAND
Central Department Store
306 Silom Road
Bangkok

TRINIDAD & TOBAGO, ANTIGUA
BARBUDA, BARBADOS,
DOMINICA, GRENADA, GUYANA,
JAMAICA, MONTSERRAT, ST.
KITTS & NEVIS, ST. LUCIA,
ST. VINCENT & GRENADINES
Systematics Studies Unit
#9 Watts Street
Curepe
Trinidad, West Indies

TURKEY
Haset Kitapevi, A.S.
Istiklal Caddesi No. 469
Beyoglu
Istanbul

UGANDA
Uganda Bookshop
P.O. Box 7145
Kampala

UNITED ARAB EMIRATES
MEMRB Gulf Co.
P.O. Box 6097
Sharjah

UNITED KINGDOM
Microinfo Ltd.
P.O. Box 3
Alton, Hampshire GU34 2PG
England

URUGUAY
Instituto Nacional del Libro
San Jose 1116
Montevideo

VENEZUELA
Librería del Este
Aptdo. 60.337
Caracas 1060-A

YUGOSLAVIA
Jugoslovenska Knjiga
P.O. Box 36
Trg Republike
YU-11000 Belgrade